The Good Housekeeping Christmas Cookbook

UPDATED WITH FESTIVE RECIPES & IDEAS

ROASTS

WREATHS * DESSERTS

GIFTS | GINGERBREAD * APPETIZERS *

DRINKS * COOKIES * TREES

The Good Housekeeping Christmas Cookbook

ROASTS

UPDATED WITH FESTIVE RECIPES & IDEAS

WREATHS ❄ DESSERTS

❄ GIFTS ❄ GINGERBREAD ❄ APPETIZERS ❄

DRINKS ❄ COOKIES ❄ TREES

HEARST
books

Contents

WHEN I WAS A KID, every Christmas seemed to burst with pent-up anticipation: presents, cookies, stockings, playing with my cousins, days off school. On Christmas Eve, I couldn't contain my excitement—it seemed morning would never come.

Fast-forward a few years (who's counting?!). I'm often so caught up in the grown-up rat race that I feel a bit of dread and anxiety mixed with that happy eagerness. I need to buy that, bake this, make that—and wrap it all up with a pretty bow! Enter the amazing team of experts here at GH (or maybe I should call them elves!). They have the power to solve all our holiday dilemmas. Amazingly, when I look through the stunning ideas and inspiring shortcuts we've pulled together in this latest edition of *The Good Housekeeping Christmas Cookbook,* I go from stressed to excited.

Here are all our best tools, tips, shortcuts, and sanity-soothers in one single book. You'll find a bounty of triple-tested holiday recipes—more than 300 of them! Appealing appetizers, gorgeous soups, and festive salads will kick off your celebration. For a sumptuous main course, choose from turkey, roast, or even vegetarian options, along with irresistible side dishes and dressings. And save room for desserts: stand-out cakes, homey pies, and puddings, plus cookies—both traditional favorites and newcomers like Dulce de Leche Sandwiches and Matcha Spritz—are all here. We've also included a nostalgic flashback to the pages of *Good Housekeeping*'s Christmases past.

But there's more to Christmas than food! You'll find ideas for creating dazzling Christmas trees and ornaments, festive garlands, welcoming wreaths and outdoor lights, cheerful centerpieces, and beautiful tabletops, plus fun and inventive gift wraps to make the season bright.

We also tell you everything you need to know about entertaining: tips on setting a formal table; the best way to make your silver gleam; a chart outlining how much food it takes to feed your crowd; the easiest ways to prep and clean up when the party's over. To get holiday-ready, start with "The Great Christmas Countdown" on page 13—an eleven-day plan that helps you break down all your holiday to-do's.

I can't wait to share the latest update of this ultimate Christmas sourcebook with you. It's guaranteed to bring back the merry, and give you a stress-free season full of happy new memories you'll cherish forever.

Jane Francisco
EDITOR IN CHIEF

Spread the Joy!

CROWD-PLEASING RECIPES, SPARKLING DECORATIONS & ENTERTAINING IDEAS TO MAKE THE HOLIDAYS FESTIVE & BRIGHT

Christmas is the most anticipated of holidays—and with good reason. The season is filled with memorable feasts, an abundance of sweets, decorations that sparkle both indoors and out, and a whirlwind of parties and presents. Most of all, no matter how you and yours celebrate, it's a time to get together—and share the joy—with family and friends.

Here at *Good Housekeeping*, we can't promise you snow, but in *The Christmas Cookbook*, we deliver all the rest.

Start with "The Great Christmas Countdown," an eleven-day plan to amp the fun factor and curtail your stress. From shopping and meal planning to setting the table, it breaks down all your to-do's leading up to the big day. Then we move on to holiday entertaining, sharing our expertise on everything from setting a formal table to how much food you'll need to feed your crowd. And in "Christmas Cleanup," we deliver strategies to whip your house into shape—both before and after the party.

In the chapters that follow, we've collected more than 300 of our all-time favorite holiday recipes, plus a glittering array of festive decorations and crafts to help you deck out your home in style. "Festive Beginnings" gets the party started with delightful appetizers, first courses, and drinks—plus how-tos for making gorgeous wreaths. "The Main Event" serves up a selection of showstopping roasts, buffet-perfect dishes, and tabletop inspiration.

Of course, we haven't forgotten the sides—or the all-important Christmas tree; "Sideshows" and "All Through the House" round up irresistible options for both. "Sweet Finales" features everyone's favorite course: dessert. From cakes, pies, and puddings to cookie recipes and decorating tips, we provide sweet satisfaction. We wrap things up with a chapter on gourmet food gifts, stunning gift wraps, and practical advice on getting presents to friends and family right on time.

Along the way, we share lots of advice on everything from stocking the bar to hosting a cookie swap. After all, we've been celebrating Christmas at the magazine since 1885—we've had a long time to develop our credentials in all things merry and bright!

Clockwise from top left: Beef Tenderloin with White Wine Sauce *(page 113)*; Pomegranate Margaritas *(page 60)*; Tree Line *(page 245)*; Lemon Meringue Drops *(page 324)*; Fresh Cranberry-Orange Mold *(page 234)*.

THE GREAT CHRISTMAS COUNTDOWN

When you were growing up, you may have been asked to help with prep and cleanup, but until you host a holiday meal yourself, you don't truly appreciate the days or even weeks of planning and prep required. To make entertaining easier, we've divided out all the to-do's over eleven days, from planning the menu to serving it. Instead of stressing out with last-minute kitchen chaos, follow this plan and you'll be able to relax and enjoy the party.

But before we launch into the countdown, check your guest list. Invite local friends and family one month before Christmas Day—make that two to three months for out-of-towners, who will need the time to make travel arrangements and hotel reservations. Or, if they're staying with you, you'll want to know ahead of time so you can figure out sleeping arrangements.

Clockwise from top left: Roasted Sweet & Sour Brussels Sprouts *(page 219)*; Dress Your Table in Red and White *(page 179)*; Pumpkin Crème Caramel *(page 296)*; Mail-Order Ham *(page 125)*.

December 15th: Check in with Your Guests

If guests haven't confirmed that they're coming, check in with them now. Make sure to ask if they're bringing any children, friends, new significant others, or pets—if furry guests are welcome in your home (if not, make it clear now). For those who can't commit yet, give them until the twentieth to confirm. If they offer to bring food, agree on what dishes they will contribute. If they need suggestions, email them a recipe once you've finalized your menu.

December 16th: Select the Menu

Will it be a formal sit-down dinner with a plated first course, entrée, side dishes, and elegant dessert? Or do you plan to pass platters around the table family style, or let guests serve themselves from a buffet? The serving style you choose will help drive your menu plan. As you select the dishes, keep in mind how much oven, stovetop, and microwave space you have available, and consider what each recipe will require.

Begin by gathering recipes for holiday favorites you like to make every year, then throw some new dishes into the mix. (You'll find more than 300 enticing options right here!) Shop for the ingredients for any new recipes today, and prepare them for your family over the next couple days—they'll let you know if they'd enjoy eating them again. If your guests agreed to bring food, be sure to include these dishes on your menu list. And, if you've invited guests with special dietary needs, work in a selection of dishes they can enjoy. That includes vegetarians, who may be used to feasting on side dishes, but would surely be grateful if you included a meatless main on your holiday menu. For more tips, see "Christmas Menu Planning" on page 14.

December 17th: Order the Turkey or Roast

Decide which type of turkey (fresh or frozen?), ham (smoked or fresh?), pork roast or beef (tenderloin or standing rib?) to serve and how much to buy (see "How Much Do I Need?" on page 23). If you're ordering a turkey or roast from your butcher, do it today. Ditto if you're ordering a precooked ham online. Place all orders for catered appetizer trays and bakery pies or desserts, too.

CHRISTMAS MENU PLANNING

Holiday meals are a time to think big. A juicy turkey, succulent ham, or standing beef rib roast are all suitably grand centerpieces—the choice often depends on family tradition.

Then make that sideboard groan with accompaniments, from mashed potatoes and stuffings to Brussels sprouts, cranberries—and don't forget the gravy! After dinner, bring on the desserts: cakes, pies, puddings, and cookies. In the chapters that follow, you'll find irresistible recipes for all of these items.

What makes for a winning Christmas menu? Plan for a variety of colors, textures, and flavors. If your main dish is a whole side of salmon, don't start the meal with a seafood pâté. And if you're serving roasted sweet potatoes with your roast beef, add a bit of crunch with broccoli.

The majority of dishes should be those you've cooked and enjoyed in the past. Take advantage of dishes that taste even better made ahead. It's also smart to include some dishes on the menu that freeze well.

Consider how much time you'll need to spend in the kitchen, and incorporate some food prep time-savers accordingly. Avoid including more than two dishes that will require your last-minute attention. Convenience foods like storebought piecrust; canned or boxed broth; peeled, deveined shrimp; and heat-and-serve ham can all free you up to enjoy the party. For meal-planning inspiration, see our "Holiday Menu Ideas" on page 400.

December 18th: Take Stock of Your Supplies (and the Guest Room)

Pull out the table linens you plan to use and the hand towels for the bathroom. Are they faded? Have they developed mysterious spots? Wash accordingly. If they're too far gone (or the thought of scrubbing a tablecloth makes you want to weep), snap up some stain-resistant tablecloths and inexpensive hand towels while you're running errands this week.

Pick up some plastic containers; they'll hold prepared items before the meal and leftovers afterward—and make good doggie bags for guests. Also get extra foil and plastic wrap, kitchen twine, trash bags, paper towels, and toilet paper (if you haven't already found this stuff on sale). Consider buying the nonperishable grocery items you need now, too, to shorten the inevitable marathon-shopping trip next week.

Inspect the guest room—by sleeping there. It's the easiest way to find out what's missing (a reading lamp? comfy pillows?). Also, straighten it up now to avoid a mad scramble later. (If guests will sleep on a sofa bed, vacuum the mattress and underneath the cushions.)

December 19th: Grocery Shop, Sharpen Your Knives (and Choose an Outfit!)

Compile a list and shop for all nonperishables, including pantry staples that may be running low. Look for sales in your local circulars and stock up on other holiday musts—paper goods, candies, mixed nuts, beverages, inexpensive toys to entertain kids, batteries for the camera.

Assess your cooking equipment, china, cutlery, and serving dishes. Is the vegetable peeler dull? Are the potholders frayed? Plan to buy or borrow what you'll need. Take inventory of your carving tools. If needed, sharpen them or buy new ones.

Choose your outfit for Christmas Day. It should look good but be comfortable enough for cooking and entertaining. Drop the clothes off at the dry cleaner's if necessary. Nothing to wear? Hit the mall. (If you don't own an apron, pick up one of those, too—prepping a Christmas dinner can get messy.)

December 20th: Purchase Wine and Beverages (and Finalize RSVPs)

Stock up on wine (or order it online, unless that's a no-no in your state). Choose a red and a white, and buy in multiples. Plan what nonalcoholic beverages to serve, for both kids and adults who don't want to drink. If you plan to serve cocktails before dinner, now is a good time to check your bar and restock as necessary (see "Stock Up Cheat Sheet" on page 70 for guidance). Do you have enough glasses? (If it's a very large group, buy cheap ones in bulk or go for recyclable plastic.) Pick up some drink tags, so guests can easily keep track of their drinks, and coasters if you're concerned about getting rings on your tables.

Wrap up the guest list: You gave any undecided guests a one-week deadline to respond—that's today!

December 21st: Prepare Make-Ahead Dishes (and Select Some Tunes)

Cook the dishes on your menu that will freeze or refrigerate well. Make as many as you can tonight, and plan on preparing the balance over the next two days. Casseroles, soups, cranberry sauce, piecrusts, and cookies are all good candidates for freezing.

Iron linens that need it and lay them out, if you have the space, so they won't rewrinkle.

Create a play list of Christmas favorites for the big day. If your kids are into music, they might enjoy taking on this task. Just be sure to screen their selections to make sure they're holiday appropriate.

December 22nd: Plan the Table Settings (and Polish Your Silver)

Set out your serving dishes and utensils and label them with Post-it notes (e.g., "Brussels sprouts here"). If you need tabletop inspiration, see "Dining Merry and Bright" on page 179. Enlist your partner or kids to make place cards, wash platters, and polish silver, if you're using it. That way, they'll be free to run errands for you and take out the trash the morning of the party. (Once silver is clean, wrap it in tissue, then place in airtight

---

CHRISTMAS DAY WINE TASTING

If your holiday menu is traditional, the dishes will run the gamut from sweet potatoes to tart cranberries to a savory gravy. With so many flavors on the table, you'll complement them better by serving several different wine varieties rather than just one.

For Starters: Begin the feast with a food-friendly Riesling. It's balance of sweetness and acidity makes it a perfect match for almost any appetizer or first course you put on the table.

Main Attraction: For the full spread, choose a white and a red and let your guests mix and match. If turkey is the centerpiece of your meal, a Sauvignon Blanc that's light but brimming with fruit flavor is a perfect partner.

If you like a hearty red, choose a peppery Shiraz. It will even harmonize with the bold spices of a chutney or cranberry sauce. Or choose a full-flavored Merlot—it'd be especially tasty with mushroom stuffing.

Final Notes: No celebratory meal is complete without dessert—a sweet wine makes it even more festive. A sweet (but not cloying) Muscat is perfect with pies, from pecan to pumpkin.

FORMAL PLACE SETTINGS

There is a proper way to set a table. Break out your china, crystal, and silver flatware, and follow this step-by-step guide to arranging your table for company.

Start off with festive table linens. It's up to you—a tablecloth, runner, or placemats all can work. Cloth napkins, whether plain white or matched to your cloth, add an elegant touch.

Each place setting should have a dinner plate or liner plate, also called a "charger." This will add a little height and a nice border to the main dishes. On top of that, place the salad plate and follow that with a folded napkin. If serving soup, place the bowl on top of the salad plate. Next, the utensils are placed in order of usage from outer to inner. To the left of the plate, place the dinner fork and to its left, the salad fork.

On the right side, place the knife with the blade facing in and then a soupspoon, if needed. The bottom edge of the utensils should be lined up with the bottom rim of the plate or charger. If you like, a small bread plate with a butter knife can be placed above the forks to the upper left of the dinner plate.

A dessert spoon can be placed directly above the dinner place setting at a perpendicular, with the handle facing to the right.

The water glass is placed directly above the tip of the knife. If serving wine, a wineglass is then placed at about a 45-degree angle to the right of the water glass and above the soupspoon. If two wines are being served, place the additional wineglass to the right of the primary wineglass.

When setting for the dessert course, remove everything except the water glass and the dessert spoon. And don't forget to provide a teaspoon for coffee or tea.

plastic bags to keep it tarnish-free.) Be sure to sharpen your knives—and not just the roast carver. All your kitchen work will go more smoothly.

If you have a frozen turkey or roast, move it from the freezer to the fridge to thaw. Prep any ingredients that will last for two to three days, like chopped onions or fried bacon for the stuffing, and bag them. Continue to make dishes that can be refrigerated or stored until Christmas Day.

December 23rd: Shop for Perishables (and Prepare for Spills)

Shop for all fresh fruits, veggies, and other perishables you'll need to complete your menu. Prepare a make-ahead gravy that will save you time on the big day (for recipe, see page 142). Chill white wine and make or buy extra ice.

Thaw frozen make-aheads in the refrigerator, like that piecrust you made two days ago. Prepare the filling and make the pies.

Finally, charge up your hand vac (or just have your broom and dustpan handy)—so you're ready to cope with those unavoidable spills.

December 24th: Cook Some More, Defrost, and Set the Table

Roast or steam the vegetables. Let them cool and then store them in resealable plastic bags in the fridge. Defrost any refrigerated pies or desserts. Decide who will carve the bird or roast; "Carving a Roast Turkey" and "Carving a Rib Roast" on pages 135 and 117 provide pointers. We've gathered all of the help lines you can call in case of a cooking emergency on the big day (see "When In Doubt" on page 22). Make sure you have easy access to this list.

You've already planned your table; now set it so you don't have to deal with that tomorrow. See "Formal Place Settings," opposite, for an overview of what goes where. Place and label trivets with what dish will go where.

Lay out your outfit for the next day, or pick it up from the dry cleaner's if you haven't already.

MAKE YOUR SILVER FLATWARE SPARKLE

Here are two methods that make polishing silver less of a chore.

The Good Way

Gather a few thick, soft cloths and silver polish. Always follow your product's label directions, but typically, you'll start by putting a dab of polish onto the cloth, dampened if needed.

Rub the polish onto one utensil at a time, going in an up-and-down, not circular, motion to avoid highlighting fine scratches. Work polish into tight areas (between fork tines and into pattern crevices). Turn the cloth frequently as you work, so tarnish isn't deposited back on your silver. Depending on the amount of tarnish, it'll take anywhere from 45 seconds to a few minutes per utensil.

Rinse the cleaned items in warm water; buff to a shine with a clean, dry, soft cloth.

The Good Enough Way

This faster method uses a reaction between aluminum foil and tarnish, where the latter "jumps" from the silver to the foil. Note: Don't use this method for pieces with hollow handles.

Line a plastic (not metal) basin with aluminum foil, shiny side up. Place the silverware inside. Make sure all pieces are contacting the foil or touching a utensil that is.

Sprinkle in ¼ cup washing soda (from grocery or hardware stores). Pour in 1 gallon boiling water. Stir and let the silver soak 10 to 15 minutes.

Wearing rubber gloves, remove the silver. Rinse, and buff with a clean, soft cloth. For very tarnished items, repeat the process.

MICROWAVE TO THE RESCUE!

Did you know that your microwave can cook a pound of just about anything in four to six minutes? And that's only one of its tricks. So when your stovetop and oven are fully occupied, here's how to do some holiday micro-management.

Steam string beans. Cook 1 pound green beans and a few tablespoons water in a covered casserole for 4 to 6 minutes until tender-crisp.

Cook cranberry sauce. In 2-quart casserole, combine a 12-ounce package of fresh cranberries, ¾ cup sugar, and ¼ cup orange juice or water. Cover with lid or vented plastic wrap, and microwave 7 to 11 minutes until cranberries pop.

Make a crunchy piecrust. Mix 4 tablespoons softened butter, 1 cup cookie or graham cracker crumbs, ¼ cup finely chopped nuts, and 2 tablespoons sugar. Press onto the bottom and side of a 9-inch glass pie plate. Microwave 2 to 3 minutes until firm.

Brown nuts. To toast nut pieces, pile ½ to 1 cup in glass measure or bowl (don't spread them out on a plate as if they were on a cookie sheet in the oven). Heat 1½ to 2½ minutes or until lightly colored and aromatic—and don't forget to stir them a couple of times during microwaving.

Poach pears. In a 2-quart casserole, heat ½ cup sugar, ¼ cup water, and 2 tablespoons lemon juice 2 minutes to dissolve sugar. Arrange 4 peeled pears on their sides in the syrup, with stems pointing to

the center. Cover with a lid or vented plastic wrap, and cook 10 to 12 minutes or until fork-tender.

Prepare bread-crumb topping. In a glass measuring cup, combine 1 cup dried bread crumbs and 1 tablespoon oil or butter. Toast 1½ to 2½ minutes until browned. It's important to stop and stir twice.

Bake sweet potatoes. Prick 4 medium sweet potatoes, then place on turntable and zap 10 to 11 minutes until soft.

December 25th: Finish Cooking (and Enjoy the Feast!)

In the morning, get the turkey or other roast into the oven, cook the potatoes (you can keep mashed ones warm in a slow cooker), and make the stuffing and any veggies you haven't prepared yet. Whip the cream for dessert; chill. And don't forget to fill a spray bottle with cold water for zapping stains when they happen.

In the afternoon, add the drippings to the gravy and bring the cranberry sauce to room temperature. If you haven't kept the potatoes warm in a slow cooker, reheat them in the microwave right before serving (see "Microwave to the Rescue!," opposite, for other convenient uses). Transfer your turkey or roast to a platter. Remove desserts from the refrigerator an hour before serving. Reheat pies in a 350°F oven for 15 minutes and prepare coffee to go with them. If you have the oven space, warm the serving plates there. Otherwise, run them under the hottest water available and quickly dry them just before dinnertime.

Serve, then sit down and enjoy the meal with your guests! You'll of course need to keep an eye out for platters that need replenishing or wineglasses that need refilling. Ask a close family member or best friend to help with that and assist in clearing the table and serving the dessert and coffee or tea. When the meal is finished, we've heard of a tradition we think all households should institute: Those who cook don't clean up!

Top: POTATO GRATIN WITH GRUYÈRE *(page 192);*
Bottom: OLD-FASHIONED PECAN PIE *(page 280).*

REMEMBER,
IT'S JUST A TURKEY

Some families traditionally serve a pork crown roast, ham, or a prime rib of beef for Christmas dinner, but for many of us, turkey's always the centerpiece of the meal. Whether you're a first-timer or a seasoned holiday cook, our tips will help you prepare and roast the Christmas bird with confidence.

What to Buy

Frozen turkeys are widely available and often on sale during the holidays. Some are prebasted to enhance juiciness. You can buy them well in advance of Christmas, but you'll need to allow enough time for them to thaw before you put them in the oven (see "How to Thaw," below).

Fresh turkeys are preferred by many people but are usually more expensive, have a shorter shelf life, and may need to be special-ordered. Don't buy one more than two days ahead of the big day.

Organic turkeys are raised and fed without the use of antibiotics, hormones, or artificial flavors or colors. It is against the law to use hormones on any turkey, so even frozen nonbranded birds will be hormone free. Free-range turkeys are allowed access to feed outdoors.

Kosher turkeys are available fresh and frozen. They're salted as part of the koshering process, so no additional salt is needed. This process makes the meat tender and juicy, similar to the results you'd get from a brined bird.

How Much to Buy

Estimate 1 pound uncooked turkey per person to ensure enough meat for Christmas dinner and for sandwiches later on. For quantities for stuffing, mashed potatoes, and other essential side dishes, see the chart "How Much Do I Need?" on page 23.

How to Thaw

Remove giblets and reserve for the gravy.

The best way: Place frozen turkey (still in packaging) in a shallow pan on the bottom shelf of the refrigerator. Allow 24 hours thawing time for every 4 to 5 pounds. A thawed bird can keep up to 4 days in the fridge.

Last-minute solution: Place a still-wrapped turkey in a large cooler or bowl and submerge in cold water. Allow 30 minutes of thawing time per pound and change the water every 30 minutes. Cook turkey immediately.

How to Stuff

The best way is to bake stuffing separately in a shallow casserole in the oven alongside the turkey. If you prefer to stuff the bird, follow these guidelines:

Make sure the turkey is fully thawed.

Mix ingredients just before using and stuff loosely into the cavity to allow room for expansion.

Roast the turkey about 30 minutes longer than an unstuffed one.

Check that the internal temperature of the stuffing reaches 165°F.

How to Roast

Place the turkey (breast side up) on a rack in a large roasting pan in an oven preheated to 325°F. If you don't have a rack, place 2 or 3 large carrots crosswise underneath the bird to ensure good heat circulation.

For moist meat, cover with foil from the start—but remove foil during the last hour of roasting for browner, crispier skin.

Basting with pan juices isn't necessary, but it will help with browning after the foil is removed.

Roast turkey 3 to 3¾ hours for a 12- to 14-pounder. (That's around 15 to 17 minutes per pound for an unstuffed bird.)

Use an instant-read meat thermometer to test doneness. Turkey should be taken out of the oven when the thickest part of the thigh (next to but not touching the bone) reaches 175°F and the breast reaches 165°F. Keep in mind that temperature will rise 5°F to 10°F upon standing.

If the turkey is fully cooked earlier than expected, wrap the entire bird and pan with foil and place a large bath towel on top to keep it hot and moist for 1 hour.

Never leave at room temperature longer than 2 hours.

How to Safely Store Turkey Leftovers

The pie has been served, the table is cleared, the dishes await. If you're tempted to curl up in front of a good movie and leave cleanup for the rest of the gang, at least put the turkey away first.

Store it within two hours of serving. "Bacteria grow rapidly at room temperature, and refrigeration will not eliminate microorganisms that have already grown," says Sandy Kuzmich, PhD, the GH Institute's Chemistry Director.

Leftover turkey can be refrigerated for 3 to 4 days. In the freezer it will keep for 4 months (plain) or 6 months (in broth or gravy). Here are some additional pointers for safe stowaways:

Take all meat off the carcass and store in serving-size packets or shallow containers. The smaller the portion, the faster you can thoroughly defrost and reheat it. (To refrigerate the packets, wrap meat in plastic wrap or foil and place in self-sealing plastic bags. To freeze, use same procedure but with freezer-weight bags.)

To thaw leftover turkey, place it in the refrigerator overnight. To warm, stir in hot gravy just to heat through. Or stir frozen turkey shreds or small pieces directly into soups at last minute; cook just until hot.

WHEN IN DOUBT

If you're having a turkey meltdown . . .

Try these phone numbers and Web sites for help.

Butterball Turkey-Talk Line
800-288-8372, November 1 to December 29; butterball.com.

USDA Meat and Poultry Hot Line
888-674-6854; www.fsis.usda.gov/education.

Reynolds Turkey Tips Hot Line
800-433-2244, November 1 to December 31; reynoldskitchens.com/holiday-central.asp.

And, if you have any cranberry-related questions, you can get help here.

Ocean Spray's Consumer Affairs Hot Line
800-662-3263; oceanspray.com.

HOW MUCH DO I NEED?

Cooking for a crowd can be daunting— you may know how much stuffing to make for eight people, but how much for twenty? Our at-a-glance guide provides quantities for holiday basics.

DISH	8 SERVINGS	10 SERVINGS	12 SERVINGS	16 SERVINGS	20 SERVINGS	24 SERVINGS
Turkey	8 pounds	10 pounds	12 pounds	16 pounds	20 pounds	24 pounds
Beef Tenderloin	3^{1}/2 pounds	4^{1}/2 pounds	5 pounds	6^{1}/2 pounds	8^{1}/2 pounds	10 pounds
Standing Beef Rib Roast	4^{1}/2 pounds	6 pounds	7 pounds	9 pounds	11^{1}/2 pounds	14 pounds
Pork Crown Roast	5 pounds	6 pounds	8 pounds	10 pounds	12 pounds	15 pounds
Fresh Ham (boneless)	5 pounds	6 pounds	8 pounds	10 pounds	12 pounds	15 pounds
Smoked Ham (bone-in)	3^{1}/2 pounds	4^{1}/2 pounds	5 pounds	7 pounds	9 pounds	10^{1}/2 pounds
Potatoes	3 pounds (6 large)	3^{1}/2 pounds (7 large)	4^{1}/2 pounds (9 large)	6 pounds (12 large)	7^{1}/2 pounds (15 large)	9 pounds (18 large)
Butternut squash	3^{1}/2 pounds (2 small)	4 pounds (2 medium)	5 pounds (2 large)	6^{3}/4 pounds (3 medium)	8 pounds (4 medium)	10 pounds (4 large)
Brussels Sprouts (10-ounce container)	2 containers	3 containers	3 containers	4 containers	5 containers	6 containers
Green Beans	2 pounds	2^{1}/2 pounds	3 pounds	4 pounds	5 pounds	6 pounds
Sweet Potatoes	3 pounds (3 large)	3^{3}/4 pounds (4 large)	4^{1}/2 pounds (5 large)	6 pounds (6 large)	7^{1}/2 pounds (8 large)	9 pounds (9 large)
Pearl Onions (10-ounce container)	2 containers	2 containers	3 containers	3 containers	4 containers	4 containers
Pie (9" to 9^{1}/2" pie)	1 to 2 pies	2 pies	2 pies	2 to 3 pies	3 pies	3 to 4 pies

KEEP OUT!
SANTA'S WORKSHOP
MAGIC BEING MADE
DO NOT ENTER
THE ELVES GREATLY APPRECIATE IT!

CHRISTMAS CLEANUP—FROM BEFORE TO BEYOND!

Decorating the house for the holidays is always a pleasure. Cleaning it up before guests arrive and after they leave—not so much. The good news: We've gotten it down to a science. See our tips for fast pre-party fixes and quick cleanup.

Ready, Set Guests!

Company's coming—in twelve minutes. Tackle these hot spots before the doorbell rings: a cluttered entryway, disheveled living room, and not-quite-spotless bathroom.

Overhaul the front hall. Grab a laundry basket, storage bin, or large shopping bag to serve as a junk receptacle, plus a plastic grocery bag and microfiber cloth. Load up your bin with any shoes, gloves, or hats that litter the foyer. Stash hall-table clutter that could get lost (mail, keys) in the plastic bag; put the bag into the bin. While you're near the door, shake doormats outside. Flip on the light for an indoor cobweb check; flick webs off with the cloth (don't worry about ones too high up—chances are, visitors won't notice them once they see your smiling face). Take your bin and keep moving—**3 minutes.**

Put the living room in order. Next stop: where guests will hang out most. Keep filling the bin with kids' toys, newspapers, and anything else that doesn't need to be here. Run your microfiber cloth over the coffee table and other dusty surfaces, like the TV screen. Pile magazines or books into neat stacks on the end tables; gather all of the stray remotes in one place. Plump up throw pillows and chair cushions (even easier: flip the latter, if possible). Use a clean corner of the microfiber cloth to nab any obvious clumps of pet hair or dust stuck to upholstery or carpeting. Drape throws to hide dingy chair arms or furniture stains. Drop off the bin in the laundry room or a nearby bedroom, or hide it in a closet; swap the cloth for a few paper towels. Move on to the bathroom—**4 minutes.**

Fake a super-clean bathroom. Tuck stuff from the vanity into the cabinet or drawers, and close the shower door or stretch out the curtain (sure, nosy guests may still snoop inside, but at least you've cut down on visual clutter). Wet a paper towel with rubbing alcohol to both clean and shine, and wipe down the mirror, faucet, sink, and countertop. Use a new alcohol-dipped towel to go over the toilet seat and rim. Clean up spots and hair from the floor with a third water-dampened paper towel. Finally, put out fresh hand towels. Make a round-trip to the kitchen with the wastebasket to dump it into the larger trash can—**5 minutes.**

MAKE IT EASIER

These organizers and cleaning supplies will make tidying up even quicker.

• **Add a shoe bag** to the inside of your entryway closet door: It makes a great stash spot for hats and gloves, unopened mail, and (yep) shoes when you're picking up in a hurry.

• **Store a pet-hair-removal tool,** in a living room drawer or cabinet, so it's handy.

• **Premoistened disinfecting wipes** like those from Clorox, which are ready for cleaning right out of the canister, will speed up any job.

Crystal-Clear Solutions

Wonder how to make your special glasses and candlesticks sparkle with all the other demands of the holiday season? Here are our fast fixes for spots on stemware, sediment inside narrow-neck vases, and melted wax stuck to candleholders. Before you begin, gather the following tools: white vinegar, a plastic basin, a lint-free towel, baking soda, dish liquid, ammonia, white rice, and a delicate scrub sponge.

Clarify cloudy glasses. Nothing dresses up a holiday dinner table more than beautiful crystal goblets. If yours are looking foggy, hard water is most likely to blame. To remove deposits—no scrubbing required—put 2 cups warm white vinegar (microwave for about two minutes) into a plastic basin. In this, place two glasses, on their sides, for about three minutes, turning to make sure they are bathed in warm vinegar all around. Remove glasses, rinse in clear water, and dry with a lint-free towel. If any spots remain, moisten the glass and sprinkle on some baking soda. With your fingertips, lightly polish it inside and out; rinse and dry.

Deep-clean decanters. When that elegant fluted wine pitcher or slim vase caught your eye in a store, you probably didn't wonder how you'd clean it. But if red wine or cut flowers have left behind sediment that's impossible to reach, try this: Fill the vessel halfway with very warm water. Squirt in a little dish liquid and add 2 tablespoons ammonia. Pour in about ½ cup white rice and swirl the mixture so the rice "scrubs" the sides of the glass. Let it sit a few minutes to dissolve the residue, and swirl again. Empty, rinse with very warm water, and dry with your lint-free towel. Place the decanter upside down on a rack to allow the interior to drip and air-dry.

Remove wax drips. Candleholders encrusted with melted wax look as if they belong in a thrift shop rather than on your holiday buffet. To quickly remove the clumps from the crevices of cut crystal, fill a basin with hot water and immerse the holders (or place them upside down if the bases are covered with cloth). Let soak several minutes, then peel off the softened wax. If needed, use a delicate scrub sponge or even your fingernail for any stuck-on bits. Wash the wax-free holders in hot, sudsy water; rinse; and dry. Another option, if you have the time: Put caked-up candlesticks in the freezer for two to three hours. The brittle wax will easily chip off; wash and dry.

DECORATING DISASTERS—SOLVED!

Whether the cause is a frisky pet, cavorting kids, or a klutzy moment of your own, sometimes holiday trimmings go down instead of up. Here are some helpful tips to make cleanup less of a chore for when they do.

Broken glass ornaments. Don rubber gloves and gather up the larger chunks of glass into a folded piece of newspaper; tape it closed and place in trash. Skip the fuss of a dustpan and brush; use pieces of soft bread or a dampened paper towel to quickly collect any remaining shards. Vacuum the spot (and a few feet around it, to ensure you've gotten everything); then search for and pick up any fallen ornament hooks before your kids or pets find them.

Spilled glitter. After you've collected mounds of glitter with your vacuum cleaner's hose—no brushes attached—either replace the bag or empty and clean the canister. These tiny particles can get stuck in the filter or clog the bag, reducing suction. Run a lint roller across the floor or carpet to pick up any remaining sparkles. Wipe the bottoms of your shoes (and also your kids') with a damp paper towel to prevent glitter from being tracked around the house.

So Long, Soot!

Old ashes piled up in the firebox? Black soot on the glass, or smoky stains on the surrounding brick, marble, or tile? If your fireplace is sending smoke signals that it needs a scrub, here's the quickest way to get it done—without putting a damper on your day.

Trash the ash. A wet/dry vacuum with a disposable bag will handle the job once the pile has cooled at least four days. But if you don't have one of those heavy-duty suckers, do this instead: After the ash is completely cool, sprinkle it with damp tea leaves or coffee grounds to cover the stale smell and keep down dust (so you won't inhale it). Then scoop the pile with a fireplace shovel (don't worry if you can't get it all—leaving an inch or two behind is fine), and dump it into a metal can or a bucket. Discard the mess outside, ideally in a metal trash container, but definitely away from the house.

Clear things up. To remove light soot or a cloudy film from glass doors, mix a solution of equal parts white vinegar and warm water and pour into a spray bottle. Spritz a bit on a paper towel and dip it into the fireplace ashes to use as a gentle abrasive. To finish, spray glass and wipe clean with a micro-fiber cloth. If soldered-on gunk won't budge (and if you really care), scrape it away with a razor blade.

Brush it off. If you have smoke stains on your fireplace facing, begin by squirting them with water—it'll keep the cleaning solution from soaking in too fast (this is particularly important with brick). Then dip a brush in a solution of ¼ cup all-purpose cleaner to 1 gallon water; give spots a quick scrub; rinse with a clean sponge; let dry. For marble or other stones, squirt with water, then go over the surface with a soft cloth dipped in mild dishwashing liquid and water. Rinse and wipe dry. One exception: If brick facing is more than 50 years old, it may crumble if you scrub with a cleaner. Just vacuum the surface with your soft-brush attachment.

MAKE IT EASIER

Buy the right equipment—or hire a pro to take care of the job.

• **Have tools at the ready.** Buy a dust mask, a metal bucket with a lid to contain ashes, and a commercial cleaner designed to remove soot and smoke stains from brick, stone, and glass (all products are available at local hardware stores or home centers).

• **Hire an expert.** Consider scheduling an appointment for an annual chimney checkup with a professional sweep certified by the Chimney Safety Institute of American (csia.org).

THE PARTY'S OVER STAIN GUIDE

Our guide to stain removal on carpets, fabric, and upholstery covers all the most common holiday spills: red wine, cranberry sauce, candle wax, chocolate, and gravy. Here's what to do—at the fatal moment and the morning after.

RIGHT AWAY	THE DAY AFTER
RED WINE Quickly blot with clean cloth before sponging with cool water, if safe for fabric. Another trick: Dab with white wine to neutralize red. If on carpet, cover with a pile of salt and let absorb overnight (cover pile with a small bowl to keep guests from tracking).	**For tablecloth or washable clothing:** Rub a little laundry pre-wash or liquid detergent into remaining stain; wash as usual with fabric-appropriate bleach. **For upholstery:** If water-safe, sponge with 1 tablespoon hand dish-washing liquid mixed with 2 cups cool water; rinse and blot dry. Otherwise, use dry-cleaning solution, like Afta Dry Cleaning Solvent and Spot Remover from Guardsman (800-516-0195, guardsman.com). **For carpet:** Vacuum salt, if used, then make a mixture of 1 tablespoon each hand dish-washing liquid and white vinegar with 2 cups warm water. Apply with sponge and blot until stain disappears; rinse and blot dry. **For all water-safe fabrics:** Try Wine Away Red Wine Stain Remover (888-946-3292, wineaway.com).
CANDLE WAX Wax is easier to remove once dry. Blow out candle and keep partying. If you're determined to stain bust immediately, freeze wax by applying ice wrapped in small plastic bag, then proceed as instructed at right.	**For tablecloth or washable clothing:** Gently scrape off as much hardened wax as possible. If colored candle, sponge drips with solvent-based dry-cleaning fluid (see "Red Wine"). Place paper towels over and under stain then press with warm iron, replacing paper towels often until all wax is transferred from carpet to towels. Rub in liquid laundry detergent, then wash in warm or hot water, adding chlorine or oxygen bleach. If any color from candle wax remains on fabric, rewash. **For upholstery and carpet:** Follow same steps as above, except for laundering; for carpet, fluff fibers when done.

RIGHT AWAY	THE DAY AFTER	
Scoop up any melted chocolate with spoon to keep it from soaking in more.	**For tablecloth or washable clothing:** Apply laundry prewash and work into stain with fingers. Launder in hot water with fabric-safe bleach. **For upholstery:** Sponge with dry-cleaning solvent (see "Red Wine") or, if safe for fabric, 1 tablespoon hand dish-washing liquid mixed with 2 cups cool water. Sponge with cold water to rinse; blot dry. **For carpet:** Sponge with dry-cleaning solvent, then use same solution as for upholstery, but with warm water. Rinse and blot dry—or better yet, leave to a pro.	**CHOCOLATE**
Scrape up excess with a spoon and sponge with cool water, if safe for fabric.	**For tablecloth or washable clothing:** Soak stain for 15 minutes in a mixture of 1 tablespoon white vinegar, ½ teaspoon liquid laundry detergent, and 1 quart cool water. Rinse. Sponge with rubbing alcohol, if necessary, then launder, using bleach if needed. **For upholstery:** If water-safe, sponge with 1 tablespoon white vinegar mixed with ⅔ cup rubbing alcohol. Sponge with cold water to rinse, then blot dry. Otherwise, use dry-cleaning solvent (see "Red Wine").	**CRANBERRY SAUCE**
Scrape off as much as you can to contain spill. If tablecloth has multiple stains, after dinner apply laundry stain remover and soak overnight in washing machine filled with warm water, enzyme detergent, and fabric-safe bleach.	**For tablecloth or washable clothing:** If tablecloth has been soaking, drain washing machine next morning; launder in hottest water possible, adding bleach if necessary (choose regular or color-safe as appropriate). If not soaking, apply laundry prewash product to stain and launder tablecloth in hottest water that's safe. **For upholstery or carpet:** Sponge with dry-cleaning solvent until stain disappears; blot dry.	**GRAVY**

Fast, After-the-Feast Cleanup

Once guests go home, it's just you—and the mess. Here's how to tackle leftovers, from a crumb-covered table to an overflowing trash can and dirty dishes in the sink.

Clear the table. If you only have the energy to get one room in shape tonight, the dining room is the easiest to accomplish. Take any remaining dishes, cups, and serving utensils into the kitchen. Then gather up the tablecloth, and shake crumbs over the kitchen sink or garbage can, or just take a step out your back door and toss the crumbs in the yard or nearest flower bed. Carry all the table linens to the washing machine. Fill it with warm water, add detergent, and leave the items to soak overnight (if you have a spare second, scan the fabrics for stains—red wine, gravy—and pretreat before soaking); you can finish the cycle in the morning.

Deal with leftovers. Food that you would normally refrigerate shouldn't sit out at room temperature for more than a couple of hours. So toss anything that's been out longer. Cover any leftovers you plan to keep with foil or plastic wrap before refrigerating (most baked goods can stay out once covered or wrapped); if needed, transfer food to smaller airtight containers the next day when you have more time.

Take out the trash. If there's room in the kitchen trash can, scrape dishes as well as cooled grease or unwanted gravy from pans into it—it's faster than emptying the sink to get at your garbage disposal, and better for your pipes, too. Seal up the bag; set by the back door. You can haul it to the outdoor garbage can in the morning.

Conquer the counters. Last, tackle what's left in and around the sink. Squirt grimy pots and pans with dishwashing liquid, and fill with very hot water. Set them aside on the counter overnight—this extended soak will make them much easier to hand-wash later. Fill empty space in the dishwasher with dirty plates, glasses, and flatware, but don't bother to prerinse, because the machine will do the work for you (yes, really). Add the detergent and start the cycle. With any remaining dinnerware items, rinse and stack neatly in the sink. They'll get their turn at the dishwasher tomorrow.

MAKE IT EASIER

Just a little bit of preplanning will save you loads of time later.

• **Double- or triple-line the trash can,** so you already have a clean bag in place when a full bag is removed.

• **Have your kids or partner unload the dishwasher** before the guests arrive, so you'll have an empty machine ready to go for the after-dinner cleanup.

• **Line broiling or roasting pans with foil** before using, so baked-on bits, grease, and drippings are easily tossed away.

Christmas Decoration Storage Ideas

The stockings may still be hung by the chimney with care, but Santa's come and gone—and it's time to un-trim the tree before every last needle drops off. So recruit the family, crank up the carols one last time, and make the takedown (and next year's put-up) less painful.

Get packing. Start by packing away decorations in customizable storage that doesn't cost a thing, such as grocery- or liquor-store castoffs. Tape an old holiday card onto each box, so you can easily spot it in the attic or basement, and add a label. That way, you don't have to look through ten boxes just to find the tree topper.

Salvage storage. If your original ornament boxes are dented disasters (or you just forgot to save them), don't worry. Ask your local liquor store for wine boxes with cardboard dividers, which you can fold and cut as needed. Then layer two to three ornaments wrapped in tissue paper into each slot, placing heavier ones on the bottom. Also, look around the house for storage ideas: egg cartons for tiny trinkets, plastic produce containers or shoeboxes for bigger baubles, paper-towel tubes for garlands.

What if you have an artificial tree but not the box it came in? Stow the faux foliage in an inexpensive, oversize duffel bag to keep the tree clean and its branches from being crushed during the off season.

Handy hanger. Treat wreaths with the same care you give your favorite party dress. Slip the hoop over the neck of a coat hanger, then cover it with a plastic dry cleaning bag to prevent a year's worth of dust from building up. Hang the wreath in a closet or from a beam in your attic.

Bright idea. Wind unwieldy strings of lights around coffee cans, and toss replacement bulbs in the cans. Cut an X in the plastic top, and stick the plug through. Label each string with masking tape and a marker to remind you which lights go on the tree and which wind around doorways.

Keep vs. Toss

• **Keep stockings**—and not the kind that hang from the mantel: Old hosiery can protect specialty candles from getting damaged. Slip knee-highs over the pillars to keep them dust-free. Then, nestle them in tissue paper to prevent dents or scratches, and stow away from heat or pressure, which can melt or warp the wax.

• **Toss newspaper padding.** While it might seem eco-friendly to wrap fragile ornaments in yesterday's news, the ink can smudge decorations. Opt for white tissue paper (colored sheets can bleed) or plastic grocery bags.

• **Keep notes about your decorations:** what worked, where they went, what you need to replace—even Santa makes a list! Stash the info in the box you'll open first.

Chapter 1

Festive Beginnings

WELCOMING APPETIZERS, FIRST COURSES, DRINKS & SETTING THE SCENE

Throw open your doors and invite friends and family to indulge in a selection of elegant holiday drinks and delectable hors d'oeuvres. Or choose a festive first-course salad or soup to whet their appetites. Either way, here are lots of tempting recipes to help you set the stage.

Stylish Appetizers & Drinks

We've rounded up an irresistible selection of cocktails, punches, and winter warmers, including old-fashioned favorites from our holiday archives. For tips on setting up a bar, see "1-2-3 Party!" and "Stock-Up Cheat Sheet" on pages 66 and 70. Pair your party drink of choice with one of our gorgeous appetizers. You'll find an option to suit every menu and occasion.

Stage-Setting Soups & Salads

Wondering what to serve before you bring out a showstopping prime rib or turkey with all the trimmings? Try crisp Mixed Winter Greens or our colorful, tart Orange-Endive Ambrosia. Or serve a creamy soup: We provide lots of options, from green pea to squash to a luscious lobster bisque.

Cheerful Holiday Crafts

Welcome guests to your front door with one of our homemade wreaths, or get things glowing with our festive ideas for outdoor lights with old-fashioned charm—no snarled strands of bulbs required!

Clockwise from top left: PROSCIUTTO-WRAPPED BREADSTICKS *(page 40)*; BLOOD ORANGE MIMOSAS *(page 65)*; HOW SWEET IT IS *(page 256)*.

Recipes

Crafts

APPETIZERS & DRINKS

Warm Crab Dip

*Provide crackers or bread or cucumber rounds
and invite your guests to take a dip!*

Active time: 10 minutes
Total time: 20 minutes
Makes: 4 cups

1 pound lump crabmeat
½ cup butter (1 stick), cut up
2 packages (8 ounces each) Neufchâtel cheese, cut up
¼ teaspoon cayenne (ground red) pepper
1 green onion, thinly sliced
Toasted bread rounds or crackers for serving

1 Pick through crabmeat to remove any shell or cartilage, making sure not to break up large pieces of meat.

2 In 3-quart saucepan, heat butter, Neufchâtel, and cayenne over medium-low heat about 6 minutes, stirring constantly, until mixture is warm and creamy.

3 Transfer dip to mini slow cooker or fondue pot to keep warm, or transfer to serving bowl. Sprinkle with green onion; serve crab dip with toasted bread or crackers.

Each 2-tablespoon serving: About 80 calories, 4g protein, 0g carbohydrate, 6g total fat (4g saturated), 0g fiber, 130mg sodium

Cocktail Meatballs with Creamy Cranberry Sauce

A pretty cranberry sauce makes these little bites perfect for the holidays. Supply toothpicks for easy dipping.

Active time: 15 minutes
Total time: 40 minutes
Makes: about 42 meatballs

Nonstick cooking spray
1¼ pounds ground beef sirloin
⅓ cup plain dried bread crumbs
¼ cup grated onion
1 large egg, beaten
¼ teaspoon ground nutmeg
½ teaspoon salt
½ teaspoon ground black pepper
½ cup sour cream
3 tablespoons mayonnaise
2 tablespoons cranberry preserves
2 tablespoons grainy Dijon mustard
1 teaspoon Worcestershire sauce
Chopped fresh parsley for garnish

1 Preheat oven to 450°F. Line 18" by 12" jelly-roll pan with foil; spray lightly with nonstick cooking spray.

2 In bowl, combine beef, bread crumbs, onion, egg, nutmeg, salt, and pepper.

3 With tablespoon-size cookie-dough scoop, scoop mixture into balls; place on prepared pan, ½ inch apart. Spray meatballs with nonstick spray. Roast 20 to 25 minutes or until cooked through (instant-read thermometer inserted into center of meatball should register 165°F).

4 In bowl, stir together sour cream, mayonnaise, preserves, mustard, and Worcestershire. Garnish meatballs with parsley; serve with sauce alongside.

Each 2-meatball serving with 2 teaspoons sauce: About 80 calories, 6g protein, 3g carbohydrate, 5g total fat (2g saturated), 0g fiber, 145mg sodium

Clockwise from top left: COCKTAIL MEATBALLS WITH CREAMY CRANBERRY SAUCE *(above)*; WARM CRAB DIP *(above)* WITH CHAMPAGNE AND LILLET COCKTAILS *(page 62)*; LAYERED WHITE BEAN AND TOMATO DIP *(page 38)*; CRANBERRY MOJITOS *(page 65)*; CHRISTMAS BALL WREATH *(page 102)*.

Layered White Bean and Tomato Dip

This healthy, flavorful appetizer is an easy, do-ahead way to please all your holiday guests.

Active time: 35 minutes
Total time: 1 hour 15 minutes plus chilling
Makes: 12 appetizer servings

1 can (28 ounces) whole tomatoes, peeled and drained
2 tablespoons olive oil
1 shallot, finely chopped
1 garlic clove, finely chopped
2 teaspoons sugar
2 sprigs fresh thyme
1/4 teaspoon salt
Pinch ground black pepper
2 cans (14 ounces each) cannellini beans, rinsed and drained
4 ounces feta cheese, crumbled (1 cup)
1/3 cup light mayonnaise
2 tablespoons fresh lemon juice
1 cup packed curly parsley leaves, finely chopped
3 green onions, dark green parts only, thinly sliced
2 tablespoons capers, drained
Fresh vegetable crudités for serving

1 In bowl, with hands, crush tomatoes and drain.

2 In 2-quart saucepan, heat 1 tablespoon oil on medium. Add shallot and garlic; cook 2 minutes or until golden, stirring. Add tomatoes, sugar, thyme, 1/8 teaspoon salt, and pepper. Cook 6 to 8 minutes or until almost dry, stirring. Remove from heat; discard thyme. Cool.

3 In food processor, pulse beans, feta, mayonnaise, lemon juice, remaining tablespoon oil, and remaining 1/8 teaspoon salt until smooth.

4 In bowl, combine parsley, green onions, and capers.

5 In 4-cup serving bowl, layer half of bean dip, all of tomato sauce, and half of herb mixture. Top with remaining bean and herb mixtures. Cover; refrigerate at least 2 hours or up to 1 day. Serve with crudités.

Each 1/3-cup serving: About 140 calories, 5g protein, 14g carbohydrate, 7g total fat (2g saturated), 3g fiber, 450mg sodium

Warm Layered Tex-Mex Bean Dip

This colorful dip is always a hit. The pinto bean, Jack cheese, and salsa layers can be assembled several hours in advance, then baked just before serving.

Active time: 35 minutes
Total time: 45 minutes
Makes: 5 1/2 cups

2 garlic cloves, peeled
1 can (15 to 19 ounces) pinto beans
2 green onions, finely chopped
1 tablespoon tomato paste
1 tablespoon water
4 ounces Monterey Jack cheese, shredded (1 cup)
1 cup mild to medium-hot salsa
2 avocados, each cut in half, pitted, and peeled
1/4 cup chopped fresh cilantro
3 tablespoons finely chopped red onion
2 tablespoons fresh lime juice
1/2 teaspoon salt
1 cup sour cream
Tortilla chips for serving

1 Preheat oven to 350°F. In 1-quart saucepan, place *1 inch water* and heat to boiling over high heat. Add garlic and cook 3 minutes to blanch; drain. With flat side of chef's knife, mash garlic; transfer to medium bowl and add beans, half of green onions, tomato paste, and water. Mash until well combined but still slightly chunky. Spread in bottom of 9-inch glass pie plate.

2 Sprinkle cheese over bean mixture, then spread salsa on top. Bake until piping hot, about 12 minutes.

3 Meanwhile, in clean medium bowl, mash avocados just until slightly chunky. Stir in cilantro, red onion, lime juice, and salt. Spoon avocado mixture over hot dip mixture and spread sour cream on top. Sprinkle with remaining green onions. Serve with tortilla chips.

Each 1-tablespoon serving: About 110 calories, 0g protein, 2g carbohydrate, 12g total fat (2g saturated), 0g fiber, 276mg sodium

HEALTHY HOLIDAY MAKEOVER: SOUR CREAM AND ONION DIP

This fresh-onion redo of the party favorite has zero MSG and one-tenth the sodium of those traditional flavoring packets. And some store-bought tubs have almost three times the calories and six times the fat. Neither option tastes nearly as good as ours. That's because we sauté vitamin C–rich onions in antioxidant-packed olive oil, then stir them into a luscious blend of sour cream and yogurt. Get ready for raves.

Active time: 10 minutes • Total time: 35 minutes plus chilling • Makes: 2 cups

1½ cups plain fat-free yogurt

2 tablespoons extra-virgin olive oil

2 yellow onions, finely chopped

¼ teaspoon sugar

¼ teaspoon salt

⅛ teaspoon ground black pepper

⅓ cup reduced-fat sour cream

Snipped chives for garnish

Fresh vegetable crudités for serving

1 Line medium sieve set over deep bowl with basket-style coffee filter or paper towel. Spoon yogurt into filter; cover and refrigerate 25 minutes. Discard liquid in bowl.

2 Meanwhile, in 12-inch skillet, heat oil on medium until hot. Add onions, sugar, salt, and pepper. Cook 15 to 17 minutes or until dark golden brown, stirring onions occasionally.

3 Line plate with double thickness of paper towels. With slotted spoon, transfer onions to plate to drain further and cool. (Onions will crisp slightly while cooling; some pieces may stick to paper towel.)

4 In medium bowl, combine sour cream, strained yogurt, and onions. Stir well. Cover, and refrigerate at least 1 hour or up to 3 days. (Dip is best when refrigerated for 24 hours; flavors develop more fully.) Garnish with chives and serve with fresh vegetable crudités.

25 CAL **Each 2-tablespoon serving:** 2g protein, 4g carbohydrate, 2g total fat (1g saturated), 1g fiber, 55mg sodium

MY MOST MAGICAL CHRISTMAS

"For three years in a row, my dad won the award from the local Lions Club for the best holiday display . . . My dad decorated our house every year with so many lights—on the roof, in front of the house, everywhere. We had the house that people would slow down to look at when they drove by. And I took such pride in that."

—Kelly Ripa

Prosciutto-Wrapped Breadsticks

These Italian-style breadsticks couldn't be easier—or more delicious! Breadsticks such as Stella d'oro brand are available at grocery stores, or purchase artisanal ones.

Total time 15 minutes • Makes: 30 sticks

30 thick breadsticks
3/4 pound very thinly sliced prosciutto
2/3 cup freshly grated Parmesan cheese

1 Place oven rack 4 inches from broiler heat source. Preheat broiler on High.

2 Wrap each breadstick from top to bottom with prosciutto. Place on cookie sheet. Sprinkle with Parmesan cheese.

3 Broil 30 seconds to 1 minute or until Parmesan has melted.

Each serving: About 70 calories, 5g protein, 7g carbohydrate, 2g total fat (1g saturated), 0g fiber, 380mg sodium

---

QUICK BITES

Here are three last-minute appetizers that everyone will love.

Tomato and Mozzarella Bites

In large bowl, whisk together **2 tablespoons olive oil**, **2 tablespoons white balsamic vinegar**, **1/4 teaspoon dried oregano**, and **1/4 teaspoon each salt and ground black pepper**; add **20 mini fresh mozzarella balls (ciliegini)** and toss until coated. Thread onto skewers, alternating mozzarella balls, **20 grape tomatoes**, and **40 basil leaves**. Makes 20 appetizer servings.

Each serving: About 95 calories, 5g protein, 1g carbohydrate, 8g total fat (4g saturated), 0g fiber, 47mg sodium

Chutney-Glazed Goat Cheese

Place **8-ounce log goat cheese** on serving platter. In small bowl, microwave **1/4 cup mango chutney** on High 1 minute; pour over goat cheese. Top with **2 tablespoons chopped walnuts**. Serve with crackers, bread, dried apricots, and grapes alongside. Makes 8 appetizer servings.

Each 2 tablespoons: About 55 calories, 3g protein, 3g carbohydrate, 4g total fat (2g saturated), 0g fiber, 115mg sodium

Spiced Citrus Olives

From **1 lemon**, with vegetable peeler, remove **3 strips peel**; then squeeze **1 tablespoon juice**. From **1 orange**, with vegetable peeler, remove **3 strips peel**; then squeeze **2 tablespoons juice**. In bowl, combine peels, juices, **2 cups mixed olives**, **1/4 cup olive oil**, **2 teaspoons fennel seeds**, **1/2 teaspoon crushed red pepper**, **1/4 teaspoon ground coriander**, and **1/4 teaspoon ground cumin**. Makes 2½ cups.

Each 2 tablespoons: About 50 calories, 0g protein, 1g carbohydrate, 5g total fat (1g saturated), 0g fiber, 191mg sodium

PROSCIUTTO-WRAPPED BREADSTICKS (*opposite*);
CHEDDAR CRAB PUFFS (*page 50*).

STYLISH STARTERS

Appetizers serve two important roles: They whet the guests' appetites and set the tone for the meal that follows. A stylish sit-down dinner calls for elegant starters that look and taste special, while fun finger foods and dips are good choices for a more casual buffet. At a cocktail party, the hors d'oeuvres are the meal; you need a generous selection.

Managing the Menu

• **Figure you'll need four or five small appetizers** before a dinner; for a cocktail party, count on ten to twelve pieces per guest. But have extras on hand; your guests may show up ravenous!

• **Prepare as many appetizers in advance** as possible. Among the best candidates are marinated olives and vegetable crudités, dips and spreads, and baked savory pastries.

• **For hors d'oeuvres that require last-minute assembly,** prepare the components and chill separately until serving time. That way, you can quickly assemble them just before the guests arrive.

• **Consider your available refrigerator space.** To make room, arrange finished appetizers on a tray and cover them with plastic wrap. Then invert a large roasting pan over the tray and place a second platter on top. Nibbles, and even dips and spreads, can be stored in resealable plastic bags.

• **Plan on serving only one or two hot appetizers.** Unless you have more than one oven, it's too difficult to juggle reheating multiple items.

• **Be sure to include some low-maintenance appetizers,** like nuts, dips, spreads, and a cheese platter (see "The Perfect Cheese Platter" on page 63). These all require no more work than setting them out and occasionally replenishing the tray.

• **Too much of a chill dulls the taste of foods,** so be sure to remove cold appetizers from the fridge 30 minutes before serving.

Serving with Flair

Make sure appetizers are easy to handle and eat— no more than a bite or two each. Set out bowls for olive pits and offer toothpicks or skewers to spear small bites—and don't forget to provide plenty of cocktail napkins and, if appropriate, small plates.

Then channel your inner stylist! Use decorative trays and serving bowls, tiered stands, and chafing dishes to create a beautiful display. Garnish hors d'oeuvres with chopped fresh herbs or toasted nuts. Top dips with a sprinkle of cayenne or paprika or a drizzle of infused oil. Spear bite-size items like mini meatballs with cocktail forks, or serve a single enticing bite in a porcelain soup spoon (you can buy these cheap at an Asian market or online). Let your menu—and your imagination—be your guide!

Stuffed Eggs

These make-ahead appetizers are perfect for a crowd. Cook a couple dozen eggs and try all our variations!

Active time: 30 minutes
Total time: 40 minutes plus chilling
Makes: 12 appetizer servings

6 large eggs
1/4 cup mayonnaise
1 tablespoon milk
1/8 teaspoon salt

1 In 3-quart saucepan, place eggs and enough *cold water* to cover by at least 1 inch; heat to boiling over high heat. Immediately remove from heat and cover tightly; let stand 15 minutes. Pour off hot water and run cold water over eggs to cool. Peel eggs.

2 Slice eggs lengthwise in half, cutting around yolks. Gently remove yolks and place in small bowl; with fork, finely mash yolks. Stir in mayonnaise, milk, and salt until evenly blended. Egg-yolk mixture and whites can be covered separately and refrigerated up to 24 hours.

3 Place egg whites in jelly-roll pan lined with paper towels (to prevent eggs from rolling). Spoon egg-yolk mixture into pastry bag fitted with star tip or resealable plastic bag with one corner cut off. Pipe about 1 tablespoon yolk mixture into each egg-white half. (Alternatively, spoon filling into eggs.) If not serving right away, cover eggs and refrigerate up to 4 hours.

Each piece: About 70 calories, 3g protein, 0g carbohydrate, 6g total fat (1g saturated), 0g fiber, 82mg sodium

Bacon-Horseradish Stuffed Eggs

Prepare yolk mixture as directed, adding **2 tablespoons crumbled crisp-cooked bacon** and **1 tablespoon bottled white horseradish.** If not serving right away, sprinkle crumbled bacon on top of stuffed eggs instead of adding to yolk mixture.

Each piece: About 80 calories, 4g protein, 1g carbohydrate, 7g total fat (2g saturated), 0g fiber, 102mg sodium

Dried Tomato-Caper Stuffed Eggs

Prepare yolk mixture as directed, adding **5 teaspoons chopped dried tomatoes packed in oil and herbs, 5 teaspoons chopped drained capers,** and **1/8 teaspoon coarsely ground black pepper.**

Each piece: About 80 calories, 3g protein, 1g carbohydrate, 7g total fat (1g saturated), 0g fiber, 143mg sodium

Lemon-Basil Stuffed Eggs

Prepare yolk mixture as directed, adding **1 tablespoon chopped fresh basil, 1/4 teaspoon freshly grated lemon peel,** and **1/4 teaspoon coarsely ground black pepper.**

Each piece: About 75 calories, 3g protein, 0g carbohydrate, 6g total fat (1g saturated), 0g fiber, 82mg sodium

Pimiento-Studded Stuffed Eggs

Prepare yolk mixture as directed, adding **2 tablespoons chopped pimientos, 2 teaspoons Dijon mustard,** and **1/8 teaspoon cayenne (ground red) pepper.**

Each piece: About 75 calories, 3g protein, 1g carbohydrate, 6g total fat (1g saturated), 0g fiber, 102mg sodium

Cranberry-Fig Conserve with Brie

*What an easy, elegant way to start off a holiday dinner.
Allowing the Brie to soften at room temperature enhances
the flavor of the cheese.*

Active time: 10 minutes
Total time: 25 minutes plus chilling and standing
Makes: 24 appetizer servings

2/3 cup packed brown sugar
2/3 cup water
1/4 cup brandy
1 lemon
1 bag (12 ounces) fresh cranberries (3 cups)
8 ounces dried figs, stems trimmed, each cut into 8 pieces
1 jalapeño chile with seeds retained, chopped
1 wheel (6 to 7 inches) ripe Brie cheese or one 1-pound
    wedge
1 loaf (16 ounces) French bread, sliced

1 In 2-quart saucepan, combine brown sugar, water, and
brandy. Heat to boiling over high heat; boil 2 minutes.

2 Meanwhile, from lemon, grate 1 teaspoon peel and
squeeze 2 tablespoons juice. Add both to saucepan, along
with cranberries, figs, and jalapeño; heat to boiling,
stirring frequently. Reduce heat to medium and cook,
stirring occasionally, until most cranberries have popped
and mixture is slightly thickened, about 5 minutes.

3 Transfer cranberry mixture to bowl or container.
Cover and refrigerate at least 3 hours or up to 1 week.
Makes about 3 cups.

4 About 1 hour before serving, remove Brie and conserve
from refrigerator; let stand at room temperature about
30 minutes to warm slightly. To serve, arrange Brie on
platter. Place conserve in small serving bowl with sliced
bread alongside.

Each serving with 2 slices bread: About 175 calories, 7g protein,
26g carbohydrate, 5g total fat (3g saturated), 2g fiber,
264mg sodium

Classic Swiss Fondue

*The name of this ever-popular hot cheese dish from
Switzerland comes from the French word* fondre *(to melt).
This luscious version uses Swiss cheese, Gruyère cheese,
and white wine to create the perfect balance of flavors.
Choose a dry, slightly acidic wine, such as Sauvignon Blanc.*

Active time: 15 minutes
Total time: 30 minutes
Makes: 6 first-course servings

1 garlic clove, cut in half
1 1/2 cups dry white wine
1 tablespoon kirsch or brandy
8 ounces Swiss or Emmental cheese, shredded (2 cups)
8 ounces Gruyère cheese, shredded (2 cups)
3 tablespoons all-purpose flour
1/8 teaspoon ground black pepper
Pinch ground nutmeg
1 loaf (16 ounces) French bread, cut into 1-inch cubes

1 Rub inside of fondue pot or heavy nonreactive 2-quart
saucepan with garlic; discard garlic. Pour wine into
fondue pot. Heat over medium-low heat until very hot
but not boiling; stir in kirsch.

2 Meanwhile, in medium bowl, toss both cheeses and
flour until mixed. Add one handful at a time to wine,
stirring constantly and vigorously, until cheese has
melted and mixture is thick and smooth. If fondue
separates, increase heat to medium, stirring just until
smooth. Stir in pepper and nutmeg.

3 Transfer fondue to table; place over tabletop heater
to keep hot, if you like. To eat, spear bread cubes using
long-handled fondue forks and dip into cheese mixture.

Each serving with bread cubes: About 595 calories, 34g protein,
56g carbohydrate, 23g total fat (13g saturated), 3g fiber,
777mg sodium

Clockwise from top left: CRANBERRY-FIG CONSERVE WITH BRIE *(above);* CLASSIC SWISS FONDUE *(above);* STUFFED EGGS *(page 43).*

Savory Blue Cheese, Walnut, and Date Rugelach

Filling rich cream-cheese dough with a mixture of blue cheese, walnuts, and dates turns rugelach into delicious appetizer pastries that go perfectly with a glass of wine.

Active time: 40 minutes
Total time: 1 hour 10 minutes plus chilling
Makes: 48 rugelach

1 cup butter or margarine (2 sticks), softened
1 package (8 ounces) cream cheese, softened
2 cups all-purpose flour
1/2 teaspoon salt
1 1/2 cups walnuts
4 ounces blue cheese, cut into small pieces
48 pitted dates (about 12 ounces)
1 large egg white
1 teaspoon water

1 In large bowl, with mixer on medium speed, beat butter and cream cheese until creamy, occasionally scraping bowl with rubber spatula. Reduce speed to low; gradually beat in flour and salt just until blended.

2 Divide dough into 4 equal pieces; shape each into disk. Wrap each disk in plastic wrap and refrigerate until firm enough to roll, at least 4 hours or overnight.

3 In food processor with knife blade attached, process 1/2 cup walnuts until finely chopped; transfer to small bowl. In same bowl, process blue cheese and remaining 1 cup walnuts just until coarse mixture forms.

4 Preheat oven to 350°F. Line two large cookie sheets with foil; grease foil.

5 On lightly floured surface, with floured rolling pin, roll one disk of dough into 10-inch round. (If dough is too cold to roll, let stand 5 to 10 minutes at room temperature to soften slightly.) With pastry wheel or knife, cut dough into 12 equal wedges but do not separate pieces. Beginning 1 inch from edge, sprinkle 1/2 cup blue-cheese mixture in 2-inch-wide ring, leaving dough in center exposed. Place 1 whole date horizontally on wide curved end of each wedge. Separate wedges, and starting at wide end, roll up

each wedge, jelly-roll fashion. Place rugelach, point side down, on cookie sheet. Repeat with remaining dough (one disk at a time), blue-cheese mixture, and dates, arranging all rugelach at least 1 inch apart on sheets.

6 In small bowl, lightly beat egg white with water. Brush rugelach with mixture and sprinkle with reserved walnuts.

7 Bake until golden, 30 to 35 minutes, rotating cookie sheets between upper and lower oven racks halfway through. Immediately transfer rugelach to wire racks to cool. Store in airtight container up to 3 days, or in freezer up to 3 months.

Each rugelach: About 125 calories, 2g protein, 10g carbohydrate, 9g total fat (4g saturated), 1g fiber, 115mg sodium

Blue Cheese-Stuffed Celery

Blue cheese and golden Calimyrna figs form a can't-miss savory-sweet stuffing.

Active time: 20 minutes
Total time: 25 minutes plus chilling
Makes: 24 pieces

4 ounces blue cheese
2 ounces Neufchâtel cheese, softened
2 tablespoons whole milk
1/4 teaspoon freshly ground black pepper
9 stalks celery hearts, cut into 3-inch pieces
1/2 cup dried chopped Calimyrna figs
1 tablespoon pure honey
Snipped chives for garnish

1 In medium bowl, with mixer on high speed, beat blue cheese and cream cheese until smooth. Add milk and pepper; beat until well combined. Cover and refrigerate 30 minutes or up to 2 hours.

2 Transfer cheese mixture to heavy-duty quart-size resealable plastic bag with one corner cut to form 1/2-inch hole. Pipe cheese mixture down centers of celery pieces. Top with figs and lightly drizzle with honey. Garnish with chives.

Each piece: 35 calories, 2g protein, 3g carbohydrate, 2g total fat (1g saturated), 1g fiber, 85mg sodium

HEALTHY HOLIDAY MAKEOVER: PIMIENTO CHEESE LOG

Your guests will love this party favorite—and its slim profile. Our version is as cheesy as the original, but a lot less fatty: By subbing goat cheese for mayo and extra roasted red peppers for the bacon (we used piquillo peppers, but other roasted red peppers will do), we've cut 290 calories and 27 grams of fat. Plus, our fresh green herb and pink pepper coating delivers holiday cheer. For extra calorie savings, serve with celery sticks instead of crackers.

Total time: 10 minutes plus chilling · Makes: 2 logs

3 tablespoons roasted, salted almonds

1/4 cup fresh flat-leaf parsley leaves, tightly packed

2 jarred, roasted piquillo peppers or
    other prepared roasted red peppers, patted dry

1 package (8 ounces) Neufchâtel cheese

4 ounces soft goat cheese

1/2 teaspoon ground coriander

1/8 teaspoon cayenne (ground red) pepper

1 teaspoon coarsely ground pink pepper
    or 1/2 teaspoon ground black pepper

Crackers or celery sticks for serving

1 In food processor with knife blade attached, pulse almonds until finely chopped. Transfer to large sheet of plastic wrap; do not wipe bowl. Pulse parsley until finely chopped; transfer to plastic wrap with almonds. Wipe bowl.

2 In cleaned food processor, pulse piquillo peppers until finely chopped. Add both cheeses, coriander, and cayenne and pulse until well mixed, occasionally scraping bowl with rubber spatula. Transfer mixture to clean large sheet of plastic wrap and form into 12-inch log.

3 Add pink pepper to parsley mixture; mix well. Spread in 12" by 5" rectangle. Using plastic wrap, place cheese log on parsley mixture. Roll and gently press log into parsley mixture. Wrap tightly in plastic. Refrigerate until firm, about 3 hours or up to 3 days. To serve, cut log crosswise to form 2 smaller logs and arrange on platter with crackers or celery alongside.

Each 2-tablespoon serving cheese: 3g protein, 1g carbohydrate, 6g total fat (3g saturated), 0g fiber, 90mg sodium

SAVORY TARTLETS WITH THREE FILLINGS

We streamlined the prep time for these two-bite tartlets by using store-bought shells.

Active time: 35 minutes • Total time: 40 minutes • Makes: 30 tartlets

30 mini phyllo (filo) pastry shells
Choice of tartlet filling (see below)

Preheat oven to 350°F. Line 18" by 12" jelly-roll pan with parchment paper. Arrange shells in single layer in pan. Bake 5 to 7 minutes or until golden brown. Cool completely in pan on wire rack. Prepare desired filling and finish tartlets as instructed in filling recipe.

Creamy Spinach-Leek Filling

In 8-inch skillet, melt 1 tablespoon butter on medium heat. Add 1 cup thinly sliced leek (white part only) and 1/8 teaspoon each salt and ground black pepper. Cook 6 minutes or until tender, stirring often. Add 1 1/2 cups packed baby spinach and 1/4 teaspoon chopped fresh thyme leaves. Cook until spinach just wilts, stirring. Stir in 1 tablespoon chopped fresh dill; cool slightly. Finely chop mixture; divide among shells. In bowl, whisk 1 large egg with 1/3 cup heavy cream, 1/8 teaspoon freshly grated nutmeg, and 1/8 teaspoon salt until smooth. Divide among shells. Bake 8 minutes or until just set. Garnish with dill.

Each tartlet: About 35 calories, 1g protein, 3g carbohydrate, 3g total fat (1g saturated), 0g fiber, 35mg sodium

Herbed Goat Cheese Filling

Separate white and green parts of 1 green onion; finely chop separately. In medium bowl, with fork, mix white part of onion; 4 ounces softened goat cheese; 1/2 teaspoon finely chopped fresh thyme leaves, 1/4 teaspoon crushed fennel seeds, and 1/8 teaspoon each salt and ground black pepper. In small bowl, combine 1 seeded and chopped tomato, 3 tablespoons finely chopped pitted Kalamata olives, 1 teaspoon olive oil, 1/2 teaspoon balsamic vinegar, green parts of onion, and 1/4 teaspoon pepper. Divide cheese mixture among shells. Top with tomato mixture. Garnish with basil and parsley.

Each tartlet: About 35 calories, 1g protein, 2g carbohydrate, 2g total fat (1g saturated), 0g fiber, 45mg sodium

Ricotta and Roasted Red Pepper Filling

In food processor with knife blade attached, combine 3/4 cup ricotta, 1 roasted red pepper, 3 tablespoons grated Parmesan, 1/8 teaspoon smoked paprika, 1/8 teaspoon cayenne pepper, and 1/8 teaspoon each salt and black pepper. Pulse until smooth; transfer to resealable plastic bag. In 8-inch skillet, combine 1 tablespoon olive oil, 2 tablespoons blanched almonds, and 1/8 teaspoon salt. Cook over medium heat 7 minutes or until golden, stirring; transfer to paper towels. Add 1 tablespoon capers to skillet. Cook 1 to 2 minutes or until crisp, stirring. Transfer to paper towels. When cool, chop almonds and capers. Snip one corner of bag with ricotta; pipe into shells. Top with almonds, capers, and snipped fresh chives.

Each tartlet: About 40 calories, 2g protein, 3g carbohydrate, 3g total fat (1g saturated), 0g fiber, 55mg sodium

Savory Tartlets with Three Fillings *(opposite)*

Cheddar Crab Puffs

These melt-in-your-mouth puffs are sure to be a hit.

Active time: 15 minutes

Total time: 40 minutes

Makes: about 42 puffs

3/4 cup water

4 tablespoons butter or margarine, cut up

1/4 teaspoon salt

1/4 teaspoon ground black pepper

3/4 cup all-purpose flour

3 large eggs

4 ounces extra-sharp Cheddar cheese, shredded (1 cup)

6 ounces lump crabmeat, picked over

1 Preheat oven to 400°F. Line two cookie sheets with parchment paper. Then, in 3-quart saucepan, combine water, butter, salt, and pepper. Heat to boiling on medium. Remove from heat. Add flour and stir until ball forms. Stir in eggs, one at a time, until dough is smooth and shiny. Stir in Cheddar and crab.

2 With tablespoon-size cookie scoop, scoop mixture into balls onto parchment, 1 inch apart. Bake 25 to 30 minutes or until golden brown, rotating sheets between upper and lower racks halfway through. Serve warm. (To make ahead, place in resealable plastic bag; freeze up to 1 month. Reheat frozen puffs in 400°F oven 8 to 10 minutes.)

Each 2-puff serving: About 75 calories, 4g protein, 4g carbohydrate, 5g total fat (2g saturated), 0g fiber, 125mg sodium

---

LIGHTER PARTY FARE

Give your guests low-cal options with these luscious high-flavor appetizers.

Artichoke and Red Pepper Bruschetta

In medium bowl, toss together **1 jar (6 ounces) marinated artichoke hearts**, drained well and coarsely chopped; **3/4 cup jarred, roasted red pepper**, chopped; **1/2 cup loosely packed fresh basil leaves**, sliced; **6 Kalamata olives**, pitted and chopped; and **2 teaspoons fresh lemon juice**. Spoon onto **24 whole-wheat flatbread crackers** just before serving. Makes 24 appetizer servings.

Each serving: About 25 calories, 1g protein, 5g carbohydrate, 1g total fat (0g saturated), 1g fiber, 80mg sodium

Greek Spinach Dip

In bowl, mash **1/2 cup feta cheese**; stir in **1 1/2 cup plain fat-free yogurt**; **1 package (10 ounces) frozen chopped spinach**, thawed and squeezed dry; **1/2 cup chopped fresh dill**; **2 teaspoons grated fresh lemon peel**; and **1/4 teaspoon salt**. Serve dip at room temperature with **sliced raw vegetables** or **whole-wheat pita**. Can be covered and refrigerated up to 2 days. Makes 2½ cups.

Each tablespoon: About 15 calories, 1g protein, 1g carbohydrate, 1g total fat (0g saturated), 0g fiber, 55mg sodium

Smoky Snack Mix

Preheat oven to 275°F. In large bowl, combine **9 cups light microwave-popped corn** (from one 11-ounce package), **2 cups multigrain squares or Multi-Bran Chex cereal**, and **1/2 cup roasted hulled pumpkin seeds (pepitas)**. In cup, stir together **1 tablespoon olive oil**, **1 1/2 teaspoons smoked mild paprika**, and **1/2 teaspoon salt**. Gradually drizzle oil mixture over popcorn mix, tossing until evenly coated. Spread mixture in two 15½" by 10½" jelly-roll pans. Bake 15 minutes or until toasted and fragrant. Can be stored in airtight containers up to 2 weeks. Makes 11 cups.

Each 1/2 cup: About 60 calories, 2g protein, 7g carbohydrate, 3g total fat (1g saturated), 2g fiber, 135mg sodium

Herbed Gougères

You'll be surprised how easy it is to create these sophisticated-looking appetizers using traditional choux pastry dough. To make ahead, see Tip.

Active time: 45 minutes
Total time: 1 hour 10 minutes
Makes: 58 gougères

1 cup water
6 tablespoons butter or margarine, cut into tablespoons
¼ teaspoon salt
Pinch cayenne (ground red) pepper
1 cup all-purpose flour
4 large eggs
6 ounces Gruyère cheese, shredded (1½ cups)
¼ cup fresh flat-leaf parsley leaves, finely chopped
2 tablespoons finely chopped fresh chives
1 teaspoon freshly grated lemon peel

1 Preheat oven to 400°F. Line two large cookie sheets with parchment paper.

2 In 3-quart saucepan, heat water, butter, salt, and cayenne to boiling on medium. Remove from heat. With wooden spoon, vigorously stir in flour all at once until mixture forms ball and leaves side of pan.

3 Add eggs, one at a time, beating well after each addition, until batter is smooth and satiny. Stir in cheese, parsley, chives, and lemon peel until well mixed. Drop batter by rounded teaspoons, about 1½ inches apart, onto prepared cookie sheets.

4 Bake 20 to 25 minutes or until puffed and golden brown, rotating sheets between upper and lower oven racks halfway through. Place sheets on wire racks to cool, 3 to 5 minutes. Serve warm.

TIP: To make ahead, cool gougères completely, then transfer to airtight containers and freeze up to 1 month. Transfer from freezer to cookie sheets; reheat in 350°F oven 10 minutes or until warm.

Each serving (4 gougères): About 140 calories, 6g protein, 7g carbohydrate, 10g total fat (7g saturated), 0g fiber, 160mg sodium

Lacy Parmesan Crisps

Called frico *in Italy, these delicious wafers are simply spoonfuls of grated cheese that are baked and cooled. Reusable nonstick baking liners, available at most kitchen supply stores, yield the best results, but you can use nonstick cookie sheets instead.*

Active time: 30 minutes
Total time: 55 minutes
Makes: 24 crisps

6 ounces Parmesan cheese, coarsely grated (1½ cups)

1 Preheat oven to 375°F. Line two large cookie sheets with reusable baking liners. Drop level tablespoons Parmesan 3 inches apart onto cookie sheets; spread into 2-inch rounds.

2 Bake Parmesan rounds until edges just begin to color, 6 to 7 minutes. Transfer crisps, still on baking liners, to wire racks to cool 2 minutes. Transfer to paper towels to drain. Repeat with remaining Parmesan.

Each crisp: About 30 calories, 3g protein, 0g carbohydrate, 2g total fat (1g saturated), 0g fiber, 114mg sodium

Sweet Potato and Zucchini Latkes

This twist on classic potato latkes yields a delightfully crispy and slightly sweet pancake. To prevent the patties from getting soggy, prepare the mixture right before cooking and pour off excess liquid while cooking, if necessary. These lacy latkes are delicate, so don't press down too hard on them once the cakes are in the pan.

Total time: 30 minutes
Makes: about 24 (2-inch) latkes

1 large egg
1 large egg white
1 medium zucchini (8 ounces)
1 medium sweet potato (12 ounces), peeled
¼ cup finely chopped onion
¼ teaspoon salt
⅛ teaspoon coarsely ground black pepper
3 tablespoons canola oil
Unsweetened applesauce (optional)

1 Preheat oven to 250°F. In medium bowl, lightly beat egg and egg white; set aside. Cut zucchini lengthwise in half and remove seeds. Coarsely grate zucchini and sweet potato; transfer to bowl with egg mixture. Stir in onion, salt, and pepper until combined.

2 In nonstick 12-inch skillet, heat 1 tablespoon oil over medium heat until hot. Add zucchini mixture by heaping tablespoons to skillet, gently flattening each latke with back of spoon. Cook 2 minutes or until edges are golden; flip and cook 2 to 3 minutes longer or until bottoms are golden. Drain on paper towels. Keep latkes warm in oven.

3 Repeat with remaining 2 tablespoons oil and remaining zucchini mixture. Serve latkes hot with applesauce alongside, if you like.

Each serving (2 latkes): About 100 calories, 4g protein, 20g carbohydrate, 1g total fat (0g saturated), 4g fiber, 220mg sodium

Top: Sweet Potato and Zucchini Latkes *(above);*
Bottom: Seafood Salad Cucumber Cups *(opposite).*

Seafood Salad Cucumber Cups

Nestle sweet shrimp and crabmeat salad in a refreshing cucumber shell and top with tart, jewel-like pomegranate seeds for an elegant holiday appetizer.

Total time: 40 minutes
Makes: 12 appetizer servings

6 sprigs fresh dill
2 lemons
2 teaspoons Dijon mustard
Pinch cayenne (ground red) pepper
1/2 teaspoon salt
3 tablespoons extra-virgin olive oil
8 ounces 16-to-20-count shelled and deveined shrimp
2 large seedless (English) cucumbers (1 pound each)
8 ounces lump crabmeat, picked over
2 tablespoons snipped chives
1/4 cup pomegranate seeds

1 Separate dill leaves from stems; reserve separately. From lemons, finely grate 1/2 teaspoon peel and squeeze 1/4 cup juice into large bowl. Reserve rinds.

2 To peel and juice, add mustard, cayenne, and salt; whisk until mixed. Whisk in oil in slow, steady stream until blended. Dressing can be refrigerated up to 3 days.

3 In 4-quart saucepan, combine dill stems, lemon rinds, and *8 cups water*. Heat to boiling. Reduce heat to maintain gentle simmer. Add shrimp; cook 3 minutes or until just opaque, stirring. Drain. Rinse under cold water until cold; drain. Discard dill and lemon. Coarsely chop shrimp. Shrimp can be refrigerated overnight.

4 Trim cucumbers; cut into 36 slices 1/2 inch thick. With melon baller, scoop out centers of slices without cutting through bottoms.

5 Finely chop 1 tablespoon dill leaves. Gently fold into dressing along with shrimp, crabmeat, and chives.

6 Fill each cucumber cup with 1 tablespoon salad mixture. Garnish with pomegranate and dill.

Each serving (3 pieces): About 75 calories, 7g protein, 3g carbohydrate, 4g total fat (1g saturated), 1g fiber, 300mg sodium

Salmon Pâté

This rich pâté is an ideal do-ahead. Make it up to two days beforehand, cover, and refrigerate.

Active time: 10 minutes
Total time: 12 minutes plus chilling and standing
Makes: 2 cups

1 lemon
1 piece salmon fillet (8 ounces), skin removed
1/4 teaspoon salt
1/8 teaspoon ground black pepper
2 tablespoons water
8 ounces smoked salmon
3 tablespoons butter or margarine, softened
2 tablespoons Neufchâtel cheese
2 tablespoons chopped fresh chives
Toasted bread rounds or unsalted crackers for serving

1 From lemon, grate 1 teaspoon peel. Cut lemon in half. From 1 half, squeeze 1 tablespoon juice; cut other half into 3 slices. Set peel and juice aside.

2 Sprinkle salmon fillet with salt and pepper on both sides. Place in microwave-safe shallow bowl. Top with lemon slices and water. Cook, covered, in microwave on High 2 minutes. Let stand, covered, 2 minutes longer. Remove from liquid and place in medium bowl; flake with fork and set aside to cool.

3 Meanwhile, in food processor with knife blade attached, pulse smoked salmon, butter, Neufchâtel, and lemon peel and juice just until smooth. Gently stir mixture and 1 tablespoon chives into flaked salmon just until combined. Wrap remaining chives in plastic and refrigerate for garnish. Spoon pâté into serving bowl; cover and refrigerate for at least 2 hours.

4 To serve, let pâté stand at room temperature 30 minutes or until soft enough to spread. Garnish pâté with remaining chives. Serve with toast rounds or crackers.

Each 2-tablespoon serving: About 60 calories, 6g protein, 0g carbohydrate, 4g total fat (2g saturated), 0g fiber, 360mg sodium

Mini Rémoulade Crab Cakes

Crab cakes are a universal favorite, and they are especially good paired with our lemon-mayo sauce. These luscious morsels can be prepared up to several hours ahead and refrigerated. Reheat the crab cakes and prepare the sauce just before serving.

Active time: 25 minutes
Total time: 45 minutes plus chilling
Makes: 50 mini crab cakes

Crab Cakes

2 tablespoons butter or margarine
1 small onion, finely chopped
1/2 red pepper, finely chopped
1 stalk celery, finely chopped
1/4 cup light mayonnaise
1 tablespoon sour cream
2 teaspoons grainy Dijon mustard
1/2 teaspoon freshly grated lemon peel
1/4 teaspoon salt
1/8 teaspoon cayenne (ground red) pepper
1 pound lump crabmeat, picked over
1 cup fresh bread crumbs (about 2 slices bread)

Lemon Sauce

1/4 cup light mayonnaise
1/4 cup sour cream
1 teaspoon freshly grated lemon peel
1 tablespoon fresh lemon juice
Pinch salt
Pinch cayenne (ground red) pepper

1 In 10-inch skillet, melt butter over medium heat. Add onion, red pepper, and celery. Cook, stirring frequently, until vegetables are tender, about 10 minutes. Let cool.

2 In large bowl, stir mayonnaise, sour cream, mustard, lemon peel, salt, and cayenne until blended; stir in crabmeat and bread crumbs just until mixed. Cover and refrigerate 30 minutes.

3 Meanwhile, prepare lemon sauce: In small bowl, combine mayonnaise, sour cream, lemon peel and juice, salt, and cayenne, stirring until blended. Makes 1/2 cup.

4 Preheat oven to 400°F. Lightly grease two cookie sheets. Drop level tablespoons crabmeat mixture onto prepared cookie sheets and press lightly to form patties. Bake until golden brown, about 15 minutes. Top each crab cake with about 1/2 teaspoon lemon sauce. Serve hot.

Each crab cake with sauce: About 30 calories, 2g protein, 1g carbohydrate, 2g total fat (1g saturated), 0g fiber, 71mg sodium

CROSTINI PLATTER

These crostini—with your choice of white bean, tuna and tomato, or caramelized onion and goat cheese topping—are great for holiday parties. You can toast the bread up to one week before you need it. Just store it in a tightly sealed container at room temperature until you're ready to spread on one or more of the tasty toppings (which can all be made ahead of time, too).

Total time: 20 to 25 minutes • Makes: 40 crostini

1 baguette (10 ounces)

Preheat oven to 400°F. Cut bread into ½-inch-thick slices; reserve ends for making bread crumbs another day. Arrange slices on two cookie sheets. Toast in oven 8 to 10 minutes or until golden brown, rotating pans between upper and lower oven racks halfway through. Cool on wire rack.

White Bean Topping

From 1 lemon, grate 1/2 teaspoon peel and squeeze 2 tablespoons juice. In food processor with knife blade attached, pulse lemon peel and juice with 2 cans (15 to 19 ounces) white kidney beans, rinsed and drained; 1 tablespoon olive oil; 1/4 teaspoon ground cumin; 1 small crushed garlic clove; 1/4 teaspoon salt; and 1/2 teaspoon ground black pepper until well blended but still slightly chunky. (Refrigerate in airtight container up to 2 days, if you like.) Spread about 1 tablespoon bean mixture on each piece of toasted bread. Sprinkle with finely chopped sage.

Each crostino: About 45 calories, 2g protein, 8g carbohydrate, 1g total fat (0g saturated), 1g fiber, 95mg sodium

Tuna and Tomato Topping

In medium bowl, with fork, gently toss 2 cans (6 ounces each) drained white tuna packed in olive oil, with 1/3 cup pitted Kalamata olives, chopped; 1/4 cup loosely packed fresh parsley leaves, chopped; 1 tablespoon drained capers, chopped; 1 tablespoon olive oil; and 16 grape tomatoes, thinly sliced crosswise, until ingredients are evenly distributed. (You can mix up topping early in day, but don't add tomatoes until ready to assemble crostini; they'll get soggy.) Place about 1 tablespoon tuna mixture on each piece of toasted bread, gently pressing mixture together without mashing tuna.

Each crostino: About 40 calories, 3g protein, 4g carbohydrate, 1g total fat (0g saturated), 0g fiber, 80mg sodium

Caramelized Onion and Goat Cheese Topping

In deep 12-inch nonstick skillet, heat 2 tablespoons olive oil on medium 1 minute. Add 2 jumbo onions (1 pound each), halved and thinly sliced; cover and cook 20 minutes, stirring occasionally. Uncover and cook 20 minutes longer or until onions are very tender and deep golden in color, stirring occasionally. Stir in 2 teaspoons fresh thyme leaves, 1/4 teaspoon salt, and 1/2 teaspoon ground black pepper. (Refrigerate in airtight container up to 2 days, if you like. Reheat onion mixture when ready to assemble crostini.) Top toasted bread slices with onion mixture. Dollop with 6 ounces soft goat cheese (1 level teaspoon cheese per crostini).

Each crostino: About 45 calories, 2g protein, 6g carbohydrate, 2g total fat (1g saturated), 1g fiber, 75mg sodium

Oysters Rockefeller

This dish, created in 1899, is truly "as rich as Rockefeller himself." The original chef's recipe was never revealed, but numerous versions followed over the years. Here, fresh oysters on the half shell are cooked until sizzling hot under a bed of seasoned chopped spinach and buttered bread crumbs.

Active time: 30 minutes
Total time: 40 minutes
Makes: 8 first-course servings

2 dozen oysters, shucked, bottom shells reserved
Kosher or rock salt
2 bunches spinach (10 to 12 ounces each), tough stems
   trimmed, washed, and dried very well
3 tablespoons plus 1 teaspoon butter or margarine
1/4 cup finely chopped onion
1/8 teaspoon cayenne (ground red) pepper
1/2 cup heavy cream
2 tablespoons Pernod or other anise-flavored liqueur
1/8 teaspoon salt
1/4 cup plain dried bread crumbs

1 Preheat oven to 425°F. Place oysters in shells in jelly-roll pan lined with ½-inch layer of kosher salt to keep them steady; refrigerate.

2 In 2-quart saucepan, cook spinach over high heat until wilted, cooking in two batches if needed; drain. Rinse spinach with cold running water; drain well and finely chop. Wipe saucepan dry with paper towels.

3 In same clean saucepan, melt 2 tablespoons butter over medium heat. Add onion; cook until tender, about 3 minutes. Stir in cayenne. Stir in spinach, cream, Pernod, and salt. Cook over high heat, stirring, until liquid has reduced and thickened. Remove from heat.

4 In small saucepan, melt remaining 4 teaspoons butter over low heat. Remove from heat; stir in bread crumbs until evenly moistened.

5 Spoon spinach mixture evenly on top of oysters. Sprinkle with buttered bread crumbs. Bake until edges of oysters curl, about 10 minutes. Transfer 3 oysters with spinach and bread crumb topping to each serving plate; serve hot.

Each serving: About 165 calories, 6g protein, 9g carbohydrate, 12g total fat (7g saturated), 0g fiber, 228mg sodium

MY FAVORITE HOLIDAY TRADITION
"We don't have any big, huge tradition. But we do watch *It's a Wonderful Life* at some point during the holidays."

—Jamie Lee Curtis

Shrimp Cocktail

Everyone loves to dip shrimp into sauce; it's fun, it's tasty— and it's easy on the cook! We've provided three sauces that are equally delicious.

Active time: 25 minutes
Total time: 40 minutes plus chilling
Makes: 8 first-course servings

1 lemon, thinly sliced
4 bay leaves
20 whole black peppercorns
10 whole allspice berries
2 teaspoons salt
24 extra-large shrimp (1 pound), shelled and deveined
Choice of dipping sauce (see opposite)
12 small romaine lettuce leaves
24 (7-inch) bamboo skewers

1 Fill 5-quart Dutch oven about half full with *water*; add lemon, bay leaves, peppercorns, allspice, and salt; heat to boiling. Cover and boil 15 minutes.

2 Add shrimp and cook just until opaque throughout, 1 to 2 minutes. Drain and rinse with cold running water to stop cooking. Cover and refrigerate shrimp 1 hour or up to 24 hours.

3 Just before serving, place bowls of sauces in center of platter; arrange romaine leaves around bowls, leaf tips facing out. Thread 1 shrimp onto each bamboo skewer and arrange skewers on romaine.

Each serving without sauce (3 shrimp): About 50 calories, 10g protein, 1g carbohydrate, 1g total fat (0g saturated), 0g fiber, 141mg sodium

Southwestern-Style Cocktail Sauce

In small serving bowl, stir **1 cup bottled cocktail sauce, 2 tablespoons chopped fresh cilantro, 2 teaspoons minced jalapeño chile,** and **2 teaspoons fresh lime juice** until well combined. Cover and refrigerate up to 24 hours. Makes about 1 cup.

Each 2-tablespoon serving: About 40 calories, 0g protein, 8g carbohydrate, 0g total fat, 0g fiber, 382mg sodium

Mustard Dipping Sauce

In a small serving bowl, stir **1 cup reduced-fat sour cream, 3 tablespoons grainy Dijon mustard, 3 tablespoons chopped fresh parsley, 1/4 teaspoon freshly grated lemon peel, 1/4 teaspoon salt,** and **1/8 teaspoon coarsely ground black pepper** until well combined. Cover and refrigerate up to 24 hours. Makes about 1 cup.

Each 2-tablespoon serving: About 60 calories, 2g protein, 2g carbohydrate, 4g total fat (2g saturated), 0g fiber, 222mg sodium

Zippy Tartar Sauce

In small serving bowl, stir **1/2 cup mayonnaise, 1/4 cup finely chopped dill pickle, 1 tablespoon chopped fresh parsley, 2 teaspoons milk, 2 teaspoons distilled white vinegar, 1/2 teaspoon finely chopped onion,** and **1/2 teaspoon Dijon mustard** until well combined. Cover and refrigerate up to 24 hours. Makes about ¾ cup.

Each 2-tablespoon serving: About 140 calories, 0g protein, 0g carbohydrate, 14g total fat (2g saturated), 0g fiber, 250mg sodium

CLASSIC AMERICAN RELISH TRAY

This retro relish tray will whet your guests' appetites without filling them up. Serve one, two, or all three, in pretty bowls, accompanied by a variety of crunchy veggies.

Corn Relish

Active time: 15 minutes
Total time: 40 minutes
plus chilling
Makes: 5 cups

In 4-quart saucepan, combine **1 package (10 ounces) frozen corn**; **1 large onion, red pepper, and green pepper**, each finely chopped; **1 cup cider vinegar**, **1/2 cup sugar**; **1 teaspoon mustard powder**; **1/2 teaspoon celery seeds**; **1/2 teaspoon crushed red pepper**; and **2 teaspoons kosher salt**. Heat to boiling on medium-high, stirring to dissolve sugar. Reduce heat to low and simmer 15 minutes. Transfer mixture to large bowl; cool to room temperature. Cover and refrigerate at least 24 hours, or up to 1 week.

Each 2-tablespoon serving:
About 25 calories, 0g protein, 6g carbohydrates, 0g total fat, 1g fiber, 95mg sodium

Marinated Olives

Active time: 5 minutes
Total time: 8 minutes plus
marinating
Makes: 2½ cups

In medium bowl, place **1¼ cups each green olives and Kalamata olives**, rinsed and drained. In 1½-quart saucepan, combine **¼ cup extra-virgin olive oil**; **6 garlic cloves**, smashed with side of chefs' knife; **4 sprigs fresh rosemary**; and **1 teaspoon fennel seeds**. Heat on medium 3 minutes or until fragrant and hot but not smoking; pour over olives. Let stand at room temperature, uncovered, up to 2 hours. Or cover and refrigerate up to 2 weeks; bring to room temperature before serving.

Each 2-tablespoon serving: About 50 calories, 0g protein, 2g carbohydrate, 5g total fat (0g saturated), 1g fiber, 335mg sodium

Quick Pickles

Total time: 10 minutes
plus chilling
Makes: 4 cups

Cut **1½ pounds Kirby (pickling) cucumbers** in half lengthwise, then slice crosswise into ½-inch-thick half-moons. Cut **1 small onion** in half through root end, then slice crosswise into ¼-inch-thick half-moons. In large bowl, spread one-third of cucumbers in single layer and sprinkle with **1 teaspoon kosher salt**. Top with one-third of onion and sprinkle with **1 teaspoon kosher salt**. Repeat layering and salting two more times until all cucumbers and onions are used.

In 4-quart saucepan, combine **1 cup distilled white vinegar**, **3/4 cup sugar**, **1 tablespoon mustard seeds**, **1 teaspoon dill seeds**, and **1/2 teaspoon celery seeds**. Heat to boiling on high, stirring to dissolve sugar. Pour over cucumber mixture in bowl. Cover with plastic wrap and refrigerate at least 24 hours or up to 1 week.

Each 1/4-cup serving: About 20 calories, 0g protein, 4g carbohydrate, 0g total fat, 1g fiber, 180mg sodium

CLASSIC AMERICAN RELISH TRAY *(opposite)*

Pomegranate Margaritas

Lower the bill at your holiday party by offering one sensational, seasonal drink: Rudolph's-nose-red pomegranate margaritas, premixed by the pitcherful. A virgin variation ensures that everyone—kids included—can join in the merrymaking.

Total time: 5 minutes
Makes: 18 servings

1 can (12 ounces) frozen limeade concentrate,
   thawed (see Tip)
2 cups water
3½ cups gold tequila
2 cups pomegranate juice
1 cup triple sec
5 limes
Ice cubes for serving
1 cup fresh pomegranate seeds (from 1 pomegranate)

1 In large pitcher, combine limeade and water until well blended. Stir in tequila, pomegranate juice, and triple sec. (Mixture can be made up to 1 day ahead and kept refrigerated until serving time.)

2 Cut each lime crosswise into ¼-inch-thick wheels; cut slit in each wheel, from center to edge. To serve, place ice cubes in glass, pour in margarita to fill, sprinkle on several pomegranate seeds, and slide lime wheel onto rim to garnish.

TIP: A budget-friendly can of concentrate contributes intense lime flavor.

Each serving: About 210 calories, 0g protein, 23g carbohydrate, 0g total fat, 1g fiber, 2mg sodium

Christmas Cranberry Juleps

Simple syrup infused with cranberry and orange peel gives this classic Southern cocktail a seasonal twist.

Active time: 5 minutes
Total time: 10 minutes plus chilling
Makes: 8 servings

1 cup water
¾ cup sugar
2 strips fresh orange peel (each 3 inches long), removed
   with vegetable peeler
1 cup fresh cranberries, plus additional for garnish
8 toothpicks
1 cup Kentucky bourbon
Crushed ice for serving
8 sprigs fresh mint

1 In 2-quart saucepan, heat water, sugar, and orange peel to boiling on high. Add cranberries and cook 2 to 3 minutes or until cranberries pop and split but still hold their shape. Remove from heat and cool to room temperature. Refrigerate syrup and cranberries until cold or up to 1 week.

2 When ready to serve, strain cranberry syrup through sieve set over 1-quart liquid measuring cup; discard solids. Spear 3 raw cranberries on each toothpick. Stir bourbon into cranberry syrup.

3 Fill 8 glasses with crushed ice. Divide bourbon mixture among glasses. Garnish with cranberry spears and mint.

Each serving: About 150 calories, 0g protein, 23g carbohydrate, 0g total fat, 0g fiber, 0mg sodium

Virgin Pomegranate Margaritas

In step 1, substitute **2 cups lemon-lime seltzer** for tequila and triple sec. Substitute **pomegranate-cranberry juice** for pomegranate juice. Proceed with step 2. (If making ahead, do not add seltzer until just before serving.)

Each serving: About 70 calories, 0g protein, 18g carbohydrate, 0g total fat, 1g fiber, 10mg sodium

CHRISTMAS CRANBERRY JULEPS (*opposite*)

Popping the cork on a champagne bottle can feel like you're shooting a rocket indoors, but it's a skill every holiday host should master.

1 Chill the bottle for a couple hours. Fridge temperature is fine, or you could submerge the bottle for an hour or two in a wine bucket filled with plenty of ice and a little cold water.

2 Remove the foil and cage, and cover the top with a cloth. (The bottle should be positioned at a 45-degree angle.)

3 Hold the cork, then twist the bottle from the base to open it.

4 Pour the bubbly and toast your guests!

TIP: For a perfect pour, polish the champagne flutes with a cloth to remove any watermarks or dust. Wrap the bottle with cloth to capture any condensation or drips. Tilt the glass slightly, and pour the champagne onto the side of the glass, not the base (this will help preserve the bubbles). Wait until the bubbles subside, then continue pouring to fill the glass. To catch any drips on the lip, twist the bottle as you remove it from the side of glass.

Champagne and Lillet Cocktails

This libation is as effortless as it is elegant. To learn how to open champagne with finesse, see box at left.

Total time: 5 minutes
Makes: 8 servings

1 cup Lillet Blanc, chilled
1 bottle (750 milliliters) champagne, chilled
2 slices navel orange, each cut into quarters

Pour 1 ounce Lillet into each of 8 champagne flutes. Fill flutes with champagne and garnish each glass with orange slice.

Each serving: About 90 calories, 0g protein, 3g carbohydrate, 0g total fat, 0g fiber, 2mg sodium

Bar Nuts

This quick-and-easy nut mix is sautéed with bits of bacon and cayenne pepper for a savory kick.

Total time: 10 minutes
Makes: 2½ cups or 10 servings

6 slices (6 ounces) bacon, chopped
2 cups roasted, salted peanuts
1 teaspoons sugar
⅛ teaspoon cayenne (ground red) pepper

1 In 12-inch skillet, cook bacon on medium heat 8 minutes or until browned.

2 Discard fat. To bacon in pan, add peanuts, sugar, and cayenne; stir to combine. Cook on medium heat, stirring, until nuts are lightly browned about 2 minutes.

Each ¼-cup serving: About 200 calories, 10g protein, 6g carbohydrate, 16g total fat (2g saturated), 1g fiber, 234mg sodium

THE PERFECT CHEESE PLATTER

A varied selection of cheeses can be the cornerstone of a cocktail party or set the stage for the feast to come. As a rule of thumb, you'll need 3 to 4 ounces of cheese per person. Your platter can mix a variety of textures and flavors or highlight one variety, like blue cheeses.

What to Buy

• **Fresh:** Uncooked, unripened cheeses are moist and mild, with just a slight tartness. Some of our favorites: sweet mascarpone and fresh goat cheeses.

• **Soft-Ripened:** With their white and bloomy rind, soft and buttery cheese like Brie and Camembert ripen from the outside in. For a real treat, serve a decadent triple-cream like Brillat-Savarin or Pierre Robert.

• **Washed Rind:** The orange-hued rind of these cheeses smells strong, but the interior is creamy and mellow. Wonderful choices include Taleggio, Limburger, and French Munster.

• **Firm:** Almost all moisture has been pressed out of these flavorful aged cheeses. Start with an American classic like Vermont or Wisconsin Cheddar. Then sample aged Gouda, Emmanthaler, and authentic Parmegiano-Reggiano.

• **Blue:** Salty and piquant, these cheeses go best with a full-bodied wine. Roquefort, Stilton, and Gorgonzola are all flavorful picks.

How to Serve and Store

• **Always bring cheese** to room temperature in original wrapping before serving.

• **Set out selection** on a board or platter, with a separate cutting utensil for each cheese.

• **Don't put strong cheeses next to mild ones;** the heavy scent will overpower the lighter one. When tasting, go from mildest to strongest.

• **Pair cheeses with crusty breads,** stoned-wheat or water crackers, cured meats like prosciutto or salami, fruit (dried or fresh), olives, an assortment of nuts, and chutneys.

• **Semihard and hard cheeses** can last up to a week, wrapped in plastic and stored in the refrigerator. After that, rewrap in parchment or waxed paper to allow the cheese to "breathe." For long-term storage, place parchment-wrapped cheese in an airtight plastic container.

Goat's and sheep's milk cheeses: ash-coated log, buttons, pyramid, ricotta salata, Bûcheron, feta.

Soft-ripened cheeses: Brie, Camembert, Explorateur.

Hard (grating) cheeses: Pecorino-Romano, Parmigiano-Reggiano,

Blue cheeses: Maytag Blue, Roquefort, Stilton, Danish Blue, Gorgonzola.

Blood Orange Mimosas *(opposite)*

Blood Orange Mimosas

Hosting a brunch? Your guests will love this festive, fruity drink.

Total time: 3 minutes
Makes: 8 servings

2 cups fresh blood orange juice, well chilled
1 bottle (750 milliliters) dry Prosecco or other dry
   sparkling wine, well chilled
Fresh blood orange slices for garnish (optional)

Into each of 8 champagne flutes or tall juice glasses, pour 2 ounces juice. Top off each glass with Prosecco and, if you like, attach slice of blood orange to rim of each glass.

Each serving: About 95 calories, 1g protein, 9g carbohydrate, 0g total fat, 0g fiber, 0mg sodium

Holiday Spritzers

Enjoy this refreshing drink as is, or add your favorite liquor.

Total time: 10 minutes plus chilling
Makes: 8 servings

1 can (8 ounces) frozen limeade concentrate, thawed
2 cups water
3 cups tart cherry, pomegranate, or cranberry juice
2 limes
2 cups lemon-lime seltzer, or more to taste
Ice cubes for serving

1 In pitcher, combine undiluted limeade concentrate and water until well blended. Stir in juice. Slice each lime crosswise into ¼-inch-thick wheels; cut a slit in each wheel, from center to edge.

2 To serve, place ice cubes in each glass; pour in about ¾ cup juice mixture and top with about ¼ cup seltzer. Place a lime wheel on the rim of each glass. Or, pour mixture into punch bowl and add 2 cups seltzer, or more to taste. Add ice cubes or ice mold.

Each serving: About 140 calories, 0g protein, 36g carbohydrate, 0g total fat, 0g fiber, 8mg sodium

Ruby Bellinis

Jewel-toned juice adds color to budget bubbly.

Total time: 5 minutes plus chilling
Makes: 8 servings

1 bottle (750 milliliters) Prosecco or sparkling white wine,
   well chilled
1 cup cranberry-pomegranate juice

Divide cranberry-pomegranate juice among 8 champagne flutes. Top off each glass with equal amounts Prosecco and serve.

Each serving: About 80 calories, 0g protein, 6g carbohydrate, 0g total fat, 0g fiber, 5mg sodium

Cranberry Mojitos

Here's a fresh twist on this popular mint-infused rum drink.

Total time: 10 minutes
Makes: 10 cups or 12 servings

4 to 5 limes
3 cups loosely packed fresh mint leaves plus additional
   mint sprigs for garnish
½ cup sugar
1 bottle (32 ounces) cranberry-juice cocktail
2 cups golden or light rum
3 cups club soda or seltzer, chilled
8 cups ice cubes for serving

1 From limes, grate 1 tablespoon peel and squeeze ½ cup juice. In blender, combine peel and juice, mint leaves, and sugar. Cover blender and pulse until mint is chopped.

2 Into large pitcher, pour mint mixture, cranberry juice, and rum. Stir in club soda.

3 To serve, add ice to pitcher or pour over ice in glasses. Garnish with mint sprigs.

Each serving: About 90 calories, 0g protein, 12g carbohydrate, 0g total fat, 1g fiber, 10mg sodium

1-2-3 PARTY!

Here are three prep steps to ensure perfect party sipping.

1. Get Situated

Before settling on what to serve and how, decide on your bar location.

Consider how many guests you expect and where people tend to congregate when they visit your home—or, rather, where you'd prefer they congregate.

Rearrange furniture so the drink station is a destination—not in the middle of everything, not right at the entrance, and not a dead end from which guests can't escape.

Envision the space with a crowd in it. Walk through it with arms outstretched so you take up more space. Will it be cozy or cramped? Adjust furniture as needed.

2. Gather the Gadgets

Festive drinks don't make themselves. With these tools, guests can self-serve.

An ice bucket or cooler: Fill it with ice to cover the bodies of the bottles, leaving necks exposed for grabbing. Have a separate bucket or bowl for the ice people will put in their drinks.

An ice scoop: If you use a glass to scoop ice and it breaks, you'll have to toss out the whole batch of ice. Scoops cost as little as two dollars—or use a large spoon, a ladle, or tongs.

A bottle opener: Sharon Franke, our test kitchen appliances and technology director, prefers a winged corkscrew—a good-quality one is virtually foolproof.

Drink stirrers: A shaker is a great tool if you have a dedicated bartender; stirrers (or iced-tea spoons) make it easier for guests to help themselves.

Glass identifiers: Stop playing the "Whose drink is it anyway?" game. Invite guests to wrap their glasses with colorful rubber bands, tie stems with presnipped ribbon scraps, or use buttons you've prethreaded with cheap hoop earrings. Or try reusable stick-on static-cling labels, which peel right off without residue.

Garnish tools: Encourage guests to deck out their drinks by offering cocktail sticks and fresh-cut fruit; set out a nutmeg grater so they can add spice to hot drinks or punch with flourish.

3. Be Stain Ready

Spills happen. Have handy:

• Absorbent clothes for when drinks are overturned.

• A small spritz bottle of water for dampening drips before blotting.

• On-the-spot stain remover to desplotch machine-washable tablecloths (and partygoers' blouses).

Holiday Champagne Punch

Refreshing and only slightly sweet, this pretty punch is a sparkling spectacle, its fruit garnish frozen into an icy ring that also helps to keep everything cold. See right for how-to photos.

Total time: 20 minutes plus freezing
Makes: 10 cups or 20 servings

1 pint strawberries
1 pound seedless green grapes
2 cups orange juice
¼ cup orange liqueur such as triple sec
1 bottle (1 liter) ginger ale, chilled
1 bottle (750 milliliters) champagne or sparkling white
    wine, chilled
1 bunch fresh mint

1 Prepare ice ring: Fill 5-cup ring mold with *¼ inch cold water*; freeze until hard, about 45 minutes. Reserve 8 strawberries; hull and slice remaining strawberries. On top of ice in ring mold, decoratively arrange half of sliced strawberries and ½ cup grapes. Add just enough *water* to cover to prevent fruit from floating. Freeze until hard, about 45 minutes. Repeat with remaining strawberry slices, another ½ cup grapes, and enough *water* to cover fruit; freeze until hard, about 45 minutes.

2 With kitchen shears, cut remaining grapes into small bunches; arrange grape bunches and reserved whole strawberries alternately on top of previous ice layer in ring mold. Add enough *water* to come to rim of mold, allowing some fruit to be exposed above water; freeze until hard, about 45 minutes or up to 6 hours.

3 About 15 minutes before serving time, in 5-quart punch bowl or bowl large enough to hold ice ring, combine orange juice and orange liqueur. Stir in ginger ale and champagne.

4 Unmold ice ring and turn fruit side up. Tuck small mint sprigs between grapes and strawberries. Add ice ring to punch bowl.

Each serving: About 85 calories, 0g protein, 14g carbohydrate, 0g total fat, 1g fiber, 7mg sodium

MAKE A FROZEN FRUIT RING

Step 1: This ring is created by freezing progressive layers of water and fruit.

Step 2: After the final layer of water and fruit is frozen solid, unmold the ice ring (run it under warm water to loosen, if necessary) and carefully turn it right side up in the bowl full of punch.

Hot Chocolate

On a wintry day, hot chocolate topped with a dollop of whipped cream is comfort-in-a-cup.

Total time: 10 minutes
Makes: 4 cups or 12 servings

1 cup heavy cream
2 tablespoons confectioners' sugar
2 teaspoons vanilla extract
6 ounces semisweet chocolate, chopped
1²/3 cups boiling water
1¹/2 cups whole milk
Whipped cream
Unsweetened cocoa for sprinkling (optional)

1 In small bowl, with mixer on medium speed, beat cream with sugar and vanilla until stiff peaks form. Cover and refrigerate until needed.

2 Place chocolate in 1-quart saucepan. Pour ¹/3 cup boiling water over chocolate and stir until chocolate melts. Whisk in milk and remaining 1 ¹/3 cups boiling water; cook over medium heat until hot but not boiling, whisking constantly.

3 Ladle hot chocolate into mugs and dollop with whipped cream. Sprinkle with cocoa, if you like, and serve.

Each serving: About 165 calories, 2g protein, 11g carbohydrate, 13g total fat (8g saturated), 1g fiber, 25mg sodium

DIY HOT COCOA DIPPERS

Stir up something special this season.

Skewer **marshmallows** on **large drinking straws**, then melt **chocolate** in a small vessel (such as a small, microwave-safe bowl). Dip marshmallows in chocolate, leaving white tops exposed; lift sticks straight up, letting excess chocolate drip off. Cool briefly on waxed paper, but dip marshmallow bottoms into **red nonpareil sprinkles** while chocolate is still slightly soft.

Hot Mulled Wine

If you wish, add other whole spices, such as cardamom, allspice, or even black peppercorns to the mulling mix.

Active time: 10 minutes
Total time: 30 minutes
Makes: 8 generous cups or 16 servings

2 cups sugar

1 cup water

1 small orange, thinly sliced

1 small lemon, thinly sliced

3 cinnamon sticks (3 inches each)

8 whole cloves

2 bottles (750 milliliters each) dry red wine

1 In nonreactive 4-quart saucepan, combine sugar, water, orange, lemon, cinnamon sticks, and cloves; heat to boiling over high heat, stirring until sugar has dissolved. Reduce heat to medium and cook 3 minutes.

2 Add wine to saucepan and heat, stirring, until hot (do not boil). Pour into mugs and serve hot.

Each serving: About 170 calories, 0g protein, 28g carbohydrate, 0g total fat, 0g fiber, 5mg sodium

Top left: HOT CHOCOLATE *(opposite)*;
Bottom left: HOT MULLED WINE *(above).*

Hot Cranberry-Cider Punch

Serve this warming drink at an open house.

Active time: 10 minutes
Total time: 30 minutes
Makes: 16 cups or 16 servings

2 teaspoons whole cloves

2 teaspoons whole allspice

5 small oranges

1/2 gallon apple cider or apple juice

2 cans (12 ounces each) frozen cranberry-raspberry
   juice concentrate

4 cinnamon sticks (3 inches each)

1/2 cup packed brown sugar

8 cups water

1 small lemon, whole cloves, and cranberries for garnish

1 Wrap cloves and allspice in cheesecloth to make a spice bag; tie with string. From 4 oranges, squeeze juice; reserve 1 orange for garnish.

2 In 6-quart saucepot over high heat, heat spice bag, orange juice, apple cider, undiluted cranberry-raspberry juice concentrate, cinnamon sticks, brown sugar, and water to boiling. Reduce heat to low; cover and simmer 20 minutes. Discard spice bag.

3 Thinly slice reserved orange and lemon. Arrange lemon slices on top of orange slices, securing with cloves and garnishing with cranberries. Pour hot punch into large (5-quart) heat-safe punch bowl. Gently place citrus slices in punch.

Each serving: 85 calories, 1g protein, 26g carbohydrate, 0g total fat, 0g fiber, 5mg sodium

MY FAVORITE HOLIDAY TRADITION

"I love to make a big pot of cider where you mix in cinnamon and all the spices and just let it simmer for a really long time. The smell fills the whole house and it just feels like Christmas."

—Lauren Conrad

Warm Spiced Cider

This holiday favorite is spiced with cinnamon, cloves, and citrus.

Active time: 10 minutes
Total time: 30 minutes
Makes: 16 cups or 16 servings

1 large orange
12 whole cloves
Peel from 1 lemon, removed in continuous 1-inch-wide strip
6 cinnamon sticks (3 inches each)
1 gallon apple cider

1 Cut two ½-inch-thick slices from center of orange. Stick cloves into skin around each orange slice. Cut remaining orange into thin slices for garnish.

2 In nonreactive 5-quart saucepot over high heat, heat orange slices with cloves, lemon peel, cinnamon sticks, and apple cider to boiling. Reduce heat to low; cover and simmer 15 minutes.

3 Pour hot cider through strainer into large (5-quart) heat-safe punch bowl. Place remaining orange slices in cider for garnish. Serve immediately.

Each serving: About 105 calories, 0g protein, 28g carbohydrate, 0g total fat, 0g fiber, 5mg sodium

Applejack Wassail

Here's a less potent version of this classic Christmas beverage made with sweet cider and apple brandy.

Active time: 10 minutes
Total time: 35 minutes
Makes: 8 cups or 16 servings

½ gallon apple cider or juice
1 lemon, thinly sliced
2 tablespoons brown sugar
2 cinnamon sticks (3 inches each)
12 whole allspice berries
12 whole cloves
6 lady apples or 1 Golden Delicious apple
1 cup applejack or apple brandy

1 In nonreactive 5-quart Dutch oven, combine cider, lemon slices, brown sugar, cinnamon sticks, and allspice berries; heat to boiling over medium-high heat. Reduce heat and simmer 20 minutes.

2 Insert 2 cloves into each lady apple or all cloves into Golden Delicious apple. Add apples and applejack to cider; cook until liquid is heated through, about 2 minutes. Remove apples, pour punch into mugs, and serve hot.

Each serving: About 110 calories, 0g protein, 18g carbohydrate, 0g total fat, 0g fiber, 5mg sodium

---

STOCK-UP CHEAT SHEET

No need to buy out the liquor store. Here's how to keep it simple (assume two to three drinks per guest).

Liquor and mixers: One liter of liquor makes about 20 drinks. (Ask if your liquor store will take back unopened products if they haven't been refrigerated; many do.) Get twice as many bottles of mixers (juice, soda, seltzer), as of liquor, plus extra for teetotalers.

A specialty cocktail: Make it even easier and premix a large batch of one drink to serve in a pitcher, punch bowl, or heated vessel. Option: Serve nonalcoholic cider or cocoa and let guests add zip with holiday-inspired liquors (schnapps, flavored vodka).

Beer and wine only: Buy a couple of types of each: one light and one dark brew, a white and a red wine (a bottle yields five to six 5-ounce glasses).

HEALTHY HOLIDAY MAKEOVER: EGGNOG

Traditional eggnog is high in fat, but only a Scrooge would give it up altogether. Our slimmed-down nog contains one-fourth the saturated fat and approximately half the cholesterol while retaining silky texture and decadent flavor. For some people, the classic version is a once-a-year indulgence. We've included both recipes so you can enjoy this holiday staple your way.

Classic Eggnog

Active time: 10 minutes

Total time: 35 minutes plus chilling

Makes: 16 cups or 32 servings

12 large eggs

1¼ cups sugar

½ teaspoon salt

2 quarts whole milk

1 cup dark rum (optional)

2 tablespoons vanilla extract

1 teaspoon ground nutmeg plus additional for
    sprinkling

1 cup heavy cream

1 In 5-quart Dutch oven, with wire whisk, beat eggs, sugar, and salt until blended. Gradually stir in 1 quart milk and cook over low heat, stirring constantly, until custard thickens and coats back of spoon well, about 25 minutes. Do not allow mixture to boil, or it will curdle. (Mixture should remain at about 160°F.)

2 Pour custard into large bowl; stir in rum, if using, vanilla, 1 teaspoon ground nutmeg, and remaining 1 quart milk. Cover and refrigerate until well chilled, at least 3 hours.

3 In small bowl, with mixer on medium speed, beat cream until soft peaks form. With wire whisk, gently fold whipped cream into custard mixture.

4 To serve, pour eggnog into chilled 5-quart punch bowl; sprinkle with nutmeg for garnish.

125 CAL **Each serving:** 5g protein, 11g carbohydrate, 7g total fat (4g saturated), 0g fiber, 90mg sodium

Healthy Makeover Eggnog

Active time: 5 minutes

Total time: 15 minutes plus chilling

Makes: 13 cups or 26 servings

6 large eggs

6 large egg whites

11 cups low-fat milk (1%)

1 cup sugar

¼ cup cornstarch

½ teaspoon salt

¼ cup vanilla

1 teaspoon ground nutmeg plus
    additional for sprinkling

⅔ cup dark Jamaican rum (optional)

1 In bowl, with whisk, beat eggs and egg whites until blended; set aside. In 5-quart Dutch oven, with heat-safe spatula, mix 8 cups milk with sugar, cornstarch, and salt. Cook on medium-high until mixture boils and thickens slightly, stirring constantly. Boil 1 minute. Remove pot from heat.

2 Gradually whisk 1 cup simmering milk mixture into eggs; pour egg mixture back into milk in saucepan, whisking constantly, to make custard.

3 Pour custard into 5-quart punch bowl; stir in vanilla, nutmeg, rum, if using, and remaining 3 cups milk. Cover and refrigerate until well chilled, at least 6 hours or up to 2 days. Sprinkle eggnog with nutmeg to serve.

105 CAL **Each serving:** 6g protein, 14g carbohydrate, 2g total fat (1g saturated), 0g fiber, 125mg sodium

GOOD HOUSEKEEPING

FROM OUR HOLIDAY ARCHIVES:
SPIRITED COCKTAILS & FESTIVE PUNCH BOWLS

The '50s and '60s were the golden age of the cocktail. Here we share some of our favorite elixirs from Christmas issues of that time, including one flaming drink and a punch with iced fruits. These swanky drinks will be as welcome at your holiday parties today as they were then.

Hot Cider Wassail

3/4 cup red cinnamon drops such as Red Hots

1/2 cup sugar

1 cup light corn syrup

1 1/2 cups water

10 crab apples or lady apples

1 gallon apple cider

4 lemons, thinly sliced

10 whole cloves

22 cinnamon sticks (3 inches each)

1 Day before or morning of party: In saucepan combine cinnamon drops, sugar, corn syrup, and water. Cook, stirring often, until mixture boils. Then cook, without stirring, until a little of the mixture, dropped in a small bowl of very cold water, separates into threads which are hard but not brittle.

2 Remove syrup from heat. In syrup, coat apples, one at a time, removing each from pan with slotted spoon and placing on greased cookie sheet to cool. Set aside in cool, dry place.

3 About 1 hour before serving: In kettle, combine apple cider, lemon slices, cloves, and 2 whole cinnamon sticks. Bring to boil; then simmer covered, about 45 minutes.

4 With slotted spoon, remove and discard lemon slices and cinnamon sticks. Pour steaming wassail into punch bowl; let apples bob on top. (Candy coating on apples will dissolve and help to flavor punch.)

5 To serve, ladle wassail into punch cups, adding cinnamon stick "swizzler" to each. Serve apples in punch, if desired. Makes about 20 (6-ounce) servings.

Old-Fashioned

1 lump sugar (see Tip)

2 dashes bitters

1 dash club soda

1 maraschino cherry

1 orange slice

2 ice cubes for serving

1 lemon slice (optional)

1 1/2 ounces whiskey (rye, bourbon, Scotch, Irish) or brandy

1 Put lump of sugar into chilled old-fashioned glass. Add bitters and club soda. With muddler, crush sugar until dissolved. Add cherry, orange slice, and ice cubes.

2 Pour in whiskey, stir well, and garnish with lemon, if desired. Serve at once. Makes 1 drink.

TIP: If you'd like to substitute simple syrup for the lump sugar, use 1 teaspoon syrup and omit the club soda.

Manhattan

1 1/2 ounces rye whiskey

3/4 ounce sweet (Italian) vermouth

1 dash bitters

1 maraschino cherry

1 Half-fill chilled cocktail shaker with shaved ice or ice cubes. Pour in whiskey, then vermouth. Add bitters. Stir quickly until blended and chilled.

2 Strain into chilled cocktail glass. Garnish with cherry. Makes 1 drink.

Café Brûlot

1 orange
Whole cloves
1 cinnamon stick (3 inches)
1 strip lemon peel (3 inches)
6 lumps sugar
1 cup brandy
¼ cup Cointreau
1 teaspoon vanilla extract
1 quart very hot, strong black coffee

1 Just before serving: From orange, cut continuous strip of orange peel, 1 inch wide, and stick cloves into it at 1-inch intervals.

2 Place orange peel in silver punch bowl or large chafing dish with cinnamon stick, lemon peel, and sugar.

3 In attractive small saucepan, heat brandy over low heat so that it does not catch fire. Meanwhile, pour Cointreau and vanilla into punch bowl; then pour in coffee (it must be hot, hot, hot!).

4 Immediately carry punch bowl and brandy to table (see Tip); for greatest impact, lower lights. Fill ladle with hot brandy; pour rest of brandy over coffee in punch bowl. Invite one guest to light brandy in ladle with long match. Then, slowly pour flaming brandy into coffee in bowl. Stir rapidly with ladle to completely extinguish flames before serving. Serve in demitasse, brûlot, or diable cups. Makes 8 servings.

TIP: Be sure the area is clear of any decorations that could catch fire. Do not place open bottles of alcohol near a flame and never pour alcohol from a bottle directly onto a flaming punch bowl (the flames may blow back).

Champagne Cocktail

1 lump sugar
1 dash bitters
Champagne, well chilled
Twist of lemon peel

1 Place lump of sugar into well-chilled champagne glass (one without hollow stem). Dash bitters onto sugar. With muddler, crush sugar well. Fill glass slowly with champagne.

2 Stir only enough to dissolve sugar mixture. Twist lemon peel over champagne glass, then drop into cocktail. Makes 1 drink.

Syllabub

2 cups white wine
1½ cups sugar
5 tablespoons grated lemon peel
⅓ cup fresh lemon juice
3 cups milk
2 cups light cream
4 egg whites
Nutmeg for garnish

1 Morning of party: In medium bowl combine wine with 1 cup sugar, lemon peel, and lemon juice; stir until sugar is completely dissolved; refrigerate.

2 In large bowl, combine milk and cream; refrigerate.

3 About 20 minutes before serving: Gradually pour chilled wine mixture into milk mixture, stirring; beat with hand beater; pour into 2½-quart punch bowl.

4 Beat egg whites until frothy; gradually add remaining ½ cup sugar, beating until stiff, but not dry. Drop by spoonfuls onto top of syllabub in punch bowl. Sprinkle with nutmeg. Makes 16 to 18 (4-ounce) servings.

Champagne Punch Fruit Bowl

Iced Fruits for Punch (see below)
4 cups fresh strawberries
1/2 cup sugar
1 bottle (750 milliliters) Sauternes
1 cup cognac
4 bottles (750 milliliters each) champagne, chilled

1 Day before: Prepare Iced Fruits for Punch.

2 At least 2 hours before serving: In large bowl, sprinkle strawberries with sugar; add Sauternes and cognac; refrigerate at least 2 hours.

3 At serving time: Arrange iced fruits in punch bowl, trapping nectarines, plums, and strawberries beneath one or two large bunches of grapes.

4 Pour strawberries with their liquid over fruit; then slowly add champagne. When serving, ladle 1 strawberry into each cup punch. Makes 36 (4-ounce) servings.

Iced Fruits for Punch: Frozen whole fruits are nice icers. They do the same job of chilling that ice rings or ice cubes do, but they are more colorful, do not dilute punch, and can be eaten later.

Before freezing, wash and dry the fruits. Arrange them on foil; then place in the freezer overnight, or until frozen. Grapes, peaches, nectarines, plums, pears, apricots, lemons, cherries, and strawberries all freeze successfully. Of these, grapes and cherries stay close to the bottom of the punch bowl, while the rest float. So always freeze one or two large bunches of grapes; you can use them to anchor smaller frozen fruits beneath them.

Make-Believe Champagne

1 cup sugar
1 cup water
1 cup grapefruit juice
1/2 cup orange juice
1 quart ginger ale, chilled

In small saucepan, boil sugar with water 5 minutes to create a sugar syrup; let cool. Stir in grapefruit juice and orange juice and refrigerate to chill. At serving time, divide juice mixture among 6 champagne glasses. Top with ginger ale and lightly stir to combine. Makes 6 (8-ounce) servings.

Pink Lady Punch

4 cups cranberry-juice cocktail
1 1/2 cups sugar
1 quart pineapple or grapefruit juice (4 cups)
2 quarts ginger ale, chilled

In medium bowl, slowly add cranberry juice to sugar; stir until sugar dissolves. Stir in pineapple juice and refrigerate to chill. At serving time, pour into punch bowl and add ginger ale. Serve in punch cups. Makes 32 (4-ounce) servings.

SALADS & SOUPS

Mixed Winter Greens

Add greens to your holiday meal with this simple salad topped with toasted almonds and Parmesan cheese.

Total time: 15 minutes
Makes: 12 side-dish servings

1/4 cup balsamic vinegar
2 tablespoons pure honey
1 tablespoon Dijon mustard
1/4 teaspoon salt
1/2 teaspoon ground black pepper
1/2 cup extra-virgin olive oil
1 head escarole, chopped (6 cups)
2 small heads or 1 large head radicchio (14 ounces total), sliced
1 package (5 ounces) baby arugula
1/2 cup slivered almonds, toasted (see page 287)
1 small wedge Parmesan cheese (3 ounces)

1 In small bowl, with wire whisk or fork, stir together vinegar, honey, mustard, salt, and pepper. Add oil in slow, steady stream, whisking constantly until well blended. Set vinaigrette aside.

2 In large bowl, combine escarole, radicchio, arugula, almonds, and vinaigrette. Toss until evenly coated. Divide salad among serving plates. With vegetable peeler, shave Parmesan directly onto each plate of salad.

Each serving: About 170 calories, 5g protein, 7g carbohydrate, 14g total fat (3g saturated), 2g fiber, 200mg sodium

Cucumber Pomegranate Salad

Sweet-tart pomegranate seeds and apples balance the light licorice flavor of fennel in this crunchy special-occasion salad.

Total time: 30 minutes
Makes: 12 side-dish servings

1 lemon
1/3 cup extra-virgin olive oil
3 tablespoons champagne vinegar
1/2 teaspoon salt
1/2 teaspoon ground black pepper
1 1/2 pounds fennel bulbs
1 seedless (English) cucumber
1 Granny Smith apple, halved, cored, and very thinly sliced
1/2 cup fresh pomegranate seeds

1 From lemon, grate 1/2 teaspoon peel and squeeze 2 tablespoons juice. In jar or container with tight-fitting lid, combine oil, vinegar, lemon peel and juice, 1/4 teaspoon salt, and pepper. Shake well. Dressing can be refrigerated up to 2 days.

2 Pluck 2 tablespoons fennel fronds from fennel tops and reserve for garnish (see Tip). Trim and core fennel. With adjustable-blade slicer or very sharp knife, very thinly slice fennel. With vegetable peeler, peel alternating strips from cucumber skin, then thinly slice cucumber crosswise at angle.

3 On large serving platter, layer fennel, cucumber, and apple. Shake dressing again and drizzle all over. Top salad with pomegranate seeds and fennel fronds. Sprinkle with remaining 1/4 teaspoon salt.

TIP: If you buy fennel bulbs without their tops, you can use 2 tablespoons fresh dill for garnish instead.

Each serving: About 85 calories, 1g protein, 8g carbohydrate, 6g total fat (1g saturated), 2g fiber, 120mg sodium

Clockwise from top left: MIXED WINTER GREENS *(above)*; BOUGH WOW *(page 105)*; CUCUMBER POMEGRANATE SALAD *(above)*; SQUASH SOUP WITH FRESH SAGE *(page 90)*.

Spinach and Mandarin Orange Salad

By using prewashed spinach, canned Mandarin orange segments, and bottled dressing, we've created a festive five-minute salad.

Total time: 5 minutes
Makes: 8 first-course servings

2 bags (5 to 6 ounces each) baby spinach
1/3 cup bottled poppy seed salad dressing
1/2 lemon
1 can (11 ounces) Mandarin orange sections, drained
1/2 cup honey-roasted sliced almonds

Place spinach in large salad bowl. Drizzle dressing on top; squeeze juice from lemon half over salad. Just before serving, toss to combine and top with orange sections and almonds.

Each serving: About 95 calories, 3g protein, 6g carbohydrate, 7g total fat (1g saturated), 5g fiber, 125mg sodium

Orange-Endive Ambrosia

For a truly authentic ambrosia, don't skimp on the coconut! It is an essential ingredient for this old-fashioned salad.

Active time: 15 minutes
Total time: 20 minutes
Makes: 8 side-dish servings

1/2 cup unsweetened coconut flakes (see Tip, page 81)
1/4 cup low-fat buttermilk
1 tablespoon sherry vinegar
1 teaspoon Dijon mustard
1 tablespoon extra-virgin olive oil
1/4 teaspoon salt
1/4 teaspoon ground black pepper
4 navel oranges
4 heads Belgian endive
1/2 cup packed fresh flat-leaf parsley leaves

1 In 12-inch skillet, toast coconut on medium 2 to 4 minutes or until golden, stirring occasionally. Remove from heat and cool completely. (Coconut can be kept at room temperature in airtight container up to 1 day.)

2 In small bowl, with fork, whisk buttermilk with vinegar, mustard, oil, salt, and pepper until well mixed. (Dressing can be covered and refrigerated up to 1 day.)

3 With knife, cut peel and white pith from oranges and discard. Cut each orange crosswise into 1/4-inch rounds; cut each round in half and transfer to bowl, keeping some rounds whole if you like. (Oranges can be covered and refrigerated up to 1 day.)

4 When ready to serve, trim endive. Cut crosswise at angle into 1-inch pieces; discard core. In large bowl, toss endive and parsley with dressing until coated.

5 On large serving platter, spread half of oranges decoratively in single layer. Top with endive salad and remaining oranges. Sprinkle with toasted coconut.

Each serving: About 100 calories, 2g protein, 12g carbohydrate, 6g total fat (4g saturated), 3g fiber, 100mg sodium

Orange-Endive Ambrosia *(opposite)*

Endive-Beet Salad with Herb-Crusted Goat Cheese

Tangy goat cheese coated in crispy, toasted bread crumbs makes an easy but elegant topping for a dinner party salad.

Active time: 45 minutes
Total time: 1 hour
Makes: 12 first-course servings

2 pounds assorted beets, peeled and cut into 1/2-inch chunks

4 teaspoons olive oil

5/8 teaspoon salt

1/4 teaspoon ground black pepper

1/2 cup panko (Japanese-style bread crumbs)

1/4 cup finely chopped flat-leaf parsley leaves

3 tablespoons finely chopped fresh dill leaves

1 cup low-fat buttermilk

1/2 cup light mayonnaise

1 tablespoon fresh lemon juice

1 tablespoon poppy seeds

1 tablespoon Dijon mustard

3 logs (4 ounces each) goat cheese, room temperature

1 package (5 ounces) baby arugula

8 heads Belgian endive, leaves separated

1 Preheat oven to 425°F. On jelly-roll pan, toss beets with 2 teaspoons oil and 1/4 teaspoon salt. Roast 20 to 25 minutes or until just tender. Beets can be refrigerated up to 2 days.

2 Meanwhile, in 10-inch skillet, heat remaining 2 teaspoons oil on medium. Add panko and 1/8 teaspoon each salt and pepper. Cook 3 minutes or until browned, stirring. Remove from heat; stir in parsley and dill. Transfer to large plate; cool completely.

3 In bowl, whisk buttermilk, mayonnaise, lemon juice, poppy seeds, mustard, and remaining 1/4 teaspoon salt and 1/8 teaspoon pepper; dressing can be refrigerated, covered, up to 5 days.

4 Roll cheese logs in crumb mixture; press to coat all sides. Reserve remaining crumbs. Cut each into 8 slices.

5 Divide arugula and endive among serving plates. Top each with beets and 2 rounds cheese. Sprinkle reserved bread crumbs on goat cheese rounds. Drizzle with dressing.

Each serving: About 185 calories, 8g protein, 13g carbohydrate, 12g total fat (5g saturated), 3g fiber, 410mg sodium

HOW WE CELEBRATE CHRISTMAS

"We make food for the reindeer. It's oatmeal, birdseed—and silver glitter. When you have girls, you have glitter. We mix it up and then we throw it all over the lawn, so that when Santa lands, the reindeer will have something to eat. And wouldn't you know, every year, amazingly, one of the reindeer drops a little silver sleigh bell onto the lawn. So the girls have a nice collection."

—Faith Hill

Citrus-Ambrosia Salad

Recalling the down-home taste of classic ambrosia (minus all the diet-deraiing mayo), this refreshing first course is only 110 calories and has a deliciously tart dressing you whip up using lime and other juices.

Active time: 10 minutes
Total time: 13 minutes
Makes: 8 first-course servings

½ cup unsweetened coconut flakes (see Tip)
1 jar (1½ pounds) refrigerated citrus segments in juice
1 to 2 limes
¼ teaspoon salt
⅛ teaspoon coarsely ground black pepper
3 tablespoons olive oil
2 bags (5 to 6 ounces) mixed baby greens or spring mix
   with herbs

1 Preheat oven to 350°F. Place coconut in 15½" by 10½" jelly-roll pan in single layer. Toast 3 minutes or until golden. (Coconut burns easily; check after 2 minutes.)

2 Drain citrus segments, reserving 1 tablespoon juice in large bowl. From limes, grate ½ teaspoon peel and squeeze 2 tablespoons juice; add to citrus juice in bowl. Whisk in salt and pepper. In thin, steady stream, whisk in oil until blended.

3 Add mixed baby greens to dressing; toss to coat. Arrange dressed greens on salad plates; top with citrus segments and toasted coconut flakes.

TIP: Unsweetened coconut flakes are large pieces of dried shaved coconut that are available in many supermarkets and specialty food stores. Sweetened flaked coconut, commonly used for baking, can be substituted, if you prefer a more sugary garnish.

Each serving: About 110 calories, 1g protein, 13g carbohydrate, 7g total fat (2g saturated), 1g fiber, 90mg sodium

Top: ENDIVE-BEET SALAD WITH HERB-CRUSTED GOAT CHEESE *(opposite); Bottom:* CITRUS-AMBROSIA SALAD *(above).*

ROASTED-BEET AND PISTACHIO SALAD *(opposite)*

Roasted-Beet and Pistachio Salad

Delight your guests with this simple but flavorful salad.
Roasting the beets enhances their natural sweetness.

Active time: 20 minutes
Total time: 1 hour 20 minutes plus cooling
Makes: 12 side-dish servings

6 beets (4 ounces each; see Tip)
1/2 cup shelled unsalted pistachios
3 tablespoons balsamic vinegar
2 teaspoons Dijon mustard
1/4 teaspoon salt
1/4 teaspoon ground black pepper
1/3 cup extra-virgin olive oil
3 bags (4 ounces each) baby greens and herbs mix
1/4 cup crumbled blue cheese
1/4 cup packed fresh mint leaves

1 Preheat oven to 400°F. Arrange beets in single layer on large sheet of foil and wrap tightly. Place in shallow glass or ceramic baking dish and bake 1 hour or until tender when pierced with tip of knife.

2 While beets bake, place pistachios in small baking pan; place in oven alongside beets until golden and toasted, about 4 minutes. Cool completely in pan.

3 When beets are done, unwrap foil and let beets sit until cool enough to handle. Peel beets and cut into 1/2-inch chunks.

4 Prepare dressing: In small bowl, with fork or wire whisk, mix vinegar, mustard, salt, and pepper until blended. In thin, steady stream, whisk in oil until blended.

5 In medium bowl, combine beets and 2 tablespoons dressing. In large serving bowl, toss greens with remaining dressing until coated. Top with blue cheese, pistachios, and beets. Tear mint leaves over salad.

TIP: No time to roast beets? Swap in packaged cooked beets.

Each serving: About 115 calories, 3g protein, 6g carbohydrate, 9g total fat (2g saturated), 2g fiber, 120mg sodium

Mesclun with Pears and Pumpkin Seeds

Instead of the pecans often used in pear salads, we're swapping in toasted pumpkin seeds, or pepitas, which have become supermarket staples in recent years.

Total time: 10 minutes
Makes: 12 side-dish servings

1/4 cup pumpkin seeds (pepitas)
3 tablespoons apple cider vinegar
1 tablespoon Dijon mustard
2 teaspoons pure honey
1/4 cup extra-virgin olive oil
3 ripe red pears, cored and thinly sliced (see Tip)
2 packages (5 ounces each) mixed baby greens
1/4 teaspoon salt
1/4 teaspoon freshly ground black pepper

1 In skillet, heat pumpkin seeds on medium 2 to 3 minutes or until toasted and some start to pop. Cool completely. Toasted seeds can be stored in airtight container up to 1 week.

2 In small bowl, with wire whisk, stir vinegar, mustard, and honey until blended. In thin, steady stream, whisk in oil until well blended. Dressing can be made ahead; cover tightly and refrigerate up to 3 days.

3 In large bowl, combine pears, greens, pumpkin seeds, dressing, salt, and pepper. Toss until evenly coated.

TIP: You can combine the dressing and pears up to 1 hour before serving to prevent the sliced pears from turning brown. When ready to serve, toss with the greens, pumpkin seeds, and seasonings.

Each serving: 100 calories, 1g protein, 9g carbohydrate, 7g total fat (1g saturated), 2g fiber, 85mg sodium

GLOSSARY OF GREENS

Salad greens fall into either of two basic categories: delicate and tender or assertive and slightly bitter. Bold-flavored or spicy greens (like escarole and watercress) are best combined with sweeter, more tender lettuces.

Arugula: Peppery arugula is also known as rugula or rocket. The older and larger the leaves, the more assertive the flavor. Milder baby arugula can be found packaged in plastic boxes at the supermarket.

Baby greens: Available in bags, in plastic containers, or in bulk at many supermarkets, this combination of very young, tender salad greens is an Americanization of the French salad mix known as *mesclun* (see below).

Belgian endive: A member of the chicory family, Belgian endive is appreciated for its crisp texture and slightly bitter flavor. The leaves should be very white, graduating to pale yellow tips.

Boston lettuce: A loose-leaf lettuce with tender floppy leaves, it is also called butterhead lettuce.

Chicory: Although chicory is an entire family of mildly bitter greens, Americans use the term to identify a dark-green variety with fringed leaves. It is also known as curly endive.

Dandelion: Tart greens that make a pungent addition to a salad. Some cooks gather the wild variety in the spring.

Escarole: Assertively flavored escarole should have curly leaves with firm stems that snap easily.

Frisée: A pale-green variety of chicory with curly, almost spiky leaves and a deliciously bitter edge.

Mesclun: From the Provençal word for "mixture," true mesclun is composed of wild baby greens and often includes herbs and edible flowers. Here, it is commonly a mix of sweet lettuces and bitter greens such as arugula, dandelion, frisée mâche, and radicchio.

Radicchio: A red-leafed Italian chicory. The most common radicchio is round with white-veined ruby-red leaves. Radicchio di Treviso has long, narrow red leaves that form a tapered head.

Romaine: Its long, crisp, dark green leaves and slightly nutty flavor make romaine the preferred lettuce for Caesar salad.

Spinach: Whether dark green and crinkled or flat, spinach leaves need to be washed thoroughly to remove all the grit. Baby spinach has very tender edible stems; it is often sold prewashed.

Watercress: Customarily sold in little bouquets covered with small, crisp, dark-green leaves, watercress adds crisp texture and a mildly spicy flavor to salads. It is very perishable, so use within one or two days of purchase.

Arugula

Boston Lettuce

Frisée

Romaine

Apple Salad with Romaine and Arugula

This make-ahead salad is the perfect choice for an open-house buffet. Mix the dressing up to three days ahead and refrigerate; whisk it again before tossing with the apples. Rinse the romaine leaves, dry them, wrap in paper towels, then store in a plastic bag for up to a day.

Total time: 25 minutes
Makes: 16 side-dish servings

2/3 cup buttermilk
1 container (6 ounces) plain low-fat yogurt (1/2 cup)
2 tablespoons cider vinegar
1 tablespoon chopped fresh tarragon leaves
1/4 teaspoon salt
1/4 teaspoon ground black pepper
4 Fuji, Gala, and/or Granny Smith apples, each cored and cut into 16 wedges
1 large head romaine lettuce (1 pound), coarsely chopped (10 cups)
2 bags (4 ounces each) watercress or 1 package (5 ounces) baby arugula

1 In medium bowl, whisk together buttermilk, yogurt, vinegar, tarragon, salt, and pepper.

2 Remove ¼ cup dressing and place in medium bowl with apple slices; toss to coat.

3 In large serving bowl, toss romaine and watercress; top with apples. Serve remaining dressing alongside.

Each serving: About 40 calories, 2g protein, 8g carbohydrate, 1g total fat (0g saturated), 2g fiber, 60mg sodium

Frisée Salad with Warm Bacon Vinaigrette

This rich bistro-style salad is sure to impress your guests. Served with the poached egg, it's perfect brunch fare.

Active time: 20 minutes
Total time: 30 minutes
Makes: 6 first-course servings

2 tablespoons olive oil
1/4 teaspoon salt
4 ounces country-style bread or French bread, cut into 1/2-inch cubes
4 thick slices bacon, cut into 1/2-inch pieces
2 tablespoons red wine vinegar
1 tablespoon Dijon mustard
1/8 teaspoon coarsely ground black pepper
2 tablespoons water
1 pound frisée, ends trimmed
6 large eggs, poached (optional)

1 Preheat oven to 400°F. In large serving bowl, combine oil and salt. Add bread cubes to oil mixture and toss to coat. Transfer bread to jelly-roll pan and bake, stirring once, until golden brown and crisp, about 10 minutes. Set pan on wire rack to cool.

2 Meanwhile, in 2-quart saucepan, cook bacon over medium heat, stirring frequently, until brown, about 8 minutes. Remove saucepan from heat. With slotted spoon, transfer bacon to paper towels to drain. Discard all but 3 tablespoons bacon drippings from saucepan.

3 With wire whisk, mix vinegar, mustard, pepper, and water into bacon drippings in saucepan.

4 To serve, tear frisée into bite-size pieces and place in serving bowl. Toss with warm bacon vinaigrette until coated. Divide salad among dinner plates. Top each with croutons, bacon, and, if you like, a poached egg.

Each serving without egg: About 210 calories, 6g protein, 13g carbohydrate, 15g total fat (4g saturated), 2g fiber, 425mg sodium

Each serving with egg: About 285 calories, 12g protein, 14g carbohydrate, 20g total fat (6g saturated), 2g fiber, 565mg sodium

Seafood Salad

For an Italian-style Christmas Eve feast (page 401), add a pound of scallops (poach 2 minutes) and a dozen clams (steam until opened).

Active time: 50 minutes
Total time: 65 minutes plus chilling
Makes: 12 first-course servings

2 lemons
2 bay leaves
1 pint grape tomatoes
1/2 cup Gaeta or Niçoise olives, pitted
1/2 cup loosely packed fresh flat-leaf parsley leaves, chopped
2 tablespoons extra-virgin olive oil
1/2 teaspoon salt
1/4 teaspoon coarsely ground black pepper
1 pound squid, cleaned
1 pound medium shrimp, shelled and deveined, with tail part of shell left on if you like

1 From 1 lemon, grate 1 teaspoon peel and squeeze 2 tablespoons juice. Cut remaining lemon in half and squeeze juice into 4-quart saucepan; add bay leaves. Fill pan with *3 inches water;* cover and heat to boiling.

2 Meanwhile, in large bowl, combine tomatoes, olives, parsley, oil, salt, pepper, and lemon peel and juice.

3 Rinse squid under cold running water. Slice squid bodies crosswise into 1/2-inch-wide rings. Cut tentacles into several pieces if large.

4 To boiling water in saucepan, add shrimp. Cook shrimp on high heat 1 to 2 minutes or just until opaque throughout. With slotted spoon, transfer shrimp to colander to drain. Add to bowl with tomato mixture.

5 Return water to boiling. Add squid; cook 30 seconds to 1 minute or just until opaque. Drain squid in colander; add to shrimp in bowl. Toss until well combined. Cover and refrigerate at least 1 hour or up to 4 hours.

Each serving: About 95 calories, 12g protein, 3g carbohydrate, 4g total fat (1g saturated), 2g fiber, 230mg sodium

Top: Seafood Salad *(above); Bottom:* Jicama and Orange Salad *(opposite).*

Jicama and Orange Salad

This refreshing salad takes advantage of low-cost, in-season oranges and jicama.

Total time: 45 minutes
Makes: 20 first-course servings

1 large jicama (2 pounds)
1 English (seedless) cucumber
4 navel oranges
3 to 4 limes
1 cup packed fresh cilantro leaves, coarsely chopped
1 tablespoon vegetable oil
1/8 teaspoon cayenne (ground red) pepper
1/4 teaspoon salt

1 Using sharp knife, trim top and bottom of jicama and peel tough brown skin; cut into matchstick-size pieces. Peel cucumber in alternating strips; cut in half lengthwise, then into 1/4-inch-thick half-moons.

2 With knife, cut peel and pith from oranges; discard. Cut each orange crosswise into 1/4-inch rounds; cut each round in half and transfer to large bowl. From limes, grate 2 teaspoons peel and squeeze 5 tablespoons juice.

3 To bowl with oranges, add jicama, cucumber, lime peel and juice, cilantro, oil, cayenne, and salt. Toss well. Serve immediately or refrigerate up to 4 hours.

Each serving: About 40 calories, 1g protein, 8g carbohydrate, 1g total fat (0g saturated), 3g fiber, 35mg sodium

Holiday Citrus Platter

A sweet sherry dressing is drizzled over citrus fruit.

Total time: 25 minutes plus chilling
Makes: 10 first-course servings

3 large navel oranges (2 pounds)
2 large ruby-red grapefruits (2 1/2 pounds)
1/4 cup cranberries or pomegranate seeds
2 tablespoons cream sherry
2 tablespoons sugar
Kumquats with leaves for garnish (optional)

1 With knife, cut off ends from oranges and grapefruits. Place 1 piece of fruit, cut end down, on cutting board and slice off peel and white pith. Repeat with remaining fruit. Slice fruit crosswise into 1/4-inch-thick rounds; cut grapefruit slices in half if large. Arrange fruit in deep platter, overlapping slices slightly.

2 Sprinkle fruit with cranberries or pomegranate seeds. In cup, stir sherry and sugar until sugar dissolves. Spoon sherry mixture over fruit. Cover and refrigerate 1 hour or up to 1 day. Garnish with kumquats if desired.

Each serving: About 55 calories, 1g protein, 14g carbohydrates, 0g total fat, 2g fiber, 1mg sodium

Ginger-Honey Fruit Salad

This quick-and-easy salad is just the thing for a brunch buffet. Toss pre-cut assorted fruit with our sweet-and-spicy dressing, chill, and serve.

Total time: 15 minutes plus chilling
Makes: 12 side-dish servings

1 lime
3 tablespoons pure honey
2 tablespoons diced crystallized ginger, finely chopped
8 cups store-bought assorted cut-up fruit (such as pineapple, strawberries, cantaloupe, and honeydew melon)
2 ripe bananas

1 From lime, grate 1 teaspoon peel and squeeze 2 tablespoons juice.

2 In serving bowl, stir together lime peel and juice, honey, and ginger. Toss dressing with cut-up fruit. Refrigerate 30 minutes.

3 To serve, peel and slice bananas; gently stir into fruit mixture.

Each serving: About 80 calories, 1g protein, 20g carbohydrate, 0g total fat, 2g fiber, 5mg sodium

Spiced Pumpkin Soup

Better grab the big bowls—this lush, velvety blend of pumpkin and fall spices will have guests wanting more. To double the yield, see Tip.

Active time: 25 minutes
Total time: 50 minutes
Makes: 6 appetizer servings

2 tablespoons olive oil
1 large onion (8 to 10 ounces), chopped
1 Granny Smith apple, peeled, cored, and chopped
1 carrot, chopped
5/8 teaspoon salt
1/2 teaspoon ground ginger
1/4 teaspoon ground cumin
1/4 teaspoon ground coriander
1 quart chicken broth
3/4 cup light coconut milk
1 can (15 ounces) pureed pumpkin
3 thick slices white bread, crusts removed, cut into
   1/2-inch cubes (3 cups)
3 tablespoons butter (no substitutions), cut up
Pinch cayenne (ground red) pepper
2 tablespoons sour cream

1 Preheat oven to 400°F.

2 In 5-quart saucepot, heat oil on medium heat. Add onion, apple, carrot, and 1/2 teaspoon salt. Cook 10 to 15 minutes or until vegetables are just tender, stirring frequently. Stir in ginger, cumin, and coriander; cook 1 minute.

3 Whisk broth, coconut milk, and pumpkin into pot. Heat to simmering on high. Reduce heat; simmer soup 20 minutes or until slightly reduced, stirring often.

4 Meanwhile, arrange bread cubes on 18" by 12" jelly-roll pan. Bake 7 to 8 minutes or until crisp and golden, stirring once. Cool; transfer to medium bowl.

5 In 10-inch skillet, heat butter on medium 3 to 5 minutes or until golden brown and fragrant, swirling pan. Drizzle butter over bread in bowl; toss to coat. (Cooled croutons can be stored in resealable bag up to 4 days at room temperature.)

6 To pot with soup, add cayenne and remaining 1/8 teaspoon salt. Working in batches, blend soup until smooth. Return to pot; heat on medium-low until hot. Serve with croutons and small dollop of sour cream.

TIP: To make 12 servings, in step 2, use 8-quart saucepot, 2 tablespoons olive oil, 2 medium onions (1 pound), 2 apples, 2 carrots, 3/4 teaspoon salt, 1 teaspoon ginger, 1/2 teaspoon cumin, and 1/2 teaspoon coriander. In step 3, use 1 1/2 quarts broth, 1 can (15 ounces) coconut milk, and 1 can (29 ounces) pumpkin. In step 4, use 5 slices bread (5 cups cubes). In step 5, use 5 tablespoons butter. In step 6, use 1/8 teaspoon cayenne, 1/4 teaspoon salt, and 3 tablespoons sour cream.

Each serving: About 250 calories, 4g protein, 26g carbohydrate, 15g total fat (6g saturated), 4g fiber, 750mg sodium

GARNISHING SOUP

As delicious as soup is unadorned, almost any bowl will be enhanced by a garnish that adds a splash of color and extra flavor.

Chopped fresh herbs are the simplest of garnishes. Choose an herb that complements the soup's flavor and color. For best results, chop or snip fresh herbs just before using. Pureed soups can accommodate more elaborate garnishes. Their smooth texture calls out for a sprinkling of grated cheese, crumbled bacon, or toasted bread or chopped nuts. Pureed vegetable soups are often topped with a drizzle of heavy cream or infused olive oil.

Spiced Pumpkin Soup (*opposite*)

Squash Soup with Cumin

We roast butternut squash until fork-tender before adding it to this spicy, smooth soup.

Active time: 25 minutes
Total time: 1 hour 15 minutes
Makes: 10 first-course servings

2 medium butternut squashes (2½ pounds each), each cut lengthwise in half, seeds removed
1 tablespoon olive oil
2 stalks celery, chopped
1 onion, chopped
1 teaspoon ground cumin
¼ teaspoon chipotle chile powder
½ teaspoon salt
¼ teaspoon ground black pepper
2 cans (14½ ounces each) chicken broth
2 cups water
Roasted salted pumpkin seeds (pepitas) for garnish
Fresh chives for garnish

1 Preheat oven to 450°F. Line 15½" by 10½" jelly-roll pan with foil. Place squash halves, cut sides down, in lined pan and roast about 45 minutes or until very tender when pierced with knife. Cool until easy to handle, then, with spoon, scoop flesh from skins and place in large bowl. Discard skins.

2 Meanwhile, in 5- to 6-quart saucepot, heat oil on medium until hot. Add celery and onion; cook 10 minutes. Stir in cumin, chipotle chile powder, salt, and pepper; cook 30 seconds, stirring. Add broth, water, and squash to saucepot; cover and heat to boiling on high. Reduce heat to low and simmer 10 minutes.

3 In batches, ladle squash mixture into blender. With center part of lid removed to allow steam to escape (drape with clean kitchen towel to avoid splatter), blend squash mixture until pureed. Transfer pureed soup into large bowl. When all soup has been processed, return to saucepot and heat through. Garnish each serving with pumpkin seeds and chives.

Each serving: About 90 calories, 3g protein, 19g carbohydrate, 2g total fat (0g saturated), 3g fiber, 350mg sodium

Squash Soup with Fresh Sage

Prepare squash as directed through step 1. In step 2, omit cumin and chipotle chile powder, and add **1 teaspoon chopped fresh sage leaves** along with salt and pepper. Complete recipe as in steps 3 and 4, but omit garnish. Top each serving with several **croutons** and **fresh sage leaves** instead, if you like.

Each serving: About 90 calories, 3g protein, 19g carbohydrate, 2g total fat (0g saturated), 3g fiber, 350mg sodium

Curried Squash Soup with Pear

Prepare squash as directed above through step 1. In step 2, omit cumin and chile powder. Add **2 Bartlett or Anjou pears**, peeled, cored, and chopped; **1 tablespoon curry powder**; and salt and pepper to saucepot after celery and onion have cooked 8 minutes. Cook 5 minutes longer. Complete recipe as in steps 3 and 4, but drizzle each serving with **low-fat yogurt** to garnish.

Each serving: About 85 calories, 2g protein, 19g carbohydrate, 1g total fat (0g saturated), 3g fiber, 270mg sodium

BUYING AND STORING WINTER SQUASH

Winter varieties like butternut, acorn, and spaghetti squash are all at their peak from October through January.

Unlike summer squash, the skin of winter squash is thick and inedible, and the seeds are rarely eaten (except for pumpkin seeds). To prepare any winter squash, rinse under cold running water. Cut in half, or as directed. Scoop out the seeds and stringy portion and discard before proceeding with recipe.

Winter squash can be refrigerated or stored at cool room temperature up to two months.

Creamy Celery Soup

This soup is velvety smooth and delicious, but we substitute potatoes for actual cream, making this a low-fat treat. To prepare ahead, see Tip.

Active time: 25 minutes
Total time: 65 minutes
Makes: 12 first-course servings

1 large bunch celery with leaves (2 pounds)
2 tablespoons olive oil
1 large onion (12 ounces), chopped
1 tablespoon fresh thyme leaves
1/2 teaspoon salt
1/4 teaspoon coarsely ground black pepper
    plus additional for garnish
1/2 cup white wine
3 cans (14 1/2 ounces each) chicken broth
2 medium all-purpose potatoes (6 ounces each),
    peeled and cut into 1-inch chunks
2 cups water

1 Trim ends from celery stalks. Reserve several celery leaves for garnish; wrap with plastic wrap and refrigerate. Slice celery stalks and remaining leaves crosswise into 1-inch pieces; transfer to colander. Rinse and drain well.

2 In 5½- to 6-quart saucepot, heat oil over medium heat. Add celery and leaves, onion, thyme, salt, and pepper, and cook 20 to 25 minutes or until celery is soft but not browned, stirring occasionally. Add wine and cook 2 minutes or until wine is mostly evaporated.

3 Add broth, potatoes, and water to saucepot; cover and heat to boiling over high heat. Reduce heat to low; cover and simmer 10 minutes or until potatoes are very tender.

4 In batches, ladle celery mixture into blender; cover, with center part of lid removed to allow steam to escape (drape with clean kitchen towel to avoid splatter), and blend very well until pureed. Pour puree into large bowl. Repeat with remaining mixture.

5 Return soup to saucepot; heat through. Ladle soup into tureen; sprinkle with pepper and garnish with reserved celery leaves.

TIP: You can make this soup up to 2 days ahead if you plan to refrigerate it, or you can freeze it for up to 1 month. Store the soup in plastic containers with tight-fitting lids. When you're ready to reheat the refrigerated soup, place it in a large covered saucepot over medium heat for about 15 minutes or until it's hot, stirring occasionally. If you're starting with frozen soup, add 2 tablespoons water to the saucepot before heating up the soup.

Each serving: About 75 calories, 2g protein, 10g carbohydrate, 3g total fat (1g saturated), 2g fiber, 600mg sodium

Chestnut Parsnip Soup *(opposite)*

Chestnut Parsnip Soup

Puree prepackaged chestnuts with potato and parsnips to create a silky, satisfying soup. See "Roasting Chestnuts," below, if you want to roast your own.

Active time: 30 minutes
Total time: 40 minutes
Makes: 12 appetizer servings

1 jar (14 ounces) peeled, roasted chestnuts
1 tablespoon plus 1 teaspoon butter or margarine
2 pounds parsnips, peeled and chopped (see Tip)
1 large onion (12 ounces), finely chopped
1 all-purpose potato, peeled and chopped
3 cups reduced-sodium chicken broth
4 cups water plus more if needed
2 tablespoons honey
1/2 teaspoon salt
1/4 teaspoon ground black pepper
1/4 cup reduced-fat sour cream
Snipped chives for garnish

1 Cut 12 whole chestnuts in half and reserve. Chop remaining chestnuts.

2 In 6- to 7-quart saucepot, melt 1 tablespoon butter on medium-high heat. Add parsnips, onion, potato, and chopped chestnuts. Cook 2 to 3 minutes or until golden, stirring. Add chicken broth and water. Heat to boiling. Reduce heat to low; cover and simmer 20 minutes or until vegetables are tender.

3 Meanwhile, in 1- to 2-quart saucepan, combine honey and remaining 1 teaspoon butter. Cook on medium heat until bubbling. Add chestnut halves and cook 5 to 7 minutes or until glazed, gently turning occasionally to evenly coat.

4 Working in batches, carefully ladle parsnip mixture into blender. Cover, with center part of lid removed to allow steam to escape (drape with clean kitchen towel to avoid splatter), and blend until smooth. (Blended soup can be covered and refrigerated up to 1 day.) Return soup to saucepot and reheat on medium-low until hot, adding additional water if thinner soup is preferred. Stir in salt and pepper.

5 Divide soup among serving bowls. Swirl 1 teaspoon sour cream into each portion. Garnish with glazed chestnut halves and snipped chives.

TIP: If the cores of the parsnips are tough and woody, cut out and discard them.

Each serving: About 180 calories, 3g protein, 37g carbohydrate, 3g total fat (1g saturated), 5g fiber, 235mg sodium

---

ROASTING CHESTNUTS

Chestnuts can be presented in many guises: tossed into almost any stuffing, added to a vegetable medley, or pureed with sugar and vanilla and served with whipped cream.

Step 1: Preheat oven to 400°F. With sharp knife, cut an X in flat side of shell of each chestnut. Place in jelly-roll pan and roast until shells open, about 20 minutes.

Step 2: Cover chestnuts with clean kitchen towel. When cool enough to handle, with paring knife, peel chestnuts, keeping unpeeled ones warm as you work for easier peeling.

French Onion Soup Gratinée

Onions, slowly cooked until deep brown and caramelized, give this classic its distinctive flavor.

Active time: 1 hour
Total time: 2 hours 20 minutes
Makes: 8 cups or 6 first-course servings

4 tablespoons butter or margarine
2½ pounds onions, each cut in half and thinly sliced
¼ teaspoon salt
1 cup dry white wine
1 can (14 to 14½ ounces) chicken broth
1 can (14 to 14½ ounces) beef broth
2 sprigs fresh thyme
2½ cups water
12 slices French bread, cut on the diagonal
   (½ inch thick each)
6 ounces Gruyère or Swiss cheese, shredded

1 In nonstick 12-inch skillet, melt butter over medium-high. Add onions and salt and cook, stirring occasionally, until golden brown, about 30 minutes. Reduce heat to medium-low and cook, stirring occasionally, until onions are deep golden brown, about 15 minutes longer. Transfer onions to 4-quart saucepan and set aside.

2 Add wine to same skillet; heat to boiling over medium-high heat. Boil until wine is reduced to ¼ cup, 3 to 5 minutes. Add reduced wine to onions. Stir in both broths, thyme, and water; cover and heat to boiling over high heat. Reduce heat to low; simmer, covered, 15 minutes.

3 Meanwhile, preheat oven to 450°F. In 15½" by 10½" jelly-roll pan, arrange bread in single layer; bake until golden brown and crisp, 8 to 10 minutes. Transfer bread to plate.

4 Place six 1½- to 2-cup oven-safe bowls in same jelly-roll pan. Remove thyme sprigs from soup and discard. Divide soup among bowls; top each with 2 bread slices. Sprinkle Gruyère evenly over bread. Bake until cheese has melted and begins to brown, 12 to 15 minutes.

Each serving: About 415 calories, 16g protein, 43g carbohydrate, 19g total fat (11g saturated), 3g fiber, 1,112mg sodium

Turkey Escarole Soup

Here's a tasty use for leftover turkey. Serve at an open house after the big meal, or just enjoy it with your family.

Active time: 15 minutes
Total time: 25 minutes
Makes: 5 main-dish servings

1 tablespoon olive oil
2 cups shredded or matchstick carrots (about two thirds of a 10-ounce bag)
1 small onion, finely chopped
2 garlic cloves, minced
3 cans (14½ ounces each) chicken broth or 5¼ cups Homemade Turkey Broth (at right)
2 cups water
2 heads escarole (1½ pounds total), cut into 1-inch pieces
½ cup orzo pasta
2 cups chopped leftover cooked turkey (10 ounces)
⅛ teaspoon coarsely ground black pepper
½ cup freshly grated Parmesan cheese

1 In 6-quart Dutch oven, heat oil over medium-high until hot. Add carrots, onion, and garlic; cook, stirring frequently, until onion softens, about 4 minutes. Stir in broth and water; heat to boiling. Stir in escarole and orzo; heat to boiling.

2 Reduce heat to medium-low; simmer until escarole and orzo are tender, about 6 minutes. Stir in turkey and pepper. Reduce heat to low; simmer until turkey is heated through, about 3 minutes.

3 To serve, divide among 5 bowls and sprinkle with grated Parmesan.

Each 2-cup serving: About 285 calories, 28g protein, 25g carbohydrate, 9g total fat (3g saturated), 6g fiber, 890mg sodium

Top left: French Onion Soup Gratinée *(opposite)*;
Bottom left: Turkey Escarole Soup *(above).*

EASY TURKEY BROTH

This homemade stock adds great flavor to stuffings, gravies, and soups.

Active time: 5 minutes
Total time: 1 hour 20 minutes
Makes: 7 cups

8 cups water
4 large carrots, cut into 2-inch chunks
4 large stalks celery, cut into 2-inch chunks
2 onions (6 to 8 ounces each), cut into quarters
2 bay leaves
Giblets and neck from 1 turkey (18 pounds)
½ teaspoon salt

1 In 8-quart stockpot, place water, carrots, celery, onions, and bay leaves. Cover and heat to boiling. Add giblets, neck, and salt. Reduce heat to medium; simmer, uncovered, 1 hour.

2 Strain stock through fine-mesh sieve into large bowl. Discard vegetables, reserving neck and giblets for another use. Cover and refrigerate stock up to 3 days, or freeze up to 4 months.

Each ½-cup serving: About 10 calories, 1g protein, 0g carbohydrate, 1g total fat (0g saturated), 0g fiber, 115mg sodium

Creamy Asparagus Soup

This simple but elegant soup makes an enchanting start to a sit-down dinner. Serve with crispy bread sticks.

Active time: 10 minutes
Total time: 35 minutes
Makes: 5½ cups or 4 first-course servings

1 tablespoon butter or margarine
1 small onion, coarsely chopped
1½ pounds asparagus, trimmed and coarsely chopped
1 can (14 to 14½ ounces) chicken or vegetable broth
   (1¾ cups)
½ teaspoon salt
⅛ teaspoon ground black pepper
1 cup water
¼ cup heavy or whipping cream
Sliced green onions and steamed thin asparagus spears
   for garnish (optional)

1 In 4-quart saucepan, melt butter over medium heat. Add onion and cook, stirring often, until tender and lightly golden, 8 to 10 minutes. Add asparagus and cook, stirring occasionally, 5 minutes.

2 Add broth, salt, pepper, and water; heat to boiling over high. Reduce heat to low; cover and simmer until asparagus is very tender, 8 to 10 minutes. Remove from heat.

3 Spoon half of asparagus mixture into blender; cover, with center part of lid removed to let steam escape, and puree until very smooth. Pour into large bowl. Repeat with remaining asparagus mixture. (Or use hand blender, following manufacturer's directions, to puree soup in pot.)

4 Clean saucepan and return asparagus puree to pan. Stir in cream and heat through over low heat (do not boil). To serve, top with green onions and asparagus spears, if you like.

Each serving: About 125 calories, 4g protein, 5g carbohydrate, 10g total fat (5g saturated), 2g fiber, 779mg sodium

BUYING AND STORING ASPARAGUS

Although the peak season for fresh asparagus is March through May, it can be enjoyed year-round.

Look for bright-green, firm, crisp stalks with compact tips and no trace of brown or rust. Buy evenly sized stalks for uniform cooking.

To prepare, hold the base of each asparagus stalk in one hand and bend back the stalk; the end will break off at the spot where the stalk becomes too tough to eat. Discard the tough portion; rinse the spears to remove any sand. Some cooks like to peel asparagus, but this is a matter of personal choice. Leave asparagus spears whole, cut diagonally into 1- to 2-inch pieces, or chop as recipe directs.

Asparagus is very perishable. To store it, stand the stalks in ½ inch cold water in a container. Refrigerate up to two days.

Creamy Asparagus Soup *(opposite)*

Lobster Bisque

When you serve lobster, as in our luscious Seafood Newburg (page 153), save the shells and cooking liquid and make this splendid soup the next day.

Active time: 15 minutes
Total time: 1 hour 15 minutes
Makes: 4 first-course servings

2 tablespoons butter or margarine
1 onion, chopped
1 carrot, peeled and chopped
1 stalk celery, chopped
1 garlic clove, finely chopped
3 tablespoons tomato paste
Leftover shells and heads from 4 steamed lobsters
2 tablespoons cognac or brandy
6 cups water
2 bottles (8 ounces each) clam juice or
    2 cups cooking liquid from steamed lobsters
3 sprigs parsley
1/8 teaspoon dried thyme
Pinch ground nutmeg
Pinch cayenne (ground red) pepper
3 tablespoons all-purpose flour
3/4 cup heavy cream

1 In 12-quart nonreactive stockpot, melt butter over medium heat. Add onion, carrot, celery, and garlic and cook until onion is tender, about 5 minutes. Stir in tomato paste.

2 Increase heat to high and add lobster shells; cook, stirring occasionally, 5 minutes. Stir in cognac and cook until liquid has evaporated. Add water, clam juice, parsley, thyme, nutmeg, and cayenne; heat to boiling. Reduce heat; cover and simmer 30 minutes.

3 Strain soup through sieve into 4-quart saucepan; discard solids. Heat to boiling over high heat; boil until reduced to 5 cups, 10 to 15 minutes.

4 In small bowl, with wire whisk, whisk flour into cream until blended and smooth. Gradually whisk cream mixture into soup; heat just to boiling, whisking constantly. Reduce heat and simmer 2 minutes.

Each serving: About 260 calories, 3g protein, 12g carbohydrate, 22g total fat (14g saturated), 0g fiber, 441mg sodium

---

STORING SOUP AND STOCK

If you're preparing soup or stock ahead of time to get a jumpstart on Christmas dinner, here's how to store it.

Soup and stock should be quickly cooled before storing in the refrigerator or freezer. To cool down a pot of soup or stock, place the pot in a sink filled with ice water and let stand, stirring until tepid. Or pour the soup into small containers and cool for thirty minutes before refrigerating.

Soup enriched with cream, yogurt, or eggs cannot be frozen because it will curdle when reheated; the soup base can be frozen, however. Freeze like any other soup, then thaw and reheat, adding the enrichment at the last minute—just long enough to heat through. Do not allow the soup to boil, or it may curdle.

Mushroom and Wild Rice Soup

Flavored with cream sherry, thyme, and a little soy sauce, this mushroom soup is a winning starter.

Active time: 45 minutes
Total time: 1 hour 45 minutes
Makes: 8 first-course servings

1/2 cup wild rice
4 1/2 cups plus 2 tablespoons water
1 package (1/2 ounce) dried mushrooms
2 tablespoons olive oil
2 celery stalks, chopped
1 large onion (12 ounces), chopped
1 package (10 ounces) mushrooms, sliced
2 cans (14 1/2 ounces each) chicken broth
1 tablespoon soy sauce
1/2 teaspoon dried thyme leaves
1/4 teaspoon coarsely ground black pepper
1/4 cup cream sherry

1 In 3-quart saucepan over high heat, heat wild rice and 2 1/2 cups water to boiling. Reduce heat to low; cover and simmer 45 minutes or until rice is tender. Meanwhile, boil 2 cups water and pour into 4-cup glass measuring cup; add dried mushrooms. Set aside.

2 In nonstick 12-inch skillet on medium, heat 1 tablespoon oil. Add celery, onion, and 2 tablespoons water; cook until vegetables are tender and lightly browned, about 10 minutes. Transfer to 4-quart saucepan.

3 In same skillet over medium-high, heat remaining 1 tablespoon oil. Add sliced mushrooms; cook until lightly browned, 10 minutes. Add to celery mixture.

4 With slotted spoon, remove dried mushrooms from soaking liquid and coarsely chop; strain liquid. Add dried mushrooms and liquid to celery mixture; stir in broth, soy sauce, thyme, pepper, and wild rice with any cooking liquid; heat soup to boiling. Stir in sherry. Reduce heat to low; cover and simmer 5 minutes.

Each serving: About 130 calories, 5g protein, 16g carbohydrate, 4g total fat (1g saturated), 0g fiber, 430mg sodium

Green Pea Soup with Radishes

This light, fresh soup makes a nice contrast to heavier holiday fare, and the brilliant green hue looks bright and festive on any table.

Active time: 20 minutes
Total time: 50 minutes
Makes: 12 appetizer servings

3 tablespoons butter or margarine
4 stalks celery, chopped (2 cups)
2 onions, chopped (3 cups)
2 large leeks, white parts only,
    cut into 1/4-inch-thick slices, well rinsed
1 1/4 teaspoons salt
1 carton (32 ounces) reduced-sodium chicken broth
4 cups water
2 pounds frozen peas, thawed
2 tablespoons fresh tarragon leaves
1/4 teaspoon ground black pepper
4 red radishes, very thinly sliced
3 tablespoons sour cream

1 In 7- to 8-quart saucepot, melt butter on medium-high. Add celery, onions, leeks, and 1/4 teaspoon salt. Cook 10 minutes or until softened, stirring occasionally.

2 Add broth and water. Cover; heat to boiling. Partially cover; reduce heat to simmer 15 minutes or until vegetables are very tender.

3 Increase heat to high. Add peas and tarragon; cook 1 to 2 minutes or until peas are heated through. Remove from heat. In batches, puree in blender until very smooth. Soup can be refrigerated in airtight containers overnight. Return soup to saucepot; stir in remaining 1 teaspoon salt and pepper. Reheat on low.

4 Divide among serving bowls; garnish with radishes and sour cream.

Each serving: About 120 calories, 6g protein, 17g carbohydrate, 4g total fat (1g saturated), 5g fiber, 440mg sodium

1

8

9

4

7

2

3

6

5

EASY-TO-MAKE WREATHS TO WELCOME YOUR GUESTS

Ring in glad tidings with creative holiday hoops that are as simple to make as they are sensational. Some use evergreen or winterberry branches you can buy at a florist, while others make use of recycled materials you can find around the house.

1. Recycled Cards Wreath

Recycle holiday cards into holly leaves for this one-of-a-kind decoration. Using a holly leaf–shaped stencil, trace onto old cards and cut out holly shapes. With a glue gun, glue a toothpick onto the backside of each of the leaves to form a 1-inch pick at the "bottom" of each leaf. Take a 10-inch Styrofoam wreath and insert these leaf picks around the shape until it is completely covered, fanning and overlapping the leaves as shown. Cut out more holly leaves as needed to cover the wreath with regifted greetings. Loop with wire in back to hang.

2. Pop out the Cork Wreath

Add pop to a dining room with wine corks wired to tiny red jingle bells. Gather about 22 corks of the same size and 22 small (⅜-inch) red bells and long green floral wire bought from the craft store. Drill a small hole (just big enough to fit your wire through) ¼ inch from the top of each cork and another ¼ inch from the bottom. (It is very important to make sure all the drilled holes at the top line up with the holes at the bottom.) Push the floral wire through all the bottom holes of the corks.

Leave enough wire at both ends when finished for tying closed later. Cut another piece of floral wire to string the tops of the corks together, alternating with the bells. Tie ends of wire at the top and bottom, twisting to close and make a wreath shape. Hang with a length of ribbon.

3. Berry Merry Christmas Wreath

A circle of winterberry branches brightens a mantel or entryway. From the florist, purchase winterberry branches. Cut 40 to 50 branches of winterberries, each 10 to 16 inches long. Using green florists' wire, attach the larger branches to a 16- to 18-inch wire frame one at a time, overlapping as you go. Continue adding smaller branches until the wreath looks full; use a hot glue gun to affix the branches when you run out of space to work with the florist wire.

4. Winter Wonderland Wreath

Matte white spray paint transforms au naturel grapevine, twigs, and pinecones into an icy-looking Arctic circle. At your craft or floral supply store, purchase an 18-inch grapevine wreath. At the floral supply area of the craft store, look for natural pods in a variety of shapes, pinecones, and seasonal nuts from an assorted-mix package (or forage these items from the outdoors) to add texture and variety to the wreath. Using a hot glue gun, add these dried decorations to the wreath. To make stick stars, use sticks from outdoors broken into 3- to 4-inch lengths or use cinnamon sticks. Glue them on top of each other to form the star shape and add them to the wreath.

When all the pieces have been added, place the wreath on newspaper or another surface you don't mind getting messy, and spray-paint the entire wreath white. Allow to dry. Loop with wire in back to hang.

5. Candy Cane Door Decor

Who said wreaths had to be hoops? Here, everyone's favorite Christmas confection provides a cheery welcome. Draw a candy cane shape onto a large piece of paper. Cut it out and trace the shape onto a 2-inch-thick piece of Styrofoam. Cut out the Styrofoam shape using a serrated knife. Wrap a piece of white felt 4 inches wider than the candy cane around the shape (use straight pins to attach it to the back). Tightly wrap a wire around the top of your candy cane and create a loop for a hanger on the back. Spread out an assortment of peppermint candies and broken candy canes on a newspaper in a well-ventilated area, like a garage. Spray the pieces with polyurethane, making sure to coat all sides of the candy well; let dry. Use a glue gun to apply the candy to the front and sides of the wreath, then give the whole thing two more coats of polyurethane. Finish by wiring on sprigs of pine and a bow.

6. Take It from Him Wreath

Turn Dad's old ties into door décor. You'll need a 14-inch wire wreath and 19 neckties. Cut all the ties but one into 15-inch lengths. Position the narrow end of the first cut tie, front side up, on a section of the wreath. Wrap the tie around the form until the pointed end is positioned as shown; hiding the rolled tie, secure with pins. Repeat, overlapping the ties slightly, until the wreath is covered. Flip the wreath over, sew rolled-up ties to the backs of points. Create a bow from the uncut tie and pin it onto the wreath.

7. Fruit Loop

Give your guests a sweet welcome with this sugar-coated fruit wreath. Gather an assortment of artificial fruit (oranges, pears, lemons, apples, and so on). Insert floral pick into each fruit. Roll them, one at a time, in tacky glue (such as Aleenes, available at craft stores), then Epsom salts, and finally white, iridescent glitter. Push the picks into a brick of Styrofoam and allow the fruits to dry completely. Wrap an 18-inch straw wreath in lime-green ribbon and pin to secure. Use a craft knife to make holes in the ribbon where you will be placing the fruit. Stick the dry fruit into the wreath, starting with the larger pieces. Use a hot glue gun to secure them. Attach an organza ribbon with wire, then loosely wrap the ribbon ends around the wreath.

8. Christmas Ball Wreath

A shimmery stunner takes Christmas ornaments off the tree and onto the wall. Buy a straw wreath about 22 inches in diameter from the craft store. Using ½ yard of white felt cut into 3-inch-wide strips, wrap each piece around the wreath, pinning to secure and overlapping the edges. Take assorted Christmas balls, small stars, snowflakes, and other ornaments and attach to the felt with a low-temperature glue gun, using the smallest ones to fill in spaces and gaps. Hang with wire, wrapped securely around the top of the wreath.

TIP: You'll need to add the wire before you cover the wreath completely.

9. Kumquat and Cranberry Garland Wreath

Kumquats and cranberries stuck into a juniper-covered wreath create a festive garland effect. Wrap a wire around a 16-inch straw wreath to create a hanger. Working diagonally around the wreath, pin rows of kumquats into the wreath with straight pins (available at fabric stores). To each side of the kumquats, add a row of cranberries (also using straight pins). Use florists' pins to attach a wide row of blue juniper in between the rows of fruit. Finish by wiring a red ribbon on top.

10. Mixed Greens Wreath

This woodsy design, studded with fruit and plants, blends faux and real. From the craft store, purchase a 16-inch grapevine wreath and artificial Granny Smith apples. Use a hot glue gun to affix the apples, spacing them evenly around the ring. Select an assortment of seasonal flora from the florist or the forest—pinecones, fragrant eucalyptus, and juniper—and weave them into the grapevine, filling in the areas between the apples.

TIP: To hang heavier wreaths, you can use a simple nail; paint it to match the door so you can leave it up year-round. For lighter wreaths (like our Recycled Cards Wreath, page 101), use a stick-on hook from 3M, which won't damage the wall.

BRIGHTEN THE NIGHT WITH FESTIVE OUTDOOR LIGHTS

Come holiday season, even normally unfazed folks feel peer pressure from the neighbors to mount a high-wattage nighttime extravaganza. But struggling with too-short extension cords, snarled strands of bulbs, and the steep utility bill afterward could bring out even Kriss Kringle's dark side.

This year, switch to simple illuminated decorations that will welcome guests to your home with old-fashioned charm. The understated displays shown here are as inexpensive as they are easy. All you need are candles, battery-powered fairy lights, and household items like canning jars and paper bags. And since there are no teetering ladders involved, even the tiniest tots can help get things glowing. If you use lighted candles, just be sure never to leave them unattended.

1. Rings of Fire

Artificial trees can't hold a candle to this woodsy Tannenbaum. How to: Pack a galzanized tub with sand and affix a grapevine wreath to its rim. Poke a trio of four-foot birch poles into the sand. Wire on gradually smaller wreaths as you go up the poles; secure candles with wire (and keep a careful eye out when they're lit!) or use LED candles that you won't have to watch. Simply trim with twinkle lights.

2. Jingle Balls

Even a birdbath can get into the spirit of the season. For this flight of fancy, fill a small bucket with snow or sand, center inside the bowl's base, and top with evergreen sprigs and battery-powered orbs. The finishing touch: pinecones.

3. Bough Wow

Bring enchantment to bare branches with sparkling votives in homespun holders. To make the handle, thread the ends of a six-inch length of 20-gauge floral wire through two slots in a hose clamp. Attach the clamps to a canning jar, and pop a candle inside. Suspend from limbs that you can easily check on.

4. Snow Motion

Guests get an anything-but-chilly reception with this sports-inspired entryway. Search eBay and flea markets for vintage winter gear, like Flexible Flyers, ice skates, and wooden skis (or you may already have

these items stashed in your garage or attic.) Attach skates to a wreath hanger, lean heavier items, like the metal-runner sleds, nearby, and accessorize with prelit artificial wreaths.

5. Yuletide Yard Tree

Give an evergreen tree the star treatment by encircling it with twinkling candlelight: Spray-paint metal buckets a jolly yuletide red, then pack them to overflowing with snow (or sand if the weather is balmy). Insert tapers, and surround with clear glass hurricanes to shield flames from the elements. Santa hat on the tree is optional (though definitely fun!).

6. Window Dressing

Sprucing up a winter-weary window planter couldn't be simpler: Position a pair of pagoda-shaped lanterns in the box (use battery operated candles for safety), then tuck in greenery all round them. To add a splash of holiday color, you can nestle bright red ornaments between the boughs.

7. Lit from Within

Highlight a window wreath (and help St. Nick and other visitors navigate the night) by lining up festive luminaris below the sill. To get this bright idea in the bag, stencil letters onto green and red paper sacks and cut out with an X-Acto knife. Fill each with a few inches of sand (to keep it from toppling over) and a votive or LED candle.

Pepper-Crusted Prime Rib *(page 117)*

Chapter 2

The Main Event

SHOWSTOPPING ROASTS, BUFFETS & TABLESCAPES

Holidays are a time to think big. A juicy turkey, succulent prime rib, a stunning crown roast, or a glistening ham are all suitably grand centerpieces for Christmas dinner. And when it comes to holiday buffets, you'll want delicious casseroles, chilis, and sandwiches to feed a crowd. In the pages that follow, we provide sure-to-please options.

Tenderloin, Turkey & Other Classic Roasts

Every family has its traditions when it comes to choosing the right roast for the big meal. So we've provided tantalizing recipes for all the favorites: Beef Tenderloin with White Wine Sauce, Pepper-Crusted Prime Rib, Pork Crown Roast with Pear Stuffing, and holiday ham, two ways.

And then there are the turkeys—from an easy but elegant Turkey Breast with Spinach-Herb Stuffing to our Buttery Herb Turkey Three Ways. If a roast duck or goose always takes pride of place on your holiday table, we offer winning recipes for those, too. Check out our tips on carving, do-ahead gravy, how much to buy, and more.

Holiday Brunches & Buffets

Whether you're throwing a Sunday brunch or an open-house buffet, our recipes are a blueprint for relaxed, cost-conscious get-togethers. Prepare our Cheddar Grits Soufflé, Northern-Style Lasagna, or Slow-Cooker Chipotle Beef Chili and let the party unfold.

Dinner Table Dazzle

Christmas is the time to pull out all the stops and make your tabletop sparkle. Our easy-to-execute ideas for festive place settings, centerpieces, and candles will help ensure that you and your guests dine bright!

Clockwise from top left: CARAMELIZED ONION–STUFFED TURKEY ROULADE *(page 136)*; THINK GREEN *(page 185)*; BACON FRENCH TOAST BAKE *(page 157)*.

Recipes

Crafts

BEEF, PORK & LAMB

Beef Tenderloin with White Wine Sauce

White wine with beef? Absolutely! The tarragon-scented sauce is lighter than a typical red-wine reduction, but it makes an oh-so-flavorful accompaniment. And, by prepping the tenderloin yourself, you'll cut the meat tab in half! See "Be Your Own Butcher" on page 116.

Active time: 45 minutes
Total time: 1 hour 35 minutes
Makes: 12 main-dish servings

3 large shallots, finely chopped (1¼ cups)
¼ cup fresh tarragon leaves, chopped, plus more for
 garnish
2 tablespoons olive oil
1½ teaspoons salt
2 teaspoons coarsely ground black pepper
1 whole beef tenderloin (5 pounds), trimmed and tied
2 tablespoons white wine vinegar
1 cup dry white wine
2 tablespoons butter or margarine
Rosemary sprigs and bay leaves for garnish

1 Preheat oven to 425°F. In small bowl, combine half of shallots, 2 tablespoons chopped tarragon, 1 tablespoon oil, salt, and pepper. Rub mixture all over tenderloin. Place tenderloin, smooth side up, on rack in large roasting pan (17" by 13½").

2 Roast tenderloin 45 to 50 minutes or until meat thermometer inserted into thickest part registers 135°F. Internal temperature of meat will rise to 145°F (medium-rare) upon standing. (If well-done meat is desired, continue roasting to desired doneness.) Transfer to platter; tent loosely with foil. Let stand 15 to 20 minutes for easier slicing.

3 Meanwhile, prepare sauce: Place roasting pan over two burners set to medium and add remaining 1 tablespoon oil and remaining shallots. Cook 1 to 2 minutes or until tender, stirring. Add vinegar and cook 1 to 2 minutes or until reduced by half, stirring and scraping pan to loosen any browned bits. Add wine, bring to simmer, and cook 4 to 5 minutes or until reduced by half, stirring and scraping pan. Remove from heat; stir in butter until melted. Carefully pour sauce through fine-mesh strainer into gravy boat. Stir in remaining 2 tablespoons tarragon and any accumulated beef juices on platter. Makes about ¾ cup sauce.

4 Remove string from tenderloin and discard. Garnish platter with rosemary sprigs and bay leaves; sprinkle tenderloin with additional chopped tarragon. Cut tenderloin into slices and serve with sauce.

Each serving: About 350 calories, 40g protein, 2g carbohydrate, 19g total fat (6g saturated), 0g fiber, 420mg sodium

Clockwise from top: ROAST PORK LOIN WITH APPLES, POTATOES, AND SAGE *(page 120)*; HOW SWEDE IT IS *(page 181)*; BEEF TENDERLOIN WITH WHITE WINE SAUCE *(above).*

Beef Tenderloin with Citrus-Red Pepper Chutney *(opposite)*.

Beef Tenderloin with Citrus-Red Pepper Chutney

Wow a holiday crowd with this flavorful entrée.

Active time: 20 minutes
Total time: 1 hour 15 minutes plus resting
Makes: 12 main-dish servings

1 tablespoon vegetable oil
2 teaspoons coarsely ground black pepper
1/2 teaspoon ground coriander
3 teaspoons mustard seeds, divided
1 trimmed and tied beef tenderloin (about 5 pounds)
Kosher salt
1/2 cup orange marmalade
1/4 cup white wine vinegar
3 tablespoons sugar
1 teaspoon fennel seeds
2 oranges
1 1/2 cup chopped roasted red peppers
Bay leaves and pink peppercorns for garnish

1 Preheat oven to 450°F. Line roasting pan or jelly-roll pan with foil. Add roasting rack to pan.

2 In medium bowl, stir together oil, pepper, coriander, and 2 teaspoons mustard seeds; rub all over tenderloin. Sprinkle beef with 1 tablespoon kosher salt. Place beef on rack and roast 40 to 50 minutes or until desired doneness (145°F for medium-rare). Cover loosely with foil and let rest at least 10 minutes. Remove and discard string.

3 Meanwhile, in 2-quart saucepan, heat marmalade, vinegar, sugar, fennel seeds, and remaining 1 teaspoon mustard seeds on medium-low just until marmalade melts, stirring to combine. Remove from heat; let cool.

4 While chutney cools, from oranges, cut and discard peel and pith; cut out segments between membranes. Stir orange segments and red peppers into chutney. Place beef on platter; garnish with bay leaves and pink peppercorns. Serve with chutney.

Each serving: About 530 calories, 34g protein, 18g carbohydrate, 36g total fat (14g saturated), 2g fiber, 625mg sodium

Coffee-Rubbed Beef Tenderloin

Collard greens are the perfect accompaniment for this down-home holiday dish.

Active time: 15 minutes
Total time: 1 hour plus marinating
Makes: 12 main-dish servings

1 trimmed beef tenderloin, tied (about 4 pounds)
1 tablespoon oil
1/4 cup brown sugar
3 tablespoons ground coffee
1/2 teaspoon cayenne (ground red) pepper
2 teaspoons smoked paprika
2 teaspoons garlic powder
2 1/2 teaspoons salt
1 teaspoon black pepper
4 cups water
Sweet Pepper Sauce (below)

1 On very large sheet of plastic wrap, brush tenderloin with oil. In medium bowl, combine brown sugar, coffee, cayenne, paprika, garlic powder, salt and black pepper; rub all over beef, patting to adhere. Wrap tightly and refrigerate at least 1 hour or up to 4 hours.

2 Preheat oven to 450°F. Remove beef from plastic and place on rack in roasting pan. Pour 4 cups water into bottom of pan. Roast 45 to 55 minutes or until desired doneness (145°F for medium-rare). Let stand at least 10 minutes before serving. Serve beef thinly sliced with Sweet Pepper Sauce.

Each serving: About 350 calories, 37g protein, 8g carbohydrate, 21g total fat (5g saturated), 2g fiber, 710mg sodium

Sweet Pepper Sauce

In food processor, pulse **1 1/2 cups roasted red peppers; 2 tablespoons tomato paste, 1/3 cup blanched sliced almonds; 1/2 cup canola or vegetable oil; 2 tablespoons sherry vinegar; 1 clove garlic** and **1/2 teaspoon salt** until smooth. Makes 2 cups.

Each 2-tablespoon serving: About 85 calories, 0g protein, 3g carbohydrate, 8g total fat (0g saturated), 1g fiber, 120mg sodium

BE YOUR OWN BUTCHER

When the test kitchen asked our market's meat department for a beef tenderloin, they offered us a beautiful five-pound roast—for $120! No way, not even for Christmas dinner. So we clarified: We wanted a whole, untrimmed tenderloin. The butcher brought out a 6½-pound slab sealed in its wholesale packaging. It wasn't pretty—but it was $45. The savings far outweigh the work of trimming it yourself. Follow our simple method below.

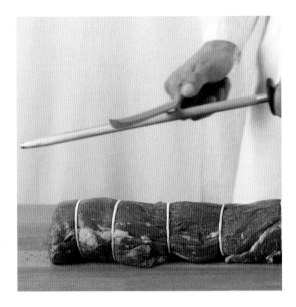

Step 1: Remove the chain. On one side of the tenderloin, the ragged, narrow chain muscle runs the length of the meat. (A shorter, smoother, rounder muscle is attached to the other side; leave that in place.) Gently pull the chain away from the loin, and with a sharp boning knife, use short strokes to cut off the muscle, starting at the narrow end. Reserve the chain for later use.

Step 2: Cut out the fat. Slice away the two large fat deposits between the shorter, intact muscle and the loin, without detaching the muscle. With your fingers, pick off any bits of fat from the surface. Discard all fat.

Step 3: Slice off the silver skin. A thin, pearlescent membrane of connective tissue covers one side of a tenderloin. To remove, slide your boning knife just under the silver skin, one inch from its narrow end, creating a one-inch-wide cut. Using a slow sawing motion, with the knife angled toward the top of the loin, separate the end of the silver skin from the meat. Hold the freed piece taut, turn the knife around, and repeat to cut off the remaining silver skin. Repeat until all of the silver skin is removed; discard it.

Step 4: Tuck and tie. Fold the two-inch tapered end under the loin. Using butcher's string or kitchen twine, tie the roast firmly, but not too tightly, at 1½-inch intervals.

Pepper-Crusted Prime Rib

Prime rib is a classic holiday entrée. While the roast rests, whisk together a simple cream sauce with roasted garlic and horseradish. No cooking required!

Active time: 15 minutes
Total time: 2 hours 10 minutes
Makes: 12 main-dish servings

1 (4-rib) beef rib roast (7 pounds), chine bone removed
2 tablespoons cracked pink or black peppercorns
2 teaspoons kosher salt
1 head garlic
½ teaspoon olive oil
½ cup reduced-fat sour cream
½ cup heavy cream
1 cup prepared horseradish, drained
¼ teaspoon salt
¼ teaspoon ground black pepper
Fresh dill sprigs for garnish

1 Preheat oven to 450°F. Place rib roast, fat side up, on rack in 14" by 10" roasting pan. Rub cracked peppercorns and kosher salt all over roast.

2 Cut top third off head of garlic, and keep both pieces intact. Drizzle oil over cut sides and place garlic top back on bottom. Wrap tightly in foil.

3 Place garlic on rack next to rib roast in oven. Roast both 20 minutes, then reset oven control to 350°F. Roast garlic 40 minutes longer, then unwrap and let cool. Roast beef 1 hour 30 minutes longer or until meat thermometer inserted into thickest part (not touching bone) registers 135°F. Internal temperature will rise to 145°F (medium-rare) upon standing. (If well-done meat is desired, continue roasting to desired doneness.) Transfer meat to large serving platter; cover loosely with foil and let stand 15 minutes for easier slicing.

4 Meanwhile, in medium bowl, with wire whisk, whip both creams together until soft peaks form. Press soft roasted garlic out of each clove into small bowl; discard skins. Add horseradish to garlic and mash with fork. Fold into cream mixture. Stir in salt and ground pepper. Spoon into small serving bowl. Garnish platter with fresh dill sprigs. Serve sauce alongside beef.

Each serving beef with 3 tablespoons sauce: About 690 calories, 40g protein, 4g carbohydrate, 56g total fat (24g saturated), 1g fiber, 550mg sodium

---

CARVING A RIB ROAST

The chine bone should be removed by your butcher so you can carve the roast between the rib bones. Carving will be easier and the meat will be juicer if the roast stands at least 15 minutes after you have removed it from the oven.

Step 1: Place the roast, rib side down, on a cutting board. With a carving knife, make a vertical cut toward the ribs, cutting a slice about ¼ inch thick.

Step 2: Release the slice by cutting horizontally along the top of the rib bone. Transfer the slice to a warm platter.

Step 3: Cut more slices. As each rib bone is exposed, cut it away and add it to the platter. This will make it easier to carve the remaining meat.

Beef Rib Roast with Creamy Horseradish Sauce and Yorkshire Pudding

*Succulent beef topped with piquant horseradish sauce and
served with a yummy Yorkshire pudding makes an old-
fashioned Christmas dinner that's sure to enchant your guests.*

Active time: 25 minutes
Total Time: 3 hours 25 minutes plus standing
Makes: 10 main-dish servings

1 (4-rib) beef rib roast from small end (7 pounds)
3 tablespoons whole tricolor peppercorns (red, green,
   and black)
1 teaspoon salt

1 Preheat oven to 325°F. In medium roasting pan
(14" by 10"), place rib roast, fat side up. In mortar, with
pestle, crush peppercorns with salt. Use to rub on fat
side of roast.

2 Roast beef until meat thermometer inserted in
thickest part of meat (not touching bone) reaches 140°F,
about 3 hours. Internal temperature of meat will rise to
145°F (medium) upon standing. Or roast until desired
doneness. About 30 minutes before roast is done,
prepare Yorkshire pudding (see Tip).

3 When roast is done, transfer to warm large platter
and let stand 15 minutes to set juices for easier carving.
Meanwhile, prepare creamy horseradish sauce.

TIP: You'll need 3 tablespons of pan drippings to make
the Yorkshire pudding. If you like, use the remaining
pan drippings to prepare an au jus sauce: Add 2 cups
of canned beef stock to the pan drippings and bring to
a boil in the roasting pan, scraping up all the flavorful
browned bits.

Each serving beef: About 315 calories, 39g protein,
1g carbohydrate, 16g total fat (7g saturated), 0g fiber,
322mg sodium

Yorkshire Pudding

Preheat oven to 450°F. In medium bowl, with
wire whisk, combine **1¹/₂ cups all-purpose flour** and
³/₄ teaspoon salt. Add **1¹/₂ cups milk** and **3 large eggs**,
beaten. Beat batter until smooth. Pour **3 tablespoons
drippings** from roast beef pan into small metal baking
pan (13" by 9"); bake 2 minutes. Remove pan from oven
and pour batter over drippings. Bake until puffed and
lightly browned, about 25 minutes. Cut into squares.
Makes 10 side-dish servings.

Each serving: About 145 calories, 5g protein, 16g carbohydrates,
6g total fat (3g saturated), 0g fiber, 197mg sodium

Creamy Horseradish Sauce

In small bowl, combine **1 jar (6 ounces) white horseradish**, drained; **¹/₂ cup mayonnaise**; **1 teaspoon sugar**;
and **¹/₂ teaspoon salt**. Whip **¹/₂ cup heavy or whipping
cream**; fold into horseradish mixture. Makes about
1²/₃ cups.

Each 1-tablespoon serving: About 50 calories, 0g protein,
1g carbohydrate, 5g total fat (2g saturated), 0g fiber,
9 mg cholesterol, 74mg sodium

Stuffed Veal Roast, Italian Style

Pancetta, unsmoked Italian bacon, lends rich flavor to this roast. If you can't find it, use the mildest regular bacon available.

Active time: 15 minutes
Total time: 1 hour 20 minutes
Makes: 8 main-dish servings

3 ounces pancetta, chopped
1 shallot, finely chopped
1/4 cup plus 1 tablespoon water
1 package (10 ounces) frozen chopped spinach, thawed
  and squeezed dry
3 ounces Fontina cheese, chopped (3/4 cup)
1 boneless veal shoulder roast (3 pounds)
1/2 cup dry white wine
2 tablespoons heavy cream
3/4 cup chicken broth
3/4 teaspoon cornstarch

1 Preheat oven to 425°F. In 10-inch skillet, combine pancetta, shallot, and 1/4 cup water; heat to boiling over medium heat. Reduce heat and simmer until pancetta is cooked through and shallot is soft, about 5 minutes. Stir in spinach until well combined. Transfer spinach mixture to medium bowl and stir in Fontina until well combined.

2 Using sharp knife, slice into roast lengthwise but do not cut whole way through; leave last quarter attached. Open roast and spread flat like a book. Spoon spinach mixture on roast, leaving 1/2-inch border all around. Roll up roast from one long side to enclose filling; tie with string at 1-inch intervals to secure.

3 Place in small roasting pan (13" by 9") and roast 30 minutes. Turn oven control to 350°F and continue cooking until meat thermometer inserted in center of roast registers 145°F, about 45 minutes longer. Internal temperature of meat will rise to 155°F (medium) upon standing. Transfer roast to warm large platter and let stand 15 minutes to set juices for easier slicing.

4 Meanwhile, skim and discard fat from roasting pan. Add wine and heat to boiling, stirring to loosen browned bits from bottom of pan. Pour into 1-quart saucepan and heat to boiling. Add cream and heat to boiling; boil until liquid has reduced by half. Add broth and heat to boiling again. In small bowl, blend cornstarch with remaining 1 tablespoon water until smooth. Stir mixture into saucepan. Heat to boiling over high heat, stirring, until sauce thickens. Slice veal and serve with sauce.

Each serving veal with 2 tablespoons sauce: About 345 calories, 38g protein, 3g carbohydrate, 19g total fat (9g saturated), 0g fiber, 501mg sodium

MY FAVORITE HOLIDAY TRADITION

"Pulling out the boxes of ornaments is a bit like a time machine, transporting you back over the years. There are all the bells, Christmas trees, and wreaths cut out of construction paper that the kids made in school. There isn't a year that they don't go up."

—Meredith Vieira

Herbed Pork Loin

The rich drippings from this roasted pork loin make for an easy pan gravy scented with fennel, thyme, and garlic. Serve with Roasted Sweet and White Potatoes with Rosemary (page 191).

Active time: 15 minutes
Total time: 1 hour 15 minutes
Makes: 12 main-dish servings

1 teaspoon fennel seeds
1 teaspoon dried thyme
3 garlic cloves, crushed with press
2 teaspoons extra-virgin olive oil
1½ teaspoons salt
1 teaspoon coarsely ground black pepper
1 boneless pork loin roast (4 pounds)
2 tablespoons all-purpose flour
½ cup dry red wine (such as Shiraz)
1 cup chicken broth
½ cup water
Fresh oregano sprigs for garnish

1 Preheat oven to 450°F. In cup, combine fennel, thyme, garlic, oil, salt, and pepper to form paste.

2 Place pork on rack in large roasting pan (17" by 11½"); rub with fennel paste. Roast pork 30 minutes.

3 Reduce oven control to 350°F and roast pork 30 to 45 minutes longer, or until meat thermometer inserted in thickest part of pork registers 145°F. (Internal temperature will rise 5°F to 10°F upon standing.) Transfer pork to platter; let stand 15 minutes.

4 Meanwhile, remove rack from roasting pan. Stir flour into drippings; cook over medium-high heat 1 minute, stirring. Add wine; heat to boiling, stirring to loosen browned bits stuck to bottom of pan. Add broth and water; heat to boiling and boil 1 minute. Strain gravy into gravy boat. Makes about 1½ cups.

5 Garnish platter with sprigs of oregano.

Each serving pork loin with 2 tablespoons gravy: About 335 calories, 31g protein, 2g carbohydrate, 20g total fat (7g saturated), 0g fiber, 465mg sodium

Roast Pork Loin with Apples, Potatoes, and Sage

This sage-infused roast pork loin is a one-dish meal—easy to cook, a snap to clean up, but so luscious, your guests won't realize it was a cinch to make.

Active time: 15 minutes
Total time: 1 hour 5 minutes plus standing
Makes: 8 main-dish servings

3 tablespoons butter or margarine, softened
2 tablespoons chopped fresh sage leaves
1 teaspoon salt
¼ teaspoon coarsely ground black pepper
1 boneless pork loin roast (3 pounds), trimmed of fat
1½ pounds baby red potatoes, cut in half
1 large onion (12 ounces), chopped
1½ pounds Gala or Jonagold apples, cored and cut into 8 wedges

1 Preheat oven to 450°F. Stir together 1 tablespoon butter, 1 tablespoon chopped sage, ½ teaspoon salt, and pepper. With hands, rub mixture all over pork loin.

2 In 15½" by 10 ½" jelly-roll pan, melt remaining 2 tablespoons butter in oven. Add potatoes, onion, and remaining ½ teaspoon salt and 1 tablespoon chopped sage to pan with butter; toss to coat. Push potatoes and onion to edges of pan and set small roasting rack in center; place pork on rack. Roast 20 minutes.

3 Arrange apples around pork, and continue roasting 30 to 40 minutes, or until thermometer inserted into thickest part of pork registers 145°F. (Internal temperature will rise 5°F to 10°F upon standing.)

4 Transfer pork to warm platter; let stand 15 minutes to set juices for easier slicing. With slotted spoon, transfer potatoes, onion, and apples to platter with pork. Pour pan drippings into small cup. Skim off and discard fat from drippings. Serve pork, sliced, with drippings.

Each serving: About 475 calories, 36g protein, 34g carbohydrate, 22g total fat (7g saturated), 4g fiber, 435mg sodium

Glazed Ham with Apricots

A simple glaze of marmalade and mustard amps the flavor of a classic ham.

Active time: 35 minutes
Total time: 2 hours 50 minutes
Makes: 16 main-dish servings

1 fully cooked bone-in smoked half ham (7 pounds; see Tip)
2 tablespoons whole cloves
6 ounces dried apricot halves
1 cup water
1/2 cup orange marmalade or apricot jam
2 tablespoons country-style Dijon mustard with seeds

1 Preheat oven to 325°F. With knife, remove skin and trim all but ⅛ inch fat from ham. Using cloves as pins, secure apricots to fat side of ham in rows, leaving some space between apricots. Place ham, fat side up, on rack in large roasting pan (17" by 11½"); add water. Cover pan tightly with foil. Bake 2 hours.

2 When ham has been baking 1 hour and 45 minutes, prepare glaze: In 1-quart saucepan, heat marmalade and mustard to boiling on medium-high. Remove foil from ham and carefully brush with some glaze. Continue to bake ham 30 to 40 minutes longer or until meat thermometer registers 135°F, brushing with glaze every 15 minutes. Internal temperature of ham will rise 5°F to 10°F upon standing. (Some apricots may fall off into pan during glazing.)

3 Transfer ham to cutting board; cover and let stand 20 minutes. Slice and serve with apricots from pan.

TIP: Ham halves are available as butt or shank. The shank half looks more like a classic whole ham because it contains the leg bone. It's also easier to carve than the butt half, and less fatty.

Each serving: About 240 calories, 29g protein, 16g carbohydrate, 7g total fat (2g saturated), 0g fiber, 1,525mg sodium

Top: Herbed Pork Loin *(opposite)*;
Bottom: Glazed Ham with Apricots *(above)*.

Pork Crown Roast with Pear Stuffing (*opposite*)

Pork Crown Roast with Pear Stuffing

This luscious marriage of meat and fruit is easy to customize. Swap in chopped apples (Galas work well) for the pears, and dried cranberries for the cherries, for tangy but equally sweet results.

Active time: 45 minutes
Total time: 2 hours 25 minutes plus marinating
Makes: 12 main-dish servings

2 tablespoons brown sugar
1 tablespoon freshly grated lemon peel
1/4 teaspoon ground nutmeg
1 tablespoon salt
2 1/4 teaspoons pepper, divided
3 tablespoons chopped fresh rosemary leaves, divided
2 tablespoons chopped fresh thyme leaves, divided
1 (10-pound) pork crown roast, trimmed
8 ounces bacon, chopped
2 medium red onions, finely chopped
4 stalks celery, finely chopped
2 pears, peeled cored and chopped
1/2 cup dried tart cherries
2 cloves garlic, chopped
10 cups 1/2-inch cubes country white bread, toasted
2 cups turkey or chicken broth
Pear slices and parsley leaves for garnish

1 In medium bowl, with fingers, rub together sugar, lemon peel, nutmeg, salt, 2 teaspoons pepper, 2 tablespoons rosemary, and 1 tablespoon thyme until well combined and fragrant; rub all over pork. Place pork on platter and wrap loosely in plastic wrap. Refrigerate at least 4 hours or up to 24 hours.

2 Arrange oven rack on bottom rung in oven. Preheat oven to 425°F.

3 Arrange pork, rib side down, on rack fitted into foil-lined large roasting pan. Roast 45 minutes.

4 Meanwhile, in 12-inch skillet, cook bacon on medium-high 8 minutes or until browned and crisp, stirring occasionally. With slotted spoon, transfer bacon to paper-towel-lined plate. Reduce heat to medium. To same skillet, add onions, celery, pears, cherries, garlic, 1/4 teaspoon pepper, and remaining 1 tablespoon rosemary and 1 tablespoon thyme. Cook 8 to 10 minutes, or until vegetables begin to soften, stirring and scraping up browned bits. Transfer to very large bowl along with bread, broth, and cooked bacon; toss until well combined. Transfer all but 4 cups stuffing to 3-quart baking dish.

5 After pork has roasted 45 minutes, remove from oven and turn pork rib side up on rack. Reduce oven temperature to 350°F. Place 4 cups reserved stuffing into center cavity of pork. Return pork to oven. Roast another 1 hour 30 minutes or until pork is cooked through (145°F). Remove from oven. Cover loosely with foil. Let rest at least 20 minutes before slicing.

6 While pork rests, increase oven temperature to 400°F. Bake stuffing in baking dish 20 minutes or until top is golden brown. Serve pork with stuffing. Garnish pork with pear slices and parsley leaves.

Each serving: About 785 calories, 65g protein, 33g carbohydrate, 41g total fat (14g saturated), 4g fiber, 1,305mg sodium

Roasted Leg of Lamb
with Pistachio-Mint Crust

*To prevent the nut crust from burning, spread it over
the roast after the lamb has cooked for one hour.*

Active time: 30 minutes
Total time: 2 hours 45 minutes
Makes: 10 main-dish servings

1 whole bone-in lamb leg (7 pounds), trimmed
2 large garlic cloves, sliced
1½ teaspoons salt
2 tablespoons butter or margarine
1 small onion, chopped
1½ slices firm white bread, torn into ¼-inch pieces
½ cup shelled pistachios, finely chopped
2 tablespoons coarsely chopped fresh mint
¼ teaspoon coarsely ground black pepper
½ cup port wine
3 tablespoons all-purpose flour
1 can (14½ ounces) chicken broth

1 Preheat oven to 325°F. Cut about 1 dozen ½-inch-long
slits in lamb and insert slice of garlic in each. Sprinkle
lamb with 1 teaspoon salt. Place lamb, fat side up, on
rack in large roasting pan (17" by 11½"). Roast 1 hour.

2 Meanwhile, in 10-inch skillet, melt butter over
medium heat. Add onion and cook until lightly browned
and tender, about 10 minutes; remove from heat. Stir
in bread, pistachios, mint, remaining ½ teaspoon salt,
and pepper. At end of first hour of roasting, carefully pat
mixture onto lamb.

3 Continue roasting lamb 1 hour 15 minutes to 1 hour
30 minutes longer, until meat thermometer inserted
in thickest part of lamb (not touching bone) registers
140°F. Internal temperature will rise to 145°F (medium)
upon standing. If well-done meat is preferred, continue
roasting to desired doneness. When lamb is done,
transfer to warm platter and let stand 15 minutes to set
juices for easier carving.

4 Meanwhile, prepare gravy: Remove rack from
roasting pan; pour pan drippings into 2-cup measuring
cup. Add port to pan, stirring until browned bits are
loosened from bottom. Add to drippings in cup; let
stand until fat separates out. Place 2 tablespoons fat
from drippings in roasting pan. Skim off and discard
any remaining fat.

5 With wire whisk, whisk flour into fat in roasting pan
over medium-high heat until well blended. Gradually
whisk in meat juice and broth and heat to boiling,
stirring constantly; boil 1 minute. Pour gravy into gravy
boat and serve with lamb.

Each serving: About 405 calories, 46g protein, 8g carbohydrate,
18g total fat (7g saturated), 0g fiber, 680mg sodium

Mustard-Glazed Fresh Ham
with Cider Sauce

*Cracklings, crunchy pieces of crisp, roasted pork skins, are a
Southern treat. If you want to try them, cook them right along
with the roast as directed below.*

Active time: 20 minutes
Total time: 5 hours 20 minutes
Makes: 24 main-dish servings

1 whole bone-in fresh ham leg (15 pounds)
1 teaspoon Chinese five-spice powder (optional)
½ cup packed brown sugar
1 tablespoon dry mustard
1 tablespoon kosher salt
1 teaspoon coarsely ground pepper
¼ teaspoon ground cloves
2½ cups apple cider
Sprig rosemary for garnish

1 Preheat oven to 350°F. With knife, remove skin from
pork, if any, and reserve. Trim excess fat from pork,
leaving ¼-inch-thick layer of fat; discard. Place pork
on rack in large roasting pan (17" by 11½"). Insert meat
thermometer into thickest part of pork, making sure
thermometer is at least ½ inch from bone. If you like, for
cracklings, sprinkle reserved pork skin with five-spice
powder. Place skin, fat side down, in 15½" by 10½" jelly-
roll pan; set aside.

2 In small bowl, combine sugar, mustard, salt, pepper, and cloves. Rub mixture on top and sides of pork, pressing lightly with hand so it adheres.

3 Roast pork and skin in same oven 4 to 5 hours (16 to 20 minutes per pound; see Tip) or until meat thermometer registers 160°F and cracklings are browned and crisp. Internal temperature of pork will rise to 165°F upon standing. (Meat near bone may still be slightly pink.)

4 When roast is done, transfer to warm, large platter; let stand 20 minutes to set juices for easier carving. Remove cracklings from pan and drain on paper towels.

5 Remove rack from roasting pan. Strain pan drippings into medium bowl. Let stand 1 minute, until fat separates. Skim and discard fat. Return pan drippings to hot roasting pan; add cider and heat to boiling over high heat, stirring until browned bits are loosened from bottom of pan. Boil about 7 minutes or until sauce thickens slightly. Strain sauce into gravy boat or serving bowl. Makes about 2¾ cups.

6 Cut or break cracklings into serving-size pieces. Thinly slice roast and serve with cider sauce and, if you like, cracklings. Garnish with rosemary.

TIP: Roasting times for fresh ham can vary by as much as an hour, depending on whether the meat contains a basting solution or was previously frozen. The best way to make sure any meat is cooked to the proper temperature is to use a meat thermometer.

Each serving pork with 1 tablespoon sauce: About 340 calories, 30g protein, 7g carbohydrates, 20g total fat (7g saturated), 0g fiber, 300mg sodium

Each ¼ cup cracklings: About 130 calories, 7g protein, 0g carbohydrate, 11g total fat (4g saturated), 0g fiber, 19g cholesterol, 365mg sodium

MAIL-ORDER HAM

Ham makes an impressive holiday centerpiece. Here's what you need to know to purchase one by mail order or online.

Like all pork cuts, ham has changed dramatically over the years. Reflecting contemporary preferences for leaner pigs, hams today are 57 percent leaner than those available twenty years ago, according to the National Pork Board. And hams come from one of the leanest parts of the pig—the leg—so they get less flavor from fat. That makes the flavors added through curing and smoking key. Enter mail-order hams, which are typically superior to supermarket hams because of the unique brining and/or smoking treatments used.

There are three types of ham to choose from: fresh, country, and city. Although most people think of ham as cured pork, a fresh ham is simply fresh pork cut from the leg; it typically requires four or five hours of roasting. Country hams are dry-cured (salt and seasonings are rubbed on the ham), smoked, then hung and aged for as long as a year to allow the flavors to develop. They are most often sold uncooked and can require substantial soaking, simmering, and baking before serving—as long as three days of preparation. City hams are wet-cured (soaked in brine). They're sold precooked (just heat—or not—and eat!), either bone-in or boned. To make the bone-in variety easy to serve, they are often sold "spiral-sliced," a process that creates thin slices down to the bone. This chapter includes recipes for fresh ham and city ham.

Lamb Shanks with White Beans and Roasted Endive

For a hearty and rustic Christmas dinner, serve lamb shanks, a Mediterranean favorite, on a bed of rosemary-scented white beans with endive that has been roasted in the oven at the same time as the lamb.

Active Time: 1 hour 30 minutes
Total Time: 3 hours 30 minutes
Makes: 8 main-dish servings

White Beans and Lamb Shanks

1 package (16 ounces) dry Great Northern beans
8 small lamb shanks (1 pound each)
2½ teaspoons salt
1 teaspoon coarsely ground pepper
2 tablespoons vegetable oil
6 garlic cloves, crushed with side of chef's knife
4 carrots, peeled and cut into 1-inch pieces
1 large (12 ounces) onion, coarsely chopped
¼ cup all-purpose flour
2 tablespoons tomato paste
2 cups dry white wine
1 can (14 to 14½ ounces) chicken broth (1¾ cups)
1 cup water
2 sprigs fresh rosemary, plus 8 sprigs for garnish

Roasted Endive

1 tablespoon olive oil
½ teaspoon salt
¼ teaspoon coarsely ground pepper
8 heads Belgian endive (1½ pounds)

1 Prepare white beans: In 4-quart saucepan, combine beans and enough *water* to cover by 2 inches; heat to boiling over high heat. Cook 3 minutes; remove from heat. Cover and set aside until beans are softened, about 1 hour. Drain and rinse beans. (Or, if you prefer, soak beans overnight in cold water. Drain and rinse.)

2 Meanwhile, prepare lamb shanks: Pat shanks dry with paper towels; sprinkle with 1 teaspoon salt and ½ teaspoon pepper. In 8-quart Dutch oven, heat oil over medium-high heat until very hot but not smoking.

Add shanks, in batches, and cook until browned, 10 to 15 minutes, using tongs to transfer shanks to large bowl as they are browned. If necessary, reduce heat to medium before adding second batch of shanks to prevent overbrowning.

3 Preheat oven to 375°F. Add garlic, carrots, and onion to Dutch oven; cook, stirring frequently, until browned and tender, about 10 minutes. Add flour, tomato paste, and remaining 1½ teaspoons salt and ½ teaspoon pepper; cook, stirring constantly, 2 minutes. Add wine and heat to boiling, stirring until browned bits are loosened from bottom of Dutch oven; boil 5 minutes. Add broth and water; heat to boiling. Stir in beans and 2 sprigs rosemary. Return shanks to Dutch oven; heat to boiling. Cover Dutch oven and bake 1 hour.

4 Meanwhile, prepare roasted endive: In large bowl, with fork, mix oil, salt, and pepper. Trim root ends of endive and cut each lengthwise in half. Add endive to oil mixture and toss until evenly coated. Arrange endive, cut sides down, in 15½" by 10½" jelly-roll pan.

5 After 1 hour, turn shanks and replace cover. Place endive in same oven. Bake shanks and endive until meat is fork-tender and easily separates from bone and endive is very tender and bottoms begin to brown, about 1 hour.

6 When shanks are done, transfer to large bowl. Skim and discard fat from liquid in Dutch oven. Remove and discard rosemary. To serve, spoon some beans and cooking liquid onto each of 8 large dinner plates. Top each with 1 lamb shank and 2 endive halves. Garnish with a rosemary sprig.

Each serving lamb and beans: About 725 calories, 67g protein, 46g carbohydrate, 28g total fat (11g saturated fat), 12g fiber, 1,110mg sodium

Each serving endive: About 30 calories, 1g protein, 3g carbohydrate, 2g total fat (0g saturated), 2g fiber, 145mg sodium

LAMB SHANKS WITH WHITE BEANS AND ROASTED ENDIVE *(opposite)*

Good
Housekeeping
Magazine

15 Cents

FROM OUR HOLIDAY ARCHIVES: FEASTING ON GAME

Although it might not occur to you to serve game for Christmas, pheasant, wild duckling, venison, and rabbit used to be popular choices, as our archives can attest. Their unique flavors will make for a special feast—and if you can roast a turkey or make a beef stew, you are up to the task! Let the huntsman dress the game birds or rabbit or butcher the venison. Refrigerate the meat for at least two or three days before cooking it to allow flavors to develop. If you're preparing pheasant, tuck a celery stalk inside the bird before refrigerating it.

Braised Pheasant with Cabbage

¼ pound piece plus 2 slices fat salt pork

2 stalks celery

4 sprigs parsley

½ bay leaf

1 sprig thyme

1 pheasant (2 to 2½ pounds), cut into quarters

1 teaspoon salt

⅛ teaspoon ground black pepper

1 onion, studded with cloves

3 cups hot water

1 medium cabbage

1 carrot, peeled and left whole

1 knockwurst or frankfurter

1 In saucepot, simmer large piece salt pork in *water* to cover, 3 to 4 minutes; drain. Using kitchen twine, tie celery, parsley, bay leaf, and thyme into bundle.

2 In Dutch oven over medium-high heat, brown remaining 2 salt pork slices; set aside. Add pheasant pieces to Dutch oven and brown, then add salt, pepper, herb bundle, clove-studded onion, browned salt pork, and 2 cups hot water. Simmer, covered, over medium heat 40 minutes.

3 Meanwhile, cut cabbage into 2-inch pieces. Add cabbage to medium pot with *water* to cover and simmer 5 minutes. Set a large bowl of cold water nearby. Drain cabbage, dip into cold water, then drain again.

4 To pheasant, add cabbage, carrot, knockwurst, and remaining 1 cup hot water and cook, covered, 45 to 60 minutes longer, or until meat is tender and leg separates from body. (Instant-read thermometer inserted into thickest part of pheasant, but not touching bone, should register 165°F.)

5 Using tongs, remove cabbage; drain thoroughly and arrange on heated platter. Add pheasant pieces on top of cabbage. Drain remaining contents of Dutch oven in colander and arrange knockwurst, carrot, and onion around pheasant. Slice large piece salt pork and add to platter. Makes 4 main-dish servings.

Wild Duck, Texas Style

1 cup diced celery

1 cup minced onion

1 cup dark seedless raisins

1 cup coarsely chopped pecans (4 ounces)

4 cups fresh bread crumbs

1½ teaspoons salt

2 eggs, beaten

½ cup scalded milk

2 wild ducks (2 to 2½ pounds each)

6 bacon slices

1 cup ketchup

½ cup chili sauce

¼ cup Worcestershire sauce

All-purpose flour (if needed)

Watercress or parsley for garnish

Thin orange slices for garnish

Currant jelly for garnish

1 Preheat oven to 500°F. In medium bowl, combine celery, onion, raisins, pecans, bread crumbs, and salt; add eggs and mix well. Stir in scalded milk.

2 Stuff neck and body cavities of birds with bread mixture. Fasten neck skin to backs; close body cavities with poultry pins or thin skewers; lace with kitchen twine. If you tie legs together, leave 3- or 4-inch opening between them.

3 Arrange 3 bacon slices across each duck breast. Place ducks on wire rack in large shallow roasting pan. Roast, uncovered, 15 minutes, then reduce heat to 350°F, cover, and roast for 1 hour 45 minutes to 2 hours 15 minutes. (Instant-read thermometer inserted into thickest part of duck, but not touching bone, should register 165°F.)

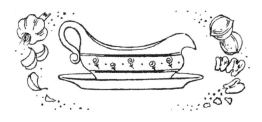

4 About 30 minutes before ducks are cooked, in a small bowl, stir together ketchup, chili sauce, and Worcestershire; pour some over ducks.

5 Just before serving, skim off fat from spicy sauce in pan. If necessary, to thicken, add 1½ tablespoons flour and *3 tablespoons water* for each cupful of sauce; whisk until smooth, then reheat over low. To serve, arrange ducks on heated platter. Garnish with watercress and orange slices topped with currant jelly. Transfer sauce to gravy boat and pass. Makes 4 to 6 main-dish servings.

Rabbit Supreme

¼ cup all-purpose flour

2 teaspoons salt

Dash ground black pepper

2 ready-to-cook rabbits (2 pounds each; see Tip)

¼ cup vegetable oil

1 cup sour cream

½ cup milk

1 cup thinly sliced onions

1 minced garlic clove

2 tablespoons cold water

1 Preheat oven to 350°F. In small bowl, toss 3 tablespoons flour with 1 teaspoon salt and pepper. Roll rabbit pieces in mixture to coat.

2 Add oil to Dutch oven over medium-high heat and brown rabbit. Stir in sour cream, garlic, and remaining 1 teaspoon salt. Transfer to oven and bake, covered, 1 hour 30 minutes, or until tender. Arrange rabbit on warm platter.

3 In cup, whisk together remaining 1 tablespoon flour with cold water; stir into sauce in Dutch oven and cook on stovetop over medium heat until sauce thickens. Pour over rabbit and serve. Makes 6 main-dish servings.

TIP: If you don't have access to wild rabbit, domestic rabbit—fresh or quick frozen—is increasingly becoming available year-round. Its meat, which is practically all white, is fine-grained and mild-flavored and can easily be substituted in many chicken recipes.

Civet of Venison

3 pounds venison shoulder, neck, or other less tender part

Basic Marinade for Game (see below)

2 stalks celery

4 sprigs parsley plus additional chopped leaves for garnish

1/2 bay leaf

1 sprig thyme

1/2 cup vegetable oil

1 cup diced fat salt pork

12 to 15 pearl onions

2 carrots, peeled and sliced

2 tablespoons packed brown sugar

1 1/2 pounds mushrooms, quartered

3 tablespoons all-purpose flour

1 garlic clove, mashed

2/3 cup red wine

Salt and ground black pepper to taste

1 Remove skin, tough sinews, and bones from meat; cut into pieces as for stew. (You can ask your butcher to do this for you, if you prefer.) Place meat in large bowl; add Basic Marinade and refrigerate 24 hours or longer.

2 When ready to cook, remove meat from marinade; strain marinade and reserve. Pat meat dry with paper towels. Using kitchen twine, tie celery, parsley sprigs, bay leaf, and thyme into bundle and set aside.

3 Heat half the oil in large skillet over medium-high heat; brown salt pork and set aside. To same skillet, add onions and cook, stirring occasionally until partially brown. Add carrots and sprinkle with brown sugar; cook until onions and carrots are browned; transfer to a bowl and set aside. Sauté mushrooms in same skillet until brown all over; add to bowl. In batches, add remaining oil and meat to skillet and brown (don't crowd skillet); transfer to large saucepan.

4 Sprinkle meat with flour; cook until flour browns. Add garlic, wine, herb bundle, reserved marinade, and just enough *water* to cover; simmer 1 hour or until meat is quite tender. Add reserved salt pork, onions, carrots, and mushrooms; cook 40 minutes longer.

5 Remove and discard herb bundle. Season stew with salt and pepper. Sprinkle with chopped parsley and serve. Makes 8 main-dish servings.

Basic Marinade for Game

2 onions, thinly sliced

1 carrot, peeled and thinly sliced

2 stalks celery

1 garlic clove

1 teaspoon salt

1/4 teaspoon dried thyme

2 bay leaves

12 whole black peppercorns

2 whole cloves

2 cups red wine

1/2 cup vegetable oil

In a large bowl, mix together all ingredients. Makes enough for 2 to 3 pounds meat.

TURKEY & OTHER POULTRY

Turkey Breast with Spinach-Herb Stuffing

For a relaxed holiday meal, serve this savory roast turkey breast with our Broccoli Pancetta Sauté (page 214) and our Potato Gratin with Gruyère (page 192).

Active time: 30 minutes
Total time: 3 hours 30 minutes
Makes: 10 main-dish servings

1 tablespoon olive oil

1 small onion, finely chopped

2 stalks celery, finely chopped

1 package (10 ounces) frozen chopped spinach, thawed and squeezed dry

1/2 teaspoon dried thyme

1/4 teaspoon dried sage

2 1/4 cups chicken broth

1/2 teaspoon salt

1/4 teaspoon coarsely ground black pepper

1/2 loaf sliced firm white bread (8 ounces), lightly toasted and cut into 1/2-inch cubes

1 whole bone-in turkey breast (7 pounds)

1/2 cup white wine

4 teaspoons cornstarch

1 Preheat oven to 350°F.

2 In 12-inch nonstick skillet, heat oil over medium heat and cook onion and celery 10 to 12 minutes or until

vegetables are lightly browned and tender, stirring occasionally. Remove skillet from heat; stir in spinach, thyme, sage, 3/4 cup chicken broth, salt, and pepper. Place bread cubes in large bowl; add spinach mixture and toss to mix well.

3 Pat turkey breast dry with paper towels. With fingertips, gently separate skin from meat on breast, being careful not to break skin. Spread stuffing mixture on meat under skin. Place turkey, skin side up, on rack in small roasting pan (13" by 9"). Cover turkey with loose tent of foil.

4 Roast turkey 1 hour and 45 minutes. Remove foil and roast 30 to 40 minutes longer. Start checking for doneness during last 30 minutes of cooking. Turkey breast is done when meat thermometer inserted into thickest part of breast (not touching bone) registers 165°F and juices run clear when thickest part of breast is pierced with tip of knife. (Internal temperature will rise 5°F to 10°F upon standing.)

5 Transfer turkey to warm platter. Let stand 15 minutes to set juices for easier carving.

6 Meanwhile, remove rack from roasting pan. Pour drippings through sieve into 1-cup liquid measuring cup or small bowl. Let drippings stand 1 minute to allow fat to separate from meat juices. Skim and discard fat. Place roasting pan on medium-high and cook 1 to 2 minutes to brown bits on bottom of pan, stirring. Carefully add wine and cook 1 minute. Stir cornstarch into remaining 1 1/2 cups broth and add with meat juices to roasting pan. Heat to boiling; boil 1 to 2 minutes or until gravy thickens, stirring to loosen brown bits from bottom of pan. Pour gravy (or strain, if you like) into gravy boat; serve with sliced turkey. Makes about 2 cups gravy.

Each serving turkey with stuffing. About 430 calories, 69g protein, 13g carbohydrate, 9g total fat (2g saturated), 0g fiber, 430mg sodium

Each 2-tablespoon serving gravy: About 5 calories, 1g protein, 1g carbohydrate, 0g total fat, 0g fiber, 85mg sodium

Clockwise from top: Roast Turkey with Wild Mushroom Gravy *(page 134);* Turkey Breast with Spinach-Herb Stuffing *(above);* Perfect Pears *(page 179).*

Roast Turkey with Wild Mushroom Gravy

We offer three gravy options for this succulent holiday bird:
wild mushroom, white wine, or roasted garlic.

Active time: 55 minutes
Total time: 5 hours
Makes: 14 main-dish servings

1 fresh or frozen (thawed) turkey (14 pounds)
1 lemon
1 cup loosely packed fresh parsley leaves, chopped
1/4 cup loosely packed fresh sage leaves, chopped
2 tablespoons fresh thyme leaves, chopped
2 teaspoons salt
1 teaspoon ground black pepper
1 tablespoon olive oil
1 carrot, peeled and coarsely chopped
1 stalk celery, coarsely chopped
2 small onions, cut into quarters
2 tablespoons butter or margarine
8 ounces sliced white mushrooms
6 ounces sliced cremini mushrooms
4 ounces sliced shiitake mushrooms
1 cup dry white wine
1 to 2 cans (14 1/2 ounces each) chicken broth
  (see Tip)
1/3 cup all-purpose flour
Fresh herbs and fruit for garnish

1 Preheat oven to 325°F. Remove giblets and neck from turkey cavity; set aside. Discard liver or save for another use. Cut neck into several large pieces. Rinse turkey inside and out with cold running water and drain well; pat dry with paper towels. Place turkey, breast side up, on small rack in large roasting pan (17" by 11½"). Scatter giblets and neck in pan around turkey.

2 From lemon, grate 1 teaspoon peel and place in small bowl. Cut lemon in half and set aside. To bowl with lemon peel, add parsley, sage, thyme, salt, and pepper, and stir until blended.

3 In medium bowl, place olive oil, carrot, and celery; stir in 2 tablespoons herb mixture to coat vegetables. Place vegetable mixture in pan around turkey. Sprinkle remaining herb mixture inside body and neck cavities, and rub all over outside of turkey. Squeeze juice from lemon halves into both cavities, and place lemon halves and 4 onion quarters in body cavity. Place remaining 4 onion quarters in pan around turkey. Fold wings under back of turkey to secure in place. If drumsticks are not held by band of skin or stuffing clamp, tie legs together with string.

4 Cover turkey with tent of foil; roast 2 hours 30 minutes. Remove foil and roast about 1 hour 15 minutes longer.

5 About 20 minutes before turkey finishes roasting, in 12-inch nonstick skillet, heat butter on medium until melted. Add all mushrooms and cook, covered, 6 minutes. Uncover and cook 11 to 12 minutes longer or until tender and golden, stirring occasionally. Remove skillet from heat; set aside until ready to complete gravy.

6 Turkey is done when temperature on meat thermometer inserted into thickest part of thigh next to body (not touching bone), registers 175°F to 180°F and breast temperature reaches 165°F. (Internal temperature will rise 5°F to 10°F upon standing.)

7 When turkey is done, carefully lift from roasting pan and tilt slightly to allow juices to run into pan. Place turkey on large platter; cover loosely with foil to keep warm.

8 Remove rack from roasting pan. Strain pan drippings into 4-cup liquid measuring cup or medium bowl, leaving giblets and neck in pan. Let drippings stand 1 minute to allow fat to separate from meat juices. Spoon 1/4 cup fat from drippings into 2-quart saucepan. Discard any remaining fat.

9 Place roasting pan over two burners on top of range and cook 2 to 4 minutes on medium-high to brown giblets, neck, and bits on bottom of pan, stirring constantly. Carefully add wine to roasting pan and boil about 3 minutes or until wine is reduced by half, stirring until browned bits are loosened from bottom of pan. Strain wine mixture into meat juices in measuring cup; pour in any additional meat juices on platter. Discard giblets and neck. Add enough broth to measuring cup to equal 4 cups total. (You may have some broth left over; save for another use.)

10 With wire whisk, mix flour into fat in pan; cook on medium 3 to 4 minutes or until mixture turns golden brown, whisking constantly. While still whisking, gradually add meat juices to pan; cook on medium-high until mixture boils and thickens, stirring frequently; boil 1 minute. Stir in mushroom mixture; heat through. Pour gravy into gravy boat and serve with turkey. Garnish turkey platter with herbs and fruit. Makes about 6 cups gravy.

TIP: To keep the gravy lovers in the crowd happy, have enough chicken broth on hand (we suggest 2 cans) to add to gravy as needed in step 9. The amount of meat juice your particular turkey gives off during roasting will determine how much chicken broth you'll need to add.

Each serving turkey without skin or gravy: About 340 calories, 57g protein, 1g carbohydrate, 11g total fat (3g saturated), 0g fiber, 415mg sodium

Each ¹/4-cup serving gravy: About 80 calories, 2g protein, 5g carbohydrate, 5g total fat (1g saturated), 1g fiber, 140mg sodium

Roast Turkey with White Wine Gravy

Prepare turkey and gravy as above, but omit butter and mushrooms and skip all of step 5. Add 1¹/2 cups white wine when wine is called for in step 9. Makes about 4 cups gravy.

Each ¹/4-cup serving gravy: About 50 calories, 1g protein, 3g carbohydrate, 5g total fat (1g saturated), 1g fiber, 140mg sodium

Roast Turkey with Roasted-Garlic Gravy

Prepare turkey and gravy as above, but omit butter and mushrooms and skip all of step 5. In step 3, separate 1 head garlic into cloves; do not peel. Add garlic to bowl with vegetable mixture. In step 8, before straining pan drippings, with spatula or back of spoon, press garlic cloves, still in roasting pan, to squeeze soft roasted garlic into pan drippings; discard peels. Complete recipe as in steps 9 and 10. Makes about 4 cups gravy.

Each ¹/4-cup serving gravy: About 50 calories, 1g protein, 4g carbohydrate, 4g total fat (1g saturated), 0g fiber, 115mg sodium

---

CARVING A ROAST TURKEY

Let the turkey stand at least fifteen minutes after you remove it from the oven. Carving will be easier and the meat will be juicier when you serve it.

Step 1: Cut through the skin where the leg is attached. To remove the leg, force it away from the body with a carving fork until it pops out of socket. Separate the thigh from the body by cutting through the joint.

Step 2: To carve the breast, make a horizontal cut above the wing joint along the length of the bird, making sure to cut down to the bone.

Step 3: With the knife parallel to the rib cage, cut the breast meat into thin slices. Cut off the wing. Repeat on the other side.

TIP: To carve the leg, slice the thigh and drumstick meat, cutting parallel to the bones. Repeat on the other side.

Caramelized Onion-Stuffed Turkey Roulade

Save 15 minutes: Ask the butcher to pound the butterflied turkey breast flat until it's ¼ inch thick—and skip this recipe's step 4 entirely!

Active time: 40 minutes
Total time: 2 hours 20 minutes plus cooling and resting
Makes: 10 main-dish servings

2 tablespoons olive oil
2 medium onions, chopped
1 teaspoon sugar
1⅛ teaspoon salt, divided
12 ounces white or cremini mushrooms
½ cup dry white wine
1½ cup coarse bread crumbs
8 medium sage leaves, thinly sliced, plus more for garnish
¼ cup plus ⅓ cup chopped fresh flat-leaf parsley leaves
1 boneless turkey breast (about 5 pounds), butterflied, skin removed
½ teaspoon pepper
4 tablespoons margarine or butter, melted
3 cups turkey or chicken broth
1 cup water

1 Preheat oven to 375°F. Arrange roasting rack in roasting pan.

2 In 12-inch skillet, heat oil on medium. Add onions; sprinkle with sugar and ⅛ teaspoon salt. Cook 20 minutes or until golden brown, stirring occasionally.

3 While onions cook, trim and chop mushrooms. Add mushrooms and wine to skillet. Increase heat to medium-high. Cook 5 minutes, or until mushrooms are tender, stirring occasionally. Transfer contents of skillet to large bowl; cool. Stir in bread crumbs, sage, and ¼ cup parsley.

4 Place turkey on large cutting board, smooth side down. On left breast, cut along right side of tenderloin to separate from breast without cutting tenderloin off completely. Fold tenderloin back until flat but still attached to breast along left side. Repeat on right breast, cutting along left side of tenderloin and folding back. Cover surface of turkey with 2 large sheets of plastic wrap. Using flat side of meat mallet or heavy rolling pin, pound turkey until about ¾ inch thick all over. Discard plastic wrap.

5 Sprinkle turkey with ½ teaspoon each salt and pepper. Spread stuffing in even layer on breast. Starting with short side, roll breast in jelly-roll fashion. Place seam side down. Using 16-inch pieces of kitchen string, tie roulade tightly at 2-inch intervals. Place roulade on rack in pan. Brush liberally with half of margarine. Sprinkle with ½ teaspoon salt. Pour broth and 1 cup water into bottom of pan. Roast 1½ to 2 hours or until turkey is cooked through (165°F), basting with remaining margarine halfway through. Remove from oven; transfer to large cutting board. Cover loosely with aluminum foil; let stand at least 10 minutes. Remove and discard strings.

6 While roulade rests, strain pan juices into gravy separator. To serve, sprinkle all but 1 tablespoon remaining parsley onto roulade, patting to adhere. Slice roulade; transfer to serving platter. Garnish with sage leaves. Sprinkle with remaining parsley. Serve with juices.

Each serving: About 350 calories, 57g protein, 8g carbohydrate, 9g total fat (4g saturated), 1g fiber, 720mg sodium

Caramelized Onion–Stuffed Turkey Roulade *(opposite)*

Sage Orange Turkey with White Wine Gravy

*This burnished bird is enhanced by a fragrant herb mixture
cooked under its skin and white wine gravy.*

Active Time: 40 minutes
Total Time: 4 hours plus standing
Makes: 12 main-dish servings; 7 cups gravy

1 fresh or frozen (thawed) turkey (12 to 14 pounds)

1 large onion (10 to 12 ounces), cut into 2-inch chunks

1/2 bunch fresh thyme

7 garlic cloves

1 large navel orange

1 small bunch fresh flat-leaf parsley

6 sprigs fresh sage

Pinch cayenne (ground red) pepper

4 tablespoons extra-virgin olive oil

1 1/4 teaspoons salt

3/4 teaspoon freshly ground black pepper

6 cups unsalted chicken broth

2 cups dry white wine

1/4 cup cornstarch

Sage sprigs, grapes, and clementines for ganish

1 Preheat oven to 325°F. Drain juices from turkey. Place
giblets and neck in large roasting pan. Pat turkey dry
with paper towels. Place turkey, breast side up, on wire
rack in pan; fold wing tips under back of turkey. Scatter
half of onion, half of thyme, and 2 garlic cloves in pan
around turkey. Pour *1 cup water* into pan.

2 From orange, finely grate 2 teaspoons peel. Transfer
peel to food processor along with 3 garlic cloves; pulse
until garlic is finely chopped. Cut whole orange into
2-inch chunks and reserve. From parsley and sage,
transfer 1 cup parsley leaves and 3 tablespoons sage
leaves to processor; pulse until very finely chopped.
Reserve herb stems. Add cayenne, 3 tablespoons oil, and
1/4 teaspoon salt to processor; pulse until well mixed.

3 Working from large-cavity end of turkey, gently run
fingers between skin and meat to loosen skin from flesh
on breast and legs. With hands, place herb mixture
under skin on both sides of breastbone and on legs.
Gently massage skin to evenly distribute mixture.

4 Rub 1/2 teaspoon salt and 1/4 teaspoon pepper inside
body cavity. Place reserved orange and herb stems and
remaining onion, thyme, and 2 garlic cloves in body
and neck cavities. Fold neck skin under back of turkey;
secure drumsticks together with kitchen string, band of
skin, or stuffing clamp. Rub remaining tablespoon oil
and 1/4 teaspoon each salt and pepper over turkey.

5 Cover turkey with loose tent of foil; roast 2 hours.
Remove foil. If pan is dry, add *1 cup water*. Roast about
1 hour longer. Turkey is done when temperature on meat
thermometer inserted into thickest part of thigh next
to body (not touching bone) reaches 175°F and breast
temperature reaches 165°F.

6 When turkey is done, carefully lift from roasting rack
and tilt slightly to allow juices to run into pan. Place
turkey on large platter and let rest while making gravy.

7 Remove rack from roasting pan. Strain pan drippings
into 8-cup liquid measuring cup or bowl, leaving solids
in pan. Let stand to allow fat to separate from meat
juices; discard fat. Add broth to drippings, then add
enough *water* to equal 8 cups total.

8 Discard thyme stems. Transfer onion, garlic, and giblets to cutting board and finely chop. When cool enough to handle, pull meat from neck; discard bones. Finely chop meat.

9 Place roasting pan over two burners on top of range; add wine and heat to boiling on medium-high. Boil 8 minutes or until wine is reduced by half, stirring until browned bits are loosened from bottom of pan. Stir broth and drippings mixture into roasting pan. Heat to boiling; boil 5 minutes. Meanwhile, in small bowl, stir cornstarch and ½ cup water to dissolve cornstarch; stir into broth mixture. Heat to boiling; simmer, stirring occasionally, 3 minutes or until thickened. Stir in chopped onion, garlic, giblets, neck meat, and ¼ teaspoon each salt and pepper. Pour into gravy boat. Garnish platter with sage and fruit.

TIP: To make 20 servings: In steps 1 and 4: Use 20- to 22-pound turkey, 2 large onions, 1 bunch thyme, 6 garlic cloves (3 each in pan and cavity). Step 2: Use 1 tablespoon freshly grated orange peel, 4 garlic cloves, 1½ cups parsley leaves, ¼ cup sage leaves, ⅛ teaspoon cayenne, ¼ cup oil, ½ teaspoon salt. Step 4: In turkey cavity, use 1 teaspoon each salt and pepper. On bird, use 2 tablespoons oil and ½ teaspoon each salt and pepper. Step 5: Roast, covered, 2 hours, then uncovered 2¼ hours. Step 7: Use 8 cups broth; add enough *water* to broth and drippings to equal 10 cups total. Step 9: Use 3¼ cups wine; boil 15 minutes. Boil with drippings mixture 10 minutes. Use ¼ cup cornstarch; simmer 6 minutes. Use ½ teaspoon each salt and pepper. Makes about 10 cups gravy.

Each serving turkey without skin or gravy: About 355 calories, 63g protein, 1g carbohydrate, 9g total fat (2g saturated fat), 0g fiber, 340mg sodium

Each ¼-cup serving gravy: About 45 calories, 5g protein, 1g total fat (0g saturated), 0g fiber, 75mg sodium

OUR FAVORITE SANDWICH IDEAS FOR COLD TURKEY

To jazz things up, stack your sliced white meat with the following items:

• **Sautéed onions and cranberry sauce** on toasted walnut-raisin bread.

• **Coleslaw and fresh tomato slices** on multi-grain bread.

• **Thinly sliced ham, American cheese,** and mustard on white bread; brown in a buttered skillet until golden.

• **Jarred roasted red peppers** and prepared pesto on Italian bread.

• **Mango chutney and Brie** on a French baguette or sourdough roll.

• **Potato salad and horseradish** on pumperknickel.

• **Thousand Island dressing, sauerkraut, and Swiss cheese** on rye; cook in an oiled skillet until golden.

• **Blue cheese dressing and apple slices** on toasted pecan bread.

• **Jalapeño-pepper Monterey Jack and salsa** between flour tortillas; pan-fry quesadilla-style in a nonstick skillet until the cheese melts.

BUTTERY HERB TURKEY *(opposite)*

Buttery Herb Turkey Three Ways

Here's an easy way to customize your holiday bird.

Active time: 30 minutes

Total time: 3 hours

Makes: 14-16 main-dish servings

1 fresh or frozen (thawed) turkey (14 to 16 pounds)

2 to 3 tablespoons kosher salt

2 cups water

Seasonings & Aromatics *(see subrecipes)*

1 Preheat oven to 350°F. Place rack in large roasting pan. Remove giblets and neck from inside turkey. Pat turkey dry. Tuck wing tips behind turkey.

2 Season under skin and all over skin with your choice of Seasonings. Sprinkle all over and inside to salt. Stuff cavity with matching Aromatics.

3 Tie legs of turkey together. Pour water into bottom of pan. Roast 2 hours. Loosely tent turkey with foil. Roast 30 minutes to 1 hour more or until thermometer inserted into thigh reads 165°F. Remove turkey from oven; let stand at least 15 minutes before carving. Serve with Gravy *(right)*.

LEMONY HERB BUTTER

Seasonings: In food processor, pulse **6 tablespoons butter, softened**; **¼ cup packed fresh parsley leaves**; **3 tablespoons fresh rosemary**; **3 tablespoons fresh thyme leaves**; **2 tablespoons lemon juice**; **1 teaspoon grated lemon peel** and **1 teaspoon black pepper** until combined.

Aromatics: **Parsley stems + rosemary springs + lemon halves**

Each Serving: About 465 calories, 69g protein, 1g carbohydrate, 19g total fat (7g saturated), 0g fiber, 735mg sodium

CHIPOTLE CINNAMON-ORANGE

Seasonings: In blender, puree **1 can (7 to 7.5 ounces) chipotles in adobo**; **⅓ cup orange juice**; **¼ cup honey**; **¼ cup olive oil**; **8 cloves garlic**; **2 teaspoons grated orange peel** and **½ teaspoon ground cinnamon** until smooth.

Aromatics: **Orange wedges + cinnamon sticks**

Each Serving: About 490 calories, 70g protein, 8g carbohydrate, 18g total fat (5g saturated), 1g fiber, 795mg sodium

SOUTHERN BBQ

Seasonings: In medium bowl, whisk together **6 tablespoons paprika**; **6 tablespoons brown sugar**; **2 tablespoons onion powder**; **2 tablespoons garlic powder**; **2 teaspoons black pepper**, and **1 teaspoon cayenne pepper**.

Aromatics: **Orange wedges + onion wedges + unpeeled garlic cloves**

Each Serving: About 460 calories, 70g protein, 9g carbohydrate, 14g total fat (4g saturated), 1g fiber, 700mg sodium

GRAVY AND MIX-INS

In 5-quart saucepot, heat **3 tablespoons vegetable oil** on medium-high. Pat turkey neck and giblets dry; add to pot. Cook 5 minutes or until browned, turning occasionally. Transfer turkey parts to plate. Reduce heat to medium. Add **2 medium carrots, chopped**; **2 medium stalks celery, chopped**; **1 medium onion, chopped**; and **pinch salt**. Cook 10 minutes, stirring occasionally. Stir in **½ cup all-purpose flour** and cook 2 minutes. Pour in **4 cups chicken or turkey broth** and **turkey parts**, scraping the bottom of pot. Bring to boiling. Simmer 15 minutes or until thickened, stirring occasionally. Remove from heat; cool slightly. To serve, scrape off and discard fat, then reheat on medium and strain, discarding all solids.

Each ¼ cup serving: About 55 calories, 1g protein, 4g carbohydrate, 4g total fat (0g saturated), 0g fiber, 250mg sodium

MIX-INS

- Add **4 ounces sliced mixed mushrooms** with vegetables. Stir in another **4 ounces sliced mushrooms** after straining.

- Add **2 medium shallots** with vegetables. Stir in **2 tablespoons lemon juice** after straining.

- Add **2 teaspoons chopped thyme**, **1 teaspoon chopped rosemary**, and **1 teaspoon chopped sage** with vegetables. Stir in **½ cup white wine** with broth.

BEST DO-AHEAD GRAVY

If you want to get a jumpstart on holiday prep, make this luscious gravy from turkey wings. You can refrigerate it up to three days.

Active time: 10 minutes • Total time: 1 hour 40 minutes • Makes: about 6 cups

1 tablespoon vegetable oil

2 turkey wings (1½ pounds), separated at joints

1 large onion, quartered

2 large carrots, each peeled and cut into 4 pieces

2 large stalks celery, each cut into 4 pieces

1 garlic clove, sliced in half

½ cup dry white wine

2 cans (14 to 14½ ounces each) chicken broth (3½ cups)

3 cups water

¼ teaspoon dried thyme

½ cup all-purpose flour

1 In deep 12-inch skillet, heat oil over medium-high heat until hot. Add turkey wings and cook 10 to 15 minutes or until golden on all sides. Add onion, carrots, celery, and garlic, and cook 8 to 10 minutes or until turkey wings and vegetables are browned, stirring frequently. Transfer turkey and vegetables to large bowl.

2 Add wine to skillet and stir until browned bits are loosened. Return turkey and vegetables to skillet. Stir in broth, water, and thyme; heat to boiling over high heat. Reduce heat to medium-low; simmer, uncovered, 45 minutes. Strain into an 8-cup liquid measuring cup or large bowl; discard solids.

3 Let broth stand 1 minute until fat separates from meat juice. Spoon ¼ cup fat from broth into 2-quart saucepan; skim and discard any remaining fat.

4 Whisk flour into fat in saucepan and cook, stirring, over medium heat, until flour turns golden brown. Gradually whisk in reserved broth and cook until gravy boils and thickens slightly, stirring constantly. Pour gravy into 2-quart container or medium bowl; cover and refrigerate up to 3 days.

5 At serving time, reheat gravy and add pan drippings from roast turkey if you like.

Each ¼-cup serving: About 50 calories, 1g protein, 2g carbohydrate, 4g total fat (1g saturated), 0g fiber, 115mg sodium

Crispy Roast Goose with Orange Sauce

This goose is the perfect thing to serve if you've been given homemade cranberry sauces or chutneys as holiday gifts. Piercing the skin helps drain off the large amount of fat and also crisps the skin as the goose cooks. But don't throw away all that flavorful fat! Pour it through a fine-mesh sieve and freeze it—it'll keep for up to four months. It's especially delicious when used for browning potatoes.

Active time: 30 minutes
Total time: 4 hours 55 minutes
Makes: 10 main-dish servings

1 fresh or frozen (thawed) goose (12 pounds)
5 navel oranges, each cut in half
1 bunch thyme
4 bay leaves
1/2 teaspoon dried thyme
1 1/4 teaspoons salt
1/2 teaspoon coarsely ground black pepper
3 tablespoons orange-flavored liqueur such as triple sec
2 tablespoons cornstarch
1/2 cup orange marmalade

1 Preheat oven to 400°F. Remove giblets and neck from goose; reserve for another use. Trim and discard fat from body cavity; trim any excess skin. Rinse goose inside and out with cold running water and drain well; pat dry with paper towels. With goose breast side up, lift wings toward neck, then fold wing tips under back of goose to hold in place. Place 6 orange halves, thyme sprigs, and bay leaves in body cavity. Tie legs and tail together with kitchen twine. Fold neck skin over back. With two-tine fork, prick skin in several places to drain fat during roasting.

2 Place goose, breast side up, on rack in large roasting pan (17" by 11½"). In cup, combine dried thyme, 1 teaspoon salt, and pepper; rub mixture over goose. Cover goose and roasting pan with foil. Roast 1 hour 30 minutes; turn oven control to 325°F and roast 2 hours longer.

3 Meanwhile, in small bowl, from remaining 4 orange halves, squeeze ¾ cup juice. Stir in 1 tablespoon liqueur, cornstarch, and remaining ¼ teaspoon salt; set

aside. In cup, mix orange marmalade with remaining 2 tablespoons liqueur.

4 With spoon or bulb baster, remove as much fat from roasting pan as possible. Remove foil and roast goose 45 minutes longer. Remove goose from oven and turn oven control to 450°F. Brush marmalade mixture over goose. Continue roasting until skin is golden brown and crisp, about 10 minutes longer. Goose is done when temperature on meat thermometer inserted in thickest part of thigh, next to body, registers 165° to 170°F; breast temperature should be 165°F. Transfer goose to warm platter; let stand at least 15 minutes for juices to set for easier carving.

5 Prepare sauce: Remove rack from roasting pan. Strain pan drippings through sieve into 8-cup measuring cup or large bowl. Let stand until fat separates from meat juice; skim and reserve fat for another use (there should be about 5 cups fat). Measure meat juice; if necessary, add enough *water* to meat juice to equal 1 cup. Return meat juice to pan and add reserved orange-juice mixture. Heat sauce to boiling over medium heat, stirring; boil 1 minute. Makes about 1¾ cups sauce.

6 Serve sauce with goose. Remove skin before eating, if desired.

Each serving with skin: About 810 calories, 66g protein, 5g carbohydrate, 57g total fat (5g saturated), 0g fiber, 472mg sodium

Each serving without skin: About 490 calories, 57g protein, 5g carbohydrate, 25g total fat (9g saturated), 0g fiber, 440mg sodium

Cornish Hens Milanese

Gremolata, a tasty Italian blend of chopped fresh parsley, freshly grated lemon peel, and pungent garlic flavors these rustic roasted hens.

Active time: 10 minutes
Total time: 1 hour
Makes: 4 main-dish servings

2 Cornish hens (1½ pounds each)
3 tablespoons chopped fresh parsley
1 teaspoon extra-virgin olive oil
¼ teaspoon salt
⅛ teaspoon ground black pepper
1 small garlic clove, minced
½ teaspoon freshly grated lemon peel

1 Preheat oven to 375°F. Remove giblets and necks from hens; reserve for another use. With poultry shears, cut each hen lengthwise in half. Rinse hen pieces with cold running water; pat dry with paper towels.

2 In small bowl, combine 2 tablespoons parsley, oil, salt, and pepper. With fingertips, carefully separate skin from meat on each hen half; spread parsley mixture under skin. Place hens, skin side up, in large roasting pan (17" by 11½").

3 Roast hens, basting with drippings three times, until juices run clear when thickest part of thigh is pierced with tip of knife, and instant-read thermometer registers 165°F when inserted into thigh, about 50 minutes.

4 Arrange hens on warm platter. In cup, combine remaining 1 tablespoon parsley, garlic, and lemon peel; sprinkle over hens.

Each serving: About 385 calories, 32g protein, 0g carbohydrate, 27g total fat (7g saturated), 0g fiber, 236mg sodium

Top: CORNISH HENS MILANESE *(above)*;
Bottom: LEMON-ROASTED CHICKEN FOR A CROWD *(opposite)*.

Spiced Grilled Turkey Breast

This breast is brined then slathered with a spicy glaze for exceptionally tender, flavorful results.

Active time: 35 minutes

Total time: 1 hour plus brining and standing

Makes: 12 main-dish servings

¼ cup sugar

¼ cup kosher salt

2 tablespoons cracked black peppercorns

2 tablespoons ground ginger

1 tablespoon ground cinnamon

4 cups water

Ice

1 small boneless turkey breast (4 pounds),
  skin removed, breast cut in half

4 garlic cloves, crushed with side of chef's knife

2 tablespoons honey

2 tablespoons Dijon mustard

1 chipotle chile in adobo, minced

1 teaspoon balsamic vinegar

1 In 2-quart saucepan, heat sugar, salt, pepper, ginger, cinnamon, and 1 cup water to boiling over high heat. Reduce heat to low; simmer 2 minutes. Stir remaining 3 cups water with ice. Remove brining solution from heat; pour ice water through sieve into brine and stir.

2 Place turkey breast in large resealable plastic bag; add brine and garlic. Seal bag, pressing out excess air. Place bag in bowl and refrigerate, turning occasionally, 24 hours.

3 Prepare outdoor grill for covered direct grilling over medium heat. Meanwhile, in small bowl, stir honey, mustard, chipotle, and vinegar until blended. Set aside.

4 Remove turkey from bag; discard brine and garlic. With paper towels, pat turkey dry and brush off most of pepper. With long-handled basting brush, oil grill rack. Place turkey on hot grill rack. Cover grill and cook turkey 20 minutes, turning over once. Brush turkey with glaze and cook 5 to 10 minutes longer (depending on thickness of breast), brushing and turning frequently, until instant-read meat thermometer inserted into thickest part of breast registers 165°F. (Internal temperature will rise 5°F to 10°F upon standing.) Place turkey on cutting board and let stand 10 minutes to allow juices to set for easier slicing.

5 Serve turkey hot, or cover and refrigerate to serve cold.

Each serving: About 170 calories, 34g protein, 4g carbohydrate, 1g total fat (0g saturated), 0g fiber, 555mg sodium

Lemon-Roasted Chicken for a Crowd

When you need a dish for a holiday buffet but you don't have time to fuss, turn to this easy crowd-pleaser.

Active time: 20 minutes

Total time: 1 hour 50 minutes

Makes: 20 main-dish servings

1½ cups fresh lemon juice (from 7 large lemons)

¼ cup vegetable oil

1 large onion (12 ounces), finely chopped

2 large garlic cloves, crushed with garlic press

5 teaspoons salt

1 tablespoon dried thyme

2 teaspoons ground black pepper

5 chickens (3 pounds each), each cut into quarters

1 Preheat oven to 375°F. In medium bowl, combine lemon juice, oil, onion, garlic, salt, thyme, and pepper. In two large roasting pans (17" by 11½"), arrange chicken pieces, skin side up. Pour lemon-juice mixture over chicken.

2 Roast chicken, basting occasionally with pan juices, about 1 hour 30 minutes, rotating position of pans halfway through. Chicken is done when meat thermometer inserted in thickest part of thigh, next to body, registers 165°F to 170°F; breast temperature should reach 165°F.

3 Transfer chicken to warm platters. Skim and discard fat from drippings in pan; pour pan drippings into medium bowl. Spoon some pan juices over chicken and serve with remaining juices alongside.

Each serving: About 380 calories, 41g protein, 3g carbohydrate, 22g total fat (6g saturated), 0g fiber, 706mg sodium

Roast Duck with Cherry-Port Sauce

Made with tart cherries, this sauce is not overly sweet. We accompanied the duck with roasted pears. You could also serve roasted potatoes, Brussels sprouts, or carrots.

Active time: 10 minutes
Total time: 2 hours 40 minutes
Makes: 4 main-dish servings

1 fresh or frozen (thawed) duck (4½ pounds; see Tip)
½ teaspoon dried thyme
¼ teaspoon salt
¼ teaspoon ground black pepper
1 can (14½ ounces) chicken broth
2 to 2½ cups water
2 Bosc pears, each cut into quarters and cored
2 teaspoons sugar
¼ cup minced shallots
⅓ cup port wine
¼ cup dried tart cherries

1 Preheat oven to 350°F. Trim and discard fat from body cavity of duck. Discard liver or reserve for another use: set neck and giblets aside for gravy. Rinse duck inside and out with cold running water; drain well. Pat dry with paper towels. Lift wings up toward neck; fold wing tips under back of duck to hold in place. With two-tine fork, prick skin in several places to drain fat during roasting. Sprinkle ¼ teaspoon thyme inside body cavity. With string, tie legs and tail together.

2 Place duck, breast side up, on rack in medium roasting pan (14" by 10"). Sprinkle salt, pepper, and remaining ¼ teaspoon thyme on outside of duck.

3 Roast, occasionally spooning off fat, 2 hours 30 minutes. Duck is done when meat thermometer inserted in thickest part of thigh, next to body, registers 165°F to 170°F; breast temperature should be 165°F.

4 Meanwhile, in 2-quart saucepan, combine reserved giblets and neck, broth, and 2 cups water; bring to boiling over high heat. Reduce heat to low; simmer, uncovered, 1 hour 30 minutes (if liquid evaporates too quickly, add remaining ½ cup water). Pour broth through strainer set over 1-cup measuring cup; discard giblets. You should have ½ to ¾ cup broth; set aside.

5 After duck has roasted 2 hours, place pears in small baking dish. Sprinkle with sugar; roast alongside duck until tender, about 30 minutes. Transfer duck and pears to platter; keep warm. Let duck stand 15 minutes to set juices for easier carving.

6 Skim and discard fat from drippings in pan. Add shallots to pan; cook over medium-high heat, stirring, 2 minutes. Stir in port, cherries, and reserved broth; boil, stirring until brown bits are loosened from bottom of pan. Simmer 5 minutes. Pour into small bowl. Serve duck with Cherry-Port Sauce and roasted pears.

TIP: The whole ducks sold frozen in supermarkets are Pekin (also known as Long Island) ducks, not to be confused with "Peking," a Chinese style of cooking them. The commercially marketed ducks generally weigh four and a half to five pounds, but because they are heavier-boned than chickens and have more fat (which is rendered during cooking), you won't get as much meat as you might expect. If you'll be serving more than four adults, roast two ducks.

Each serving: About 790 calories, 39g protein, 25g carbohydrate, 57g total fat (19g saturated), 4g fiber, 685mg sodium

POULTRY SENSE

Want to know how many birds you need to buy for your holiday dinner? See this chart, which also tells you how much stuffing to prepare on the side.

POULTRY	READY-TO-COOK WEIGHT	SERVINGS	STUFFING
Broiler-fryer	2 1/2 to 4 1/2 pounds	2 to 4	1 to 3 cups
Roasting chicken	5 to 7 pounds	5 to 7	3 to 6 cups
Capon	6 to 8 pounds	6 to 8	3 to 6 cups
Cornish hen	1 to 2 pounds	1 to 2	3/4 to 1 1/2 cups
Turkey	8 to 12 pounds	6 to 8	6 to 9 cups
	12 to 16 pounds	12 to 16	9 to 12 cups
	16 to 20 pounds	16 to 20	12 to 15 cups
	20 to 24 pounds	20 to 24	15 to 18 cups
Turkey breast (bone in or boneless)	4 to 6 pounds	5 to 8	3 to 6 cups
Duck	4 1/2 to 5 pounds	4	3 to 4 cups
Goose	10 to 12 pounds	6 to 8	6 to 9 cups

FISH & SHELLFISH

Salmon with Mustard Glaze

Let this luscious side of salmon star at your buffet—it takes only 30 minutes from start to finish. Pair it with the Herbed Rice Pilaf on page 201.

Active time: 10 minutes
Total time: 30 minutes
Makes: 12 main-dish servings

2 lemons, thinly sliced, plus lemon wedges for garnish
1/2 cup spicy brown mustard
1/4 cup light mayonnaise
2 tablespoons sugar
2 tablespoons cider vinegar
1/2 cup loosely packed chopped fresh dill, plus additional
    for garnish
1 whole boneless side of salmon (3 1/4 pounds)
1/4 teaspoon salt
1/4 teaspoon freshly ground black pepper
3/4 cup reduced-fat sour cream

1 Preheat oven to 450°F. In 18" by 12" jelly-roll pan, arrange lemon slices in row in single layer from one corner to the diagonally opposite corner.

2 In medium bowl, stir mustard, mayonnaise, sugar, vinegar, and half of dill until sugar dissolves.

3 Place salmon, skin side down, on lemons in prepared pan. In medium bowl, set aside half of mustard mixture; spread remaining mixture on top of salmon. Sprinkle salt and pepper on top. Roast 13 to 15 minutes or until just opaque throughout (see Tip). Instant-read thermometer inserted horizontally into thickest part of salmon should register 145°F.

4 Meanwhile, stir sour cream and remaining dill into remaining mustard mixture. Place salmon on large serving platter; garnish with lemon wedges and dill. Serve salmon with sauce.

TIP: If you're lucky enough to be using wild Alaskan salmon in this recipe, the roasting time may be a bit longer than we specify.

Each serving: About 255 calories, 28g protein, 3g carbohydrate, 12g total fat (3g saturated), 0g fiber, 255mg sodium

DEBONING AND SERVING WHOLE COOKED SALMON

Step 1: Remove skin from top of fish. Slide metal spatula under front section of top fillet; lift off and transfer to platter.

Step 2: Lift backbone away from bottom fillet; discard backbone. Slide spatula between bottom fillet and skin; transfer fillet to platter.

Clockwise from top left: ITALIAN-SPICED SHRIMP CASSEROLE *(page 152)*; SALMON WITH MUSTARD GLAZE *(above)*; MUSSELS WITH TOMATO AND WHITE WINE SAUCE *(page 152)*; GREEN AND GOLD STUNNER.

Chilled Salmon with Green Olive Sauce

This dish looks and tastes very elegant, yet it's ready in just fifteen minutes. The yield is easily doubled if your microwave can accommodate a 9" by 13" baking dish.

Active time: 13 minutes
Total time: 15 minutes
Makes: 4 main-dish servings

1 medium bulb fennel (1½ pounds), cored and thinly
   sliced, plus fronds for garnish
4 skinless salmon fillets (6 ounces each, about 1 inch thick)
3/8 teaspoon salt
1/8 teaspoon freshly ground black pepper
1/4 cup dry white wine
1/4 cup water
1 cup plain low-fat yogurt
1/4 cup pitted green olives, finely chopped, plus olives
   for garnish
1/4 cup packed finely chopped fresh chives, plus chives
   for garnish
1 tablespoon fresh lemon juice
1 tablespoon extra-virgin olive oil

1 In 8" by 8" glass baking dish, arrange fennel in single layer, then place salmon fillets on top. Sprinkle with ¼ teaspoon salt. Add wine and water to dish. Cover with vented plastic wrap and microwave on High 8 minutes or until fish just turns opaque throughout.

2 With slotted spatula, transfer salmon to paper towels to drain. Let cool to room temperature. Reserve sliced fennel in baking dish.

3 Meanwhile, in bowl, combine yogurt, olives, chives, lemon juice, oil, and ⅛ teaspoon each salt and pepper. Cover; refrigerate up to 2 days.

4 To serve, divide fennel among 4 serving plates. Top with fennel fronds, then salmon and sauce. Garnish with chives and whole olives.

Each serving: About 415 calories, 51g protein, 9g carbohydrate, 19g total fat (4g saturated), 2g fiber, 585mg sodium

Top: CHILLED SALMON WITH GREEN OLIVE SAUCE *(above);*
Bottom: SOLE ROLL-UPS WITH CRAB STUFFING *(opposite).*

Sole Roll-Ups with Crab Stuffing

In this stylish entrée, thin sole or flounder fillets are rolled around a luscious crabmeat stuffing seasoned with bread crumbs, parsley, and lemon juice. A flavorful creamy tomato sauce completes the dish.

Active time: 20 minutes
Total time: 55 minutes
Makes: 6 main-dish servings

2 tablespoons butter or margarine
1/4 cup finely chopped shallots
8 ounces lump crabmeat, picked over
1/2 cup fresh bread crumbs (about 1 slice bread)
1 tablespoon chopped fresh parsley
2 teaspoons fresh lemon juice
5/8 teaspoon salt
1/8 teaspoon plus pinch ground black pepper
6 sole or flounder fillets (6 ounces each)
1 can (14 to 16 ounces) tomatoes, drained
1/4 cup heavy cream
1 teaspoon chopped fresh tarragon

1 Preheat oven to 400°F. Grease 13" by 19" baking dish.

2 In nonstick 10-inch skillet, melt 1 tablespoon butter over medium heat. Add 2 tablespoons shallots; cook until tender, about 2 minutes. Transfer to medium bowl. Add crabmeat, bread crumbs, parsley, lemon juice, 1/4 teaspoon salt, and 1/8 teaspoon pepper; toss with fork until evenly combined.

3 Sprinkle skinned side of sole fillets with 1/4 teaspoon salt. Spoon crabmeat mixture evenly over fillets. Roll up fillets; place, seam side down, in prepared baking dish. Bake until just opaque throughout, about 25 minutes.

4 Meanwhile, in blender, puree tomatoes until smooth. In same 10-inch skillet, melt remaining 1 tablespoon butter over medium heat. Add remaining 2 tablespoons shallots; cook until tender, about 2 minutes. Add pureed tomatoes, remaining 1/8 teaspoon salt, and remaining pinch pepper. Increase heat to high; cook, stirring frequently, until liquid has almost evaporated, about 5 minutes. Stir in cream and heat to boiling. Remove from heat and stir in tarragon.

5 With wide slotted spatula, transfer fish to platter. Stir any juices in baking dish into tomato sauce; spoon sauce over fish.

Each serving: About 298 calories, 41g protein, 7g carbohydrate, 11g total fat (5g saturated), 0g fiber, 665mg sodium

Swordfish Steaks Broiled with Maître d'Hôtel Butter

For even more richness and flavor, top each steak with an additional tablespoon of herb butter just before serving.

Active time: 15 minutes
Total time: 25 minutes
Makes: 4 main-dish servings

4 swordfish steaks (6 ounces each, 1 inch thick)
4 teaspoons Maître d'Hôtel Butter (recipe below)

1 Prepare maître d'hôtel butter.

2 Preheat broiler. Place swordfish on rack in broiling pan. Spread 1/2 teaspoon maître d'hôtel butter on each side of each fish steak. Place pan in broiler, 4 inches from heat source. Broil swordfish, without turning, until just opaque throughout, 8 to 10 minutes. Spoon pan juices over fish to serve.

Each serving: About 220 calories, 30g protein, 0g carbohydrate, 10g total fat (4g saturated), 0g fiber, 175mg sodium

Maître d'Hôtel Butter

In medium bowl, beat **1/2 cup (1 stick) butter or margarine,** softened with wooden spoon until creamy. Mix in **2 tablespoons chopped fresh parsley, 1/4 teaspoon freshly grated lemon peel,** and **1 tablespoon fresh lemon juice** until thoroughly incorporated. Transfer flavored butter to waxed paper and shape into 6-inch-long log, twisting ends of paper to seal. Overwrap in plastic or foil before refrigerating up to 2 days or freezing up to 1 month. Makes 12 servings.

Italian Spiced Shrimp Casserole

This quick but crowd-pleasing shrimp dish on rice gets its flavor from diced tomatoes and a variety of Italian herbs and spices.

Active time: 20 minutes
Total time: 40 minutes
Makes: 6 main-dish servings

1 cup long-grain white rice
1³/4 cups hot water
1 tablespoon olive oil
1 small onion, finely chopped
1 tablespoon fresh oregano leaves, minced
¹/2 teaspoon crushed red pepper, or to taste
2 garlic cloves, crushed with garlic press
1 cup dry white wine
1 can (14¹/2 ounces) no-salt-added diced tomatoes,
    drained well
¹/2 teaspoon salt
¹/2 teaspoon ground black pepper
1 pound 16- to 20-count shrimp, shelled and deveined, tail
    part of shell left on if you like
8 leaves basil, very thinly sliced, for garnish

1 Preheat oven to 400°F.

2 In 3-quart shallow baking dish, combine rice and water. Cover tightly with foil and bake 20 minutes.

3 Meanwhile, in 5- to 6-quart saucepot, heat oil over medium heat. Add onion, oregano, and crushed red pepper; cook 3 minutes, stirring occasionally. Add garlic and cook 30 seconds or until golden, stirring. Add wine and heat to boiling; reduce heat to medium-low and simmer, stirring occasionally, 6 minutes or until wine is reduced by half. Stir in tomatoes, salt, and black pepper. Remove from heat.

4 Arrange shrimp on top of rice in baking dish, in single layer. Pour tomato mixture evenly over shrimp; cover tightly with foil and bake 10 to 15 minutes or until shrimp turn opaque. Garnish with basil.

Each serving: About 245 calories, 16g protein, 35g carbohydrate, 4g total fat (1g saturated), 2g fiber, 300mg sodium

Mussels with Tomato and White Wine Sauce

This irresistibly saucy dish should be served with plenty of good crusty bread for dipping.

Active time: 20 minutes
Total time: 45 minutes
Makes: 8 first-course or 4 main-dish servings

1 tablespoon olive or vegetable oil
1 small onion, chopped
2 garlic cloves, finely chopped
¹/4 teaspoon crushed red pepper
1 can (14 to 16 ounces) tomatoes
³/4 cup dry white wine
4 pounds large mussels, scrubbed and debearded
2 tablespoons chopped fresh parsley

1 In nonreactive 5-quart Dutch oven, heat oil over medium heat. Add onion and cook until tender and golden, 6 to 8 minutes. Add garlic and crushed red pepper and cook 30 seconds longer. Stir in tomatoes with their juice and wine, breaking up tomatoes with side of spoon. Heat to boiling; boil 3 minutes.

2 Add mussels; heat to boiling. Reduce heat; cover and simmer until mussels open, about 5 minutes, transferring mussels to large bowl as they open. Discard any mussels that have not opened. Pour mussel broth over mussels and sprinkle with parsley.

Each first-course serving: 105 calories, 9g protein, 6g carbo-hydrate, 3g total fat (1g saturated), 0g fiber, 277mg sodium

Moules à la Marinière

Prepare as directed in recipe, substituting **butter** for olive oil, if you like, and **¹/3 cup chopped shallots** for onion. Omit crushed red pepper and tomatoes; use **1¹/2 cups dry white wine.**

Seafood Newburg

Lobster Newburg was first served at Delmonico's restaurant in New York City in 1876. As the tale goes, Charles Delmonico named it Lobster à la Wenberg in honor of one of his best customers, Ben Wenberg, a West Indies sea captain. Later, when the two men quarreled, Charles changed the name by reversing the first three letters to make it Newberg (later the spelling was changed to Newburg). In this recipe, we've added shrimp and scallops, making it Seafood Newburg.

Active time: 20 minutes
Total time: 35 minutes
Makes: 8 main-dish servings

1 tablespoon butter or margarine
¼ cup finely chopped shallots
1 pound medium shrimp, shelled and deveined
½ pound sea scallops, halved if large
½ teaspoon salt
⅛ teaspoon ground black pepper
¼ cup sherry
2 teaspoons tomato paste
1½ cups heavy cream
½ cup clam broth
½ teaspoon paprika
2 large egg yolks
¾ pound cooked lobster meat, cut into chunks (see Tip)
1 tablespoon chopped fresh parsley
Hot cooked rice (optional)

1 In large skillet, melt butter over medium-high heat. Add shallots; cook until tender, about 2 minutes. Stir in shrimp, scallops, ¼ teaspoon salt, and pepper. Cook, stirring, until seafood just begins to color but is not cooked through, 2 to 3 minutes. With slotted spoon, transfer seafood to plate; cover and keep warm.

2 Stir sherry and tomato paste into skillet; heat to boiling. Cook until reduced by half. Stir in 1 cup cream, clam broth, paprika, and remaining ¼ teaspoon salt. Reduce heat to medium; cook 3 minutes.

3 In small bowl, beat egg yolks and remaining ½ cup cream until blended. Add to skillet along with reserved seafood and lobster. Bring to simmer; simmer 1 minute (do not boil). Stir in parsley. Serve with rice if you like.

TIP: If cooking whole lobsters for meat, two 1½-pound lobsters will yield about ¾ pound meat.

Each serving: About 305 calories, 25g protein, 4g carbohydrate, 20g total fat (12g saturated), 0g fiber, 498mg sodium

MY FAVORITE HOLIDAY TRADITION
"Christmas Eve is the big day in my family. My mom makes the traditional Italian fish dinner, with cold fish salad. We make pasta with lobster."

—Alyssa Milano

Bacon French Toast Bake

Our gift to you—make-ahead French toast for Christmas morning. Now go focus on the fun stuff—like unwrapping presents!

Active time: 20 minutes
Total time: 1 hour 15 minutes plus drying and soaking
Makes: 10 servings

1 loaf (about 1 pound) challah or brioche bread, cut into
  1/2-inch-thick slices
6 large eggs
2 cups half-and-half
2 cups grated Gruyère cheese (about 8 ounces)
1/4 cup plus 1 tablespoon maple syrup
1/2 teaspoon ground cinnamon
1/2 teaspoon salt
1/2 teaspoon pepper
4 slices bacon, chopped

1 Leave bread slices spread out on rack or platter at room temperature at least 2 hours or until slightly stale. Grease 3-quart baking dish.

2 Arrange bread in prepared baking dish, slightly overlapping. In large bowl, whisk eggs, half-and-half, Gruyère, 1/4 cup maple syrup, cinnamon and 1/2 teaspoon each salt and pepper until well combined. Pour all over bread in baking dish. With hands, press down on bread to submerge. Cover baking dish with plastic wrap. Refrigerate at least 4 hours or up to 1 day.

3 Preheat oven to 375°F. Remove plastic. Sprinkle bacon all over top of bread mixture. Bake 45 to 50 minutes or until golden brown and set. Drizzle with remaining 1 tablespoon maple syrup before serving.

Each serving: About 410 calories, 18g protein, 33g carbohydrate, 23g total fat (10g saturated), 0g fiber, 655mg sodium

Clockwise from top left: Season's Bounty (*page 181*); Bacon French Toast Bake (*above*); Peppermint Twist (*page 185*); Pineapple-Pom Fruit Melange (*above*).

BRUNCHES & BUFFETS

Pineapple-Pom Fruit Melange

Add sweet-tart taste and vibrant color to your holiday brunch buffet table with this salad.

Active time: 20 minutes
Total time: 25 minutes
Makes: 8 servings

1/4 cup sugar
1 spring fresh rosemary, slightly bruised with side of knife
1/2 teaspoon vanilla extract
Pinch salt
1/4 cup water
4 large navel oranges
1 pound fresh pineapple chunks
1 pound large seedless grapes, halved
1 1/2 cups pomegranate seeds

1 In small saucepan, combine sugar, rosemary, vanilla, salt, and water. Heat on medium-high just until sugar dissolves. Remove from heat; cool completely.

2 With sharp paring knife, cut off tops and bottoms of oranges, then cut off peel. Working over large bowl, cut segments out of oranges into bowl; discard membranes. To bowl with orange segments, add pineapple, grapes, pomegranate seeds, and rosemary syrup, tossing until combined. Serve immediately, or cover and refrigerate up to 1 day.

Each serving: About 160 calories, 2g protein, 40g carbohydrate, 0g total fat (0g saturated), 4g fiber, 310mg sodium

Winter Veggie Tart

A holiday entrée doesn't have to be turkey or a roast. This festive tart fills the bill. Serve with butternut squash soup.

Active time: 45 minutes
Total time: 1 hour 45 minutes
Makes: 10 servings (2 tarts)

3 cups all-purpose flour

1 1/4 teaspoons salt, divided

1 1/2 cup butter (3 sticks), cut up and cold

3/4 cup ice water

8 ounces radishes (about 10 medium) trimmed and quartered

8 ounces Brussels sprouts, halved

2 medium carrots, chopped

2 small red onions, cut into very thin wedges

3 tablespoons extra virgin olive oil

4 cloves garlic, chopped

2 bunches Swiss chard (about 1 1/4 pounds total), thinly sliced

8 ounces Gruyère cheese, grated

1 Preheat oven to 400°F. In food processor, pulse flour and 3/4 teaspoon salt until combined. Add half of butter, pulsing until fine crumbs form. Add remaining butter, pulsing just until coarse crumbs form. Drizzle half of ice water over flour mixture, pulsing to incorporate. Drizzle in remaining ice water; pulse until dough mostly comes together. Transfer dough to large bowl; knead 3 or 4 times until dough fully comes together. Divide into two equal-size disks; wrap in plastic. Refrigerate at least 30 minutes or up to 2 days.

2 Meanwhile, in large bowl, toss radishes, Brussels sprouts, carrots, and onions with 2 tablespoons oil and 1/2 teaspoon salt; arrange in single layer on 2 large, rimmed baking sheets. Roast 25 minutes or until browned and almost tender, stirring once. Vegetables can be made up to 1 day ahead.

3 In 5-quart saucepot, heat remaining oil on medium. Add garlic; cook 1 minute, stirring. Add chard. Cook 5 to 8 minutes or until chard wilts, stems are tender and chard dries out a bit, stirring occasionally.

4 On large sheet of floured parchment paper, roll 1 disk pastry into 14-inch circle; place parchment with pastry on it onto 1 large rimmed baking sheet. In center of pastry, arrange half of cheese, leaving a 2-inch rim on pastry's perimeter. Next, arrange half of chard, then half of vegetables mixture, over cheese. Fold edges of pastry up and over. With remaining pastry disk, cheese, and vegetables, repeat rolling, filling, and folding process.

5 Bake 50 minutes to 1 hour or until bottoms are golden brown, switching racks halfway through. Remove from oven. Let stand 10 minutes before slicing.

Each serving: About 550 calories, 13g protein, 36g carbohydrate, 40g total fat (23g saturated), 3g fiber, 15mg sodium

Winter Veggie Tart *(opposite)*

Smoked Salmon Spread and Bagels

Instead of topping bagel toasts with large slices of expensive smoked salmon, treat your guests to this flavorful spread. It delivers big taste without the big bucks. Prepare the salmon spread up to one day ahead to give the flavors a chance to blend.

Active time: 15 minutes

Total time: 20 minutes plus chilling

Makes: 32 toasts

4 ounces Neufchâtel cheese, softened

4 ounces smoked salmon, chopped

1 container (8 ounces) reduced-fat sour cream

2 tablespoons fresh dill, chopped

1 tablespoon capers, drained and chopped

1/4 teaspoon salt

1/4 teaspoon ground black pepper

1 lemon

2 bagels, preferably sesame seed and poppy seed

1/2 small red onion, thinly sliced

1/2 English (seedless) cucumber, thinly sliced

4 red radishes, thinly sliced

1 In large bowl, stir cream cheese until light and fluffy. Fold in salmon, sour cream, dill, capers, salt, and pepper. From lemon, grate 1 teaspoon peel and squeeze 1 teaspoon juice; stir juice and peel into spread. Transfer to serving bowl. Cover and refrigerate at least 1 hour and up to overnight.

2 Preheat oven to 375°F. Cut bagels in half to form 4 crescents. Place bagel halves with cut side down, and cut each lengthwise into four slices to form 16 flat C shapes. Cut each in half crosswise to form 32 triangular shapes.

3 On large cookie sheet, arrange bagel slices in single layer; bake 8 to 10 minutes or until golden and crisp. Transfer to wire rack to cool completely.

4 Serve toasts with spread and onion, cucumber, and radish slices for topping.

Each toast with 1 scant tablespoon spread: About 35 calories, 2g protein, 3g carbohydrate, 2g total fat (1g saturated), 0g fiber, 140mg sodium

Cheddar Grits Soufflé

Savory soufflé featuring grits and Cheddar cheese is a perfect brunch dish for special occasions.

Active time: 30 minutes

Total time: 1 hour 15 minutes plus cooling

Makes: 8 side-dish servings

6 1/2 ounces extra-sharp Cheddar cheese, shredded (1 1/2 cups)

2 cups water

2 tablespoons butter or margarine

1/2 teaspoon salt

2 1/2 cups whole milk

1 cup quick-cooking grits

1/4 teaspoon freshly grated nutmeg

1/8 teaspoon cayenne (ground red) pepper

3 large eggs, separated

3 large egg whites

1 Preheat oven to 375°F. Grease 3-quart soufflé dish and sprinkle 2 tablespoons shredded Cheddar onto side.

2 In 4-quart saucepan, heat water, butter, salt, and 1 1/2 cups milk to boiling on medium-high. Whisk in grits. Cover, reduce heat to low, and simmer 5 minutes or until thick. Whisk well, then whisk in nutmeg, cayenne, remaining 1 cup milk, and remaining Cheddar. Whisk in egg yolks; transfer to bowl and cool to room temperature.

3 In large bowl, with mixer on medium-high speed, beat all egg whites until stiff peaks form. Add one-third whites to grits mixture; beat until blended. Fold in remaining whites. Transfer to soufflé dish.

4 Bake 45 to 50 minutes or until puffed and golden brown on top.

Each serving: About 280 calories, 13g protein, 20g carbohydrate, 17g total fat (8g saturated), 1g fiber, 415mg sodium

CHEDDAR GRITS SOUFFLÉ *(opposite)*

Pumpkin Popovers

We take our popovers seriously at GH, having served them to every president, royal, and other A-lister who's dined in the iconic Hearst building for over 70 years. When we found out that Harry Connick Jr., host of his own daytime show, Harry, loved cooking, we invited him to help us tweak this favorite to start the holiday season.

Active time: 10 minutes
Total time: 1 hour
Makes: 6 servings

3 large eggs
1 cup milk
3 tablespoons melted butter, plus more for greasing
1 cup all-purpose flour
1 1/4 teaspoons pumpkin pie spice
1/2 teaspoon salt
Confectioners' sugar, for dusting

1 Preheat oven to 375°F. Generously grease six (6-ounce) custard cups or cups of popover pan with melted butter. Set on rimmed baking sheet.

2 In blender, combine eggs, milk, 3 tablespoons melted butter, all-purpose flour, pumpkin pie spice, and salt; blend until smooth. Pour about 1/3 cup batter in each custard cup, or fill popover pan cups half full.

3 Bake 50 minutes, then quickly cut small slit in top of each popover to release steam; bake 10 minutes longer. Immediately remove popovers from cups, loosening with spatula if necessary. Serve hot, dusted with confectioners' sugar.

Each serving: About 205 calories, 7g protein, 18g carbohydrate, 12g total fat (7g saturated), 1g fiber, 280mg sodium

TEST KITCHEN SECRET: Psst . . . there's no pumpkin in our popovers. We baked up many versions, with from 2 tablespoons to 1/4 cup pumpkin, but they were more pudding than popover. When we whipped up the recipe with just the classic spice blend, the look and texture were spot-on and won in our blind taste test.

Classic Popovers

Amaze guests with these stunning (and surprisingly easy) popovers—now in more flavors than ever!

Active time: 10 minutes
Total time: 1 hour
Makes: 6 servings

3 large eggs
1 cup whole milk
1 cup all-purpose flour
3 tablespoons butter, melted
½ teaspoon salt

1 Preheat oven to 375°F. Generously grease cups of popover pan or eight 6- to 8- ounce ramekins.

2 In blender, puree eggs, milk, flour, butter, and salt until smooth.

3 Divide evenly among cups. Bake 40 minutes.

4 With small paring knife, cut small slit in top of each popover. Bake 10 minutes more. Remove from oven; immediately transfer from cups to wire rack. Serve warm. Cooled popovers can be kept at room temperature up to 3 hours or frozen up to 1 month. Reheat at 350°F until crisp.

Each serving: About 205 calories, 7g protein, 18g carbohydrate, 12g total fat (6g saturated), 1g fiber, 310mg sodium

TIP: For gluten-free popovers, swap in gluten-free flour instead of all-purpose.

MORE POP HITS

Try these delicious new variations— chocolately, smoky, bacon-filled!—with one of our flavored butters (bottom).

SWEET COCOA
Reduce flour to ¾ cup. Blend ¼ cup unsweetened cocoa and 3 tablespoons sugar into batter.

BACON CHEESE
Reduce salt to ¼ teaspoon. Blend 4 strips chopped cooked bacon, ½ cup shredded sharp Cheddar cheese, and ¼ cup finely grated Parmesan cheese into batter.

SAVORY SPICED
Blend 1½ teaspoons ground cumin, 1 teaspoon smoked paprika, and ¼ teaspoon black pepper into batter.

Seasoned Butters

Beat ¾ cup (1½ sticks) softened butter with choice of:

SWEET CINNAMON
¼ cup dark brown sugar
+ ½ teaspoon ground
cinnamon

LEMON-CHIVE
1 tablespoon snipped fresh chives + 1 teaspoon grated lemon zest + ⅛ teaspoon black pepper

ROSEMARY-GARLIC
2 cloves garlic, crushed with press + 1 tablespoon fresh rosemary, finely chopped, all cooked in 1 tablespoon olive oil until garlic is golden.

SETTING UP A CROWD-PLEASING BUFFET

Buffets have long been a popular and convenient way to feed a holiday crowd. The host sets out an assortment of dishes, along with serving utensils, dishes, and silverware. The guests line up and help themselves, moving from one end of the serving station to the other.

The advantages are many: The host can serve a large number of people at a relatively low cost while being freed up to join the party too. The guests can choose exactly what they want to eat and, because a buffet requires movement, they naturally mingle. It's casual entertaining at its best, but that doesn't mean it doesn't require some planning. Here are our tips on how to make it all come off without a hitch.

Choosing the Menu

Select dishes that can be cooked ahead and warmed for serving or partially prepared then assembled at the last minute. Casseroles are often a part of the menu, since they're cooked and served in a single dish that retains its heat. Limit the number of dishes you serve, but provide generous quantities of each: If guests return to the buffet for seconds, or even thirds, of your favorite family lasagna, you don't want them to wind up with an empty plate.

Make sure the entire main course and sides will fit on a single dinner plate. Food that you can eat with a fork—no large pieces that must be cut with a knife—are most convenient for the guests. You can certainly serve cakes, pies, or puddings for dessert, but cookies and fruit that can be eaten out of hand make it easy on both guests and host.

Setting Up the Buffet (and Routing Traffic)

A buffet can be set up in the dining room, living room, or kitchen on a table, on a sideboard, or even on top of a chest of drawers. The table can be set in the center of the room or pushed against a wall—the important thing is that guests can move around the table easily.

Arrange food and tableware so guests can serve themselves in a logical order, such as: napkin roll with utensils, dinner plate, hot dishes, cold dishes, salad, bread, and condiments. Be sure to place an appropriate serving utensil beside each dish, on a saucer to collect drips. Keep hot foods hot in a chafing dish or slow cooker. Warming the plates before service is always a nice touch. Can you use paper plates and cups and plastic utensils to save on dishwashing time? Yes, if it's an informal, family-style affair, although china and silver will make the meal holiday-special.

When the buffet is ready, invite guests to help themselves; offer to fix plates for elderly guests or children who may appreciate help. Replenish food when necessary, and invite guests to return for seconds.

Who Will Sit Where?

Unlike at a sit-down meal, buffet guests will load their plates and then settle in to eat on sofas, in armchairs, or even on the staircase, using any surface they can find—coffee tables, end tables, even their laps—to hold their plates. If there's room, or you invited a large crowd, consider setting up some folding tables in the living room, or even just folding chairs for extra seating.

Beverage and Dessert Stations

Set up a separate table for beverages, somewhat away from the main buffet. This not only reduces traffic jams, but also encourages guests to select their food at the buffet, then put down their plates before pouring drinks, maximizing ease and minimizing spills. A bowl of festive punch surrounded by punch glasses makes self-service especially easy. Check this station sporadically, replenishing ice, seltzer, and any mixers, and clearing any empty glasses that may have collected.

Desserts can also be set up on a separate buffet if you have the space. Put out serving dishes, coffee cups, and utensils pre-party, but wait until the main buffet is cleared to bring out the sweet stuff. Ask a friend to remove dinner plates while you clear the buffet table and reset it for dessert and coffee service—or arrange the desserts on a separate preset dessert buffet.

Pedestals are a great way to serve not only cakes and pies, but also cookies, bars, and candies: multi-layers of treats make for an eye-catching sweet finale. If you're serving coffee, a self-serve urn keeps it hot; provide hot water and assorted tea bags for tea drinkers, along with cream, sugar, and sliced lemons.

Andouille-Shrimp Gumbo (*opposite*)

Andouille-Shrimp Gumbo

This okra-thickened Creole classic delivers a hit of New Orleans spice to any party. The recipe is easily doubled to satisfy a larger group.

Active time: 30 minutes
Total time: 1 hour 10 minutes
Makes: 11 cups or 6 main-dish servings

1/3 cup plus 1 tablespoon vegetable oil

1/2 cup all-purpose flour

2 celery stalks, chopped

2 garlic cloves, minced

1 green pepper, chopped

1 onion, chopped

2 cans (14 1/2 ounces each) chicken broth (3 1/2 cups)

1 can (14 1/2 ounces) stewed tomatoes

1 pound skinless, boneless chicken thighs, cut into
   thin strips

8 ounces andouille or chorizo sausage, cut into
   1/4-inch-thick slices

6 ounces okra, left whole or cut into 1/2-inch-thick slices

1 cup loosely packed fresh parsley leaves, chopped

1 tablespoon minced fresh thyme leaves

1 tablespoon minced fresh sage leaves

3/4 teaspoon salt

1/2 teaspoon coarsely ground black pepper

4 cups water

1 1/2 pounds shelled and deveined medium shrimp, with
   tail part of shell left on (see Tip)

1 cup long-grain white rice, cooked as label directs

1 In 6-quart Dutch oven or saucepot, heat 1/3 cup oil over medium low. Gradually stir in flour until blended and cook, stirring, until mixture is dark brown, about 15 minutes.

2 Meanwhile, in nonstick 12-inch skillet, heat remaining 1 tablespoon oil over medium until hot.
Add celery, garlic, green pepper, and onion and cook, stirring occasionally, until vegetables are tender.

3 When flour mixture is ready, gradually stir in broth until blended and smooth. Add tomatoes, chicken, andouille, okra, parsley, thyme, sage, salt, pepper, cooked vegetables, and water; heat to boiling over high heat. Reduce heat to low; simmer, uncovered, 40 minutes.

4 Skim off fat and discard. Add shrimp and cook, uncovered, until shrimp turn opaque throughout, about 5 minutes longer.

5 Ladle gumbo into large bowls. Top with a scoop of hot rice.

TIP: For convenience, we call for shrimp that have already been cleaned. But if you have the extra time and want to cut your costs, buy them with shells on and clean them yourself.

Each serving: About 525 calories, 40g protein, 46g carbohydrate, 19g total fat (6g saturated), 3g fiber, 1,515mg sodium

Sausage Calzones

*Hot and golden from the oven, this express-lane dish uses
refrigerated pizza dough (you could also buy the dough from
a local pizzeria), bottled marinara sauce, and zesty chicken
sausage. If you're making calzones for a crowd, double (or
even triple) the recipe. They are sure to disappear fast!*

Active time: 5 minutes
Total time: 30 minutes
Makes: 4 main-dish servings

1 cup part-skim ricotta cheese
1 link fully cooked Italian
    chicken sausage (3 ounces),
    diced
3/4 cup frozen peas
2 ounces part-skim mozzarella cheese,
    shredded (1/2 cup)
1 tube (13 to 14 ounces) refrigerated pizza dough
1 cup prepared marinara sauce, warmed

1 Preheat oven to 400°F. In medium bowl, stir together
ricotta, sausage, peas, and mozzarella.

2 Spray large cookie sheet with nonstick cooking spray.
Unroll pizza dough on center of cookie sheet. With
fingertips, press dough into 14" by 10" rectangle. Cut
dough lengthwise in half, then cut each piece crosswise
in half to make 4 rectangles in all.

3 Place one-fourth ricotta filling on half of one dough
rectangle. Fold other half of dough over filling and pinch
edges together to seal. Repeat with remaining filling
and dough.

4 Bake calzones 25 minutes or until well browned on
top. Serve with marinara sauce.

Each serving: About 485 calories, 25g protein, 59g carbohydrate,
16g total fat (7g saturated), 4g fiber, 1,210mg sodium

Roasted Red and Green Pepper Quesadillas

Serve savory quesadilla appetizers alongside our Slow-Cooker Chipotle Beef Chili (page 171). A creamy guacamole is part of the recipe. Check your local store for five-count bags of avocados at a fraction of the usual price.

Active time: 1 hour
Total time: 1 hour 45 minutes
Makes: 48 appetizers

4 poblano peppers
2 large red peppers (8 to 10 ounces each)
1 large onion (12 ounces), cut into 1/4-inch pieces
1 pint grape tomatoes
1 teaspoon vegetable oil
16 (8-inch) flour tortillas
1 pound Monterey Jack cheese, shredded (4 cups)
1/2 cup packed fresh cilantro leaves, chopped
5 ripe avocados
3 tablespoons fresh lime juice
1/2 teaspoon salt

1 Arrange oven rack 5 inches from heat source. Preheat broiler. In broiling pan lined with foil, arrange poblanos and red peppers in single layer. Broil 15 to 20 minutes or until blackened all over, turning occasionally to evenly blacken. Wrap peppers in foil; let cool.

2 In 15½" by 10½" jelly-roll pan, toss onion and tomatoes with oil until coated; arrange in single layer. Broil 12 to 15 minutes or until onion is brown and tomatoes begin to burst, stirring once. Remove from broiler and cool in pan. Reset oven control to 200°F. Remove peppers from foil; peel off skin and discard. Remove and discard stems and seeds; finely chop peppers (see Tip).

3 On large work surface, arrange 8 tortillas in single layer. Divide cheese, cilantro, and chopped peppers among tortillas. Top with remaining tortillas.

4 Heat 10-inch skillet on medium until hot. (If two skillets are available, cook 2 quesadillas at once.) Place 1 quesadilla in skillet and cook 1 to 3 minutes or until bottom browns. Carefully turn over and cook 1 to 3 minutes or until bottom browns. Transfer to clean large cookie sheet and keep warm in oven. Repeat until all quesadillas are cooked.

5 Cut avocados in half. Remove and discard seeds and peel, then transfer to large serving bowl. Add lime juice, onion and tomatoes, and salt. Using potato masher or fork, mash until just slightly chunky. Makes about 5 cups guacamole.

6 Cut each quesadilla into sixths and serve with guacamole alongside.

TIP: You can prepare the peppers and the onion and tomatoes through the end of step 2 up to two days ahead. Wrap and refrigerate them separately.

Each serving: About 120 calories, 4g protein, 12g carbohydrate, 7g total fat (2g saturated), 1g fiber, 200mg sodium

FAVORITE HOLIDAY TRADITIONS

"On Christmas Eve, we have everyone over and make a potful of meatballs for submarine sandwiches. Then we each open one present. But on Christmas morning it's carnage—wrapping paper flying everywhere."

—Melissa McCarthy

Salsa Verde Enchiladas

This south-of-the-border casserole is always welcome on a buffet.

Active time: 50 minutes
Total time: 1 hour 10 minutes
Makes: 2 casseroles, 8 main-dish servings total

2 rotisserie chickens, meat removed from bones and
    coarsely shredded (5½ cups)
2 jars (16 to 18 ounces) mild salsa verde
6 green onions, thinly sliced
¼ cup fresh lime juice
¼ cup chopped fresh cilantro leaves
16 (6-inch) corn tortillas
1 container (8 ounces) reduced-fat sour cream
½ cup reduced-sodium chicken broth
1 package (8 ounces) reduced-fat (2%) shredded Mexican
    cheese blend (2 cups)

1 In medium bowl, combine chicken and ½ cup salsa
verde. Preheat oven to 350°F. Grease two 13" by 9"
glass or ceramic baking dishes. In 12-inch skillet, heat
remaining salsa verde, green onions, and lime juice to
boiling. Boil 2 minutes, stirring occasionally. Stir in
2 tablespoons cilantro; keep warm over very low heat.

2 With tongs, place 1 tortilla in salsa verde mixture;
heat 10 seconds. Place tortilla on waxed paper; top with
about ⅓ cup shredded-chicken mixture. Roll up tortilla
and place, seam side down, in prepared baking dish.
Repeat with remaining tortillas and chicken mixture,
arranging 8 tortillas in each dish.

3 Stir sour cream and broth into remaining salsa verde
mixture; spoon over filled tortillas. Cover baking dishes
with foil and bake 15 minutes. Remove foil; sprinkle
each casserole with 1 cup cheese and 1 tablespoon
cilantro. Bake 5 minutes longer or until cheese melts.

Each serving (2 enchiladas): About 465 calories, 39g protein,
36g carbohydrate, 18g total fat (7g saturated), 3g fiber,
785mg sodium

Top: Salsa Verde Enchiladas *(above)*;

Bottom: Slow-Cooker Chipotle Beef Chili *(opposite)*.

Slow-Cooker Chipotle Beef Chili

A variety of inexpensive beans supplement the relatively small amount of beef in this super-satisfying chili. The chili keeps very well; it can be made a day ahead and refrigerated. To reheat it, transfer it to a Dutch oven and heat on medium until the chili comes to a simmer; reduce the heat to low, cover, and simmer 30 minutes to heat through.

Active time: 35 minutes
Total time: 6 hours 35 minutes
Makes: 10 main-dish servings

2 cans (15 to 19 ounces each) different beans, such as
   pinto and black or red beans
1 chipotle chile in adobo, finely chopped
1 tablespoon adobo sauce from chiles
1 can (28 ounces) diced fire-roasted tomatoes
1 large onion (12 ounces), finely chopped
1 green pepper, finely chopped
2 garlic cloves, crushed with garlic press
2 1/2 pounds beef chuck, cut into 1-inch chunks
1 tablespoon ground cumin
1/2 tablespoon dried oregano
1/8 teaspoon salt
1/8 teaspoon ground black pepper
2 ounces Monterey Jack cheese, shredded (1/2 cup)
1/2 cup reduced-fat sour cream
1/2 cup packed fresh cilantro leaves, coarsely chopped
1 lime, cut into wedges

1 In large colander, drain beans. Rinse well and drain again. Place chopped chipotle chile in large bowl with 1 teaspoon adobo.
2 Add tomatoes with their juice, onion, pepper, and garlic to bowl with chipotle; mix well. In another large bowl, combine beef, cumin, oregano, salt, and pepper.

3 In 7-quart slow-cooker bowl, spread generous layer of tomato mixture. Layer on beef, then beans, and top with remaining tomato mixture. Cover slow cooker with lid and cook as manufacturer directs on High 6 hours.

4 Using slotted spoon, transfer solids to large serving bowl. Transfer cooking liquid from slow cooker to 4-cup liquid measuring cup. Remove and discard fat. Pour off and discard all but 2 cups cooking liquid. Stir remaining 2 teaspoons adobo into cooking liquid in cup; pour over chili and stir to combine. Serve with Monterey Jack, sour cream, cilantro, and limes alongside.

Each serving: About 325 calories, 32g protein, 23g carbohydrate, 12g total fat (5g saturated), 7g fiber, 515mg sodium

DON'T POISON THE GUESTS!

Here are numbers you need to know when you are hosting a buffet.

140 DEGREES

The temperature at which hot food needs to be held until it is served. Set the oven high enough so that the thickest part of the roast or middle of the casserole reads 140°F.

165 DEGREES

The internal temperature a chicken or turkey must reach, according to the latest guidelines from the USDA.

2 HOURS

How long you can keep hot dishes on the buffet table. Put out small batches and replace with fresh helpings in clean serving bowls—don't just top off what's out there. Same goes for cold foods.

3 TO 4 DAYS

How long you can keep leftovers in the fridge (after that, freeze them). Reheat to 165°F; sauces and soups should reach a rolling boil.

Northern-Style Lasagna

This is the classic lasagna of nothern Italy where a rich béchamel replaces ricotta cheese. Here, noodles layer with full-flavored meat sauce, béchamel, and a blend of cheeses. Dried porcini mushrooms add additional flavor.

Active time: 1 hour 15 minutes
Total: 2 hours 5 minutes plus standing
Makes: 10 main-dish servings

Meat Sauce
1/2 cup boiling water
1/2 ounce dried porcini mushrooms (1/2 cup)
2 tablespoons extra-virgin olive oil
3 large garlic cloves, finely chopped
2 carrots, peeled and finely chopped
1 large onion (12 ounces), chopped
8 ounces lean (90%) ground beef
8 ounces ground pork
8 ounces ground veal
1/2 cup dry red wine
1 can (28 ounces) diced tomatoes
1/2 teaspoon salt

Béchamel
4 tablespoons butter or margarine
1/3 cup all-purpose flour
1/2 teaspoon ground black pepper
1/2 teaspoon salt
1/4 teaspoon ground nutmeg
2 1/2 cups milk

Cheese Filling and Assembly
8 ounces Fontina cheese, shredded (2 cups)
1/2 cup freshly grated Parmesan cheese
1 package (8 to 9 ounces) no-boil lasagna noodles
(6 1/2" by 3 1/2" each)

1 Prepare meat sauce: In small bowl, pour boiling water over porcini mushrooms; let stand 15 minutes.

2 Meanwhile, in 12-inch skillet, heat oil over medium heat until hot. Add garlic, carrots, and onion and cook, stirring occasionally, until vegetables are tender, about

15 minutes. Increase heat to high. Add beef, pork, and veal and cook, breaking up meat with side of spoon, until meat is browned, about 10 minutes.

3 Meanwhile, with slotted spoon, remove porcini from soaking liquid, reserving liquid. Rinse mushrooms to remove any grit, then coarsely chop. Strain mushroom liquid through sieve lined with paper towels; set aside.

4 Add wine to meat in skillet and heat to boiling; boil until most liquid has evaporated, 2 to 3 minutes. Stir in tomatoes with their juice, salt, mushrooms, and reserved soaking liquid; heat to boiling. Reduce heat to medium-low; simmer, uncovered, until sauce thickens slightly, about 20 minutes, stirring occasionally.

5 Preheat oven to 375°F. Meanwhile, prepare béchamel sauce: In nonreactive 2-quart saucepan, melt butter over low heat. With wire whisk, stir in flour, pepper, salt, and nutmeg and cook 1 minute. Whisking continuously, gradually add milk and heat to boiling. Remove saucepan from heat; set aside.

6 Prepare filling: In small bowl, toss Fontina and Parmesan until well combined.

7 Assemble lasagna: In bottom of 13" by 9" baking dish, evenly spread 1 cup meat sauce. Arrange 4 noodles over sauce, overlapping slightly to fit and making sure they do not touch sides of dish. (If your package of has only 12 lasagna noodles, use 3 noodles per layer and do not overlap them.) Spoon about 1 1/2 cups meat sauce over noodles. Spread about 2/3 cup béchamel sauce over meat sauce and sprinkle with about 1/2 cup cheese filling. Repeat layering three more times with remaining noodles, meat sauce, béchamel sauce, and cheese.

8 Cover lasagna with foil and bake 30 minutes. Remove foil and bake until heated through and cheese is lightly browned, about 20 minutes longer. Let stand 15 minutes for easier serving.

Each serving: About 460 calories, 2g protein 34g carbohydrate, 23g total fat (11g saturated), 2g fiber, 933mg sodium

FINGER FOOD FEAST

Dipping food is fun for kids and adults alike. In this buffet-friendly recipe, panko-breaded chicken drumsticks and fresh veggies are paired with a lemon-and-basil yogurt dip.

Active time: 35 minutes • Total time: 55 minutes • Makes: 6 main-dish servings

3 tablespoons Dijon mustard

3 tablespoons light mayonnaise

12 large chicken drumsticks (3½ pounds),
   skin removed

1 lemon

1 cup panko (Japanese-style bread crumbs)

½ cup finely grated Parmesan cheese

2 tablespoons olive oil

⅛ teaspoon cayenne (ground red) pepper

⅞ teaspoon salt

⅜ teaspoon ground black pepper

⅓ cup plain nonfat yogurt

¼ cup packed fresh basil leaves, finely chopped

1 pound asparagus

Carrots, celery sticks, green beans, and sliced
   peppers, for serving

1 Arrange oven rack in top third of oven. Preheat oven to 450°F. Line 18" by 12" jelly-roll pan with foil.

2 In large bowl, stir mustard and mayonnaise until well combined; add chicken pieces and toss until evenly coated. Set aside.

3 Grate 1 teaspoon lemon peel into 9-inch pie plate and squeeze 1 tablespoon juice into small bowl. In pie plate with peel, combine panko, Parmesan, oil, cayenne, ⅛ teaspoon salt, and ⅛ teaspoon pepper. Dredge 1 drumstick in crumb mixture until coated, shake off excess, and place on prepared pan. Repeat with remaining chicken and crumbs. Bake 30 minutes or until crust is golden brown and meat thermometer registers 165°F.

4 Meanwhile, in small bowl with lemon juice, stir yogurt, ¼ teaspoon salt, and remaining ¼ teaspoon pepper until smooth. Stir in basil.

5 Fill 12-inch skillet with *1 inch water*. Cover and heat to boiling. Add asparagus and remaining ½ teaspoon salt. Cook, uncovered, 4 to 5 minutes or until bright green and tender-crisp, turning occasionally. Rinse under cold water; drain.

6 Serve chicken with asparagus and assorted raw vegetables, along with dipping sauce on the side.

TIP: Kids love carrots that have been boiled for 3 to 4 minutes; they're extra-sweet, but still crunchy. To make it simple, cook them in the same water used for the asparagus. If you'd like, make the drumsticks a day ahead—they're tasty either cold or reheated in a 400°F oven for 10 minutes.

Each serving: About 335 calories, 37g protein, 11g carbohydrate, 15g total fat (4g saturated), 1g fiber, 560mg sodium

Salmon Noodle Bake

Fresher and more elegant than the traditional tuna noodle casserole (and almost as frugal), this veggie-packed dish is loaded with chunks of seafood-counter salmon (less than a pound stretches to feed six) flavored with leeks, mushrooms, and herbs. Subbing for the canned condensed soup: a less fatty, chicken-broth-based sauce that you can make from scratch in minutes.

Active time: 25 minutes
Total time: 45 minutes
Makes: 6 main-dish servings

1½ cups low-fat milk (1%)
1 large leek (1 pound)
10 ounces sliced mushrooms
1 tablespoon reduced-sodium soy sauce
2 tablespoons plus 1 teaspoon olive oil
2 large stalks celery, finely chopped
1 teaspoon fresh thyme leaves, chopped
3 tablespoons all-purpose flour
1 can (14½ ounces) reduced-sodium chicken broth
8 ounces curly egg noodles
12 ounces skinless salmon fillet, cut into 1-inch chunks
1 cup frozen peas
½ teaspoon salt
¼ teaspoon ground black pepper
⅓ cup panko (Japanese-style bread crumbs)
1 tablespoon chopped fresh flat-leaf parsley
   leaves for garnish

1 Preheat oven to 350°F. Grease 3-quart shallow baking dish. Heat large covered saucepot of *water* to boiling on high. In glass measuring cup, microwave milk on High 2 minutes or until warm.

2 Meanwhile, trim and discard root and dark green top from leek. Discard any tough outer leaves. Cut leek lengthwise in half, then crosswise into ¼-inch-wide slices. Place leek in large bowl of cold water; swish well to remove sand. Transfer leek to colander. Repeat process with fresh water, changing water several times until all sand is removed. Drain leek well and set aside.

3 In 12-inch skillet, combine mushrooms and soy sauce. Cook 5 to 6 minutes on medium-high until mushrooms are tender and sauce evaporates, stirring occasionally. Transfer to large bowl.

4 In same skillet, heat 2 tablespoons oil on medium-high. Add leek, celery, and half of thyme. Cook 2 minutes or until golden and just tender, stirring occasionally. Add flour and cook 1 minute, stirring. Continue stirring and add broth, then warm milk, in steady stream. Heat to boiling, stirring, and cook 2 minutes or until thickened, continuing to stir constantly. Transfer to bowl with mushrooms.

5 While sauce cooks, add noodles to boiling water; cook 1 minute. Drain well.

6 To bowl with mushroom mixture, add noodles, salmon, peas, salt, and pepper. Gently stir to combine. Spread mixture in prepared dish.

7 In small bowl, combine panko with remaining ½ teaspoon thyme and 1 teaspoon oil. Sprinkle evenly over top of noodle mixture. Bake 17 to 18 minutes or until topping turns golden brown. Garnish with parsley.

Each serving: About 370 calories, 22g protein, 43g carbohydrate, 12g total fat (2g saturated), 4g fiber, 570mg sodium

SALMON NOODLE BAKE *(opposite)*

Country Captain Casserole

Though the exact origin of this well-known dish is often debated, its great flavor is never in dispute. It's sure to be well received on your holiday buffet.

Active time: 20 minutes
Total time: 45 minutes
Makes: 6 main-dish servings

2 tablespoons vegetable oil
2 green onions, thinly sliced, plus additional for garnish
2 cups long-grain white rice
3 cups water
4 carrots, peeled and cut into ¼-inch-thick half-moons
1 large sweet onion (12 ounces), finely chopped
1 large yellow pepper (8 to 10 ounces), finely chopped
2 garlic cloves, finely chopped
1 tablespoon grated, peeled fresh ginger
1 tablespoon curry powder
1 teaspoon garam masala or ground cumin
2 cans (14½ ounces each) no-salt-added diced tomatoes
½ cup golden raisins
¼ teaspoon salt
¼ teaspoon ground black pepper
1½ pounds skinless boneless chicken thighs
¼ cup sliced almonds, lightly toasted (page 287)

1 Preheat oven to 350°F.

2 In 7-quart Dutch oven or other heavy, ovenproof pot with lid, heat 1 tablespoon oil on medium-high. Add 2 thinly sliced green onions and rice and cook 2 minutes or until onions soften, stirring. Add water and heat to boiling. Cover and bake 15 minutes.

3 Meanwhile, in 12-inch skillet, heat remaining 1 tablespoon oil on medium-high. Add carrots, onion, pepper, and garlic. Cook 6 minutes or until golden and tender, stirring occasionally.

4 Add ginger, curry, and garam masala. Cook 1 minute, stirring. Add tomatoes with their juice and raisins. Heat to boiling.

5 Sprinkle salt and pepper all over chicken. Add chicken thighs to pan, submerging in vegetable mixture. Heat mixture to boiling and cook 2 to 4 minutes, or until chicken just loses its pink color throughout.

6 Uncover rice and pour chicken mixture over, spreading in even layer. Cover and bake 25 minutes longer. Garnish with almonds and additional chopped green onions.

Each serving: About 575 calories, 31g protein, 84g carbohydrate, 12g total fat (2g saturated), 6g fiber, 250mg sodium

Classic Italian Hero

Why pay more to buy a giant hero when you can put together your own and tailor it to taste? Whether you call it a hero, sub, hoagie, or grinder, this toothsome sandwich is a crowd-pleaser.

Total minutes: 15 minutes
Makes: 12 appetizer servings or 6 main-dish servings

1 large (16-inch) loaf Italian bread (12 ounces)
¼ cup vinaigrette of choice
4 ounces thinly sliced hot and/or sweet capocollo, prosciutto, soppressata, and/or salami
4 ounces thinly sliced mozzarella cheese, preferably fresh mozzarella
Shredded romaine lettuce or arugula, peperoncini, basil leaves, roasted red peppers, very thinly sliced red onions, pesto, olivada, and/or sliced ripe tomatoes

1 Cut bread horizontally in half. Remove enough soft center from each half to make 1-inch-thick shell. (Reserve soft bread for another use.)

2 Brush vinaigrette evenly over cut sides of bread. Layer meats and cheese on bottom half of bread. Top with additional ingredients of your choice. Replace top half of bread.

3 If not serving right away, wrap sandwich in foil and refrigerate up to 4 hours. Cut into serving-size pieces and arrange on platter, or present whole sandwich on cutting board and let guests slice off desired amount.

Each appetizer serving: About 145 calories, 7g protein, 12g carbohydrate, 8g total fat (2g saturated), 1g fiber, 408mg sodium

Baked Rigatoni and Peas for a Crowd

This easy meatless pasta is baked in two dishes; put one out on the buffet and keep the other warm in the oven until you need it.

Active time: 45 minutes
Total time: 1 hour 15 minutes
Makes: 20 main-dish servings

8 tablespoons (1 stick) butter or margarine
½ cup all-purpose flour
7 cups milk, warmed
2 cups freshly grated Parmesan cheese
2 teaspoons salt
2 packages (16 ounces each) rigatoni or ziti
1 bag (20 ounces) frozen peas, thawed
2 cans (14½ ounces each) diced tomatoes
1 cup loosely packed fresh basil leaves, thinly sliced
½ cup plain dried bread crumbs

1 Prepare cheese sauce: In heavy 4-quart saucepan, melt 6 tablespoons butter over low heat. Add flour and cook, stirring, 2 minutes. Gradually whisk in warm milk. Cook over medium heat, stirring constantly with wooden spoon, until sauce has thickened and boils. Reduce heat and simmer, stirring frequently, about 5 minutes. Stir in 1½ cups Parmesan and salt. Remove from heat.

2 Meanwhile, in 12-quart saucepot, cook pasta as label directs; drain. Return rigatoni to saucepot.

3 Preheat oven to 350°F. Pour cheese sauce over rigatoni in saucepot, stirring to combine. Stir in peas, tomatoes with their juice, and basil. Spoon pasta mixture into two 13" by 9" baking dishes.

4 In small saucepan, melt remaining 2 tablespoons butter over low heat. Remove from heat and stir in bread crumbs and remaining ½ cup Parmesan. Sprinkle topping over pasta. Bake until casserole is bubbling and topping is golden, 30 to 35 minutes.

Each serving: About 390 calories, 15g protein, 48g carbohydrate, 15g total fat (9g saturated), 3g fiber, 703mg sodium

Top: CLASSIC ITALIAN HERO *(opposite);*
Bottom: COUNTRY CAPTAIN CASSEROLE *(opposite).*

DINING MERRY & BRIGHT

Here's an assortment of stylish ideas to make your holiday tabletop sparkle. Choose from place settings decked out in classic red and white Swedish country style, or all tied up with a huge gold bow. If you're feeling crafty, make your own napkin rings out of gift wrap and rickrack or turn pears into place cards—all with minimal fuss and maximum festivity.

1. Perfect Pears

With the simple addition of a pearl-topped pin, ripe pears can serve as edible name-card holders for your guests. Try arranging them with greenery and tiny ornaments too, for a DIY-on-a-dime centerpiece.

2. Dress Your Table in Red and White

Striped runners made with ticking fabric set the scheme for this color-coordinated table. (You can stitch up the runners in minutes using a sewing machine.) Santa suit-red ribbons, chargers, and winter berries continue the harmonious hues. Sprigs of evergreen tucked into the napkin rolls add a refreshing burst of green.

3. Hat Trick

You might not have elves on call to set the table, but you can honor December's employees of the month by turning napkins into Santa's helpers' hats. To do: Gather square napkins that are on the stiff side, then go to goodhousekeeping.com/elfhat for our quick video on how to fold them. To accessorize, stick a jingle bell looped onto a short piece of craft wire into the point of each hat.

4. All Tied Up

Make place settings look like a gift with napkin rings crafted from leftover wrapping paper, rickrack, and double-sided tape. Snip strips of paper roughly 1½" by 5" (test one on your linens, as the size varies depending on your rolled-up napkin's thickness). Wrap the paper around the napkins, using double-sided tape to affix. Cut out 6-inch lengths of rickrack and tie them around the bands for a finished look.

5. Bow Show

Here's a simple yet stunning way to dress up your tabletop for sit-down gatherings. It couldn't be quicker—just wrap each place setting with a length of wide, pretty ribbon. Do it in satin for a graphic statement, or in a loose organza for an elegant finish. Once the meal is over, you can save the ribbons (the still clean ones, anyway) to wrap presents.

FESTIVE CENTERPIECES— IN 15 MINUTES OR LESS!

Centerpieces are usually last on the Christmas to-do list. Time is tight, the food comes first, and really, how different can a vase of flowers look each year? But this Christmas, you don't have to default to a boring, been-there bouquet, or leave a bare spot beside the breadbasket and hope no one notices—not when you can whip up any one of the following holiday-worthy centerpieces in fifteen minutes or less.

Whether you choose to display stalks of wheat, evergreens and berries, or an assortment of fresh fruit (see "Ripe for the Picking" on page 182), the season's bounty plays a starring role. If you prefer to feature fresh-cut flowers in your centerpiece, turn the page: "Skip the Vase" offers a quick alternative to the business-as-usual bouquet. See also "Blooms That Last" for our tips on selecting fresh flowers and keeping them vibrant.

1. Christmas Bulbs

Potted narcissus (see Tip), swaddled in burlap and tied with red twine, bring botanical beauty—and fragrance—to your dining room table or sideboard. Or use multiple pots to line a stairwell, as shown here. Time invested: five minutes. The payoff: a low-maintenance arrangement that'll stay fresh for several weeks.

TIP: Buy paperwhites from a florist, or force the quick-growing bulbs starting in mid-November. By Christmas, you'll have flowers that will bloom and perfume the air into the New Year. But paperwhites aren't the only potted plants available in late December; you can achieve a similar effect with pots of poinsettias, cyclamens, hollies, or even mini Christmas trees.

2. How Swede It Is

To make this no-fuss natural centerpiece, loosely cinch craft-store wheat stalks with red and white ribbon. Place faux snow inside a clear glass vase and nestle the bouquet of stalks on top. Surround with almonds in the shell and evergreen cuttings for easy organic elegance in under ten minutes.

3. Season's Bounty

A sap bucket is spray-painted red to add a hit of seasonal cheer, then filled to the brim with evergreen branches and berries. Total time—minus allowing the paint to dry!—twelve minutes. Purchase the holiday greens at a florist or select a loose assortment when your buy your Christmas tree; any variety of greens and berries will create a festive arrangement.

White burlap, bought by the yard and fringed at the ends, serves as an easy and affordable tablecloth. Here, its simplicity downplays the formality of the china and ornate dining table.

4. Skip the Vase

To create this bold bouquet, trim the stems of a dozen roses to 10 inches and strip off the leaves; with a rubber band, gather the stems just below the heads. Splay out the stems and snip to form a sturdy base; tie with ribbon to secure the arrangement's shape. (We chose a red velvet ribbon that's as plush as the rose petals.) The flowers will be fine without water for a few hours—well worth the fifteen minutes of prep time.

5. Branch Out

The patina of tarnished pewter contrasts with fall foliage in this rustic-meets-refined grouping. Tuck acorns, viburnum, and crab apple cuttings (find at a florist or gather from the yard) in a trio of staggered-size containers, corralled on a tray. Total time: eight minutes.

6. Ripe for the Picking

Elegant turns easy when you think outside the vase. In this fresh update of the classic cornucopia, clear glass vases overflow with apples, pears, tangerines, and both ripe and green pomegranates. Accent with ribbon curling in and around the fruit—to run out the time to thirteen minutes—and invite guests to grab some produce post-dinner.

BLOOMS THAT LAST

You can purchase ready-made holiday bouquets from the florist or grocery store, but why not roll up your sleeves, get out your clippers, and create a seasonal arrangement yourself? The following tips help ensure long-lasting flowers.

Get into Condition: Before arranging your flowers, allow them to soak in a bucket one-third filled with warm water for at least four hours but preferably overnight. Known as conditioning, this step makes the stems fill up with water and the flowers become crisp.

Snip Those Stems: Add warm water to a clean vase. Under running water, cut 1 to 2 inches off the stems at an angle so they'll soak up as much water as possible. Arrange the blossoms.

Keep It Cool: Display your bouquet in a cool, draft-free area. Avoid direct sunlight—no surprise, it causes the flowers to droop and die more quickly.

Watch Your Water: To prevent bacterial growth, remove any leaves submerged in water (they can produce flower-killing organisms). Change the water at least every two days and add a preservative—either a mix from the florist or this homemade life extender: 1/2 teaspoon sugar and 1 dash bleach for every gallon of water.

Steer Clear of the Fridge: You may have heard that the fridge is the best place to keep your flowers cool overnight. But unlike florists' refrigerators, yours isn't set to the right temperature or humidity level. Plus, your fruits and vegetables emit ethylene gas, which will kill the blooms.

LET IT GLOW

Candles and Christmas go hand in hand. Get glowing with our ideas for unique and festive candle holders.

1. Go Nuts

A cylinder vase heaped with walnuts, cranberries, and kumquats holds a pillar candle in position.

2. Let It Shine

Sophisticated yet stress-free to assemble, this candlelit centerpiece will last until you ring in the New Year. Just place several snowy tapers in short candlesticks in the center of a store-bought boxwood wreath. To keep greenery looking fresh, spritz occasionally with water; you can do this in the bathtub to avoid getting water stains on your dining room table.

3. Think Green

Empty glass bottles become holiday-ready candleholders when tied at the middle with big velvet or satin bows. Gather a cluster of them to create a centerpiece.

4. Peppermint Twist

A sleek, simple tray festooned with small candles and peppermint puffs is part decoration, part dessert— and a less traditional take on the classic candy dish.

CANDLING WITH CARE

Votives, tealights, pillars, tapers— candles are everywhere during the holidays. Buy and burn them wisely.

Eye Before You Buy: When shopping, check that the wick is tightly braided and feels secure (give it a tug). Loosely twisted or poorly anchored wicks cause candles to burn unevenly or flames to flicker wildly. Inspect jars or votives, too: Thicker glass is less likely to crack.

Location, Location, Location: Place candles so their flames are at least 3 inches apart (to keep one from melting another) and away from flammable décor and walls. Always put candles on heat-resistant plates or in stable holders. Never leave burning candles unattended.

Mind Your Measurements: Trim wicks to ¼ inch—every time you use them. A short wick means a more controlled flame. A flame should be only an inch or two high, and steady.

TIP: Got a half-burned jar or pillar candle with a hard-to-reach wick? Light the end of a piece of dry spaghetti to use as a long-handled match.

Watch the Clock: Don't burn pillar candles more than one hour for every inch of diameter—longer, and the pool of liquid wax can get so big that the candle can lose its shape and spring a leak. And never burn any candle (except tealights) all the way down, lest the surface underneath be damaged.

TIP: Add a few drops of water to holders before inserting candles; stubs will lift out more easily.

Up to Snuff: To put out candles, use a candle snuffer. Or, when (gently) blowing out any candle, place your hand behind the flame to keep wax droplets from scattering.

Chapter 3

Sideshows

SENSATIONAL SIDE DISHES & RELISHES

It's no secret that everyone relishes the sides as much as the turkey or roast. Our delicious recipes for potatoes, Brussels sprouts, cranberries, and all the other trimmings are sure to please your crowd. If you want to serve old-fashioned favorites, try Orange-Candied Sweets, Corn Fritters Southern Style, and other recipes from our holiday archives.

Potatoes, Stuffings & Breads

Christmas dinner isn't complete without an ample supply of potatoes and stuffing. Here, we share our favorites, including Sour Cream Smashed Potatoes and Savory Bread Stuffing with Pears. And, to ensure that everyone at the table is satisfied, we've included recipes for savory scones, spoonbread, and holiday pilafs studded with dried fruits and nuts.

Vegetables, Relishes & Cranberry Sauce

Green Bean Casserole, New World Succotash, Maple-Ginger-Glazed Carrots, and Tarragon Peas with Pearl Onions—these are just a sampling of our classic vegetable sides.

And, of course, we haven't forgotten the cranberries: Choose from a variety of tart sauces to round out your Christmas dinner.

Clockwise from top: Tarragon Peas with Pearl Onions *(page 213)*; Red, White, and Blue Beauty *(page 252)*; Maple-Cranberry Sweet Potatoes *(page 200)*.

Recipes

3 Return potatoes to saucepot. With potato masher, coarsely mash potatoes with sour cream. Gradually add warm milk; continue to mash until potatoes are well blended but still slightly chunky. Stir in snipped chives, remaining 1 teaspoon salt, and pepper.

4 Spoon potatoes into serving bowl and garnish with additional snipped chives.

Each serving: About 185 calories, 4g protein, 32g carbohydrate, 5g total fat (2g saturated), 3g fiber, 295mg sodium

POTATOES & PILAFS

Sour Cream Smashed Potatoes

Smashing small red potatoes with a combination of sour cream and milk yields a perfect texture and flavor. For color, garnish with chives.

Active time: 15 minutes
Total time: 1 hour 15 minutes
Makes: 12 side-dish servings

4 pounds small (not baby) red potatoes, well-scrubbed
2 teaspoons salt
1 cup whole milk
2 tablespoons butter or margarine
1 cup reduced-fat sour cream
1/4 cup snipped chives plus additional for garnish
1/2 teaspoon ground black pepper

1 In 8-quart saucepot, combine potatoes, 1 teaspoon salt, and *water* to cover; heat to boiling on high. Reduce heat to low; cover and simmer 45 to 55 minutes or until potatoes are tender when pierced with tip of knife. Drain well.

2 Meanwhile, in microwave-safe cup, microwave milk and butter on High 1 minute or until butter is melted and milk is warm.

Roasted Sweet and White Potatoes with Rosemary

This low-maintenance mix of roasted sweet and white potatoes makes for a pretty platter.

Active time: 12 minutes
Total time: 1 hour 30 minutes
Makes: 12 side-dish servings

2 tablespoons olive oil
1 tablespoon butter or margarine
2 pounds sweet potatoes, peeled and cut into 2-inch chunks
2 pounds all-purpose potatoes, cut into 2-inch chunks
2 tablespoons chopped fresh rosemary leaves
1 1/2 teaspoons salt
1/2 teaspoon ground black pepper

1 Preheat oven to 350°F. To 15 1/2" by 10 1/2" jelly-roll pan, add oil and butter. Place pan in oven while it preheats and butter melts.

2 Remove pan from oven; add both kinds of potatoes, rosemary, salt, and pepper; toss to coat. Roast 1 hour 15 minutes or until golden and tender, stirring occasionally.

Each serving: About 150 calories, 2g protein, 28g carbohydrate, 3g total fat (1g saturated), 3g fiber, 315mg sodium

Clockwise from top left: SOUR CREAM SMASHED POTATOES *(above)*; SWEATER STOCKINGS *(page 245)*; HERBED RICE PILAF WITH CRANBERRIES AND THYME *(page 201)*; ROASTED SWEET AND WHITE POTATOES WITH ROSEMARY *(above)* SHOWN WITH HERBED PORK LOIN *(page 120)*.

Twice-Baked Celery Root Potatoes

These stuffed potatoes are an easy self-service option for the holiday buffet table.

Active time: 30 minutes
Total Time: 1 hour 40 minutes
Makes: 12 side-dish servings

6 medium baking potatoes
1 pound celery root, peeled and cut into 1-inch chunks
1/2 cup milk
4 tablespoons butter or margarine
3/4 teaspoon salt
1/4 teaspoon ground black pepper
1/2 cup freshly grated Parmesan cheese
Chopped parsley for garnish

1 Preheat oven to 450°F. Place potatoes in oven, directly on rack, and bake 45 to 50 minutes or until tender when pierced with knife. Set potatoes aside until cool enough to handle. Reset oven temperature to 400°F.

2 Meanwhile, in 3-quart saucepan, place celery root and enough water to cover; heat to boiling on high. Reduce heat to low; cover and simmer 15 minutes or until celery root is tender. Drain.

3 In food processor with knife blade attached, blend celery root with milk, butter, salt, and pepper until pureed. Transfer puree to large bowl.

4 When potatoes are cool enough to handle, cut 1/4-inch slice from each end, then cut each potato crosswise in half. Stand potatoes on narrow ends. With spoon, scoop potato from skins into bowl with celery root puree, leaving about 1/4 inch potato with skin and being careful not to break through bottom of potato. Reserve potato-skin cups. With potato masher, mash potato with celery root until almost smooth. Stir in Parmesan.

5 Spray 15½" by 10½" jelly-roll pan with nonstick cooking spray. Spoon potato mixture into potato-skin cups, mounding slightly. Place cups in prepared pan. Bake 25 minutes or until heated through and lightly browned. (If not baking right away, cover and refrigerate filled potatoes overnight; bake 35 to 40 minutes.) Sprinkle with parsley to serve.

Each serving: About 160 calories, 4g protein, 25g carbohydrate, 5g total fat (2g saturated), 2g fiber, 290mg sodium

Potato Gratin with Gruyère

This classic French side dish—made with nutty Gruyère cheese—is the perfect accompaniment to roasted meat or poultry.

Active time: 15 minutes
Total time: 1 hour 5 minutes
Makes: 8 side-dish servings

2 cups half-and-half or light cream
1/4 teaspoon cayenne (ground red) pepper
1 teaspoon salt
3 pounds Yukon Gold potatoes, peeled and thinly sliced
6 ounces Gruyère cheese, shredded (1½ cups)

1 Preheat oven to 350°F. Grease shallow 8-cup baking dish. Set aside.

2 In 5-quart saucepan, combine half-and-half, cayenne, and salt; heat to boiling over medium-high heat.

3 Add potatoes and cook 2 minutes or until half-and-half mixture thickens slightly, stirring gently with heat-safe spatula.

4 Transfer half of potato mixture to prepared dish; sprinkle evenly with half of Gruyère. Top with remaining potato mixture and remaining Gruyère.

5 Bake 40 to 45 minutes or until potatoes are fork-tender and top is golden and bubbly.

Each serving: About 295 calories, 11g protein, 33g carbohydrate, 14g total fat (8g saturated), 2g fiber, 395mg sodium

POTATO GRATIN WITH GRUYÈRE (*opposite*)

Accordion Potatoes

Bake this attractive side dish on the oven rack underneath the holiday roast or ham. To achieve the accordion effect, cut whole potatoes almost all the way through in a series of close vertical slices; the potatoes will fan out as they cook. Choose potatoes that weigh no more than six ounces each so they'll finish cooking by the time your roast is done.

Active time: 20 minutes
Total time: 1 hour 40 minutes
Makes: 8 side-dish servings

8 medium red potatoes (6 ounces each)
32 (3-inch) thyme sprigs
4 tablespoons butter or margarine, melted
½ teaspoon salt
½ teaspoon coarsely ground black pepper
1 tablespoon chopped fresh parsley
1 tablespoon snipped fresh chives

1 Preheat oven to 325°F. Grease 13" by 9" baking pan.

2 Set 1 potato on cutting board. With large knife, starting at one end of potato, cut a series of vertical slices about ⅛ inch apart, making sure not to cut all the way through (see photo). Repeat with remaining potatoes.

3 Insert a thyme sprig into four of the cuts in each potato. Arrange potatoes in prepared pan, cut side up; drizzle butter over tops. Sprinkle potatoes with salt and pepper; cover baking pan tightly with foil.

4 Place pan on lowest rack in oven and bake potatoes 1 hour 15 minutes or until fork-tender. Remove pan from oven and remove foil.

5 Turn oven control to broil. Place pan with potatoes on rack in broiler at closest position to heat source. Broil until browned on top, 5 to 7 minutes. Sprinkle with parsley and chives.

Each serving: About 205 calories, 3g protein, 35g carbohydrate, 16g total fat (4g saturated), 3g fiber, 219mg sodium

Top: ACCORDION POTATOES *(above)*; *Bottom:* SMASHED POTATOES WITH YOGURT AND CHIVES *(opposite)*.

Roasted Garlic and Root Vegetable Mash

For an enticing alternative to mashed potatoes, we smashed together Yukon Golds, sweet potatoes, and rutabagas with plenty of roasted garlic. An herb-flecked topping of toasted bread crumbs and Pecorino-Romano makes this dish irresistible.

Active time: 25 minutes
Total time: 1 hour 30 minutes
Makes: 12 side-dish servings

1 head garlic, sliced in half horizontally
2 tablespoons vegetable oil
2½ pounds Yukon Gold potatoes
1½ pounds sweet potatoes
2 pounds rutabagas
1¼ cups whole milk
4 tablespoons butter, melted
½ cup reduced-sodium chicken broth
1 teaspoon salt
½ teaspoon ground black pepper
¾ cup plain bread crumbs
½ cup grated Pecorino-Romano cheese
6 large fresh sage leaves, finely chopped
½ teaspoon fresh thyme leaves

1 Preheat oven to 400°F. On sheet of foil, drizzle garlic with 1 tablespoon oil. Wrap tightly; roast 40 to 50 minutes or until soft.

2 Meanwhile, peel all potatoes and rutabagas; cut into 1½-inch chunks.

3 In 8-quart saucepot, place Yukon Gold potatoes, rutabagas, and enough *water* to cover by 2 inches. Cover; heat to boiling on high. Reduce heat; add sweet potatoes. Simmer, uncovered, 20 minutes or until vegetables are very tender. Drain; return to pot.

4 Remove and discard garlic skins from cloves. To vegetables, add garlic, milk, 3 tablespoons butter, broth, salt, and pepper. Mash until smooth. Transfer to 3-quart baking dish. (If you like, refrigerate, covered, up to overnight; bake in 400°F oven for 15 minutes or until warm before continuing.)

5 In bowl, combine crumbs, cheese, sage, thyme, and remaining oil and butter. Sprinkle over mash. Bake 15 to 20 minutes or until top is golden brown.

Each serving: About 245 calories, 7g protein, 34g carbohydrate, 9g total fat (4g saturated), 4g fiber, 425mg sodium

Smashed Potatoes with Yogurt and Chives

Instead of the classic sour cream and butter, we combined Yukon Gold potatoes with nonfat yogurt and chives for a lower-fat smashup that still tastes rich and tangy. For even cooking in the microwave, choose potatoes that are approximately the same size.

Active time: 8 minutes
Total time: 15 minutes
Makes: 8 side-dish servings

3 pounds Yukon Gold potatoes
2 tablespoons butter or margarine
¾ teaspoon salt
¼ teaspoon ground black pepper
2 containers (6 ounces each) plain nonfat yogurt
    (1⅓ cups)
¼ cup chopped chives

1 Place unpeeled potatoes (do not pierce) in very large microwave-safe bowl. Cover with vented plastic wrap. Microwave on High 15 to 16 minutes or until fork-tender. Uncover (leaving any accumulated liquid in bowl); add butter, salt, and pepper. With potato masher, coarsely mash potatoes.

2 Stir in yogurt and half of chives until combined. Spoon into serving bowl; cover with plastic wrap to keep warm. If necessary, reheat in microwave just before serving. Sprinkle with remaining chives to serve.

Each serving: About 220 calories, 7g protein, 42g carbohydrate, 3g total fat (1g saturated), 4g fiber, 280mg sodium

Sweet Potato and Cauliflower Mash

Lighten up sweet potatoes with cauliflower for a slender side dish heavy on flavor.

Active time: 20 minutes
Total time: 1 hour
Makes: 12 servings

3 pounds sweet potatoes, peeled and cut into 1-inch
   chunks
3 tablespoons plus ¼ teaspoon salt
1 large head cauliflower (2½ pounds), cut into florets
   (about 8 cups)
⅓ cup extra virgin olive oil
6 leaves fresh sage
2 small cloves garlic, crushed with press
¼ cup low-fat (1%) milk

1 In 7- to 8-quart saucepot, combine sweet potatoes, enough cold water to cover by 1 inch and 3 tablespoons salt. Partially cover and heat to simmering on high. Remove cover and add cauliflower. Simmer 15 minutes or until vegetables are very tender but not falling apart, stirring occasionally.

2 Meanwhile, in 1-quart saucepot, heat oil on medium-low. Add sage and garlic. Cook 4 to 5 minutes or until garlic is golden, stirring occasionally. Remove from heat. Remove and discard sage leaves.

3 Drain vegetables well; return to empty pot. In batches, in food processor, puree vegetables until smooth; transfer to large bowl. To pureed vegetables, add oil mixture, milk, and ¼ teaspoon salt, stirring to combine.

Each serving: About 140 calories, 3g protein, 19g carbohydrate, 7g total fat (1g saturated), 4g fiber, 180mg sodium

Top: SWEET POTATO AND CAULIFLOWER MASH *(above);*
Bottom: KALE-AND-HORSERADISH POTATOES *(opposite).*

Kale-and-Horseradish Potatoes

Kale makes this dish trendy and horseradish gives it a kick.

Active time: 10 minutes
Total time: 1 hour
Makes: 12 servings

4 pounds Yukon gold potatoes, peeled and cut into halves
3 tablespoons plus 1 teaspoon salt
1/2 cup butter (1 stick), cut up
1 bunch curly kale, tough stems removed, chopped
1 tablespoon water
3 green onions, thinly sliced
1 cup whole milk
1/2 cup reduced-fat sour cream
1/4 cup prepared horseradish, drained

1 In 7- to 8-quart saucepot, combine potatoes, enough cold water to cover by 1 inch and 3 tablespoons salt. Partially cover and heat to simmering on high. Remove cover and simmer 20 to 25 minutes or until potatoes are very tender but not falling apart, stirring occasionally.

2 Meanwhile, in 3-quart saucepot, melt butter on medium. Add kale, 1 tablespoon water, and 1/2 teaspoon salt. Cover and cook 3 to 4 minutes or until tender, stirring occasionally. Stir in green onions; cook 2 minutes. Remove from heat.

3 Drain potatoes well; return to empty pot. Mash potatoes or put through ricer. Stir in milk, sour cream, kale mixture, horseradish, and 1/2 teaspoon salt. Serve warm.

Each serving: About 245 calories, 7g protein, 32g carbohydrate, 10g total fat (6g saturated), 3g fiber, 360mg sodium

Super-Creamy Potatoes

Cream, butter, and milk combine to work their magic in this amped-up classic.

Active time: 15 minutes
Total time: 40 minutes
Makes: 12 servings

4 pounds Yukon gold potatoes
3 tablespoons plus 1/2 teaspoon salt
3/4 cup heavy cream
3/4 cup whole milk
6 tablespoons butter, cut up

1 In 7- to 8-quart saucepot, combine potatoes, enough cold water to cover by 1 inch and 3 tablespoons salt. Partially cover and heat to simmering on high. Remove cover and simmer 20 to 25 minutes or until potatoes are very tender but not falling apart, stirring occasionally.

2 Meanwhile, in 4-cup measuring cup, combine cream, milk, and butter. Microwave on High 1 minute or until butter melts.

3 Drain potatoes well; return to empty pot. Mash potatoes or put through ricer. Stir in milk mixture and 1/2 teaspoon salt. Serve warm.

Each serving: About 235 calories, 4g protein, 28g carbohydrate, 12g total fat (7g saturated), 2g fiber, 260mg sodium

SWEET POTATOES WITH MARSHMALLOW MERINGUE (*opposite*)

Sweet Potatoes with Marshmallow Meringue

To modernize this dish, we microwaved the potatoes before mashing and topped them with meringue mounds—a less-sugary substitute for the mini marshmallows made popular in the 1950s.

Active time: 30 minutes
Total time: 50 minutes plus cooling
Makes: 12 side-dish servings

3 pounds sweet potatoes
2 tablespoons pure maple syrup
1 tablespoon packed dark brown sugar
1 tablespoon fresh lemon juice
1/8 teaspoon ground allspice
1/4 teaspoon salt
3 large egg whites
1/4 teaspoon cream of tartar
1/3 cup granulated sugar

1 Prepare potatoes: Preheat oven to 400°F. Pierce sweet potatoes all over with tip of knife; place in large microwave-safe bowl. Cover with vented plastic wrap and microwave on High 15 to 17 minutes or until very tender when pierced with fork; drain. When potatoes are cool enough to handle, peel and return to bowl.

2 To bowl with sweet potatoes, add maple syrup, brown sugar, lemon juice, allspice, and salt. Mash with potato masher until smooth. Transfer potatoes to 2-quart casserole dish. (If making ahead, cover and refrigerate up to overnight; to rewarm potatoes, bake in 400°F oven for 15 minutes or until heated through.)

3 Prepare meringue: In large bowl, with mixer on high speed, beat egg whites and cream of tartar until soft peaks form. Sprinkle in granulated sugar, 2 tablespoons at a time, beating until sugar dissolves and meringue stands in stiff, glossy peaks when beaters are lifted.

4 Transfer meringue to large piping bag fitted with 1/2-inch plain tip or to gallon-size resealable plastic bag with one corner cut to form 1/2-inch hole. Starting at one side of casserole dish, pipe meringue in small mounds onto surface of sweet potatoes, covering entire surface. Bake 6 to 8 minutes or until meringue is golden.

Each serving: About 100 calories, 2g protein, 23g carbohydrate, 0g total fat, 2g fiber, 90mg sodium

BUYING AND STORING SWEET POTATOES

These root vegetables are available year-round, although their peak season is October through January.

There are many varieties of sweet potatoes, but what most Americans are familiar with is a rather sweet, moist, orange-fleshed potato with a very dark skin. However, in the rest of the world, sweet potatoes have rather dry, slightly sweet, white or yellow flesh. Look for sweet potatoes that feel heavy for their size and have no bruises, soft spots, or sign of sprouting. They are quite perishable. Store in a cool, dark place up to one week. Do not refrigerate.

Maple-Cranberry Sweet Potatoes

Sophisticated syrups focus the flavor of this no-fuss side dish and its ginger-almond and butterscotch-spice variations. Assemble the day before the dinner.

Active time: 20 minutes
Total time: 1 hour
Makes: 10 servings

4 pounds sweet potatoes, peeled (see Tip)
1½ teaspoons salt
1 cup pure maple syrup
1½ cups cranberries
3 tablespoons butter (no substitutions)

1 In covered 6-quart saucepot over high heat, bring whole sweet potatoes with 1 teaspoon salt and enough *water* to cover to boil. Reduce heat to low; simmer, covered, about 30 minutes or just until potatoes are fork-tender. Drain and set aside until cool enough to handle.

2 Meanwhile, in 1-quart saucepan, heat maple syrup to boiling on high. Reduce heat to medium, and boil gently 10 to 15 minutes or until reduced to ½ cup. Stir in cranberries, butter, and remaining ½ teaspoon salt, and cook just until cranberries pop, about 5 minutes longer.

3 Preheat oven to 400°F. Cut cooled sweet potatoes crosswise into 1-inch-thick slices and arrange in shallow 3-quart ceramic or glass baking dish, overlapping slices if necessary.

4 Spoon maple-cranberry syrup evenly over potatoes. Bake, uncovered, 20 to 25 minutes or until hot.

TIP: Select sweet potatoes of the same size so they cook evenly. You can prepare them (even arrange them in a casserole) and the syrup up to 1 day ahead, but refrigerate them separately. Allow both to come to room temperature before baking. Reheat syrup; pour over potatoes and pop in the oven when the roast comes out.

Each serving: About 260 calories, 2g protein, 55g carbohydrate, 4g total fat (2g saturated), 5g fiber, 230mg sodium

Ginger-Almond Sweet Potatoes

Prepare sweet potatoes as directed in step 1. In step 2, instead of maple-cranberry syrup, prepare ginger syrup: In 1-quart saucepan, melt **1 tablespoon butter or margarine** on medium heat. Add **2 teaspoons grated, peeled fresh ginger**; cook 1 minute, stirring. Stir in **½ cup apricot preserves, ¼ cup orange juice**, and **½ teaspoon salt**; heat to boiling, stirring. Complete recipe as in steps 3 and 4, spooning ginger syrup over potatoes and sprinkling with **½ cup toasted sliced natural almonds** before baking.

Each serving: About 230 calories, 4g protein, 45g carbohydrate, 4g total fat (1g saturated), 5g fiber, 210mg sodium

Butterscotch-Spice Sweet Potatoes

Prepare sweet potatoes as directed in step 1. In step 2, instead of maple-cranberry syrup, prepare butterscotch-spice syrup: In 1-quart saucepan, combine **½ cup packed brown sugar, 3 tablespoons butter (no substitutions), 2 tablespoons water, 1 teaspoon pumpkin pie spice, ¼ teaspoon salt**, and **⅛ teaspoon cayenne (ground red) pepper**. Heat to boiling, stirring until smooth. Complete recipe as in steps 3 and 4, spooning butterscotch-spice syrup over potatoes before baking.

Each serving: About 210 calories, 2g protein, 43g carbohydrate, 4g total fat (2g saturated), 4g fiber, 175mg sodium

Herbed Rice Pilaf with Cranberries and Thyme

Dried mushrooms add a savory note to this fruit-studded wild and brown rice pilaf.

Active time: 35 minutes
Total time: 1 hour 25 minutes
Makes: 12 side-dish servings

1 ounce dried porcini mushrooms
3½ cups water
1 cup wild rice (6 ounces), rinsed
½ cup dried cranberries
3 tablespoons butter or margarine
2 carrots, peeled and chopped
1 small onion, chopped
2 teaspoons fresh thyme leaves,
    chopped, plus sprigs for garnish
¾ teaspoon salt
¼ teaspoon ground black pepper
3 cups reduced-sodium chicken broth
2 cups long-grain brown rice

1 In medium bowl, combine mushrooms and 1¾ cups water. Microwave on High 2 minutes; let stand 10 minutes to rehydrate.

2 With slotted spoon, transfer mushrooms to cutting board; set aside. Pour enough cooking liquid through fine-mesh sieve to fill 2-cup liquid measuring cup.

3 In covered 2-quart saucepan, heat ¼ cup mushroom cooking liquid and remaining 1¾ cups water to boiling on high. Add wild rice; reduce heat to low. Cover and simmer 50 to 55 minutes or until tender. Add cranberries and let stand 10 minutes. If making ahead, cool completely, transfer to resealable plastic bag, and refrigerate up to 2 days.

4 While wild rice cooks, in 5- to 6-quart saucepot, melt butter on medium heat. Add carrots, onion, thyme, ½ teaspoon salt, and pepper; cook 4 minutes, stirring occasionally. Finely chop mushrooms; add to carrot mixture, along with broth and remaining 1 cup mushroom cooking liquid. Heat to boiling on high, covered. Stir in brown rice; reduce heat to low. Cover and simmer 50 to 55 minutes or until rice is tender. If necessary, drain rice and return to pot. Stir in wild rice mixture and remaining ¼ teaspoon salt. Cook on medium until heated through. Spoon into serving bowl; garnish with thyme sprigs.

Each serving: About 230 calories, 6g protein, 43g carbohydrate, 4g total fat (1g saturated), 4g fiber, 310mg sodium

Fruited Multigrain Pilaf with Almonds

Serve a double dose of grain goodness (brown rice and bulgur) in this delicious fruit-and-nut pilaf.

Active time: 5 minutes
Total time: 40 minutes plus standing
Makes: 6 side-dish servings

1 teaspoon olive oil
1 onion, chopped
½ cup quick-cooking brown rice
1 can (14½ ounces) chicken broth
½ cup water
½ cup bulgur (cracked wheat)
½ cup dried fruit bits
½ cup sliced almonds, toasted

1 In 3-quart saucepan, heat oil over medium heat. Add onion and cook until lightly browned, about 4 minutes, stirring. Stir in rice; cook 1 minute. Add broth and water; heat to boiling. Reduce heat to low; cover and simmer 15 minutes.

2 Stir in bulgur; heat to boiling over high heat. Reduce heat to low; cover and simmer until rice and bulgur are tender and liquid is absorbed, 10 to 12 minutes.

3 Remove from heat. Stir in fruit; cover and let stand 5 minutes, then stir in almonds.

Each serving: About 180 calories, 5g protein, 28g carbohydrate, 7g total fat (1g saturated), 4g fiber, 295mg sodium

STUFFING & BREADS

Wild Rice and Mushroom Stuffing

This recipe makes an elegant alternative to ordinary bread stuffing. It's richly flavored with two kinds of mushrooms and root vegetables. To make ahead, see Tip.

Active time: 40 minutes
Total time: 1 hour 30 minutes
Makes: 16 side-dish servings

1 cup wild rice (6 ounces), rinsed
3¾ cups water
1 cup dried cranberries or raisins
4 tablespoons butter or margarine
3 carrots, peeled and cut into ¼-inch dice
2 stalks celery, cut into ¼-inch dice
1 onion, cut into ¼-inch dice
1 teaspoon salt
½ teaspoon dried thyme
¼ teaspoon coarsely ground black pepper
8 ounces shiitake mushrooms, stems discarded, caps sliced
10 ounces white mushrooms, trimmed and sliced
2 cups long-grain brown rice
1 can (14½ ounces) chicken broth (1¾ cups)

1 In 2-quart saucepan, heat wild rice and 2 cups water to boiling on high heat. Reduce heat to low; cover and simmer until wild rice is tender, 35 to 40 minutes. Stir in cranberries; heat 1 minute. Drain wild rice mixture if necessary.

2 Meanwhile, in nonstick 5- to 6-quart Dutch oven, melt 2 tablespoons butter on medium heat. Add carrots, celery, and onion, and cook until tender and golden, 12 to 15 minutes. Stir in salt, thyme, and pepper, and cook 1 minute; transfer to medium bowl.

3 In same Dutch oven, melt remaining 2 tablespoons butter on medium heat. Add shiitake and white mushrooms, and cook until mushrooms are tender and golden, and liquid evaporates, about 12 minutes; transfer to bowl with vegetables.

4 Preheat oven to 325°F.

5 In same Dutch oven, heat brown rice, broth, and remaining 1¾ cups water to boiling on high heat. Reduce heat to low; cover and simmer until tender, 35 to 40 minutes. Stir wild rice and vegetable mixtures into rice.

6 Spoon stuffing into 13" by 9" glass baking dish or shallow 3½-quart casserole. Cover with foil and bake until heated through, about 20 minutes.

TIP: To cut down on last-minute cooking, prepare the components of this dish up to two days before serving. Increase the baking time to 1 hour or microwave until heated through, stirring once.

Each serving: About 120 calories, 3g protein, 23g carbohydrate, 2g total fat (0g saturated), 2g fiber, 190mg sodium.

Clockwise from top left: WINTRY GARLAND *(page 245)*; CRANBERRY-CORNMEAL BISCUITS *(page 210)*; WILD RICE AND MUSHROOM STUFFING *(above)*; SAUSAGE-FENNEL STUFFING *(page 206)*.

Vegetable-Herb Stuffing

Our trio of stuffings all call for toasting and cubing the bread first—it makes the stuffing less gummy. To free up your oven for pies and the Christmas turkey or roast, you may prepare these dishes up to a week ahead.

Active time: 25 minutes
Total time: 1 hour 25 minutes
Makes: 12 side-dish servings

1¹/2 loaves (16 ounces each) sliced firm white bread
1 tablespoon olive oil
2 carrots, peeled and finely chopped
2 stalks celery, finely chopped
1 onion, finely chopped
¹/2 cup loosely packed fresh parsley leaves,
   coarsely chopped
³/4 teaspoon poultry seasoning
¹/2 teaspoon salt
¹/4 teaspoon ground black pepper
2¹/2 cups chicken broth

1 Preheat oven to 400°F. Grease shallow 3- to 3½-quart ceramic or glass baking dish; set aside. Arrange bread on two large ungreased cookie sheets and toast in oven 16 to 17 minutes or until golden and dry, turning slices over halfway through. Reset oven control to 325°F.

2 Meanwhile, in 12-inch nonstick skillet, heat oil on medium heat 1 minute. Add carrots, celery, and onion, and cook about 12 minutes or until vegetables are tender and lightly browned, stirring occasionally. Remove skillet from heat; stir in parsley, poultry seasoning, salt, and pepper.

3 With serrated knife, cut bread into ¹/2-inch cubes and place in very large bowl. Add chicken broth and vegetable mixture to bread in bowl; toss until bread mixture is evenly moistened.

4 Spoon stuffing into prepared baking dish. Cover dish with foil and bake 30 minutes. Remove foil and bake 15 to 20 minutes longer or until heated through and lightly browned on top.

Each 1-cup serving: About 180 calories, 6g protein, 32g carbohydrate, 4g total fat (0g saturated), 2g fiber, 540mg sodium

Whole-Grain Apple-Fennel Stuffing

Prepare stuffing as directed in step 1, but substitute **1 loaf (24 ounces) sliced whole-grain bread** for white bread. In step 2, increase oil to **2 tablespoons olive oil**, and omit carrots and celery. Trim and chop **1 bulb fennel (1 pound)** and cook in skillet along with onion 10 minutes or until tender. Omit parsley and poultry seasoning. Stir in **2 Golden Delicious apples**, peels left on, each cored and cut into ¹/2-inch chunks, and **2 teaspoons chopped fresh thyme leaves** along with salt and pepper. In step 3, to bread cubes in bowl, add apple mixture, **¹/2 cup dried cranberries**, and **¹/2 cup water** along with broth. Complete recipe as in step 4. Makes about 13 cups.

Each 1-cup serving: About 170 calories, 8g protein, 32g carbohydrate, 4g total fat (0g saturated), 10g fiber, 340mg sodium

Sausage, Chestnut, and Mushroom Stuffing

Prepare stuffing as directed in step 1, except use only 1 loaf bread. In step 2, omit oil. Remove casings from **1 pound sweet Italian sausage links**; cook meat in skillet on medium heat 10 minutes or until browned, stirring and breaking up sausage with side of spoon. With slotted spoon, transfer   to small bowl. Omit carrots and chop only **1 stalk celery**. Leaving sausage drippings in skillet, add onion and celery; cook 8 minutes. Stir in **1 package (10 ounces) sliced white mushrooms**, and cook 10 minutes or until golden. Omit parsley, poultry seasoning, and salt; stir in **¹/4 teaspoon dried thyme** with pepper. In step 3, to bread in bowl, add sausage, vegetable mixture, and **1¹/2 cups chopped roasted, peeled chestnuts** (page 93) along with broth. Complete recipe as in step 4. Makes about 12 cups.

Each 1-cup serving: About 270 calories, 10g protein, 26g carbohydrate, 14g total fat (4g saturated), 2g fiber, 620mg sodium

Tex-Mex Cornbread Stuffing

Put a little South in your holiday dinner guests' mouths.

Active time: 20 minutes

Total time: 1 hour 20 minutes

Makes: 12 servings

2 cups coarsely ground cornmeal

2 teaspoons baking powder

1 teaspoon baking soda

1 teaspoon salt

1½ cups reduced-fat sour cream

4 tablespoons butter, melted

¼ cup honey

2 large eggs

1 cup whole milk

2 cups fresh or frozen (thawed) corn kernels

8 ounces Cheddar cheese, shredded

½ cup finely chopped pickled jalapeños

1 tablespoon snipped chives, for garnish

1 Preheat oven to 400°F. Line 8" by 8" baking pan with foil. Spray foil with nonstick cooking spray.

2 In large bowl, whisk cornmeal, baking powder, baking soda and ½ teaspoon salt. In medium bowl, whisk sour cream, butter, honey, and 1 egg; stir into cornmeal mixture just until well mixed. Pour into prepared pan. Bake 25 to 30 minutes or until golden on top and brown around edges. Cool slightly on wire rack.

3 Meanwhile, in medium bowl, whisk milk and remaining egg. Stir in corn, cheese, jalapeños and remaining ½ teaspoon salt; set aside.

4 Cut cornbread into 1-inch chunks. Arrange in single layer in 3-quart baking dish. Pour milk mixture over cornbread, spreading cheese and jalapeños in an even layer. Bake 25 to 30 minutes or until top is golden. Let stand at least 5 minutes before serving. Garnish with chives.

Each serving: About 310 calories, 11g protein, 30g carbohydrate, 17g total fat (10g saturated), 2g fiber, 655mg sodium

Herb and Chestnut Stuffing

Spread your wings beyond the usual when it comes to the stuffing for this year's turkey.

Active time: 20 minutes

Total time: 1 hour

Makes: 12 servings

12 cups cubed (¾-inch) good-quality white Pullman bread (from about 1-pound loaf)

3 tablespoons vegetable oil

4 stalks celery, finely chopped

2 medium carrots, finely chopped

2 medium onions, finely chopped

10 large fresh sage leaves, finely chopped

2 tablespoons fresh thyme leaves, chopped

½ teaspoon salt

½ teaspoon pepper

1 package (6 to 8 ounces) cooked chestnuts, chopped

1½ cups turkey or vegetable broth

2 large eggs, beaten

1 Preheat oven to 375°F. Lightly grease 3-quart baking dish. Arrange bread in single layer on 2 large rimmed baking sheets; toast 15 minutes or until dry and crunchy.

2 In 6- to 7-quart saucepot, heat oil on medium. Add celery, carrots, onion, sage, thyme, and salt and pepper. Cook 8 to 10 minutes or until vegetables begin to soften, stirring occasionally. Remove from heat.

3 To pot, add toasted bread, chestnuts, broth and eggs. Toss until well combined. Transfer mixture to prepared baking dish. Bake 30 to 35 minutes or until edges and top are golden brown and crunchy.

Each serving: About 210 calories, 6g protein, 32g carbohydrate, 7g total fat (1g saturated), 3g fiber, 470mg sodium

Savory Bread Stuffing with Pears

This golden brown stuffing is studded with pancetta, pears, fennel, and dried cranberries. No pancetta? No problem—just substitute an equal amount of bacon.

Active time: 25 minutes
Total time: 1 hour 25 minutes
Makes: 12 side-dish servings

1 large loaf (22 ounces) Italian bread (preferably day-old),
   cut into ½-inch cubes (14 cups)
2 tablespoons olive oil
3 ounces pancetta, cut into ¼-inch pieces
2 fennel bulbs (1 pound each), trimmed and chopped
1 large onion (12 ounces), chopped
2 garlic cloves, crushed with garlic press
2 Bartlett or Anjou pears, chopped
1 cup dried cranberries
3 cups reduced-sodium chicken broth
½ cup packed fresh flat-leaf parsley
1 tablespoon finely chopped fresh sage leaves
1 tablespoon finely chopped fresh rosemary leaves
½ teaspoon salt
½ teaspoon ground black pepper

1 Preheat oven to 400°F. Divide bread between two 15½" by 10½" jelly-roll pans or large cookie sheets and bake 15 minutes or until golden, rotating pans between upper and lower racks halfway through. Remove bread from oven; set aside to cool. Reset oven control to 350°F.

2 Meanwhile, in 5-quart Dutch oven or heavy saucepot, heat oil on medium-high. Add pancetta and cook 4 minutes or until golden brown and crisp, stirring occasionally. With slotted spoon, transfer pancetta to paper-towel-lined plate; do not remove Dutch oven from heat.

3 To same Dutch oven, add fennel, onion, and garlic. Cook 7 minutes or until vegetables are golden and tender, stirring frequently. Add pears and cranberries and cook 4 minutes or until softened, stirring frequently. Add broth and heat to boiling; reduce heat to medium-low and simmer 5 minutes.

4 In large bowl, combine bread and broth mixture. Stir in parsley, sage, rosemary, salt, pepper, and reserved pancetta. In shallow 3-quart glass or ceramic baking dish, spread mixture in an even layer. Cover with foil and bake 25 minutes. Uncover and bake 15 minutes longer or until top of stuffing is golden brown.

Each serving: About 275 calories, 7g protein, 46g carbohydrate, 7g total fat (2g saturated), 5g fiber, 515mg sodium

Sausage-Fennel Stuffing

Preheat oven to 375°F. Lightly grease a 3-quart baking dish. Arrange **12 cups cubed fruit-nut bread such as raisin-pecan or cranberry-walnut (about 1 pounds)** on 2 large rimmed baking sheets in a single layer. Toast 15 minutes or until dry and crunchy. Meanwhile, in 6- to 7-quart saucepot, heat **2 tablespoons vegetable oil** on medium. Add **12 ounces sweet Italian sausage**, casings removed; cook 5 to 6 minutes or until browned, breaking up with back of wooden spoon. With slotted spoon, transfer to medium bowl. To same pot, add **2 medium trimmed fennel bulbs, 2 medium onions, 4 cloves garlic, all finely chopped,** and **¼ teaspoon salt**. Cook 6 to 8 minutes or until vegetables soften, stirring occasionally. Remove from heat. Add sausage to pot along with toasted bread, **2 cups turkey or chicken broth,** and **½ cups chopped fresh flat-leaf parsley leaves**. Toss until well combined. Transfer mixture to prepared baking dish. Cover baking dish with foil and bake 20 minutes. Remove foil and bake 10 minutes or until top is crunchy.

Each serving: About 185 calories, 10g protein, 27g carbohydrate, 6g total fat (1g saturated), 6g fiber, 490mg sodium

SAVORY BREAD STUFFING WITH PEARS *(opposite)*

Double-Corn Spoonbread

Stone-ground cornmeal plus corn kernels equals twice the corn flavor in every spoonful. This recipe is easily doubled; bake in a shallow 2½ - to 3-quart casserole.

Active time: 15 minutes
Total time: 1 hour 15 minutes
Makes: 6 side-dish servings

1½ cups water
½ teaspoon salt
1½ cups whole milk
¾ cup stone-ground cornmeal
1½ tablespoons butter or margarine
2 large eggs
½ teaspoon baking powder
2 green onions, finely chopped, plus more for garnish
1½ cups fresh or thawed frozen corn kernels
3 tablespoons finely grated Parmesan cheese
¼ teaspoon ground black pepper

1 Preheat oven to 400°F. Grease 1½-quart casserole.

2 In 4-quart saucepan, heat water, salt, and ¾ cup milk to boiling over high heat. Reduce heat to medium-low and whisk in cornmeal in a slow, steady stream. Cover and simmer 10 minutes or until mixture is very thick and pasty, whisking frequently.

3 Remove from heat and whisk in butter until melted. Continue whisking and add remaining ¾ cup milk in a slow, steady stream. Whisk in eggs, one at a time, then baking powder.

4 Stir in green onions, corn, Parmesan, and pepper until mixed. Transfer to prepared dish and spread in smooth, even layer.

5 Bake 45 minutes to 1 hour or until cornbread is golden and knife inserted in center comes out clean. Garnish with green onions.

Each serving: About 185 calories, 8g protein, 22g carbohydrate, 8g total fat (3g saturated), 2g fiber, 350mg sodium

Top: DOUBLE-CORN SPOONBREAD *(above)*;
Bottom: BUTTERNUT SQUASH STUFFING *(opposite)*.

Butternut Squash Stuffing

The sweetness of the squash is balanced by the smokiness of the bacon and fresh sage.

Active time: 50 minutes
Total time: 1 hour 35 minutes
Makes: 13 side-dish servings

1 pound sourdough bread, cut into 1/2-inch cubes (12 cups)
8 ounces bacon, cut crosswise into 1/2-inch pieces
1 butternut squash (2 pounds), peeled, seeded, and cut into 1/2-inch chunks
3 stalks celery, chopped
8 ounces (4 large) shallots, finely chopped (1 1/2 cups)
2 tablespoons chopped fresh sage leaves
1/4 teaspoon salt
1/4 teaspoon ground black pepper
3 cups chicken broth

1 Preheat oven to 325°F. Divide bread between two 15 1/2" by 10 1/2" jelly-roll pans or large cookie sheets. Place pans on two oven racks and toast bread 30 to 35 minutes or until golden, stirring bread and rotating pans between upper and lower racks halfway through toasting. Cool bread in pans on wire racks.

2 Meanwhile, in 12-inch skillet, cook bacon on medium heat until crisp, 10 to 15 minutes, stirring occasionally. With slotted spoon, transfer bacon to very large bowl.

3 Remove all but 3 tablespoons bacon fat from skillet. Add squash, celery, and shallots, and cook on medium-high heat, stirring frequently, 15 minutes or until vegetables are tender and shallots are lightly browned. Remove skillet from heat; stir in sage, salt, and pepper.

4 To bowl with bacon, add bread cubes and broth; toss to mix well. Add vegetable mixture and toss.

5 Spoon squash mixture into greased 13" by 9" glass baking dish. Cover dish with foil and bake stuffing in preheated 325°F oven 20 minutes. Remove foil and stir stuffing. Bake 25 minutes longer or until heated through and lightly browned on top.

Each 1-cup serving: About 240 calories, 6g protein, 28g carbohydrate, 10g total fat (4g saturated), 2g fiber, 620mg sodium

Herbed Oyster Stuffing

Just a cup of oysters transforms this bread stuffing.

Active time: 25 minutes
Total time: 2 hours 30 minutes
Makes: 12 side-dish servings

1 pound French country bread, cut into 1/2-inch cubes (12 cups)
6 stalks celery
4 large shallots (2 to 3 ounces each)
4 cloves garlic
2 tablespoons fresh thyme leaves
1/2 cup packed fresh flat-leaf parsley leaves
3 slices thick-cut bacon
1 cup shucked oysters
1/4 cup butter or margarine
1/4 teaspoon freshly ground pepper

1 Preheat oven to 350°F. In 18" by 12" jelly-roll pan, spread bread. Bake 30 minutes or until golden, stirring once. Cool completely; transfer to large bowl.

2 Meanwhile, finely chop celery, shallots, garlic, thyme, and parsley. Cut bacon crosswise into 1/4-inch pieces. Coarsely chop oysters, cover, and refrigerate. Strain oyster liquid into liquid measuring cup (you should have 1 cup; add stock if needed); cover and refrigerate. Generously grease 3-quart shallow glass or ceramic baking dish.

3 In 12-inch skillet, cook bacon on medium heat, stirring occasionally, 8 minutes or until browned and crisp. With slotted spoon, transfer to bowl with bread. Drain all but 2 tablespoons fat from skillet. To skillet, add celery and shallots. Cook on medium heat 5 minutes, stirring occasionally. Transfer to bowl with bread. In same skillet, melt butter. Add garlic and thyme; cook 1 to 2 minutes or until fragrant and golden, stirring. Transfer to bowl with bread, along with parsley, oysters and liquid, and pepper. Stir until well mixed.

4 Transfer stuffing to prepared baking dish and spread in even layer. Cover with foil and bake 30 minutes. Uncover and bake 20 minutes longer or until top is golden brown.

Each serving: About 245 calories, 6g protein, 48g carbohydrate, 4g total fat (1g saturated), 4g fiber, 245mg sodium

Cranberry-Cornmeal Biscuits

These drop-style biscuits complement any holiday meal. For a breakfast treat, serve with a softened sweet-cream butter and fruit preserves.

Active time: 15 minutes
Total time: 30 minutes plus cooling
Makes: 12 biscuits

1¼ cups cornmeal
¾ cup all-purpose flour
½ cup dried cranberries
2 tablespoons sugar
2 teaspoons baking powder
½ teaspoon salt
4 tablespoons butter or margarine, melted
¾ cup milk

1 Preheat oven to 400°F. Grease large cookie sheet.

2 In medium bowl, combine cornmeal, flour, cranberries, sugar, baking powder, and salt. Stir butter, then milk into cornmeal mixture just until mixture forms soft dough.

3 Drop dough by scant ¼ cups, 2 inches apart, on prepared cookie sheet. Bake biscuits 15 minutes or until golden. Cool biscuits slightly on wire rack to serve warm, or cool completely to serve later. Reheat before serving if you like.

TIP: To make ahead, wrap cooled biscuits in foil in a single layer. Leave at room temperature overnight or put in a resealable plastic bag and freeze up to 1 month.

Each biscuit: About 150 calories, 3g protein, 24g carbohydrate, 5g total fat (3g saturated), 2g fiber, 210mg sodium

Dill-Pepper Buttermilk Biscuits

The savory combination of dill and black pepper gives these biscuits a sophisticated flavor that makes them a perfect accompaniment to salads and soups.

Active time: 20 minutes
Total time: 32 minutes
Makes: 18 biscuits

2 cups all-purpose flour
2½ teaspoons baking powder
½ teaspoon baking soda
½ teaspoon freshly ground black pepper
¼ teaspoon salt
¼ cup vegetable shortening
¾ cup buttermilk
3 tablespoons chopped fresh dill

1 Preheat oven to 450°F. In large bowl, combine flour, baking powder, baking soda, pepper, and salt. With pastry blender or two knives used scissor-fashion, cut in vegetable shortening until mixture resembles coarse crumbs. In cup, combine buttermilk and dill; stir into flour mixture just until mixture forms soft dough that leaves side of bowl.

2 Turn dough onto lightly floured surface; knead six to eight times or just until smooth. With floured rolling pin, roll dough ¼ inch thick.

3 With floured 2-inch biscuit cutter, cut out rounds without twisting cutter. Arrange biscuits on ungreased cookie sheet, 1 inch apart.

4 Press trimmings together; reroll and cut out additional biscuits. Bake 12 to 14 minutes or until golden. Serve warm.

Each biscuit: About 80 calories, 2g protein, 11g carbohydrate, 3g total fat (1g saturated), 0g fiber, 135mg sodium

Cranberry and Pumpkin Seed Scones

These delectable scones are topped with crunchy pumpkin seeds for extra flavor and color.

Active time: 20 minutes
Total time: 50 minutes
Makes: 12 scones

3 cups all-purpose flour
3 tablespoons sugar
1 tablespoon baking powder
1/2 teaspoon salt
3/4 cup (11/2 sticks) butter or margarine, chilled and cut into pieces
1 cup dried cranberries
1 cup milk
1 large egg, separated
3 tablespoons shelled unsalted pumpkin seeds

1 Preheat oven to 400°F. In large bowl, combine flour, sugar, baking powder, and salt. With pastry blender or two knives used scissor-fashion, cut in butter until mixture resembles coarse crumbs. Stir in cranberries.

2 In small bowl, with fork, mix milk with egg yolk. Stir milk mixture into flour mixture just until blended. With hands, divide dough in half and place on opposite corners of ungreased large cookie sheet (17" by 14"). Pat each half into 7-inch round. With floured knife, cut each round into 6 wedges (do not separate wedges).

3 In cup, with fork, lightly beat egg white; use to brush tops of scones. Arrange pumpkin seeds on scones, pressing gently so they will stick to dough.

4 Bake scones 25 to 27 minutes or until golden. Separate scones into wedges; transfer to wire rack to cool slightly. Serve scones warm, or cool completely to serve later. Reheat before serving if you like.

Each serving: About 290 calories, 5g protein, 37g carbohydrate, 14g total fat (3g saturated), 2g fiber, 365mg sodium

Savory Bacon and Green Onion Scones

Who says scones have to be sweet? These are packed with crispy bacon and fresh green onion for bite. Serve up a basket at your holiday dinner or breakfast buffet.

Active time: 10 minutes
Total time: 25 minutes
Makes: 20 scones

6 slices bacon (6 ounces)
2 cups all-purpose flour
1 tablespoon baking powder
1/4 cup finely chopped green onions
1/4 teaspoon salt
1/4 teaspoon ground black pepper
3/4 cup milk

1 Preheat oven to 450°F. In 12-inch skillet, cook bacon over medium heat until browned. Reserve 1/4 cup cooking fat. Drain bacon on paper towels; crumble.

2 Transfer bacon and and fat to large bowl. Add flour, baking powder, green onions, salt, and pepper, stirring to combine. Stir in milk.

3 Drop batter by heaping tablespoons onto ungreased cookie sheet. Bake 12 minutes or until golden brown. Serve hot, or rewarm in a 325°F oven 6 to 8 minutes before serving.

Each scone: About 90 calories, 2g protein, 10g carbohydrate, 4g total fat (2g saturated), 0g fiber, 175mg sodium

VEGETABLE SIDES

Green Beans with Mixed Mushrooms

This simple side borrows the classic casserole's basic flavors, but gives them grabbed-from-the-garden goodness using fresh green beans, thinly sliced onions, and earthy criminis and shiitakes.

Active time: 30 minutes
Total time: 45 minutes
Makes: 12 side-dish servings

2 tablespoons olive oil
4 sprigs fresh thyme
2 large onions (12 ounces each), thinly sliced
1 garlic clove, crushed with garlic press
8 ounces cremini mushrooms, thinly sliced
4 ounces shiitake mushrooms, stems discarded, thinly sliced
2½ teaspoons salt
½ teaspoon ground black pepper
3 pounds green beans, trimmed

1 Heat covered 7- to 8-quart saucepot of *water* to boiling on high.

2 Meanwhile, in 12-inch skillet, heat oil on medium-high. Add thyme and onions; cook 10 to 12 minutes or until browned and very tender, stirring occasionally. Stir in garlic and cook 1 minute. Add all mushrooms and cook 5 minutes or until tender, stirring occasionally.

Stir in ½ teaspoon each salt and pepper. Remove and discard thyme.

3 Add green beans and remaining 2 teaspoons salt to boiling water. Cook, uncovered, 8 to 9 minutes or until tender, stirring occasionally. Drain and rinse with cold water. (If making ahead, transfer mushroom mixture to medium bowl. Cover; refrigerate up to overnight. Transfer beans to resealable plastic bag; refrigerate up to overnight.)

4 Combine green beans and mushroom mixture in saucepot and cook on medium heat until beans are heated through, stirring occasionally.

Each serving: About 80 calories, 3g protein, 14g carbohydrate, 3g total fat (0g saturated), 4g fiber, 125mg sodium

Tarragon Peas with Pearl Onions

Fresh tarragon adds a perky licorice flavor to these frozen peas and pearl onions.

Active time: 5 minutes
Total time: 15 minutes
Makes: 8 side-dish servings

2 tablespoons butter or margarine
1 bag (16 ounces) frozen pearl onions
1 bag (16 ounces) frozen peas
¼ cup water
½ teaspoon salt
¼ teaspoon ground black pepper
1 tablespoon chopped fresh tarragon leaves

In 12-inch nonstick skillet, heat butter on medium-high until melted. Add pearl onions and cook 6 to 7 minutes or until browned. Add peas, water, salt, and pepper. Cover and cook 3 to 4 minutes longer or until onions and peas are tender. Stir in tarragon and spoon into serving bowl.

Each serving: About 85 calories, 4g protein, 12g carbohydrate, 3g total fat (1g saturated), 4g fiber, 260mg sodium

Clockwise from left: MAPLE-GINGER-GLAZED CARROTS *(page 223)*; GREEN BEANS WITH MIXED MUSHROOMS *(above)*; CAVORTING CARIBOU *(page 255)*; BROCCOLI PANCETTA SAUTÉ *(page 214)*.

Broccoli Pancetta Sauté

Ready in a flash, this broccoli is sautéed with zippy lemon juice, crushed red pepper, and pancetta.

Active time: 10 minutes
Total time: 15 minutes
Makes: 12 side-dish servings

2 tablespoons olive oil
1½ ounces pancetta, chopped
2 garlic cloves, crushed with garlic press
¼ teaspoon crushed red pepper
2 pounds broccoli flowerets, cut into small pieces
½ teaspoon salt
½ cup water
1 tablespoon fresh lemon juice
Lemon wedges for serving

1 In 12-inch skillet, heat 1 tablespoon oil on medium-high. Add pancetta and cook 1 to 2 minutes or until browned and crisp, stirring. With slotted spoon, transfer to paper towels to drain.

2 To same skillet, add garlic and crushed red pepper. Cook 10 seconds, stirring, then raise heat to high and add broccoli and salt. Cook 2 minutes, then add water. Cover and cook broccoli 3 to 5 minutes or until most of water evaporates.

3 Meanwhile, in small bowl, with wire whisk, stir together lemon juice and remaining 1 tablespoon oil. Drizzle over broccoli and gently toss to coat. Transfer to serving bowl. Top with pancetta and serve with lemon wedges on the side.

Each serving: About 55 calories, 3g protein, 4g carbohydrate, 4g total fat (1g saturated), 2g fiber, 130mg sodium

Braised Wild Mushrooms and Peas

An effortlessly elegant side that only tastes extravagant.

Active time: 15 minutes
Total time: 30 minutes
Makes: 12 side-dish servings

2 packages (10 ounces each) sliced white mushrooms (see Tip)
8 ounces shiitake mushrooms, stems discarded, caps cut into ½-inch-thick slices
8 ounces oyster mushrooms, tough ends trimmed, separated into lobes
½ cup water
2 tablespoons butter or margarine
4 green onions
1 package (16 ounces) frozen peas
1 tablespoon reduced-sodium soy sauce
¼ teaspoon salt
½ teaspoon ground black pepper

1 In 12-inch skillet, combine all mushrooms, water, and 1 tablespoon butter. Cover and cook on medium 10 minutes. Uncover and cook 15 minutes or until mushrooms are tender and browned, stirring occasionally.

2 Meanwhile, finely chop white and pale green parts of green onions; thinly slice green tops, set aside. Stir chopped green onions and peas into mushroom mixture. Cook 2 to 3 minutes or until vegetables are heated through and liquid in pan returns to boiling, stirring occasionally.

3 Stir in soy sauce, salt, and pepper. Add remaining 1 tablespoon butter; stir until melted. Remove skillet from heat and stir in reserved sliced green onions. Transfer mixture to serving bowl.

TIP: We stretch the mushroom flavor by adding inexpensive white mushrooms to our mix of oysters and shiitakes. If you like, you can clean and sauté the mushrooms the day before, then just cover and refrigerate them. Reheat the mushrooms in a 12-inch skillet on medium before proceeding with step 2.

Each serving: About 80 calories, 5g protein, 11g carbohydrate, 2g total fat (0g saturated), 3g fiber, 175mg sodium

BRAISED WILD MUSHROOMS AND PEAS *(opposite)*

HEALTHY HOLIDAY MAKEOVER: NEW GREEN BEAN CASSEROLE

Here's a fresh take on this holiday classic—no soup can in sight! We switched to low-fat milk and reduced-sodium broth and traded canned french-fried onions for oven-fried ones, trimming the total fat by 8 grams and dropping the sodium by 257 milligrams. Seconds, anyone?

Active time: 30 minutes • Total time: 45 minutes • Makes: 8 side-dish servings

Olive oil nonstick cooking spray
1 large onion (12 ounces), cut into ½-inch-thick rings
5 tablespoons all-purpose flour
⅝ teaspoon salt
1½ pounds green beans, trimmed
1 tablespoon butter or margarine

1 large shallot, finely chopped (¼ cup)
1 container (10 ounces) sliced cremini or white mushrooms
¼ teaspoon freshly ground black pepper
1 cup reduced-sodium chicken broth
½ cup low-fat milk (1%)

1 Preheat oven to 425°F. Line large cookie sheet with foil; spray with nonstick spray.

2 In bowl, toss onion with 2 tablespoons flour and ⅛ teaspoon salt. Spread onion in single layer on prepared foil; spray onion with nonstick spray. Bake 14 minutes; toss to rearrange, then spray again. Bake 15 minutes or until crisp.

3 Meanwhile, heat 5-quart saucepot of water to boiling on high. Add beans and cook, uncovered, 5 minutes or until tender-crisp. Drain beans in colander; rinse under cold water. Drain again.

4 In 4-quart saucepan, melt butter on medium heat. Add shallot; cook 2 minutes, stirring. Add mushrooms; cook 7 to 8 minutes or until tender, stirring often. Stir in remaining ½ teaspoon salt and 3 tablespoons flour, along with pepper; cook 1 minute. Add broth and milk; heat to boiling on high, stirring. Reduce heat to low and cook 2 minutes. Add beans.

5 Transfer mixture to 2-quart baking dish; bake 15 minutes. Stir mixture; top with reserved onion; continue baking 15 minutes or until sauce is bubbly.

95 CAL **Each serving:** 5g protein, 16g carbohydrate, 2g total fat (0g saturated), 4g fiber, 285mg sodium

Tarragon Vegetables Julienne

Here's a colorful side with a French accent. Leeks, carrots, and zucchini are julienned, then sautéed with butter and fresh tarragon, which contributes a distinctive aniselike flavor. An adjustable-blade slicer, food processor, or julienne peeler makes the job easier, but if you don't own these tools, you can slice the vegetables with a chef's knife.

Active time: 40 minutes
Total time: 50 minutes
Makes: 6 cups or 12 side-dish servings

½ pound leeks (2 medium)
1½ pounds carrots (8 large), peeled
1½ pounds zucchini and/or yellow summer squash (3 medium)
3 tablespoons butter or margarine
1½ teaspoons salt
⅛ teaspoon ground black pepper
1 tablespoon chopped fresh tarragon leaves

1 Cut off roots and trim dark-green tops from leeks. Discard any rough outer leaves. Cut each leek lengthwise in half, then crosswise into 2-inch pieces. Cut each piece lengthwise into ⅛-inch-thick matchstick strips. Rinse leeks thoroughly in large bowl of cold water, swishing to remove sand. Transfer leeks to colander to drain, leaving sand in bottom of bowl. Repeat process, changing water several times, until all sand is removed.

2 Cut carrots and zucchini crosswise into 2-inch-long pieces. With adjustable-blade slicer, julienne peeler, or very sharp knife, cut carrots and zucchini into ⅛-inch-thick matchstick strips.

3 In 12-inch skillet, melt butter over medium-high heat. Add leeks, carrots, salt, and pepper; cook 4 to 5 minutes, stirring frequently, until carrots are tender-crisp. Add zucchini and tarragon and cook 3 minutes longer, stirring frequently, until all vegetables are tender.

Each serving: About 65 calories, 2g protein, 10g carbohydrate, 3g total fat (1g saturated), 3g fiber, 355mg sodium

Savory Broccoli-Cauliflower Roast

Citrus and green olives garnish this roasted cauliflower and broccoli side dish, a simple and savory addition to the holiday table.

Active time: 20 minutes
Total time: 45 minutes
Makes: 12 side-dish servings

4 heads broccoli (1½ pounds each), cut into medium florets
5 tablespoons extra-virgin olive oil
⅜ teaspoon salt
⅛ teaspoon plus pinch freshly ground black pepper
2 heads cauliflower (1¼ pounds each), cut into medium florets
1 orange
1 lemon
¼ cup green olives, pitted and thinly sliced
1 tablespoons chopped fresh flat-leaf parsley leaves for garnish

1 Arrange two oven racks in bottom half of oven. Preheat oven to 450°F.

2 On 18" by 12" jelly-roll pan, toss broccoli with 2 tablespoons oil, ¼ teaspoon salt, and ⅛ teaspoon pepper. On another 18" by 12" jelly-roll pan, toss cauliflower with 1 tablespoon oil, ¼ teaspoon salt, and ⅛ teaspoon pepper.

3 Roast 30 to 35 minutes or until vegetables are browned and just tender, rotating pans between oven racks halfway through roasting.

4 Meanwhile, from orange, grate ½ teaspoon peel and squeeze ¼ cup juice into medium bowl. Into same bowl, from lemon, grate ¼ teaspoon peel and squeeze 2 tablespoons juice. Whisk in 2 tablespoons oil, remaining ⅛ teaspoon salt, and pinch pepper.

5 Arrange broccoli and cauliflower on serving platter. Scatter olives over vegetables. Whisk dressing again and drizzle all over dish. Garnish with parsley.

Each serving: About 115 calories, 5g protein, 12g carbohydrate, 7g total fat (1g saturated), 5g fiber, 215mg sodium

Roasted Sweet & Sour
Brussels Sprouts (*opposite*)

Roasted Sweet & Sour Brussels Sprouts

Sweet and tangy balsamic vinegar is the surprise ingredient in this Chinese-inspired side.

Active time: 10 minutes
Total time: 35 minutes
Makes: 12 servings

3 pounds Brussels sprouts, trimmed and halved
2 tablespoons olive oil
¼ cup lower-sodium soy sauce
¼ cup balsamic vinegar
¼ cup brown sugar
½ teaspoon ground ginger
¼ teaspoon black pepper
¼ cup loosely packed fresh parsley leaves, finely
   chopped

1 Preheat oven to 450°F. On 2 large rimmed baking sheets, toss sprouts with oil; spread out in single layers. Roast 20 to 25 minutes or until deep golden brown, stirring and rotating sheets on oven racks halfway through.

2 Meanwhile, in 2-quart saucepan, heat soy sauce, vinegar, brown sugar, ginger, and black pepper to boiling on medium-high. Reduce heat to maintain simmer; simmer 12 to 15 minutes or until syrupy. Remove from heat. Toss sprouts with parsley and enough sauce to coat. Serve remaining sauce on the side.

Each serving: About 90 calories, 4g protein, 15g carbohydrate, 3g total fat (0g saturated), 4g fiber, 210mg sodium

HOW WE CELEBRATE CHRISTMAS

"I'm a true guy. Christmas Eve, I'm at Walmart trying to finish up. Procrastinator, big-time. Sometimes it's cash and gift cards from me. But Amy's really great at thinking through the big gift that Santa's going to leave. And she's a big stocking stuffer. She loves for each of the kids to have a stocking crammed full of silly stuff. . . . You never know what's in there."

—Vince Gill

Kale Salad with Glazed Onions and Cheddar

With glazed onions, dried cherries, pine nuts, and crunchy kale, the flavor of this salad is as bright as its colors.

Active time: 30 minutes
Total time: 40 minutes
Makes: 6 side-dish servings

1 bunch curly kale (8 ounces) curly, tough ribs and stems removed and discarded, leaves very thinly sliced

1 tablespoon fresh lemon juice

2 teaspoons extra-virgin olive oil

1/8 teaspoon salt

1/8 teaspoon freshly ground black pepper

8 ounces frozen pearl onions, thawed

1 tablespoon butter or margarine

2 tablespoons water

2 teaspoons Worcestershire sauce

1 teaspoon sugar

1 tablespoon cider vinegar

1/3 cup dried tart cherries

1/4 cup pine nuts (pignoli)

2 ounces extra-sharp white Cheddar cheese (1/2 cup), shredded

1 In large bowl, toss kale with lemon juice, oil, and salt and pepper; set aside.

2 In 12-inch skillet, combine pearl onions, butter, 1 tablespoon water, Worcestershire sauce, and sugar. Cook on medium heat 8 to 10 minutes or until onions are tender and most of the liquid has evaporated, stirring occasionally.

3 Add vinegar to skillet. Increase heat to medium-high. Cook 3 to 4 minutes, stirring frequently, until onions are browned. Add remaining 1 tablespoon water. Cook 1 minute longer, swirling pan constantly. (Onions can be refrigerated, covered, up to overnight.) Transfer onions to bowl with kale.

4 To kale, add cherries and pine nuts; toss vigorously to combine. Add cheese; toss. Transfer to serving platter.

TIP: To make 12 servings. Step 1: Use 1 large bunch kale (about 12 ounces), 2 tablespoons lemon juice, 1 tablespoon extra-virgin olive oil, 1/4 teaspoon each salt and pepper. Step 2: Use 12 ounces frozen pearl onions, thawed; 2 tablespoons water; 1 tablespoon Worcestershire sauce; 2 teaspoons sugar. Step 3: Use 2 tablespoons cider vinegar. Step 4: Use 1/2 cup dried cherries, 1/3 cup pine nuts, 4 ounces extra-sharp white Cheddar cheese, shredded (1 cup).

Each serving: About 165 calories, 4g protein, 13g carbohydrate, 11g total fat (3g saturated), 3g fiber, 160mg sodium

Red Cabbage and Apples

We love this colorful Christmas-spiced side.

Active time: 15 minutes
Total time: 30 minutes
Makes: 12 side-dish servings

2 tablespoons butter or margarine

1 red onion, cut in half and thinly sliced

1 small head red cabbage (1 3/4 pounds), cored and thinly sliced

2 Granny Smith apples, each peeled, cored, and cut into 1/2-inch chunks

1/2 cup water

2 tablespoons packed brown sugar

2 tablespoons red wine vinegar

1/8 teaspoon ground cloves

1/2 teaspoon salt

1 In deep nonstick 12-inch skillet, melt butter over medium heat. Add onion; cook 5 minutes or until softened, stirring occasionally.

2 Stir in cabbage, apples, water, brown sugar, vinegar, cloves, and salt. Cover skillet and cook 10 minutes or just until cabbage and apples are tender, stirring occasionally. Uncover; cook 5 minutes or until most of liquid evaporates.

Each serving: About 55 calories, 1g protein, 10g carbohydrate, 2g total fat (0g saturated), 2g fiber, 130mg sodium

New World Succotash

We've updated the classic with edamame—young, green soybeans that taste like a sweeter, livelier version of limas. We're celebrating succotash heritage, too, with fresh carrots and corn—and, of course, bacon.

Active time: 10 minutes
Total time: 25 minutes
Makes: 12 side-dish servings

2 slices thick-cut bacon
4 carrots, peeled
¼ cup water
3 cups fresh corn kernels (from 4 ears)
1 bag (16 ounces) frozen shelled edamame
1 lemon
¼ cup snipped fresh chives
⅛ teaspoon cayenne (ground red) pepper
½ teaspoon salt

1 In 12-inch skillet, cook bacon on medium 8 minutes or until browned and crisp, turning over occasionally. While bacon cooks, peel and cut carrots into quarters lengthwise, then cut crosswise at angle into 1½-inch pieces. Drain bacon on paper towels. Remove and discard all but 1 tablespoon fat from skillet.

2 To fat in skillet, add carrots and water. Cover and cook 6 minutes. Add corn and edamame and cook, uncovered, 8 to 10 minutes or until vegetables are tender, stirring occasionally.

3 Meanwhile, from lemon, grate 1 teaspoon peel and squeeze 1 tablespoon juice into large bowl. Add vegetable mixture, snipped chives, cayenne pepper, and salt; toss to combine.

4 To serve, crumble bacon and sprinkle over succotash.

Each serving: About 100 calories, 6g protein, 12g carbohydrate, 4g total fat (1g saturated), 3g fiber, 160mg sodium

Top: NEW WORLD SUCCOTASH *(above)*;
Bottom: RED CABBAGE AND APPLES *(opposite)*.

Creamed Spinach

Parsley adds fresh flavor to frozen spinach, while cream cheese and sour cream add a comforting richness and a delicate tang. The Indian-style variation would pair nicely with our Country Captain Casserole (page 176) on a holiday buffet. The yield is easily increased to feed however many guests you've invited to the party.

Active time: 20 minutes
Total time: 35 minutes
Makes: 6 side-dish servings

2 tablespoons butter or margarine

3 large shallots, finely chopped (3/4 cup)

2 tablespoons all-purpose flour

1/2 cup milk

3/4 teaspoon salt

1/4 teaspoon coarsely ground black pepper

1/8 teaspoon ground nutmeg

1 small package (3 ounces) cream cheese, softened and cut into pieces

3 packages (10 ounces each) frozen chopped spinach, thawed and squeezed dry

1 cup loosely packed fresh parsley leaves

1/4 cup sour cream

1 In 4-quart saucepan, melt butter over medium-low heat. Add shallots and cook, stirring frequently, until tender, about 3 minutes. Add flour and cook, stirring, 1 minute. With wire whisk, gradually whisk in milk; heat to boiling, whisking constantly. Reduce heat and simmer, stirring occasionally with wooden spoon, until sauce has thickened and boils, about 2 minutes. Stir in salt, pepper, and nutmeg.

2 Remove from heat; stir in cream cheese until smooth. Stir in spinach, parsley, and sour cream; heat through, stirring frequently (do not boil).

Each serving: About 180 calories, 7g protein, 14g carbohydrate, 12g total fat (7g saturated), 5g fiber, 500mg sodium

Indian-Style Creamed Spinach

Cook shallots as directed in step 1, but stir in 2 1/2 teaspoons minced, peeled fresh ginger, 2 finely chopped garlic cloves, 3/4 teaspoon each ground coriander and cumin, and 1/8 teaspoon cayenne (ground red) pepper. Cook, stirring, 1 minute. Omit flour, milk, nutmeg, and cream cheese. Stir in spinach and 1/4 cup heavy cream and heat through. Stir in sour cream.

Each serving: About 120 calories, 4g protein, 9g carbohydrate, 9g total fat (5g saturated), 4g fiber, 415mg sodium

MY FAVORITE HOLIDAY TRADITION

"We all get in a circle and go around and say something we're most thankful for. Of course, the high school kids will say something goofy, like 'I'll be glad when this circle is over.' But we've had a kindergartner say, 'I'm grateful for the troops who are serving us when they're away from their families.' Out of the mouths of babes, right? And then it's always ended with my dad saying a prayer."

—Amy Grant

Maple-Ginger-Glazed Carrots

Fresh ginger adds zip to these simple glazed carrots.
For best maple flavor, look for a dark grade B syrup.

Active time: 30 minutes
Total time: 1 hour
Makes: 12 side-dish servings

4 pounds carrots, peeled and cut diagonally into
   1/4-inch-thick slices
1/4 cup water
1 tablespoon grated, peeled fresh ginger
3 tablespoons butter or margarine
1/3 cup dark pure maple syrup (such as grade B)
1 tablespoon cider vinegar
1/2 teaspoon salt
1/4 teaspoon ground black pepper
Chopped fresh parsley leaves for garnish

1 In 5- to 7-quart saucepot, combine carrots, water, ginger, and 2 tablespoons butter. Cover and cook on medium 10 minutes, stirring occasionally. Uncover and cook 10 to 12 minutes or until liquid has evaporated and carrots are almost tender.

2 Add maple syrup, vinegar, salt, and pepper, and heat to boiling on medium-high. Boil 8 to 10 minutes or until syrup is thick and carrots are tender and coated with glaze, stirring frequently. Remove pan from heat; stir in remaining 1 tablespoon butter. Spoon carrots into serving bowl and garnish with parsley.

Each serving: About 105 calories, 1g protein, 20g carbohydrate, 3g total fat (1g saturated), 4g fiber, 185mg sodium

Oven-Browned Carrots and Parsnips

This duet of sweet root vegetables is subtly accented by the flavors of fresh lemon peel and orange liqueur.

Active time: 20 minutes
Total time: 1 hour 20 minutes
Makes: 10 side-dish servings

2 pounds carrots, peeled and cut into 3" by 1/2" matchsticks
2 pounds parsnips, peeled and cut into 3" by 1/2" matchsticks
4 strips fresh lemon peel (3" by 1" each)
2 tablespoons orange-flavored liqueur
1 teaspoon sugar
1/2 teaspoon salt
1/4 teaspoon coarsely ground black pepper
3 tablespoons butter or margarine, cut into pieces
Fresh parsley leaves for garnish

1 Preheat oven to 425°F. In bowl, toss carrots and parsnips with lemon peel, liqueur, sugar, salt, and pepper.

2 Divide the mixture between two 15½" by 10½" jelly-roll pans (or use 1 jelly-roll pan and 1 large shallow roasting pan) and dot with butter.

3 Roast vegetables until tender and browned, about 1 hour, stirring occasionally and rotating pans between upper and lower oven racks halfway through roasting time. Garnish with parsley to serve.

Each serving: About 135 calories, 2g protein, 24g carbohydrate, 4g total fat (3g saturated), 4g fiber, 190mg sodium

EASY-ROAST VEGETABLES

Prepare veggies (2 pounds per recipe) as directed, then toss with 1 tablespoon olive oil and roast at 450°F on rimmed cookie sheet. Serves 8.

❶ POTATOES

Toss 1-inch chunks and 1 tablespoon chopped rosemary leaves; roast 35 minutes.

❷ BRUSSELS SPROUTS

Roast halved sprouts 20 minutes. Toss with ¼ cup finely chopped walnuts and 1 tablespoon chopped parsley.

❸ RED ONIONS & FENNEL

Toss ½-inch wedges with 1 teaspoon chopped thyme leaves; 2 cloves garlic, thinly sliced; and ¼ teaspoon black pepper. Roast 30 minutes.

❹ TURNIPS & SQUASH

Roast 1-inch chunks 35 minutes. Sprinkle with 1 tablespoon chives.

❺ BROCCOLI & CAULIFLOWER

Roast 2-inch florets 20 minutes. Sprinkle with ¼ cup finely grated Parmesan cheese and 1 teaspoon grated lemon.

Spice-Roasted Carrots

Give regular roasted carrots a wake-up call with this zesty, tangy, crunchy recipe.

Active time: 15 minutes
Total time: 1 hour 15 minutes
Makes: 8 servings

8 very large carrots (about 3 pounds), peeled
3 tablespoons olive oil
2 tablespoons packed fresh oregano leaves, chopped
1 teaspoon smoked paprika
½ teaspoon ground nutmeg
½ teaspoon salt
¼ teaspoon pepper
2 tablespoons butter, melted
1 tablespoon red wine vinegar
⅓ cup roasted salted pistachios, shelled and finely chopped

1 Preheat oven to 450°F.

2 In roasting pan, toss carrots with oil, oregano, paprika, nutmeg, salt, and pepper. Roast 1 hour or until tender but not falling apart. Transfer to serving platter. Drizzle with butter and vinegar and garnish with pistachios.

Each serving: About 165 calories, 3g protein, 16g carbohydrate, 11g total fat (3g saturated), 5g fiber, 295mg sodium

Green Bean–Cheddar Casserole

Ready for a break from the classic holiday green-bean casserole? Try this one, with two kinds of cheese.

Active time: 30 minutes
Total time: 1 hour 20 minutes
Makes: 10 servings

3 pounds green beans, trimmed
2 cups stale bread, torn into small chunks
3 tablespoons olive oil
3 green onions, thinly sliced
3 tablespoons cornstarch
2½ cups whole milk
⅛ teaspoon ground nutmeg
½ teaspoon salt
½ teaspoon pepper
8 ounces Cheddar cheese, shredded
¼ cup finely grated Parmesan cheese (1 ounce)

1 Heat covered 7- to 8-quart saucepot of salted water to boiling on high. Preheat oven to 375°F. Add green beans to boiling water. Cook 2 minutes. Drain well; set aside.

2 In food processor, pulse bread into coarse crumbs. Transfer to medium bowl along with oil and green onions. Toss to combine; set aside.

3 In 4-quart saucepan, whisk cornstarch and ½ cup milk until smooth. Add nutmeg, salt and pepper. Slowly whisk in remaining 2 cups milk. Heat to boiling on medium-high, whisking frequently. Boil 2 minutes, whisking. Reduce heat to medium-low. Stir in cheese one handful at a time, waiting until cheese melts before adding next handful. Stir in green beans until well-coated. Transfer with reserved crumb mixture. Bake 25 to 30 minutes or until crumbs are golden brown.

Each serving: About 245 calories, 11g protein 19g carbohydrate, 15g total fat (7g saturated), 4g fiber, 375mg sodium

Top: SPICE-ROASTED CARROTS *(opposite);*
Bottom: GREEN BEAN–CHEDDAR CASSEROLE *(above).*

Roasted Acorn Squash

A traditional accompaniment to roasted turkey and pork, this squash side dish is as colorful as it is tasty.

Active time: 10 minutes
Total time: 40 minutes
Makes: 8 side-dish servings

4 small acorn squashes (1 pound each)
4 tablespoons butter or margarine, melted
1/4 cup packed brown sugar
1 teaspoon salt
1/4 teaspoon coarsely ground black pepper

1 Preheat oven to 450°F. Spray 15½" by 10½" jelly-roll pan with nonstick cooking spray. Cut each squash lengthwise in half; scoop out seeds and discard. Cut to make 16 equal-size wedges total.

2 Place squash pieces in pan. In cup, stir together butter, brown sugar, salt, and pepper. Brush cut sides of squash with butter mixture.

3 Bake 30 minutes or until lightly browned and fork-tender. (Let each person scoop tender flesh from wedges and discard skin.)

TIP: You can save time by cooking this squash in the same oven with one of our roasts. Just place the pan with the squash on the shelf below the meat for the last 30 minutes of the roasting time. While the roast rests, increase oven temperature to 450°F and cook squash another 10 to 15 minutes, until tender and browned.

Each serving: About 150 calories, 2g protein, 26g carbohydrate, 6g total fat (1g saturated), 3g fiber, 375mg sodium

Herb-Roasted Acorn Squash

Prepare as directed, but omit brown sugar and stir **2 tablespoons freshly chopped herbs**, such as rosemary, sage, or thyme, into butter mixture in step 2.

Pepper-Roasted Acorn Squash

Prepare as directed, but omit brown sugar and use **1 teaspoon black pepper** in step 2.

Spice-Roasted Acorn Squash

Prepare as directed, but add **1/2 teaspoon ground cinnamon** or **1/4 teaspoon ground nutmeg** to butter mixture in step 2.

Sautéed Swiss Chard with Golden Raisins and Capers

Here's a side with an Italian accent. Serve it with our Stuffed Veal Roast, Italian Style (page 119).

Active time: 30 minutes
Total time: 50 minutes
Makes: 8 side-dish servings

4 pounds Swiss chard (about 3 bunches)
2 tablespoons olive oil
2 small onions, chopped
1/3 cup golden raisins
1/4 cup capers, rinsed and drained

1 Trim tough stem ends from Swiss chard. Cut stems crosswise into 1-inch pieces; cut leaves into 2-inch pieces, keeping stems and leaves separate. Rinse leaves and stems; drain well.

2 In nonstick 12-inch skillet, heat oil over medium heat. Add onions and cook about 6 minutes or until pieces begin to brown. Add chard stems and cook, covered, 5 to 7 minutes or until tender. Stir in raisins. Add leaves to stems in batches, covering skillet after each batch; cook 7 to 10 minutes total or until leaves are tender and wilted, stirring often. Remove from heat; stir in capers.

Each serving: About 120 calories, 4g protein, 20g carbohydrate, 4g total fat (1g saturated), 5g fiber, 555mg sodium

ROASTED ACORN SQUASH (*opposite*)

Good Housekeeping

FEBRUARY
1929

25 CENTS

35 CENTS IN CANADA

FROM OUR HOLIDAY ARCHIVES: DOWN-HOME SIDES

For a cozy Christmas dinner with family, serve a selection of these Southern-style sides, straight from our archives. Potato Pie and Okra and Corn in Cream would be delicious alongside our Mustard-Glazed Fresh Ham with Cider Sauce (page 124).

Okra and Corn in Cream

4 tablespoons butter or margarine

1½ cups corn, cut from cob, or thawed frozen corn

8 ounces okra, cut into ½-inch-thick slices (2 cups)

1 teaspoon salt

Dash ground black pepper

½ cup light cream

Melt butter in 9-inch skillet. Add corn and cook over low heat until just beginning to brown. Add okra; cover skillet tightly and cook over very low heat 10 minutes, stirring occasionally. Remove cover and sprinkle vegetables with salt and pepper. Add cream and cook, stirring occasionally, until heated through. Serve immediately. Makes 4 side-dish servings.

Corn Fritters, Southern Style

1 cup all-purpose flour

1 teaspoon baking powder

1 teaspoon salt

2 eggs

¼ cup milk

2 teaspoons vegetable oil plus more for frying

2½ cups frozen cut corn, thawed

1 Sift flour with baking powder and salt into small bowl. In medium bowl, beat eggs, milk, and 2 teaspoons oil. Stir flour mixture into egg mixture, then stir in corn.

2 In deep skillet over medium-high, heat 1½ inches of oil. Drop batter by tablespoonful into hot oil and fry 3 to 5 minutes, turning over once, until golden brown. Drain on paper-towel-lined plate; serve hot. Makes about 60 fritters.

Orange-Candied Sweets

8 sweet potatoes

4 tablespoons butter or margarine

1 cup packed brown sugar

2 tablespoons honey

½ cup orange juice

1 teaspoon freshly grated orange peel

1 Early in day: Peel potatoes and halve lengthwise. Melt butter in large skillet over medium-high heat; add potatoes and cook until browned, 4 to 5 minutes. Transfer to 2-quart casserole, along with any butter left in skillet. Stir in brown sugar, honey, and orange juice and peel. Refrigerate.

2 About 1 hour before serving: Preheat oven to 450°F. Bake sweet potatoes, covered, 45 minutes. Uncover and baste with pan juices; bake 20 minutes longer, basting often, or until potatoes are tender and golden brown. Makes 8 side-dish servings.

Pineapple Sweets

Substitute 1 can (8 ounces) crushed pineapple, undrained, for honey, orange juice, and peel.

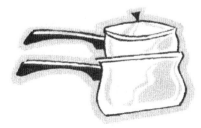

Potato Pie

2¼ cups sifted all-purpose flour

3¼ teaspoons salt

1 tablespoon sugar

½ cup vegetable shortening

6 tablespoons butter or margarine

3 tablespoons water

6 medium potatoes, peeled and thinly sliced (7 cups)

⅛ teaspoon ground black pepper

1 large onion (12 ounces), thinly sliced

1 tablespoon chopped fresh parsley leaves

Milk for brushing

1 cup heavy cream

1 Preheat oven to 375°F.

2 Into medium mixing bowl, sift flour, 1¼ teaspoons salt, and sugar.

3 With two knives or pastry blender, cut in shortening until mixture is as fine as cornmeal, then cut in 4 tablespoons butter until particles are pea size.

4 Sprinkle water, a little at a time, over flour mixture, mixing thoroughly with fork. When mixture forms dough that leaves sides of bowl clean, use hands to press gently into smooth ball; wrap in waxed paper and refrigerate for 30 minutes to chill.

5 Meanwhile, in large bowl, toss potatoes with remaining 2 teaspoons salt, pepper, onion, and parsley.

6 Roll out one half of dough so it is 1½ inches larger and same shape as 1½-quart shallow baking dish and fit dough into dish. Fill with potato mixture, dot with remaining 2 tablespoons butter, then trim pastry even with edge of dish.

7 Roll out second half of dough. Lay dough over potato mixture and trim so it extends 1 inch beyond edge of dish. Fold edges under bottom crust and press firmly together to create stand-up rim; make crimped edge (see Tip, page 280). Cut a few slits in top of pie and brush top with a little milk.

8 Bake pie 1 hour to 1 hour 15 minutes or until potatoes are tender when pierced with tip of knife. Remove from oven; make small hole in crust and pour in cream (a baster works well). Let stand a few minutes then cut into squares or wedges. Makes 8 side-dish servings.

Crisp Cabbage 'n' Bacon

4 bacon slices

6 cups coarsely chopped cabbage (1¾ pounds)

½ teaspoon salt

⅛ teaspoon ground black pepper

1 In large skillet over medium-high heat, cook bacon slices 6 to 8 minutes until crisp; remove from skillet and place on paper-towel-lined plate to drain.

2 Pour off bacon fat; return 2 tablespoons to skillet. Add cabbage and sprinkle with salt and pepper. Cover and cook 5 to 6 minutes, stirring once.

3 Crumble bacon over cabbage and serve. Makes 4 side-dish servings.

Celery au Gratin

2 small bunches celery (1½ pounds total)
⅓ cup milk
6 ounces Cheddar cheese, shredded (1½ cups)
1 cup day-old bread crumbs
1 tablespoon melted butter or margarine

1 Cut celery stalks lengthwise into quarters. (If stalks are very long, cut into halves crosswise as well.)

2 In covered ovenproof skillet with a little *salted water*, gently simmer celery 20 minutes; drain. (Do not overcook.)

3 Meanwhile, in small saucepan, heat milk over low heat until warm, then melt cheese in milk, whisking until smooth. Toss bread crumbs with melted butter. Pour cheese sauce over celery and sprinkle with buttered bread crumbs.

4 Preheat broiler.

5 Place skillet under broiler until casserole is bubbly and brown. Makes 4 to 6 side-dish servings.

Winter Squash with Cranberries

2 packages (12 ounces each) frozen squash, thawed and mashed, or 4 cups mashed, cooked Hubbard squash
2 eggs, beaten
5 tablespoons melted butter or margarine
¼ cup sugar
1½ cups fresh or thawed frozen cranberries, halved
½ teaspoon salt
⅛ teaspoon ground black pepper
Dash nutmeg

1 Early in day: In large bowl, with egg beater, beat squash with eggs and 3 tablespoons melted butter until well combined. Stir in sugar, cranberries, salt, and pepper (taste and adjust seasoning if needed). Spoon into 2-quart casserole, drizzle remaining 2 tablespoons butter over top, and sprinkle with nutmeg. Refrigerate.

2 Fifteen minutes before serving: Preheat oven to 400°F. Bake casserole 45 minutes, until browned on top and cooked through. Set on wire rack to cool slightly before serving. Makes 8 side-dish servings.

Turnips in Parsley-Lemon Butter

6 white turnips, pared and cut into large cubes
2 tablespoons butter or margarine
1 tablespoon lemon juice
2 tablespoons chopped fresh parsley leaves
Dash ground black pepper

1 In medium pot, cook turnips in *1 inch boiling salted water*, covered, 20 to 30 minutes, or until tender. Drain turnips, return to pan, and shake over heat a few times to dry off slightly.

2 Melt butter in small saucepan over medium heat; add lemon juice and parsley and heat briefly. Pour lemon butter over turnips; stir in pepper and serve immediately. Makes 4 or 5 side-dish servings.

RELISHES & CRANBERRY SAUCES

Caramelized Onion and Fennel Relish

*This flavor combination is luscious served alongside our
Herbed Pork Loin (page 120).*

Active time: 15 minutes
Total time: 40 minutes
Makes: 4 cups

4 teaspoons olive oil
1½ pounds red onions, thinly sliced (6 cups)
1 fennel bulb (2 pounds), trimmed, cut into quarters, and
    thinly sliced (8 cups)
2 teaspoons sugar
1 teaspoon salt
¼ teaspoon ground black pepper

1 In deep nonstick 12-inch skillet or 5-quart saucepot,
heat oil over medium heat.

2 Add onions, fennel, sugar, salt, and pepper; cover and
cook 15 minutes, stirring occasionally.

3 Remove cover and cook 10 to 15 minutes longer or
until vegetables are tender and deep golden brown,
stirring frequently.

Each 2-tablespoon serving: About 20 calories, 1g protein,
4g carbohydrate, 1g total fat (0g saturated), 1g fiber, 85mg sodium

Creamed Pearl Onions

*Our luscious recipe for this holiday favorite features a white
sauce seasoned with just a pinch of nutmeg.*

Active time: 20 minutes
Total time: 40 minutes
Makes: 10 side-dish servings

2 baskets (10 ounces each) pearl onions
3 tablespoons butter or margarine
3 tablespoons all-purpose flour
2 cups milk, warmed
¼ teaspoon salt
⅛ teaspoon ground black pepper
Pinch ground nutmeg

1 In 10-inch skillet, heat *1 inch water* to boiling over
high heat. Add onions; heat to boiling. Reduce heat;
cover and simmer until tender, 10 to 15 minutes. Drain.

2 When cool enough to handle, peel onions, leaving
a little of root end attached to help onions hold
their shape.

3 Meanwhile, prepare white sauce: In heavy 2-quart
saucepan, melt butter over low heat. Add flour and
cook, stirring, 1 minute. With wire whisk, gradually
whisk in warm milk. Cook over medium heat, stirring
constantly with wooden spoon, until sauce has
thickened and boils. Reduce heat and simmer, stirring
frequently, 3 minutes. Stir in salt, pepper, and nutmeg;
remove from heat.

4 Return onions to skillet. Add white sauce and cook,
stirring, until heated through.

Each serving: About 85 calories, 2g protein, 8g carbohydrate,
5g total fat (3g saturated), 1g fiber, 121mg sodium

Clockwise from top left: FRONT-DOOR GREENERY; GINGER AND PEAR CRANBERRY SAUCE *(page 237);* LET IT SHINE *(page 185);*
PINEAPPLE-CRANBERRY CHUTNEY *(page 235).*

Fresh Cranberry-Orange Mold

This decked-out version of the classic holiday condiment looks gorgeous on the table.

Active time: 20 minutes
Total time: 25 minutes plus standing and chilling
Makes: 12 servings

1 can (11 ounces) Mandarin orange segments
2 cups water
½ cup sugar
4 whole cloves
2 sticks cinnamon (3 inches each)
1 (2-inch) piece fresh ginger, peeled and sliced
2 packages (4 servings each) cranberry-flavor gelatin
2 cups fresh cranberries
2 teaspoons grated fresh orange peel
Kumquats and fresh mint sprigs for garnish

1 Strain syrup from Mandarin orange segments into 2-quart saucepan. Cover segments and set aside in refrigerator. Add water, sugar, cloves, cinnamon, and ginger to syrup in saucepan; heat to boiling on high. Remove from heat and let stand 10 minutes for spice flavor to develop. Reheat to boiling, then strain liquid into medium bowl; discard solids. Stir in gelatin until completely dissolved, about 1 minute.

2 Refrigerate until mixture mounds slightly when dropped from spoon, 1 hour 30 minutes to 1 hour 45 minutes.

3 Meanwhile, in food processor with knife blade attached, pulse cranberries and orange peel about 15 times or until cranberries are chopped.

4 With rubber spatula, gently fold cranberry mixture and Mandarin orange segments into thickened gelatin until well mixed; pour into shallow 6-cup mold or bowl. Cover and refrigerate until set, at least 8 hours or overnight.

5 To serve, dip mold up to rim in bowl of warm, not hot, water for several seconds. Dry outside of mold. Carefully insert small metal spatula around edge of mold to release gelatin. Invert onto serving plate; lift off mold. Garnish with kumquats and mint.

TIP: Prepare this dish up to 3 days ahead and leave it in the mold, keeping it well chilled. Invert it onto a platter and add garnishes just before serving.

Each serving: About 110 calories, 2g protein, 27g carbohydrate, 0g total fat, 1g fiber, 50mg sodium

Southwestern-Style Cranberry Relish

A finely chopped jalapeño pepper adds unexpected heat to this relish. It'd be perfect partnered with our Spiced Grilled Turkey Breast (page 145).

Active time: 10 minutes
Total time: 25 minutes plus chilling
Makes: 2 cups or 8 servings

1 lemon
1 bag (12 ounces) cranberries, picked over and rinsed
1 pickled jalapeño chile, finely chopped
½ cup honey
¼ cup cider vinegar
1 teaspoon mustard seeds
½ teaspoon salt
½ teaspoon ground black pepper

1 From lemon, with vegetable peeler, remove peel in 1-inch-wide strips. Cut strips crosswise into slivers.

2 In nonreactive 2-quart saucepan, combine cranberries, lemon peel, pickled jalapeño, honey, vinegar, mustard seeds, salt, and pepper; heat to boiling over high heat. Reduce heat; simmer, stirring occasionally, until most cranberries have popped and mixture has thickened slightly, about 10 minutes.

3 Cover and refrigerate until well chilled, about 3 hours or up to 4 days.

Each ¼-cup serving: About 90 calories, 0g protein, 24g carbohydrate, 0g total fat, 1g fiber, 174mg sodium

Pineapple-Cranberry Chutney

Cook a double batch of this versatile condiment the week before Christmas (it'll keep).

Active time: 20 minutes
Total time: 45 minutes
Makes: 4 cups

2 navel oranges
1 ripe pineapple
1 jalapeño chile, seeded and minced
½ small red onion, chopped
1 cup dried cranberries
½ cup granulated sugar
½ cup cider vinegar
2 tablespoons minced, peeled fresh ginger
½ teaspoon salt

1 From 1 orange, grate 1 teaspoon peel. Cut off peel and pith from both oranges; slice flesh into ½-inch pieces. Cut off crown and bottom from pineapple; slice off rind and eyes. Cut pineapple lengthwise into quarters; slice flesh into ½-inch chunks.

2 In 4-quart saucepan, place orange peel and pieces, pineapple, jalapeño, onion, cranberries, sugar, vinegar, ginger, and salt; heat to boiling on medium-high, stirring. Cook, uncovered, 20 minutes or until thickened, stirring occasionally. Serve warm or cover and refrigerate up to 1 week.

Each ¼-cup serving: About 75 calories, 0g protein, 19g carbohydrate, 0g total fat, 1g fiber, 75mg sodium

---

TASTY WAYS TO SERVE CRANBERRY SAUCE OR CHUTNEY

If you have leftovers from the big dinner, here's how to make the most of them.

• **Stir into mayonnaise** for a delicious spread for turkey or ham sandwiches.

• **Puree in a blender** until smooth and use as a glaze for roast ham or chicken.

• **Serve with** grilled cheese sandwiches.

• **Swirl into softened cream cheese** or goat cheese and serve with crackers or apple slices.

• **Stir in a little Dijon mustard** and use as a dipping sauce for shish kabobs or mini frankfurters.

Citrus-Apricot Cranberry Sauce *(opposite)*

Citrus-Apricot Cranberry Sauce

Orange juice and apricots, fruits that were uncommon in most kitchens when this recipe first ran in the magazine in 1887, temper the tang of the cranberries in this easier-than-it-seems side—a single saucepan and some simmering is all it takes.

Active time: 5 minutes
Total time: 20 minutes
Makes: 3 cups

1 lemon
½ cup chopped dried apricots
½ cup orange juice
½ cup sugar
½ cup water
2 whole star anise
⅛ teaspoon ground black pepper
1 bag (12 ounces) cranberries (3 cups)

1 With vegetable peeler, remove all peel from lemon in strips; reserve strips and squeeze 2 tablespoons juice.

2 In 2- to 3-quart saucepan, stir together lemon juice, dried apricots, orange juice, sugar, water, star anise, and pepper. Heat to boiling over medium-high, stirring occasionally.

3 To saucepan, add cranberries and lemon peel. Return to boiling. Reduce heat to medium; simmer 3 to 4 minutes or until half of cranberries pop and mixture thickens. Let cranberry sauce cool before serving, or cover and refrigerate up to 4 days. Discard star anise and lemon peel before serving, if you like.

Each ¼-cup serving: About 65 calories, 0g protein, 17g carbohydrate, 0g total fat, 1g fiber, 0mg sodium

Ginger and Pear Cranberry Sauce

Cranberry sauce takes a walk on the spicy side with the addition of fresh ginger. Try the sweet orange marmalade variation, too.

Active time: 10 minutes
Total time: 20 minutes
Makes: 3 cups

3 Bosc or Anjou pears
1 bag (12 ounces) cranberries (3 cups)
1 tablespoon grated, peeled fresh ginger
¾ cup sugar
¼ cup water

1 Peel, core, and chop 2 pears and place in 3-quart saucepan. Add cranberries, ginger, sugars, and water and heat to boiling on high, stirring occasionally.

2 Reduce heat to medium and cook, uncovered, 5 to 7 minutes or until most cranberries pop and pears are tender, stirring occasionally.

3 Spoon sauce into serving bowl; cover and refrigerate 3 hours or up to 4 days. (Mixture will thicken as it chills.) Core remaining pear and cut into slices to use as garnish.

Each ¼-cup serving: About 75 calories, 0g protein, 20g carbohydrate, 0g total fat, 2g fiber, 10mg sodium

Marmalade-Cranberry Sauce

Prepare cranberry sauce as directed above in step 1, except omit pears and ginger and use only ½ cup sugar. In step 2, cook only 3 to 4 minutes or until most cranberries pop. After removing from heat, stir in ½ cup sweet orange marmalade. Complete recipe as in step 3. Makes about 2¼ cups.

Each ¼-cup serving: About 105 calories, 0g protein, 27g carbohydrate, 0g total fat, 2g fiber, 25mg sodium

Cranberry-Port Ring

As delicious as it is stunning, this ring is the perfect upgrade to canned cranberry sauce.

Active time: 10 minutes
Total time: 25 minutes plus chilling
Makes: 12 servings

6 cups fresh or frozen cranberries
1³/4 cups sugar
3 thin coins fresh unpeeled ginger
2 sticks cinnamon
3¹/4 cups cold water
1 cup ruby port
3 envelopes unflavored gelatin (7¹/2 teaspoons)
Vegetable oil, for greasing

1 In 5- to 6-quart saucepot, combine cranberries, sugar, ginger, cinnamon, 2½ cups water and ¾ cup port. Heat to boiling on high. Reduce heat to maintain simmer; cook 10 to 15 minutes or until most cranberries pop, stirring occasionally.

2 Meanwhile, to small bowl, add ½ cup water and sprinkle gelatin evenly over it. Let stand 10 minutes. Lightly grease decorative mold with oil.

3 Into large bowl, strain cranberry mixture through fine-mesh sieve, pressing on solids to extract liquid; discard solids. Stir in gelatin mixture until dissolved, then stir in remaining ¼ cup port and ¼ cup water. Pour liquid into prepared mold. Refrigerate overnight or up to 4 days. To remove from mold, place serving plate facedown on top of it and invert plate and mold together, then lift and remove mold.

Each serving: About 155 calories, 2g protein, 36g carbohydrate, 0g total fat (0g saturated), 0g fiber, 5mg sodium

Top: CRANBERRY-PORT RING *(above)*; *Bottom:* EVA LONGORIA'S CRANBRRY-POACHED PEARS *(opposite)*.

Eva Longoria's Cranberry-Poached Pears

Spiced pears cooked with sweet-tart cranberries are a dynamic alternative to cranberry sauce.

Active time: 15 minutes
Total time: 30 minutes plus chilling
Makes: 8 servings

8 small pears (such as Seckel or Forelle)
4 cups water
5 tablespoons honey
3 tablespoons sugar
1 strip orange zest
1 strip lemon zest
1 teaspoon fresh lemon juice
1 stick cinnamon
1 vanilla bean
1 bag fruit tea (tropical green or passion fruit)
2¼ cups fresh or frozen cranberries

1 Place pears in saucepan large enough to hold them snugly. Add water to barely cover. Add honey, sugar, orange and lemon zest, lemon juice, and cinnamon stick.

2 Using tip of paring knife, scrape vanilla seeds out of pod and add to pan. Toss in pod and add tea bag. Bring to a boil over medium high heat, stirring until sugar has dissolved. Reduce heat and simmer until pears are tender when pierced with tip of knife, about 10 minutes.

3 Add cranberries and return to simmer until they burst, about 3 minutes. Remove and discard tea bag.

4 Transfer pears to large bowl and pour cranberries and syrup over them. Cover and refrigerate overnight or up to 3 days.

5 Remove and discard citrus zest, cinnamon stick, and vanilla bean. To serve, arrange pears on platter. Spoon cranberries and as much of poaching liquid as desired over pears. Serve.

Each serving: About 155 calories, 0g protein, 41g carbohydrate, 0g total fat (0g saturated), 6g fiber, 3mg sodium

Maple-Orange Cranberry Sauce

If you're hunting for an easy recipe, look no further.

Active time: 5 minutes
Total time: 20 minutes
Makes: 8 servings

2 (12-ounce) bags fresh or frozen (thawed) cranberries
½ cup sugar
½ cup maple syrup
½ cup orange juice
1 tablespoon finely grated orange peel
¼ teaspoon salt
¼ teaspoon pepper

1 Simmer all ingredients in medium saucepan on medium-high 10 to 15 minutes, until slightly thickened.

Each serving: About 150 calories, 0g protein, 38g carbohydrate, 0g total fat (0g saturated), 3g fiber, 77mg sodium

Chapter 4

All Through The House

DAZZLING CHRISTMAS TREES, FESTIVE GARLANDS & STOCKINGS

There's no place like home for the holidays, especially when it's decorated with inspired touches brimming with Christmas spirit. We've rounded up our favorite ideas for brightening your hearth, plus a chorus of trees, from playful to regal to au naturel.

Change of Hearth

Make your fireplace the most festive spot in the house with our easy, wallet-friendly transformations. Repurpose mittens or old sweaters to create cozy Christmas stockings, or line your mantelpiece with mini spruce trees. Festoon your banisters or an entryway with an evergreen garland; store-bought straw ornaments add a formal country touch.

Trees That Dazzle

The Christmas tree should be the crowning glory of a holiday home. To inspire you, we share ten different takes on the traditional tannenbaum, featuring a variety of palettes from red and white to regal jewel tones to a perky pink and green.

Ornament Inspirations

There's no need to spend a bundle on trimmings for your tree. With a little imagination, you can see everyday objects in a festive new light. Velvet ribbons, candy garlands, or spray-painted pinecones can all be transformed into dashing decor for your tree. Or see our other ideas for charming DIY tree ornaments starting on page 255.

Clockwise from top left: Assorted Ornaments; Green and Gold Stunner; Woven-Ribbon Ornament *(page 255).*

Crafts

1

4

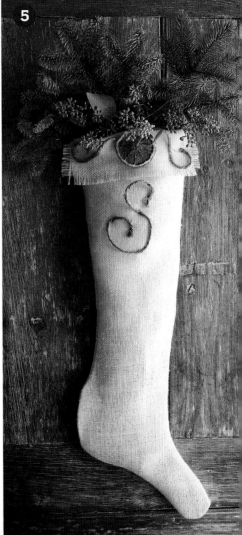

5

2

3

HEARTH & HOME

Stockings are the most time-honored way to decorate the mantel, but why stop there? Our festive garlands, mini trees, and candles enhance the seasonal glow.

1. Tree Line

Supermarket spruce seedlings, popped into pails and arrayed along a candlelit mantel, create a wintry woodland scene.

2. Sweater Stockings

A row of no-sweat sweater stockings—stitched up quickly from secondhand cable knits and Fair Isles—are ready to be stuffed with presents, while silver glass holders glow on the mantel (for safety, use LED candles).

To make these clever stockings, use old sweaters from your basement or a consignment shop. Create a stocking-shaped template in desired size—making sure to leave a ½-inch allowance for the seam. Cut out sweater for the front, and for the back, use felt in a corresponding color. Sew the two pieces right sides together, then turn inside out to finish. Sew a ribbon loop into the top for hanging.

3. Wintry Garland

Embellish an evergreen garland (fresh cut or fake) with berry branches and ornaments that resemble pinecones and snowflakes. Drape the greenery along a doorway, mantelpiece, or staircase handrail, then hang the ornaments from ribbon loops.

4. Give Them a Hand

Assist stockings with the annual gift-dispensing duties by transforming mittens into hanging holders for tiny treats—simply stitch on loops made from ribbons.

5. Stocking Feat

Customized with an initial and brimming with greenery, a rough-hewn bootie adds primitive chic to a hearth or door. All it takes to make this folk-art facsimile: burlap, twine, and minimal sewing skills.

Create a stocking-shaped template and trace two stocking shapes onto white burlap. Cut out your shapes and, with right sides together, sew starting 3 inches down on both sides from the top (the top will fold over to make a cuff, as shown here). Turn right side out and press, creating the cuff. Fray the cuff edges by pulling at the loose threads of the burlap. Use twine to form a monogram letter and border at the top. Secure with a pin once you create a design you like, and sew in place. We threaded the twine through a dried orange slice for added interest.

Fill your new stocking with a layer of bubble wrap, to give it bulk and weight. Cut a manila folder or piece of stiff cardboard to fit in the top half, and place it behind the bubble wrap. Place a branch of spruce between the bubble wrap and folder, and add a few other light sprigs of seeded eucalyptus or other stocking stuffers of your choice. To hang, string a piece of wire through the back top of the burlap.

1

2

3

O, CHRISTMAS TREE!

Spruce it up! Create a personalized tree with handcrafted decorations, natural ornaments like pinecones and dried fruit, or a limited color palette ranging from regal jewel tones or greens and golds to classic red and white or preppy pink and lime green.

1. Royal Highness
Rich jewel tones of violet, gold, blue, and green give this tree an air of royalty. A gold bead garland wraps it in luxury. To create a harmonious tableau, we extended the bold color palette to the under-the-branches display. The gifts are dazzling in violet and gold wrapping; a coordinating tree skirt ties it all together.

2. Have a Ball
Traditional Christmas tree ornaments have a whole life away from the evergreen. Display extra ornaments in clear glass bowls or in baskets, as shown here, for simple (and thrifty!) holiday decorating.

3. Tart and Tiny Tree
This tabletop feather tree is ripe with tiny lady apple, Seckel pear, and nut ornaments. Kumquat garlands wreath it with color. To make the playful tree topper, thread alternating kumquats and lady apples on thin wire and shape into a ring. A tableau of rustic pottery filled with fresh and dried fruit completes the look.

WEE TREES

Whether you live in an apartment that can't accommodate a full-size tree, or simply want to dress up a mantel or buffet, miniature tabletop trees are a fun and festive solution.

Artificial versions are available in a range of sizes, designs, and colors, online or wherever Christmas decorations are sold. Or purchase a small potted evergreen instead: Water it regularly and it will last into the new year. Miniature spruces look great in multiples along a mantelpiece or windowsill; check out Tree Line on page 245 for inspiration.

A wee tree requires wee decorations. Select tiny balls, colorful candies, or petite fruits, as shown in the Tart and Tiny Tree, opposite. For added sparkle, wind the branches with strands of Mardi Gras beads or small blinking lights.

4

4. Tree of Plenty

Set the scene for this Scandinavian-style tree with a smorgasbord of cool, crisp trimmings—from store-bought straw stars and mock cross-stitch ornaments to fabric caribou you can make yourself (see Cavorting Caribou, page 255). Completing the look: A tree skirt of sheepskin and gifts wrapped in solid-hued paper.

5. Fit for a King Tree

A regal palette presides over this opulent tree, which pairs metallics with sapphire and amethyst hues. Instead of garlands wrapping around the tree, short strands of pearls, gold beads, and rhinestone spirals dangle from its branches. Candy-filled gold-paper cones are ornaments now, party favors later.

TREE-TRIMMING TOOL KIT

Get ready for the holiday season:

Keep the following tree-trimming essentials in a small toolbox to ensure the decorating process comes off without a hitch: wire cutter, glue, scissors, nylon fishing line, paper clips, narrow ribbon, and invisible tape.

6. All-Natural Noël

Crowned by a twig star and decked with a garland of red burlap, this towering tree delights with DIY ornaments: dried orange slices and lady apples (page 255), brown paper horns of plenty filled with berries (Holly Cornucopias, page 256), walnuts gilded with gold paint, mini cranberry wreaths, and large pinecones tucked into the boughs. Underneath, presents are adorned with equally organic flourishes, including holly and kumquats.

7. Birds' Nest Tree

Create a cozy perch for some feathered friends by placing twigs, wreaths, and juniper berries among the boughs. A grapevine wreath studded with bright berries creates a rustic topper.

7

TREE-DECORATOR'S CALCULATOR: HOW MUCH IS ENOUGH?

Follow these guidelines to strike a balance between bare branches and ornament overload. As a rule, you'll need one set of 50 lights per foot of tree.

TREE HEIGHT	NUMBER OF BULBS	NUMBER OF DECORATIONS
2 feet	100 to 150	25 to 35
3 feet	150 to 250	35 to 50
4 feet	200 to 350	50 to 75
6 feet	300 to 450	100 to 150
7 feet	350 to 550	150 to 200

8. Think Pink (and Green) Tree

What's good for Lilly Pulitzer is even better for a tree! Hot-pink and lime-green bows are tied directly to the boughs; grosgrain ribbons form a preppy garland encircling the tree.

9. Red, White, and Blue Beauty

A candy-cane-inspired palette really pops when a blue spruce is trimmed with touches of turquoise and teal. Presents are wrapped in pristine white paper and tied with red-and-white-striped ribbons. The DIY ornaments are made from fabric (rosettes, covered cookie cutters) and candy (ribbon curliques and peppermint garland); see Candy-Striper Ornaments, page 257, for how-to.

ECO-SMART TREES

Support local agriculture and buy a Christmas tree grown in your area. You can find nearby farms at localharvest. org. Afterward compost the tree.

Or purchase an artificial tree that you can use and store year after year. Unlike the forthrightly fake imposters of the past, the best of today's faux trees could pass for freshly chopped. Another big improvement: Most artificial Christmas trees are pre-lit, so you can skip the temper-fraying ritual of detangling wires and distributing lights evenly around the branches. Disassembly is also easier: The trunk separates into sections; then you fold up the branches, which are hinged.

ORNAMENTS WITH HOMEMADE CHARM

No need to spend a bundle on trimmings for your tree. You can make your own ornaments; inspiration—and instructions—provided below.

1. Woven-Ribbon Ornaments

Weave high-contrast ribbon to create these simple ornaments. Layer lengths within mini embroidery hoops, using double-stick tape around the inner hoop to hold the ribbon in place.

2. Clearly Christmas

For a fresh way to deck the halls, look no further than your own Tannenbaum to make these simple, stunning ornaments. Start by snipping sprigs of greenery off your tree and gathering some ribbon and red beads (these will be the berries). Purchase plain glass ornaments from a hobby store or online. Carefully remove the ornament tops, place the sprigs and beads inside, and replace the tops. Hang with ribbon, adding a holiday greeting on a strip of paper, if you like.

3. Cavorting Caribou

Follow our online template (goodhousekeeping.com/holidays/christmas-ideas) or draw your own to craft these charming fabric caribou. The star ornament above comes together in minutes with leftover wheat reeds, wooden craft shapes, a red marker, and some hot glue.

To make 24 caribou, you'll need ½ yard fabric, stiff iron-on fusible backing from a fabric store, wire for hanging, an X-Acto knife, and sharp scissors. Choose a cotton patterned fabric, and follow the manufacturer's instructions to iron it onto the fusible web. Download our pattern and trace it onto the back of the webbing. Using your sharp scissors, cut it out. Pierce a small slit on top of the caribou back with your X-Acto knife and slide a 3-inch wire through to create a hanger.

4. Seasonal Fruit Ornaments

If the commercialized razzle-dazzle of Christmas is leaving you feeling more frenzied than festive, try these rustic ornaments made from seasonal fruit.

Dried Oranges: Cut oranges crosswise into ¾-inch slices, keeping them as uniform as possible in thickness. Lay them on a baking sheet or aluminum foil in the oven set at the lowest temperature (around 150°F). Leave them to bake for about four hours, then turn with a spatula, checking them every hour until they seem almost dry with a bit of moisture left so they still have an orange color (they will continue to dry at room temperature). Create a tiny hole in the top of each slice with a small paring knife and string twine through each to hang on your tree.

Sweet Lady Apples: When selecting these mini apples, try to choose the ones that are 2 inches across or smaller so they're not too bulky (or heavy) to hang from the branches of your tree. To hang: Take a piece of floral wire long enough to poke about one third of the way through the apple (or until it feels secure), and leave enough wire to hook at the top to hang on your tree.

5. Holly Cornucopia

Add these horn-of-plenty ornaments to your tree as vessels for sprigs of holly and berries. Use a 12- to 14-inch bowl to trace circles on brown paper or brown grocery bags. Cut out each circle, then cut it in half. Fold each semicircle into thirds to form a triple-thick flattened cone. Cut through the three layers along the top to create a scalloped edge. Fold over the scallops in the "front" of the cone (this will be the side that faces you, if the cone is lying flat on a surface, and the overlapping "corners" are underneath). Squeeze in the sides to create a three-dimensional cone shape; staple together in back to secure. Thread with twine to hang. Fill with holly and berries.

6. Smart Cookies

Classic store-bought butter cookies can easily become enticing ornaments. Purchase a box or tin of them plus narrow velvet ribbon; cut ribbon into lengths of about 10 inches. Fold each length of ribbon in half, making a loop, pull it through a cookie's center, and pull the ribbon's ends through the loop, knotting the ends. Just make sure to hang them out of reach of pets and hungry tykes.

7. Horse Play

Gingerbread cookies in the shape of Dala horses—ponies that are a Swedish icon—make for the sweetest ornaments. Finish this edible décor with a white icing bridle and saddle, and hang with light-blue ribbon.

8. How Sweet It Is!

Fill shiny gold cones with foil-wrapped *baci*—delectable Italian hazelnut-chocolate balls—and dangle them from your tree. To make the cones, cut out a semicircle of gold metallic poster board and staple to form a cone. Line the top edge with velvet ribbon (we used teal for contrast), then staple a gold ribbon on the cones to make a hanger. Then, most important, fill with chocolates.

9. Doves in Flight

These elegant three-dimensional birds, shown here on an evergreen wreath, are surprisingly simple to make. All you need is white printer paper, some scissors, and a pencil. For a template and instructions, visit goodhousekeeping.com/holidaycrafts.

MAKE MERRY UNDER THE MISTLETOE

Encourage seasonal smooches with this no-fuss mistletoe ball. The ancient Druids considered this evergreen a sacred plant with mysterious medicinal powers. Now we know it's powerful enough to elicit a kiss!

Wrap a **4-inch Styrofoam ball** in a **14-inch fabric square**; secure with a **rubber band**. Thread the end of a **1½-yard length of ribbon** down through the rubber band, around the ball, and up through the rubber band's other side so the ribbon ends match up (knot them to hang the ball). Wrap **14 inches of ribbon** around the ball's other side (crossing the first ribbon, as shown), and tuck the ends into the rubber band. Hide the rubber band with **a shimmery bow** and **mistletoe, holly,** or **other festive sprigs** (faux or fresh).

CANDY-STRIPER ORNAMENTS

These easy-to-make ornaments deck out your tree in a tried-and-true Christmas combo—red and white! From a perky ribbon and button rosette to a sugary garland of peppermint candies, these are great projects to make with the kids. For a beauty shot of the complete, decorated tree, see page 253.

1. Give It a Whirl: With a bright button and a few fast folds, fabric ribbons turn into colorful Christmas rosettes. For each ornament you'll need: 17-inch length of 1½-inch ribbon, a to-scale felt disc (cut from a sheet of felt), a button of your choice, a short length of ⅛-inch ribbon (to loop as the ornament hanger), double-stick tape, a stapler, and a hot glue gun. Lay out the 1½" ribbon right side up and attach double-stick tape along the entire top edge. Starting at the left end, fold the ribbon at a slight angle in ½-inch increments, making sure to keep the center tight while flaring out the edges—this is how you make a circle; the tape keeps it intact. When you've completed the circle, secure the ends with a stapler. Next, grab a felt disc and glue it to the front center. Affix a cute button on top of the felt and attach a narrow ribbon loop to the back to hang.

2. Candy Land: The eye-catching curlicued crimps of ribbon candy don't require any extra enhancement—simply attaching a shiny ribbon transforms them into instant edible ornaments.

3. Cookie-Cutter Redux: Dressed up in a dainty dot print, favorite holiday cookie cutters can double as décor. Trace the cutter onto patterned wrapping paper, snip out the shape, and attach to the back of the cutter with clear tape.

4. Sugar Rush: All you need for this festive, no-fuss candy garland are cellophane-wrapped peppermints and clear tape. Attach candies end-to-end and drape from branch to branch—assembly is so effortless even your little elves can get in on the action.

Chapter 5

Sweet Finales

BEST-LOVED CAKES, PIES, PUDDINGS & COOKIES

Everyone at the table may say they're stuffed, but they'll always make room for dessert! Select a grand finale from our buffet of sweet and sensational options—or bake an assortment of cookies and other goodies so guests can indulge in more than one. From simple Wine-Poached Pears to a Ganache Tart with Salted-Almond Crust, you'll find treats here to please both you and your guests.

Cakes, Pies & Tarts

Choose from our Sticky Toffee Bundt Cake or Orange Custard Tart, Dulce de Leche Christmas Wreath or Chocolate-Raspberry Roll: Our step-by-step instructions make baking even the most impressive-looking cakes and pies easy. Consider organizing a dessert buffet that features a couple of these gorgeous desserts center stage. An assortment of cookies and bars—plus hot and cold beverages—are all you need to round out the party. For tips on finishing your pies with fancy fluted edges, see "A Trio of Decorative Crusts" on page 280.

Puddings & Fruity Desserts

Sweet finales like Cranberry Trifle, Wine-Poached Pears, and Pumpkin Crème Caramel are welcome at any holiday meal. Or delight your guests with figgy pudding, fruitcake, or one of the other nostalgic desserts from our holiday archives.

Cookies, Brownies & Bars

Who isn't sweet on these delightful holiday treats? From Pinwheels to Whole-Grain Gingersnaps to White-Chocolate-Dipped Peppermint Sticks, our cookie recipes are a pleasure to bake, give—and eat! Our tips on cookie decorating will help you elevate this fun craft to an art form, while our cookie-swap party plan ensures that all of your friends go home with an array of beautiful holiday cookies.

Clockwise from top left: CRANBERRY TRIFLE *(page 301)*; TIRAMISÙ *(page 305)*; WREATH HUNG WITH A FESTIVE STRIPED RIBBON.

Recipes

Crafts

CAKES

Chocolate-Raspberry Roll

This raspberry- and mascarpone-filled cake is our contemporary take on the traditional Bûche de Noël. The chocolate-frosted jelly-roll shape looks like a yule log; slicing it reveals a swirl of delectable raspberry filling.

Active time: 40 minutes
Total time: 55 minutes plus cooling and chilling
Makes: 12 servings

1 tablespoon water
1/3 cup plus 4 tablespoons granulated sugar
2 half-pints raspberries (6 ounces each)
6 squares (6 ounces) bittersweet chocolate, chopped
2 tablespoons butter or margarine
1/4 teaspoon salt
1/4 cup raspberry liqueur
6 large eggs, separated
3 tablespoons confectioners' sugar
1 cup heavy cream
1/2 cup mascarpone cheese

1 Preheat oven to 350°F. Grease 18" by 12" jelly-roll pan. Line with parchment paper; grease paper.

2 In medium bowl, stir water and 2 tablespoons granulated sugar. Fold in berries. Let stand while preparing cake.

3 Fill 4-quart saucepan with *2 inches water*. Heat to simmering. In large heatproof bowl, combine chocolate, butter, salt, and 2 tablespoons liqueur; set bowl over pan, stirring until smooth. Remove from heat. Stir in egg yolks, one at a time, beating after each addition.

4 In large mixer bowl, with mixer on medium-high speed, beat egg whites until frothy. Gradually add 1/3 cup granulated sugar; beat until stiff peaks form. Gently fold whites into chocolate, one-third at a time, until incorporated. Spread batter evenly in pan.

5 Bake 15 minutes or until toothpick inserted in center comes out nearly clean. Cool in pan on wire rack 10 minutes. Dust top of cake with 2 tablespoons confectioners' sugar; place sheet of waxed paper on top of cake. Set cutting board over cake, then flip board and pan together. Remove pan and peel off parchment. Cool.

6 In large bowl, with mixer on medium-high speed, beat cream and mascarpone until soft peaks form. Add remaining 2 tablespoons each granulated sugar and liqueur. Beat until stiff; spread over cake, leaving 1/2-inch border.

7 Starting from 1 long side, roll cake, peeling off paper in process. (Cake may crack slightly during rolling.) Place on platter, cover with plastic wrap, and refrigerate at least 1 hour or up to 1 day. (Refrigerate berries if making ahead.)

8 Dust with remaining 1 tablespoon confectioners' sugar. Serve with raspberries.

Each serving: About 305 calories, 6g protein, 26g carbohydrate, 22g total fat (12g saturated), 3g fiber, 115mg sodium

Clockwise from top left: CINNAMON CRUMB CAKE *(page 275)*; CHOCOLATE-RASPBERRY ROLL *(above)*; CRANBERRY-VANILLA CAKE WITH WHIPPED CREAM FROSTING *(page 271)*; WINDOW DRESSING *(page 106)*.

Amaretto Apricot Cake

Almond paste helps keep this fruit-studded Bundt moist. The cake can be made ahead of time and glazed just before serving. Garnish with raspberries and fresh mint for a holiday touch.

Active time: 25 minutes
Total time: 1 hour 35 minutes plus cooling and standing
Makes: 16 servings

2½ cups all-purpose flour
1 teaspoon baking powder
¼ teaspoon baking soda
½ teaspoon salt
1 tube (7 ounces) almond paste
1½ cups granulated sugar
6 ounces dried apricots, preferably California
   (1¾ cups; see Tip)
1½ sticks butter or margarine, softened
5 large eggs, lightly beaten
2 tablespoons amaretto or 1 teaspoon vanilla extract
8 ounces sour cream, at room temperature
1 cup confectioners' sugar
1 to 2 tablespoons fresh lemon juice
Raspberries for garnish
Fresh mint leaves for garnish

1 Preheat oven to 325°F. Coat 10-cup (10-inch) fluted baking pan (such as Bundt) with baking spray with flour.

2 On large sheet of waxed paper, combine 2 cups flour, baking powder, baking soda, and salt.

3 In food processor with knife blade attached, pulse almond paste and sugar until finely ground. Transfer to large bowl. In same food processor (no need to wipe bowl), pulse apricots and remaining ½ cup flour until finely chopped.

4 Add butter to bowl with almond sugar. With mixer on medium-high speed, beat 7 minutes or until pale and fluffy. With mixer on medium speed, add eggs gradually and then add amaretto until incorporated, occasionally scraping bowl with rubber spatula.

5 With mixer on low speed, add flour mixture alternately with sour cream, beginning and ending with flour mixture, scraping bowl occasionally, until batter is smooth. With rubber spatula, fold in apricot mixture until blended.

6 Transfer batter to prepared pan. Bake 1 hour 15 minutes or until toothpick inserted in center of cake comes out clean. Cool cake in pan on wire rack 15 minutes, then invert onto rack and cool completely. Cake can be kept at room temperature in airtight container up to 3 days. Cake can also be frozen, tightly wrapped in plastic wrap, up to 1 month.

7 To serve, place cake on serving plate. In small bowl, stir confectioners' sugar and 1 tablespoon lemon juice until well mixed. Add more lemon juice if necessary to achieve consistency of honey. Pour over cake to glaze. Garnish with raspberries and mint leaves. Allow glaze to set about 5 minutes before slicing.

TIP: California apricots have a wonderful tart flavor and bright orange color. This cake would also be delicious made with dried tart cherries.

Each serving: About 390 calories, 6g protein, 55g carbohydrate, 17g total fat (8g saturated), 2g fiber, 225mg sodium

AMARETTO APRICOT CAKE *(opposite)*

Lemon-Ricotta Cheesecake

Lighter than a classic cheesecake—in texture and calories—this luscious cake makes a pretty and refreshing finish to any holiday meal.

Active time: 40 minutes
Total time: 1 hour 30 minutes plus cooling, standing, and chilling
Makes: 16 servings

1 cup graham cracker crumbs
4 tablespoons butter or margarine, softened
3 to 4 lemons
1¼ cups sugar
¼ cup cornstarch
2 packages (8 ounces each) Neufchâtel cheese, softened
1 container (15 ounces) part-skim ricotta cheese
4 large eggs
2 cups half-and-half or light cream
2 teaspoons vanilla extract

1 Preheat oven to 375°F. Wrap outside of 9-inch springform pan with heavy-duty foil to prevent batter from leaking out during baking.

2 In springform pan, with fork, mix graham cracker crumbs and butter until crumbs are moistened. With hand, press mixture firmly onto bottom of pan. Bake crust 10 minutes. Cool on wire rack about 15 minutes.

3 Reset oven to 325°F. Meanwhile, from 2 lemons, grate 2 teaspoons peel and squeeze ⅓ cup juice. In small bowl, stir together sugar and cornstarch until blended. In large bowl, with mixer on medium speed, beat Neufchâtel and ricotta until smooth, about 5 minutes. Slowly beat in sugar mixture. Reduce speed to low; beat in eggs, half-and-half, vanilla, and lemon peel and juice just until blended, scraping bowl often with rubber spatula.

4 Pour batter onto crust. Bake cheesecake 1 hour. Turn off oven; let cheesecake remain in oven 1 hour.

5 Remove cheesecake from oven. To help prevent cracking during cooling, run a thin knife between edge

Top: LEMON-RICOTTA CHEESECAKE *(above);*
Bottom: DARK CHOCOLATE–RASPBERRY LAYER CAKE *(opposite).*

of cheesecake and pan as soon as cheesecake comes out of oven. Cool cake in pan on wire rack 2 hours. Cover and refrigerate cheesecake at least 6 hours or overnight, until well chilled.

6 To serve, remove foil and side of pan and place cake on plate. From remaining lemons, with sharp knife, cut 8 very thin center slices; use to garnish top of cheesecake.

Each serving: About 300 calories, 9g protein, 26g carbohydrate, 18g total fat (10g saturated), 0g fiber, 235mg sodium

Dark Chocolate-Raspberry Layer Cake

This celebratory showstopper brings together tangy cream-cheese frosting flavored with raspberries and three layers of intensely chocolaty cake.

Active time: 1 hour 5 minutes
Total time: 1 hour 25 minutes
Makes: 12 servings

Unsweetened cocoa, for dusting
9 ounces bittersweet chocolate (60 to 70 percent cacao; see Tip, page 289), chopped
3 ounces unsweetened chocolate, chopped
1 tablespoon vanilla extract
1/4 teaspoon salt
1 1/2 cups granulated sugar
1 cup plus 6 tablespoons (2 3/4 sticks) butter or margarine
6 tablespoons butter or margarine
8 large eggs, separated
1/2 cup all-purpose flour
1 pint raspberries
12 ounces cream cheese, softened
1/2 cup confectioners' sugar

1 Preheat oven to 350°F. Grease three 9-inch round cake pans. Line bottoms with parchment paper; grease paper. Lightly dust with cocoa, tapping out excess.

2 Fill 4-quart saucepan with *2 inches water*. Heat to simmering. In large heatproof bowl, combine both chocolates, vanilla, salt, 1 1/4 cups granulated sugar, and 10 tablespoons butter. Set over simmering water.

Gently stir occasionally until chocolates and butter melt. Remove from heat. While stirring, add egg yolks, one at a time, beating well after each addition. Gently fold in flour just until incorporated.

3 In another large bowl, with mixer on medium-high speed, beat egg whites until frothy. Gradually add remaining 1/4 cup granulated sugar and continue beating until stiff peaks form. Gently fold egg whites into chocolate mixture, one-third at a time, just until incorporated. Divide batter among prepared pans.

4 Bake 15 minutes or until cakes are set and toothpick inserted in centers comes out clean. Cool in pans on wire racks 10 minutes. Invert onto racks; remove pans (see Tip). Discard parchment paper; cool completely.

5 Place 1/2 cup raspberries in fine-mesh sieve set over small bowl. With wooden spoon, mash raspberries to extract 2 tablespoons juice; discard solids. In large bowl, with mixer on medium speed, beat cream cheese and remaining 12 tablespoons butter until smooth and fluffy. Beat in confectioners' sugar, then raspberry juice, until blended. If thin and runny, refrigerate 5 minutes to achieve frosting consistency. Transfer to piping bag fitted with 1/2-inch plain tip.

6 Place one cake layer on cake stand. Decoratively pipe on one-third of frosting. Top with another cake layer and one-third of frosting. Repeat, piping remaining frosting on final layer. Decorate top of cake with raspberries and serve slices with any remaining raspberries. Refrigerate up to 1 day. Bring to room temperature before serving.

TIP: During one of our recipe tests, a layer of this dense yet delicate cake cracked when turned out of its pan. To prevent that mishap, we found that the best way to invert any cake and remove it from a pan is this: Place a wire rack directly over the top of the cake pan first. Then hold the pan and rack together and flip both over. Carefully lift off the pan; peel off the parchment paper and let cool as directed.

Each serving: About 670 calories, 10g protein, 57g carbohydrate, 47g total fat (28g saturated), 4g fiber, 205mg sodium

Double-Chocolate Bundt

In this tribute to the classic cake, coffee amps up the cocoa, and buttermilk makes slices nice and moist.

Active time: 25 minutes
Total time: 1 hour 25 minutes
Makes: 16 servings

Cake

1 cup unsweetened cocoa, divided
2¼ cup all-purpose flour
1¾ cup granulated sugar
2 teaspoons baking soda
1 teaspoon baking powder
1 teaspoon salt
1 cup buttermilk
1 cup strong coffee, cold
2/3 cup vegetable oil
2 large eggs
1½ teaspoon vanilla extract

Glaze

3 ounces semisweet chocolate, melted
4 tablespoons butter, melted
¼ cup confectioners' sugar
¼ cup sour cream
2 tablespoons strong coffee, cold
¼ teaspoon vanilla extract
1/8 teaspoon salt

1 Prepare Cake: Preheat oven to 350°F. Generously grease 12-cup Bundt pan; dust with ¼ cup cocoa. Into large bowl, sift flour, sugar, baking soda, baking powder, salt and remaining ¾ cup cocoa.

2 In medium bowl, with mixer on medium speed, beat buttermilk, coffee, oil, eggs, and vanilla until smooth. Gradually beat flour mixture into buttermilk mixture just until blended. Transfer to prepared Bundt pan. Bake 45 to 55 minutes or until toothpick inserted comes out clean.

3 Cool completely in pan on wire rack. Loosen sides with offset spatula. Invert onto wire rack and remove pan.

4 Prepare Glaze: In medium bowl, whisk chocolate and butter. Add confectioners' sugar, sour cream, coffee, vanilla and salt; stir until smooth. Pour over chocolate cake. Let stand at room temperature until set, about 4 hours.

Each serving: About 335 calories, 5g protein, 44 g carbohydrate, 17g total fat (5g saturated), 3g fiber, 405mg sodium

Midnight Mocha Cheesecake

This indulgent, gluten-free cheesecake recipe is perfect for those who crave a little coffee with their sweet treats.

Active time: 15 minutes
Total time: 2 hours, 20 minutes plus cooling and chilling
Makes: 16 servings

2 cups gluten-free crispy chocolate cookie crumbs
4 tablespoons butter
2 tablespoons sugar, plus 1 cup
1/8 teaspoon salt
8 ounces bittersweet chocolate
¼ cup cold strong coffee
1 tablespoon instant espresso powder
1 teaspoon vanilla extract
3 packages cream cheese
¼ cup unsweetened cocoa
4 large eggs

1 Preheat oven to 325°F. Spray 9-inch springform pan with nonstick cooking spray. In medium bowl, combine crumbs, butter, 2 tablespoons sugar, and salt; transfer to prepared pan. Press into even layer that comes up side of pan slightly. Place on rimmed baking sheet. Bake 10 minutes. Cool completely.

2 Meanwhile, in small microwave-safe bowl, microwave 6 ounces chocolate on high in 30-second intervals or until mostly melted, stirring in between; let cool. In small bowl, stir together coffee, espresso powder, and vanilla. With mixer on medium-high speed, beat cream cheese until smooth. Reduce speed to low. Beat in cocoa and remaining 1 cup sugar, scraping down side of bowl occasionally. Beat in coffee mixture. Increase speed to medium. Add eggs one at a time, beating well between additions, scraping down side of bowl occasionally. Beat in melted chocolate just until well mixed. Pour batter into cooled crust. Bake 50 minutes on rimmed baking sheet.

3 Turn oven off and prop door open with wooden spoon. Let cheesecake stand in oven 1 hour. With small icing spatula or knife, loosen side of cheesecake from pan. Refrigerate, uncovered, 2 hours or up to 2 days.

4 When ready to serve, loosen cheesecake once more from side of pan; remove springform ring. In small microwave-safe bowl, microwave remaining 2 ounces chocolate on high 30 seconds or until just melted, stirring. Drizzle over cheesecake.

Per serving: About 400 calories, 6g protein, 32g carbohydrate, 28g total fat (16g saturated), 1g fiber, 300mg sodium

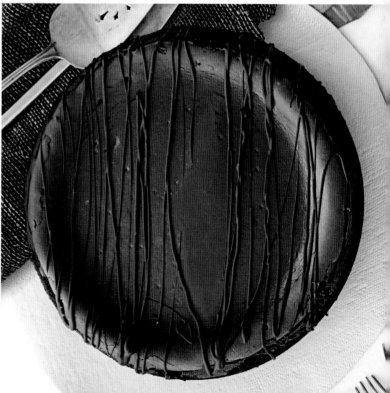

Top: DOUBLE-CHOCOLATE BUNDT *(opposite)*;
Bottom: MIDNIGHT MOCHA CHEESECAKE *(opposite)*.

Cranberry-Vanilla Cake
with Whipped Cream Frosting

This pretty cake features three delectable layers slathered with a cranberry filling, all topped with gobs of creamy whipped frosting. To make it extra festive, we finished it with a candied cranberry garnish.

Active time: 50 minutes
Total time: 1 hour 40 minutes plus cooling and chilling
Makes: 16 servings

Vanilla Cake

3 cups cake flour (not self-rising)
1 tablespoon baking powder
1/4 teaspoon salt
1 cup (2 sticks) butter or margarine, at room temperature
2 cups granulated sugar
5 large eggs, at room temperature
2 teaspoons vanilla extract
1 1/4 cups low-fat buttermilk

Cranberry Filling

1 bag (12 ounces) fresh or thawed frozen cranberries (3 cups)
1 cup granulated sugar
1/3 cup apricot jam
1/4 teaspoon ground cinnamon

Candied Cranberry Garnish

1/4 cup water
3/4 cup granulated sugar
1 cup fresh or thawed frozen cranberries

Whipped Cream Frosting

2 cups heavy cream
1 cup confectioners' sugar
1/3 cup crème fraîche or sour cream
1 teaspoon vanilla extract

1 Prepare cake: Preheat oven to 350°F. Line bottoms of three 8-inch cake pans with parchment paper. Grease sides of pans and parchment. Into large bowl, sift flour, baking powder, and salt.

2 In large mixer bowl, with mixer on medium-high speed, beat butter and sugar until smooth and fluffy. Beat in eggs, one at a time, until incorporated. Beat in vanilla. Reduce speed to low; alternately add buttermilk and flour mixture in two or three parts, beating well after each addition.

3 Divide batter evenly among pans; smooth tops. Tap pans firmly against counter. Bake 40 to 45 minutes or until toothpick inserted in center comes out clean. Cool on wire rack 10 minutes. Invert cakes onto rack; remove pans and peel off parchment. Cool completely. Cakes may be wrapped in plastic and stored at room temperature up to 1 day.

4 Prepare filling: In 3-quart saucepan, combine cranberries, sugar, jam, and cinnamon. Cook on medium 8 to 10 minutes or until most berries burst, stirring often. Transfer to bowl; refrigerate until cold.

5 Prepare garnish: In 1-quart saucepan, combine water and 1/4 cup sugar. Heat to boiling on high. Stir in cranberries. Cool completely, then drain. Place remaining 1/2 cup sugar on plate. Toss berries in sugar to coat. Place on wire rack; let dry 1 hour.

6 To assemble: Place 1 cake layer on cake stand; spread half of filling on top. Repeat with another layer and remaining filling. Top with third layer.

7 Prepare frosting: With mixer on medium speed, whisk cream until soft peaks form. Reduce speed to low; add confectioners' sugar, crème fraîche, and vanilla. Whisk until stiff peaks form. Spread frosting all over cake. Garnish with sugared berries. Cake can be covered and refrigerated up to 1 day. Remove from refrigerator 30 minutes before serving.

Each serving: About 590 calories, 6g protein, 85g carbohydrate, 26g total fat (16g saturated), 2g fiber, 300mg sodium

Clockwise from top: Cranberry-Vanilla Cake with Whipped Cream Frosting *(above)*; Sticky Toffee Bundt Cake *(page 274)*; Chocolate-Raspberry Roll *(page 263)*.

Dulce de Leche Christmas Wreath

This cream-puff pastry wreath, filled with caramel and cream, is special-occasion-worthy.

Active time: 40 minutes
Total time: 1 hour 45 minutes
Makes: 12 servings

½ cup butter or margarine (1 stick)
1 cup water
¼ teaspoon salt
1 cup all-purpose flour
4 large eggs, at room temperature
1 cup heavy cream
1 can (13 to 14 ounces) dulce de leche
1½ cups sliced almonds (6 ounces) toasted (page 287)
2 tablespoons confectioners' sugar
Raspberries for garnish
Fresh mint leaves for garnish

1 Preheat oven to 425°F. Line large cookie sheet with parchment paper. Using 8-inch plate or cake pan as guide, with pencil, trace circle on parchment. Flip parchment over on cookie sheet so pencil line does not touch food.

2 In 3-quart saucepan, heat butter, water, and salt to boiling on medium-high. Reduce heat to medium-low and add flour. Stir continuously 1 minute or until mixture leaves side of pan and forms ball. Continue stirring 2 to 3 minutes or until mixture begins to coat bottom of saucepan. Transfer to large mixer bowl and cool 2 minutes.

3 With mixer on medium speed, beat mixture 1 minute. Continue beating and add eggs, one at a time, then beat 2 to 3 minutes longer or until satiny. Mixture should still be warm and cling to side of bowl. Transfer dough to large piping bag fitted with ¾-inch plain tip or to large resealable plastic bag with one corner cut off to form ¾-inch hole.

4 Using circle traced on parchment as guide, pipe dough onto parchment in 1-inch-thick ring just inside circle. Pipe second ring inside of first, making sure dough rings touch. With remaining dough, pipe third ring on top of center seam of first two rings. With moistened finger, gently smooth dough rings where ends meet.

5 Bake 20 minutes. Reset oven control to 375°F and bake 25 minutes longer, or until golden. Remove wreath from oven and, with tip of small knife, make several small slits all over to release steam. Return to oven to bake 10 minutes longer. Cool wreath completely on cookie sheet on wire rack. (Cooled wreath can be stored in resealable plastic bag at room temperature for up to 2 days. Before serving, recrisp in 325°F oven for 10 minutes and allow to cool before proceeding.)

6 While wreath is cooling, whip cream until soft peaks form. In large bowl, with mixer or wooden spoon, beat dulce de leche 5 minutes or until soft. Gently fold almonds into dulce de leche. With long serrated knife, slice wreath horizontally in half; remove and discard moist dough from inside. With spoon or spatula, spread almond mixture into bottom of wreath; top with whipped cream. Replace top of wreath.

7 To serve, dust wreath with confectioners' sugar and garnish with raspberries and mint leaves.

Each serving: About 370 calories, 8g protein, 31g carbohydrate, 25g total fat (11g saturated), 2g fiber, 160mg sodium

CHOUX PASTRY

Compared with more elaborate pastry recipes, choux pastry is almost laughably easy to make.

It is cooked twice, first in a saucepan on the stovetop and then in the oven. It makes a light, airy hollow pastry that is perfect for filling with pastry cream, whipped cream, or ice cream. Here we sandwich it with dulce de leche and whipped cream.

Dulce de Leche Christmas Wreath (*opposite*)

Sticky Toffee Bundt Cake

If you love traditional sticky toffee pudding, then you'll love this cake featuring the same flavors, including a gooey caramel glaze.

Active time: 35 minutes
Total time: 1 hour 40 minutes plus cooling
Makes: 16 servings

1 cup chopped pitted dates (5 ounces)
1 cup water
2 teaspoons ground ginger
1 teaspoon baking soda
2 cups all-purpose flour
1 teaspoon baking powder
1/8 teaspoon plus pinch salt
1 cup (2 sticks) butter or margarine, at room temperature (see Tip)
1¼ cups packed dark brown sugar
1¼ cups granulated sugar
3 large eggs, at room temperature
2½ teaspoons vanilla extract
1 tablespoon light corn syrup
1/3 cup heavy cream
Red and green grapes for garnish

1 In 2-quart saucepan, combine dates and water. Heat to boiling on high. Remove from heat. Stir in ginger and baking soda. Cool completely.

2 Preheat oven to 350°F. Grease and flour 10-cup Bundt pan. Into large bowl, sift flour, baking powder, and 1/8 teaspoon salt; set aside.

3 In another large bowl, with mixer on medium speed, beat ¾ cup butter and 1 cup each brown and granulated sugars until very well combined. Beat in eggs, one at a time, scraping side of bowl occasionally. Beat in 2 teaspoons vanilla extract. Add flour mixture and date mixture in alternation in two or three parts, beating well in between additions, until combined.

4 Pour batter into prepared pan. Bake 55 minutes to 1 hour or until toothpick inserted in center comes out clean. Cool in pan on wire rack 15 minutes. Invert pan onto wire rack. Cool completely. At this point, cooled cake can be wrapped tightly in plastic and stored at room temperature up to 1 day.

5 In 3-quart saucepan, combine corn syrup and remaining 4 tablespoons butter and ¼ cup each brown sugar and granulated sugar. Cook on medium 3 minutes or until sugar has dissolved and syrup bubbles, stirring constantly. Stir in cream, remaining ½ teaspoon vanilla extract, and pinch of salt. Cook another 2 minutes, stirring constantly. Let cool 5 minutes.

6 Place sheet of waxed paper under cake. Pour caramel sauce over top of cooled cake and allow sauce to drip down sides. Let caramel set. Transfer cake to serving plate. Garnish with grapes.

TIP: If you're using margarine for the glaze, refrigerate it until it thickens before pouring it over the cake.

Each serving: About 355 calories, 3g protein, 54g carbohydrate, 14g total fat (9g saturated), 1g fiber, 265mg sodium

Cinnamon Crumb Cake

The perfect choice for a buffet-style holiday brunch, this freeze-with-ease coffee cake can be completed a month in advance. Just be sure to wrap it tightly before freezing.

Active time: 25 minutes

Total time: 1 hour 15 minutes plus cooling

Makes: 10 servings

½ cup pecans, toasted (page 287) and chopped

⅓ cup packed dark brown sugar

1¾ cups all-purpose flour

½ teaspoon ground cinnamon

6 tablespoons butter or margarine, softened

1 teaspoon baking powder

¼ teaspoon baking soda

¼ teaspoon salt

¾ cup granulated sugar

1 teaspoon vanilla extract

2 large eggs

⅔ cup sour cream

1 In small bowl, mix pecans, brown sugar, ¼ cup flour, and cinnamon until well blended. With fingertips, work in 2 tablespoons butter until mixture resembles marbles. Set aside.

2 Preheat oven to 350°F. Grease 9-inch springform pan (see Tip); dust with flour. On sheet of waxed paper, mix remaining 1½ cups flour, baking powder, baking soda, and salt until combined.

3 In large bowl, with mixer on medium speed, beat granulated sugar, remaining 4 tablespoons butter, and vanilla 5 to 6 minutes or until mixture is fluffy, occasionally scraping bowl with rubber spatula. Reduce speed to low; add eggs one at a time, beating well after each addition.

4 With mixer on low speed, add flour mixture alternately with sour cream, beginning and ending with flour mixture, scraping bowl occasionally, until batter is smooth.

5 Pour batter into prepared pan. Sprinkle with crumb topping and gently press into batter. Bake 40 to 45 minutes, until toothpick inserted in center of cake comes out clean. To serve warm, cool cake in pan on wire rack 15 minutes. With small metal spatula, loosen cake from side of pan and remove, then cool an additional 30 minutes. To serve later, cool cake completely in pan, then cover tightly with plastic wrap.

TIP: A springform pan allows you to remove the sides and bottom so you can display the finished product to full advantage on a cake stand. If you don't own a springform one, you can use a regular 9-inch cake pan. Line the bottom with parchment for easy release.

Each serving: About 300 calories, 5g protein, 37g carbohydrate, 15g total fat (7g saturated), 1g fiber, 225mg sodium

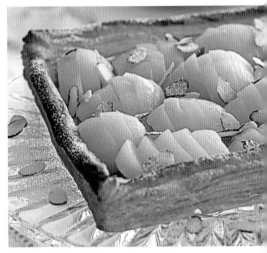

Merry Christmas

PIES & TARTS

Cherry Hazelnut Linzer Tart

Here, sour cherry preserves step in for the more traditional raspberry filling. For a playful touch, we've decorated the top of the tart with stand-up Christmas tree cookies made from the tart dough.

Active time: 30 minutes
Total time: 1 hour 10 minutes plus chilling and cooling
Makes: 12 servings

2/3 cup hazelnuts (filberts, toasted, skinned, and cooled (page 287)
1 1/4 cups all-purpose flour
1/4 teaspoon baking powder
1/4 teaspoon salt
1/2 cup butter (1 stick), softened (no substitutions)
1/2 cup granulated sugar
1/4 teaspoon ground cinnamon
1/4 teaspoon ground cloves
1 large egg, separated
1 teaspoon vanilla extract
1 cup sour cherry preserves
3 tablespoons confectioners' sugar

1 Preheat oven to 375°F.

2 In food processor with knife blade attached, pulse nuts, flour, baking powder, and salt until finely ground.

3 In large bowl, with mixer on medium-high speed, beat butter, sugar, cinnamon, and cloves 3 minutes or until pale and fluffy. Set aside 1 tablespoon egg white. With mixer on medium, beat in remaining egg white and yolk, then vanilla, until blended, occasionally scraping bowl.

4 With mixer on low speed, gradually add nut mixture. Beat 2 minutes or until blended. Transfer two-thirds of dough to 9-inch tart pan with removable bottom; transfer remaining to pastry bag fitted with 1/3-inch plain round tip. Press dough evenly into bottom and up side of pan. Freeze 20 minutes. Brush reserved egg white on bottom crust. Spread preserves evenly over tart. Pipe dough in bag in straight lines, 1 inch apart, across top. Pipe additional straight lines, 1 inch apart, diagonally over first lines to form lattice pattern. Bake 35 minutes or until browned.

5 Meanwhile, line cookie sheet with parchment. Transfer remaining dough onto sheet of waxed paper; cover with second sheet. Roll to 1/8-inch thickness. Freeze 5 minutes. With 2" by 1" tree cookie cutter, cut out as many cookies as possible; transfer to cookie sheet. Bake 7 to 9 minutes or until golden brown.

6 Cool cookies and tart in pan completely on wire racks. Remove side of pan. Dust cookies and tart with confectioners' sugar. Insert cookies upright into tart.

Each serving: About 265 calories, 3g protein, 38g carbohydrate, 12g total fat (5g saturated), 1g fiber, 120mg sodium

Clockwise from top left: ORANGE CUSTARD TART *(page 288);* DOUBLE-CRUST APPLE PIE *(page 285);* PEAR-FRANGIPANE TART *(page 286);* CHERRY HAZELNUT LINZER TART *(above);* CLEARLY CHRISTMAS *(page 255).*

Black-Bottom Chocolate Cream Pie

This pie is seriously decadent—a luscious chocolate custard fills a crust made of crushed chocolate cookies.

Active time: 45 minutes
Total time 50 minutes plus cooling and chilling
Makes: 12 servings

24 chocolate wafer cookies
6 tablespoons butter or margarine
1 cup plus 3 tablespoons sugar
1/3 cup cornstarch
1/4 teaspoon salt
3 1/2 cups milk
4 large egg yolks
3 ounces unsweetened chocolate, finely chopped
1 cup heavy or whipping cream

1 Preheat oven to 375°F. In food processor, pulse wafers into very fine crumbs. (You should have 1 1/4 cups.) In medium bowl, melt 4 tablespoons butter; add crumbs and 1 tablespoon sugar. Stir until moistened. Firmly press mixture into bottom and up side of 9-inch pie plate. Bake 10 to 12 minutes or until set. Cool on wire rack.

2 In heavy 3-quart saucepan, whisk cornstarch, salt, and 1 cup sugar. While whisking, gradually add milk. Cook on medium-high, whisking constantly, 7 to 8 minutes or until boiling and thickened. Remove from heat.

3 In large bowl, whisk egg yolks until blended. Whisk in hot milk mixture in steady stream. Return mixture to saucepan and cook on medium heat, stirring constantly, 4 to 6 minutes or until mixture boils and thickens. Remove from heat and add chocolate. Stir until melted, then stir in remaining 2 tablespoons butter until melted.

4 Pour mixture into cooled pie crust and spread evenly. Press sheet of plastic wrap directly against surface. Refrigerate at least 4 hours, or up to overnight.

5 When ready to serve, beat cream until thickened; gradually beat in remaining 2 tablespoons sugar. Beat until soft peaks form. Dollop whipped cream to cover.

Each serving: About 365 calories, 5g protein, 39g carbohydrate, 22g total fat (13g saturated), 2g fiber, 185mg sodium

Cranberry Almond Pie

This dessert will surely satisfy a sweet tooth! It's easy to make and just right for the holidays.

Active time: 30 minutes
Total time: 1 hour 35 minutes plus chilling and cooling
Makes: 12 servings

1 tube (7 ounces) almond paste
4 tablespoons butter or margarine, softened
1/2 cup plus 2/3 cup sugar
3 large eggs
1/4 cup all-purpose flour
Pinch salt
9-Inch Baked Pie Shell (see opposite), baked and cooled
1 bag (12 ounces) cranberries (3 cups)
1/3 cup water
1/2 teaspoon grated fresh orange peel, plus additional for garnish

1 Preheat oven to 350°F. In food processor with knife blade attached, blend almond paste, butter, and 1/2 cup sugar until smooth. Add eggs, flour, and salt; blend until well mixed, occasionally scraping down side of processor bowl with rubber spatula.

2 Pour almond filling into pie shell. Bake 30 to 33 minutes or until filling is slightly puffed and golden. Cool completely on wire rack, about 3 hours.

3 Meanwhile, in 2-quart saucepan, combine 1 1/2 cups cranberries with remaining 2/3 cup sugar, water, and 1/2 teaspoon orange peel; heat to boiling on high. Reduce heat to medium-low; simmer 5 minutes or until mixture thickens slightly and most cranberries have popped, stirring occasionally. Stir in remaining cranberries. Set cranberry topping aside to cool to room temperature.

4 Spoon cranberry topping over almond filling just before serving; garnish with additional orange peel. Refrigerate any leftovers up to 4 days.

Each serving: About 350 calories, 5g protein, 43g carbohydrate, 18g total fat (7g saturated), 2g fiber, 170mg sodium

9-INCH BAKED PIE SHELL

Use this foolproof basic crust as the foundation for as many pies as you can dream up.

Active time: 20 minutes · Total time: 40 minutes plus chilling and cooling · Makes: 1 (9-inch) pie shell

1¹⁄₃ cups all-purpose flour
¹⁄₄ teaspoon salt
5 tablespoons cold butter or margarine, cut up

3 tablespoons vegetable shortening
4 to 5 tablespoons ice water

1 In food processor with knife blade attached, blend flour and salt. Add butter and shortening, and pulse until mixture resembles coarse crumbs. Sprinkle in ice water, 1 tablespoon at a time, pulsing after each addition, until large, moist crumbs just begin to form.

2 Shape dough into disk; wrap in plastic and refrigerate 30 minutes or overnight. (If chilled overnight, let dough stand 30 minutes at room temperature before rolling.)

3 Preheat oven to 425°F. On lightly floured surface, with floured rolling pin, roll dough into 12-inch round. Ease dough round into 9-inch glass or ceramic pie plate. Gently press dough against bottom and up sides of plate without stretching. Trim dough edge, leaving 1-inch overhang. Fold overhang under; pinch to form stand-up edge, then make decorative edge (see "A Trio of Decorative Crusts" on page 280). Freeze pie shell 15 minutes.

4 Line pie shell with foil or parchment and fill with pie weights, dried beans, or uncooked rice. Bake 10 to 12 minutes or until beginning to set. Remove foil with weights, and bake 13 to 15 minutes longer or until golden. If shell puffs up during baking, gently press it down with back of spoon. Cool on wire rack until ready to fill.

9-Inch Double Piecrust

To make crust for a double-crust pie, increase ingredients to 2¹⁄₂ cups all-purpose flour, ¹⁄₂ teaspoon salt, 10 tablespoons cold butter or margarine, 6 tablespoons vegetable shortening, and 6 to 7 tablespoons ice water. Follow mixing instructions above, then divide dough into 2 disks, making one slightly larger. Follow instructions for rolling and baking dough for bottom crust, using larger disk. When ready to place top crust on pie, roll remaining disk into 12-inch round and proceed as recipe directs.

Each ¹⁄₁₀ pie shell: About 150 calories, 2g protein, 14g carbohydrate, 10g total fat (5g saturated), 1g fiber, 120mg sodium

Deep-Dish Baked Pie Shell

Prepare 9-Inch Baked Pie Shell as directed, but increase all-purpose flour to 1½ cups and vegetable shortening to ¼ cup. Ease dough into 9½-inch deep-dish pie plate.

Each ¹⁄₁₀ pie shell: About 165 calories, 2g protein, 14g carbohydrate, 11g total fat (5g saturated), 1g fiber, 120mg sodium

Old-Fashioned Pecan Pie

Flaky homemade crust and copious amounts of dark corn syrup give this traditional pecan pie a leg up on the competition.

Active time: 25 minutes
Total time: 1 hour 25 minutes plus chilling and cooling
Makes: 10 servings

3/4 cup dark corn syrup

1/2 cup packed dark brown sugar

3 tablespoons butter or margarine, melted

1 teaspoon vanilla extract

Pinch salt

3 large eggs

1 1/2 cups pecan halves, toasted (page 287)

9-Inch Baked Pie Shell (page 279), baked and cooled
    at least 10 minutes

1 Preheat oven to 350°F.

2 In large bowl, with wire whisk, mix corn syrup, sugar, butter, vanilla, salt, and eggs until blended. With spoon, stir in pecans.

3 Pour filling into baked pie shell. Bake 43 to 45 minutes or until filling is set around edge but center jiggles slightly. Cool on wire rack at least 3 hours for easier slicing. Refrigerate leftovers up to 1 week.

TIP: For a grown-up version of this classic, add 2 tablespoons bourbon and 1/4 teaspoon freshly grated nutmeg to the egg mixture in step 2.

Each serving: About 410 calories, 5g protein, 41g carbohydrate, 27g total fat (9g saturated), 2g fiber, 220mg sodium

---

A TRIO OF DECORATIVE CRUSTS

These fancy, fluted edges are easier to create than you might think.

Crimped: Push one index finger against outer edge of rim between the index finger and thumb of other hand, as shown; pinch to make crimp. Repeat.

Forked: Fold overhanging dough under and press edge to lie flat. With floured fork, press dough to rim of plate; repeat around edge.

Turret: With kitchen shears, make cuts, 1/2 inch apart, around edge of crust. Fold cut sections alternately toward center and toward rim.

Old-Fashioned Pecan Pie *(opposite)*

Brown Sugar Pecan Pie

*A slice of this sweet, seasonal pie is the perfect finish to
Thanksgiving dinner.*

Active time: 40 minutes
Total time: 1 hour 20 minutes plus chilling and cooling
Makes: 12 servings

All-purpose flour
1 recipe 9-Inch Baked Pie Shell (page 279, complete
 through step 2)
1 cup packed dark brown sugar
 cup pure maple syrup
3 large eggs
3 tablespoons butter
1 tablespoon bourbon
¼ teaspoon salt
1 large egg white
2 cups pecan halves

1 Preheat oven to 375°F. On lightly floured surface,
with floured rolling pin, roll dough into 12-inch round.
Ease dough round into 9-inch glass or ceramic pie
plate. Gently press dough against bottom and up side
of plate without stretching. Trim dough edge, keeping
overhang intact. Transfer overhang to work surface.
From overhang, with ¾-inch decorative cookie cutter,
cut 40 shapes, rerolling if necessary, for decorating rim
of pie later. Refrigerate pie shell 15 minutes. Refrigerate
cut shapes until ready to use.

2 Line pie shell with foil or parchment and fill with
pie weights, dried beans, or uncooked rice. Bake 12 to
14 minutes or until beginning to set. Remove foil with
weights and bake 13 to 15 minutes longer or until golden.

3 Meanwhile, in large bowl, with wire whisk, mix sugar,
syrup, whole eggs, butter, bourbon, and salt until well
blended.

Top: Brown Sugar Pecan Pie *(above);*
Bottom: Sparkly Apple Slab Pie *(opposite).*

4 Place hot pie shell in 18" by 12" jelly-roll pan. Lightly brush rim of pie shell with egg white. Gently and carefully press cut shapes around rim. Spread pecans evenly in pie shell, then pour sugar mixture over them.

5 Bake 35 minutes or until filling is golden brown, puffed, and set around edge, but center still jiggles slightly. Cool completely on wire rack.

Each serving: About 395 calories, 5g protein, 43g carbohydrate, 24g total fat (7g saturated), 2g fiber, 180mg sodium

Sparkly Apple Slab Pie

Sparkling with sugar, this is a magical, must-try holiday treat.

Active time: 25 minutes

Total time: 1 hour 30 minutes plus chilling and cooling

Makes: 12 servings

3 cups all-purpose flour

1½ tablespoons granulated sugar

1½ teaspoons salt

1½ cups very cold butter, cubed

¾ cup cold water

⅓ cup cornstarch

½ teaspoon ground cinnamon

½ teaspoon ground ginger

¼ teaspoon ground allspice

3 pounds Golden Delicious apples, peeled and chopped

½ cup brown sugar

4 teaspoons lemon juice

2 tablespoons heavy cream or milk

2 tablespoons coarse sanding or turbinado sugar

1 In food processor, pulse flour, sugar, and 1 teaspoon salt until combined. Add half of butter; pulse until fine crumbs form. Add remaining butter; pulse just until coarse crumbs form. Add water in 2 batches, pulsing between additions and scraping side of bowl. Pulse just until dough starts to come together. Transfer dough to large bowl; gently knead 2 or 3 times until dough comes together. Divide into 4 equal-size mounds; shape into flat rectangles and wrap each tightly in plastic. Refrigerate at least 30 minutes or up to 2 days.

2 Preheat oven to 400°F. Line 15" by 10" rimmed baking sheet with parchment paper. Spray lightly with nonstick cooking spray. In large bowl, whisk together cornstarch, cinnamon, ginger, allspice, and remaining ½ teaspoon salt. Add apples, brown sugar, and lemon juice, tossing until apples are well coated; set aside.

3 Place 1 piece dough on lightly floured work surface. Lightly flour dough and roll into 12" by 9" rectangle, lightly flouring and scraping as needed to prevent sticking. Transfer to prepared baking sheet, placing 9-inch side along longest side of pan. Repeat rolling with another piece of dough. Transfer to other side of prepared baking sheet, overlapping slightly with first piece of dough. Press seam together to seal. Spread apple mixture over dough in even layer.

4 Repeat rolling process with third piece of dough. Place rectangle on top of one side of apple mixture, arranging 9-inch side along longest side of pan. Repeat rolling process with remaining piece of dough. Place rectangle on top of other side of apple mixture, overlapping slightly with other piece of dough. Press seam together to seal. Pinch edges of dough together to enclose filling. Brush top with cream and sprinkle with sugar. Cut 4 slits in top crust. Bake 1 hour and 10 minutes or until top is deep golden brown. Cool on wire rack before serving. Pie can be made up to 1 day ahead and kept at room temperature, covered.

Each serving: About 430 calories, 4g protein, 52g carbohydrate, 24g total fat (15g saturated fat), 2g fiber, 430mg sodium

DOUBLE-CRUST APPLE PIE *(opposite)*

Double-Crust Apple Pie

People with a passion for piecrust will appreciate this double-crust delight: Flaky layers of pastry encase a gently spiced apple filling. For a delectable tart-and-sweet flavor, use a mix of Granny Smith, Braeburn, and Golden Delicious apples.

Active time: 45 minutes
Total Time: 2 hours plus chilling and cooling
Makes: 10 servings

2/3 cup plus 1 teaspoon sugar
1/3 cup cornstarch
1/2 teaspoon ground cinnamon
1/4 teaspoon nutmeg
1/4 teaspoon salt
3 1/2 pounds Granny Smith, Golden Delicious, and/or Braeburn apples, each peeled, cored, and cut into 16 wedges
1 tablespoon fresh lemon juice
Unbaked dough for 9-Inch Double Piecrust (page 279)
2 tablespoons butter or margarine, cut up
1 large egg white, lightly beaten

1 Place cookie sheet on rack in lower third of oven and preheat oven to 400°F.

2 In large bowl, combine sugar with cornstarch, cinnamon, nutmeg, and salt. Add apples and lemon juice, and toss to coat evenly.

3 On lightly floured surface, with floured rolling pin, roll larger disk of chilled dough into 12-inch round. Ease dough into 9½-inch deep-dish glass or ceramic pie plate. Gently press dough against bottom and up side of plate without stretching. Trim dough edge, leaving 1-inch overhang; reserve trimmings. Spoon apple mixture into piecrust; dot with butter.

4 Roll remaining disk for top crust into 12-inch round. Center round over filling in bottom crust. Trim pastry edge, leaving 1-inch overhang; reserve trimmings. Fold overhang under; bring up over pie-plate rim and pinch to form stand-up edge, then make decorative edge (page 280). Brush crust with some egg white. Reroll trimmings. With knife or cookie cutters, cut out apple and leaf shapes; arrange on pie. Cut short slashes in round to allow steam to escape during baking. Brush cutouts with egg white, then sprinkle crust and cutouts with remaining 1 teaspoon sugar.

5 Bake pie 1 hour 10 minutes or until apples are tender when pierced with knife through slits in crust. To prevent overbrowning, cover pie loosely with tent of foil after 40 minutes. Cool pie on wire rack 3 hours to serve warm. Or cool completely to serve later.

Each serving: About 455 calories, 4g protein, 61g carbohydrate, 23g total fat (11g saturated), 4g fiber, 330mg sodium

Pear-Frangipane Tart

Packaged marzipan (a paste made of almonds and sugar)
makes this phyllo tart a snap to fill and bake.

Active time: 15 minutes
Total time: 40 minutes
Makes: 12 servings

1 sheet frozen puff pastry (half 17.3-ounce package), thawed
1/3 cup marzipan (half 7-ounce tube)
1 large egg white
1/4 cup sugar
2 tablespoons all-purpose flour
1 tablespoon dark Jamaican rum
1 can (28 ounces) pear halves in light syrup
2 tablespoons sliced almonds, toasted
1 tablespoon confectioners' sugar

1 Preheat oven to 400°F. On lightly floured surface,
unfold puff pastry sheet. With floured rolling pin, roll
pastry into 11" by 11" square. Cut ¾-inch-wide strips
from each side of pastry square. Transfer square to
lightly greased (or parchment-lined) baking sheet. Brush
edges of square with *water*. Place pastry strips on edges
of square to form border, trimming as necessary. Prick
center of square in many places with fork to reduce
puffing during baking. Bake shell 14 to 15 minutes or
until somewhat puffed and lightly browned.

2 Meanwhile, in food processor with knife blade attached,
mix marzipan, egg white, sugar, flour, and rum until
smooth. Remove from oven. Immediately spread marzipan
mixture evenly in shell. Return to oven and bake 9 to
10 minutes longer. Cool on cookie sheet on wire rack.

3 Drain pear halves and place on baking sheet lined with
paper towel. Keeping pear shape intact, thinly slice each
half crosswise into about 8 pieces. Arrange pear halves on
marzipan mixture, spreading slices slightly. To serve, top
tart with almonds and sprinkle with confectioners' sugar.

Each serving: About 210 calories, 3g protein, 28g carbohydrate,
11g total fat (2g saturated), 1g fiber, 27mg sodium

Top: PEAR-FRANGIPANE TART *(above)*;
Bottom: PUMPKIN PIE WITH PECAN BRITTLE *(opposite)*.

Pumpkin Pie with Pecan Brittle

Pure pumpkin filling, rather than prepared pie mix, gives this pie its ultra-fresh taste. Wow guests by topping each slice with our easier-than-it-looks pecan brittle.

Active time: 25 minutes
Total time: 1 hour 40 minutes plus cooling and chilling
Makes: 30 servings

Pumpkin Pie
Deep-Dish Baked Pie Shell (page 279)
3/4 cup sugar
3 large eggs
1 can (15 ounces) pure pumpkin (not pumpkin pie mix)
1 cup half-and-half or light cream
1 1/2 teaspoons pumpkin pie spice
1/2 teaspoon salt

Pecan Brittle (optional)
1/2 cup sugar
2 tablespoons water
2 tablespoons chopped pecans

Whipped Cream (optional)
1/2 cup heavy or whipping cream
1 tablespoon sugar

1 Prepare pie shell. Cool on wire rack at least 10 minutes. Reset oven control to 350°F.

2 In large bowl, with wire whisk, mix sugar and eggs until blended. Mix in pumpkin, half-and-half, pumpkin pie spice, and salt until smooth.

3 Pour filling into pie shell (see Tip). Bake 48 to 50 minutes or until edge is set but center still jiggles slightly. Cool pie completely on wire rack, about 4 hours to serve at room temperature. Or cool slightly, about 1 hour, then cover and refrigerate to serve cold later.

4 Prepare pecan brittle, if desired: Line large cookie sheet with foil; place sheet on wire rack. (Note: foil and cookie sheet will get very hot when topped with caramel.) In heavy 2-quart saucepan, heat sugar and water on medium heat until boiling. Cook about 5 minutes or until mixture turns golden. With heat-safe spatula, stir in pecans and cook 30 seconds. Working quickly and carefully, pour hot caramel onto foil and carefully lift and tilt cookie sheet slightly (holding foil in place) to spread caramel into a thin, even layer. Let brittle cool completely, about 30 minutes. When cool, peel foil away, and break brittle into 10 pieces to garnish pie.

5 When ready to serve, if you like, in medium bowl, with mixer on medium speed, beat cream with sugar until soft peaks form. Serve each slice of pie with a dollop of sweetened whipped cream, and garnish with a piece of pecan brittle. Refrigerate any leftovers up to 4 days.

Each serving without whipped cream and brittle: About 290 calories, 5g protein, 34g carbohydrate, 16g total fat (7g saturated), 2g fiber, 270mg sodium

TOASTING NUTS

These instructions work for walnuts, pecans, almonds, and hazelnuts.

• **Preheat the oven** to 350°F and position rack in the middle.

• **Spread out nuts** in a single layer on a rimmed baking pan; place it in the oven.

• **Bake** until the nuts are lightly browned, 10 to 15 minutes, stirring occasionally, moving the nuts in the center of the pan to the edges, where they will brown faster.

• **Immediately transfer** the nuts to a cool platter or baking pan to stop the browning.

• **If you're toasting just a few nuts,** heat them in a dry skillet over low heat for 3 to 5 minutes or until fragrant, stirring frequently.

TIP: To remove the bitter skins from hazelnuts, toast them as directed above until any portions without skin begin to brown. Transfer the nuts to a clean, dry kitchen towel and rub them until the skins come off.

Orange Custard Tart

Fill a vanilla-scented crust with a creamy citrus custard, and you have a beautiful tart that will brighten any holiday party. For an easy shortcut, see Tip.

Active time: 30 minutes
Total time: 1 hour 15 minutes plus chilling,
     freezing, and cooling
Makes: 8 servings

Vanilla Tart Crust
1¼ cups all-purpose flour
2 tablespoons sugar
¼ teaspoon salt
½ cup (1 stick) butter (no substitutions), chilled and cut up
1 large egg yolk
¼ teaspoon vanilla extract
2 to 3 tablespoons ice water (or more as needed)

Orange Custard Filling
¾ cup plus 6 tablespoons whole milk
2 large egg yolks
⅓ cup sugar
2 tablespoons cornstarch
2 tablespoons all-purpose flour
1 tablespoon butter (no substitutions)
⅛ teaspoon salt
1 vanilla bean or ¼ teaspoon vanilla extract
3 medium navel oranges (1¼ pounds)
2 tablespoons apple jelly
2 teaspoons triple sec
Red currants for garnish

1 Make crust: In food processor with knife blade attached, pulse flour, sugar, and salt until blended. Add butter. Pulse until mixture resembles coarse meal. Add egg yolk and vanilla; pulse until combined. Add ice water, 1 tablespoon at a time, pulsing until mixture holds together when pinched. Gather dough into ball; flatten into disk, wrap disk in plastic, and refrigerate until firm, at least 1 hour or up to 2 days.

2 Preheat oven to 400°F. On lightly floured surface, with floured rolling pin, roll disk into 12-inch round.

Gently roll dough to drape over rolling pin to transfer to 9-inch tart pan with removable bottom. Gently press dough onto bottom and side of pan. Run rolling pin along top of tart pan to trim away excess dough. Freeze 30 minutes or until very firm.

3 With fork, pierce dough all over. Line tart shell with foil and fill with pie weights or dry beans. Bake 15 minutes. Reduce oven temperature to 350°F. Remove foil and weights. Bake crust another 15 to 20 minutes or until golden. Cover rim with foil if browning too quickly. Cool in pan on wire rack.

4 While crust cools, make filling: In 2-quart saucepan, heat ¾ cup milk to simmering on medium. In heatproof medium bowl, whisk together egg yolks, remaining 6 tablespoons milk, and sugar until blended; whisk in cornstarch and flour until smooth. Slowly whisk hot milk into egg mixture. Return to same saucepan.

5 Cook mixture on medium 4 minutes or until very thick, whisking constantly. Remove from heat. Whisk in butter and salt until smooth. With knife, cut vanilla bean lengthwise in half; scrape out seeds and whisk into milk mixture (or whisk in vanilla extract). Transfer mixture to small bowl. Place plastic wrap directly on surface to prevent skin from forming. Refrigerate until cool, about 45 minutes. (Can be refrigerated up to 1 day; remove from refrigerator 30 minutes before using.)

6 With sharp paring knife, cut peel and white pith from oranges. Thinly slice crosswise. Spread pastry cream evenly in cooled tart shell. Arrange orange slices in one layer on pastry cream, overlapping slightly. Can be refrigerated, covered, up to 2 hours.

7 In 1-quart saucepan, combine jelly and triple sec. Heat on medium until melted, whisking. Cool slightly and brush fruit with jelly. Garnish with currants.

TIP: If you like, you can use refrigerated store-bought ready-to-unroll piecrust. You can skip steps 1 through 3—just follow the baking instructions on the box before filling with pastry cream.

Each serving: About 330 calories, 5g protein, 42g carbohydrate, 16g total fat (10g saturated), 2g fiber, 240mg sodium

Ganache Tart with Salted-Almond Crust

Silky smooth and sprinkled with sea salt, this truffle-like tart gets its richness from deep, dark chocolate and heavy cream. Poured warm into a crisp, buttery almond crust, the filling firms up fast in the fridge.

Active time: 45 minutes
Total time: 55 minutes plus freezing, cooling, and chilling
Makes: 12 servings

½ cup roasted salted almonds
¾ cup (1½ sticks) butter (no substitutions), cut into
    tablespoons and softened
½ cup confectioners' sugar
¼ teaspoon salt
1 large egg yolk
½ teaspoon vanilla extract
1¼ cups all-purpose flour
1 cup heavy or whipping cream
1 pound highest-quality bittersweet chocolate
    (60 to 70 percent cacao; see Tip), very finely chopped
Flaky sea salt for garnish (optional)

1 Preheat oven to 350°F.

2 In food processor, pulse almonds until finely ground. Transfer to bowl. In same processor (do not clean), pulse 6 tablespoons butter until creamy. With rubber spatula, scrape bottom and side of bowl, then add confectioners' sugar and salt and pulse until smooth. Scrape bowl, then add egg yolk and vanilla and pulse until smooth. Scrape bowl, then add flour and ground almonds and pulse until mixture forms fine crumbs. Pour mixture into 11-inch tart pan with removable bottom.

3 With fingers, firmly press crumb mixture into bottom and up side of pan to form even crust. Freeze 10 minutes or until firm.

4 Bake crust 25 minutes or until golden brown. Cool completely on wire rack.

5 In 3-quart saucepan, heat cream to bubbling on medium. Remove from heat. Add chocolate and let stand 1 minute. With rubber spatula, stir gently until smooth. Add remaining 6 tablespoons butter, 1 tablespoon at a time, gently stirring after each addition until blended. Pour mixture into cooled crust. Gently shake tart pan to create smooth, even top.

6 Refrigerate 30 minutes to set, then let stand at room temperature until ready to serve, up to 6 hours. Garnish with sea salt if desired.

TIP: Premium baking chocolate, once the province of pastry chefs, is now a supermarket staple. With higher-quality cacao—from single-origin beans or a blend—these bars will consistently produce stellar creations. The best indicator of quality: not a high price tag, but a short ingredient list. Any chocolate labeled "dark," "bittersweet," or "semisweet" should ideally contain only chocolate, sugar, cocoa butter, soy lechithin, and vanilla. Unsweetened chocolate should have a single ingredient—chocolate.

Each serving: About 485 calories, 6g protein, 29g carbohydrate, 39g total fat (22g saturated), 3g fiber, 95mg sodium

15 Cents

January 1913

Good Housekeeping Magazine

FROM OUR HOLIDAY ARCHIVES: NOSTALGIC CHRISTMAS DESSERTS

We're delighted to share these recipes for old-fashioned favorites from our holiday archives. Desserts like figgy pudding, old-fashioned fruitcake, and mincemeat tarts are sure to evoke memories of Christmases past for the elders at your table, while the younger set will be delighted by these old-school desserts because they're so very good.

Old-Fashioned Fruitcake

1/2 pound dried figs

1/2 pound dried apricots plus additional for garnish

4 cups sifted all-purpose flour

2 teaspoons baking powder

1/2 teaspoon salt

1 cup butter or margarine (2 sticks)

2 cups packed brown sugar

3 large eggs

2/3 cup light corn syrup plus additional for brushing

1 1/2 cups sweet wine

4 cups walnuts (16 ounces), coarsely broken

1 jar (16 ounces) orange marmalade

1 container (16 ounces) candied cherries plus additional cut-up cherries for garnish

2 containers (4 ounces each) diced preserved citron

2 jars (4 ounces each) diced preserved pineapple

1 container (4 ounces) diced candied orange peel

4 ounces diced candied lemon peel

1 package (15 ounces) golden raisins

1 Begin several weeks before holidays and start early in day. Thoroughly grease 4-quart fluted mold, about 4 inches high (or 10-inch angel-food pan and 9" by 5" by 3" loaf pan); then flour well.

2 Coarsely snip dried figs and apricots with kitchen scissors. Sift flour with baking powder and salt.

3 Meanwhile, in large bowl, with mixer at medium speed, mix butter with brown sugar until light and fluffy. Add eggs, beating until very light and fluffy; then beat in 2/3 cup corn syrup.

4 Preheat oven to 275°F.

5 At low speed, beat flour mixture into butter mixture, alternating with wine. Now remove this mixture to a large mixing bowl. Into it fold walnuts and marmalade. Then stir in snipped figs and apricots, cherries, citron, pineapple, orange and lemon peels, and raisins. Turn into prepared mold (or pans).

6 Bake mold 6 hours (angel-food pan, 4 hours, and loaf pan, 3 hours), or until cake tester inserted in center comes out clean. Cool on wire rack 10 minutes; remove from mold, cool completely. Wrap in double layer of foil; refrigerate or freeze for at least 2 weeks.

7 On serving day: If frozen, thaw fruitcake at room temperature, still wrapped, about 6 hours. If desired, brush top and sides of cake with corn syrup. Place apricots in ring around top center of cake; sprinkle with candied cherries. Makes 9 servings.

Mincemeat Tarts

2 packages frozen double-crust pie dough, thawed, or
  2 recipes unbaked dough for 9-Inch Double Piecrust
  (page 279)
1½ cups Colonial Mincemeat (see right)
1½ cups chopped apples
¼ cup chopped walnuts
2 tablespoons butter or margarine, softened
1 to 2 tablespoons brandy (optional)
1 egg white, beaten, or 2 tablespoons milk
Vanilla ice cream for serving

1 Early in day or 1 hour 30 minutes before serving: Line four 4½-inch pie plates or six 4-inch fluted tart pans with pastry. Cut out 4 or 6 pastry rounds for top crusts; set aside.

2 Preheat oven to 425°F.

3 In medium bowl, mix mincemeat with apples, walnuts, butter, and brandy, if using. Spoon filling into pastry-lined pans.

4 Moisten edges of pastry with water and cover with pastry rounds. Trim edges and seal with fork or press to flute. Make slits in top crusts; brush tops with beaten egg white or milk.

5 Bake 10 minutes, then lower oven temperature to 375°F and bake about 35 minutes longer, or until crusts are golden brown. Set pans on wire racks to cool slightly.

6 To serve, gently remove tarts from pans. Serve warm, topped with vanilla ice cream. Makes 4 to 6 servings.

Colonial Mincemeat

At least 2 days before making tarts, in food grinder with medium blade, grind **1 package (15 ounces) dark seedless raisins, 1 pound chopped lean beef, 1 container (4 ounces) citron, and 1 package (11 ounces) dried currants**. In Dutch oven, combine meat mixture with **1 tablespoon ground cinnamon, 1 tablespoon ground mace, ½ teaspoon ground nutmeg, 1½ teaspoons ground allspice, 1½ teaspoons salt, 1 cup white wine, and 2¼ cups packed light brown sugar (16 ounces)**; mix thoroughly. Bring to a boil over medium-high heat, then add **½ cup orange juice** and simmer over low heat 1½ hours, stirring occasionally. Pack mincemeat in clean preserve jars; cover tightly and refrigerate at least 2 days or up to 1 week. Makes about 3 pints.

Coffee Soufflé

2 tablespoons butter or margarine
2 tablespoons all-purpose flour
¼ teaspoon salt
2 tablespoons instant coffee granules or powder
¾ cup water
3 eggs, separated
½ cup granulated sugar
½ teaspoon vanilla extract

1 Preheat oven to 350°F. In saucepan, melt butter over medium heat. Add flour, salt, coffee, and water; stir until smooth. Cook mixture until it has thickened; remove from heat.

2 In medium bowl, beat egg yolks until thick and lemon-colored; gradually beat in sugar. With a rubber spatula, stir in coffee mixture and vanilla. In large bowl, beat egg whites until they hold soft peaks; fold in coffee and egg yolk mixture.

3 Turn soufflé into greased 1-quart casserole. Place in pan with enough hot water to go about halfway up sides. Bake 45 to 50 minutes. Serve immediately with cream. Makes 6 servings.

Indian Pudding

1 quart milk
1/4 cup cornmeal
1/2 cup molasses
1/4 cup sugar
1 tablespoon butter or margarine
1 teaspoon ground cinnamon
1 teaspoon ground nutmeg
1 teaspoon salt
1/2 cup chopped dates, nuts, or seedless raisins (optional)
Coffee ice cream, Hard Sauce (see right), or heavy cream
    for serving

1 Preheat oven to 275°F.

2 Scald milk in double boiler. Stir in cornmeal slowly and cook 20 minutes, stirring occasionally. Stir in molasses, sugar, butter, cinnamon, nutmeg, salt, and dates, nuts, or raisins, if using, until well combined.

3 Bake in greased 1½-quart casserole, uncovered, 3 hours, stirring once after 1 hour 30 minutes.

4 Serve warm or cold with ice cream, hard sauce, or heavy cream. Makes 8 to 10 servings.

Gingery Indian Pudding

Use 6 tablespoons molasses instead of the larger amount; add **2 additional tablespoons sugar**. Substitute **1 teaspoon ground ginger** for cinnamon and nutmeg.

Holiday Figgy Pudding

1 cup dried figs (4 ounces)
2 cups sifted all-purpose flour
1 tablespoon ground ginger
1 teaspoon baking soda
1/4 teaspoon salt
1 egg, beaten
1 cup light molasses
1/2 cup melted vegetable shortening
1 cup boiling water
Hard Sauce (see below) or vanilla ice cream for serving

1 About 3½ hours before serving: With kitchen scissors, remove stems from figs. In medium saucepot, simmer figs, with *water* to cover, 30 minutes; drain and finely snip figs.

2 Meanwhile, thoroughly grease 2-quart mold with tight-fitting cover.

3 Sift together flour, ginger, baking soda, and salt into medium bowl. In large bowl, stir together figs, egg, molasses, and shortening until well combined.

4 Alternately add flour mixture and *boiling water* to fig mixture; mix well. Turn into mold and cover tightly.

5 Place mold on trivet in deep Dutch oven. Add boiling water to come halfway up sides of mold; cover Dutch oven. Steam on stovetop over medium-low heat 2 hours, adding *boiling water* as necessary.

6 Unmold pudding and serve hot with Hard Sauce or ice cream. Makes 8 to 10 servings.

Hard Sauce

With spoon or electric mixer, beat **1/2 cup (1 stick) butter or margarine** with **1 cup confectioners' sugar** until fluffy. Stir in **1/2 teaspoon vanilla extract** and refrigerate until serving time.

PUDDINGS & FRUITY DESSERTS

Simple Vanilla Crème Brûlée

This classic baked custard gets a last-minute broil to create the smooth, crackable sugar crust.

Active time: 12 minutes
Total time: 45 minutes plus chilling
Makes: 6 servings

1 cup light cream or half-and-half
1 cup heavy cream
1 1/2 teaspoons vanilla extract
5 large egg yolks
1/3 cup granulated sugar
2 tablespoons packed dark brown sugar

1 Preheat oven to 325°F.

2 In microwave-safe 2-cup liquid measuring cup, heat creams in microwave on Medium (50% power) 5 minutes. Stir in vanilla.

3 Meanwhile, in 4-cup liquid measuring cup, whisk egg yolks and granulated sugar until well blended. Slowly whisk in warm cream until combined; with spoon, skim off foam.

4 Place six 4-ounce ramekins in 13" by 9" metal baking pan. Pour cream mixture into ramekins, filling almost to tops. Partially pull out oven rack and place pan on rack; fill with enough *boiling water* to come halfway up sides of ramekins. Carefully push in rack and bake custards 30 minutes or until custard is just set but center still jiggles slightly. Remove ramekins from water and place on wire rack; cool 30 minutes. Cover and refrigerate until custards are well chilled, at least 4 hours or overnight.

5 Up to 1 hour before serving, position rack as close as possible to heat source and preheat broiler. Place brown sugar in coarse sieve; with spoon, press through sieve to evenly cover tops of chilled custards. Place ramekins in jelly-roll pan for easier handling. Broil custards 2 to 3 minutes or just until brown sugar melts. Refrigerate immediately 1 hour to cool custards.

Each serving: About 365 calories, 4g protein, 18g carbohydrate, 31g total fat (18g saturated), 0g fiber, 35mg sodium

Cappuccino Crème Brûlée

Prepare crème brûlée as instructed, adding **4 teaspoons espresso coffee powder** along with vanilla to warm cream mixture in step 2.

Each serving: About 370 calories, 4g protein, 18g carbohydrate, 31g total fat (18g saturated), 0g fiber, 35mg sodium

Clockwise from top left: WINE-POACHED PEARS *(page 304)*; SIMPLE VANILLA CRÈME BRÛLÉE *(above)*; FIT FOR A KING TREE *(page 248)*; MEYER LEMON PUDDING CAKES *(page 304)*.

Pumpkin Crème Caramel

We swapped in coconut milk for evaporated milk in
this lush, creamy alternative to pumpkin pie.

Active time: 15 minutes
Total time: 1 hour 5 minutes plus chilling
Makes: 12 servings

1/4 cup water

11/4 cups sugar

1 can (14 ounces) coconut milk (not cream of coconut),
    well shaken

3/4 cup heavy cream

1 cup solid-pack pumpkin

6 large eggs

2 teaspoons vanilla extract

1/8 teaspoon salt

2 tablespoons dark or coconut rum (optional)

Freshly whipped cream for serving

Toasted, shredded coconut for garnish

Freshly grated nutmeg for garnish

1 Preheat oven to 350°F.

2 In 1-quart saucepan, heat water and ¾ cup sugar
to boiling on medium-high, stirring to dissolve sugar.
Continue to cook, without stirring, 5 to 9 minutes
or until caramel is just amber in color. Pour caramel
into 9-inch-round, 2-inch-deep ceramic or metal pan,
swirling to evenly coat bottom of pan.

3 In 2-quart saucepan, heat coconut milk, cream, and
remaining ½ cup sugar just to boiling on medium-high,
stirring to dissolve sugar.

4 Meanwhile, in large bowl, with wire whisk, mix
together pumpkin, eggs, vanilla, salt, and rum, if using,
until blended.

5 Gradually whisk hot milk mixture into pumpkin
mixture until blended. Pour pumpkin mixture through
fine-mesh sieve into 8-cup glass measuring cup, then
into caramel-coated pan. Place pan in roasting pan;
set on oven rack. Pour *boiling water* into roasting pan
to come three-quarters up side of custard pan. Bake
45 to 55 minutes (if using metal pan, start checking for

doneness at 35 minutes) or until knife comes out clean
when inserted 1 inch from edge of custard (center will
still jiggle slightly).

6 Carefully remove pan from water. Allow crème
caramel to cool 1 hour in pan on wire rack. Cover and
refrigerate crème caramel overnight or up to 2 days. To
unmold, run small spatula around side of pan; invert
crème caramel onto serving plate, allowing caramel
syrup to drip down from pan (some caramel may remain
in pan). Swirl whipped cream onto dessert, and sprinkle
with coconut and nutmeg.

Each serving: About 240 calories, 5g protein, 24g carbohydrate,
15g total fat (11g saturated), 1g fiber, 70mg sodium

BAIN MARIE

A bain marie (hot water bath) is the
best way to ensure that delicate custard
mixtures cook evenly. Here's how to do it:

Place custard cups or a baking dish in a baking
or roasting pan. Place the pan on the oven rack.
Pour in enough very hot (not boiling) water to
come halfway up the sides of the cups or dish.
Bake custard as directed.

PUMPKIN CRÈME CARAMEL (*opposite*)

Chocolate Soufflé

This recipe takes less than half the time of a traditional soufflé and is every bit as impressive. If you've never tried your hand at a soufflé, this light and chocolaty version will make you feel like a four-star chef.

Active time: 10 minutes
Total time: 25 minutes
Makes: 4 servings

Nonstick baking spray with flour
4 ounces bittersweet chocolate chips (scant 1 cup)
1/3 cup sweetened condensed milk
3 large eggs, separated
2 tablespoons confectioners' sugar

1 Preheat oven to 375°F. Generously coat four 4-ounce ceramic or glass ramekins with nonstick baking spray.

2 In microwave-safe large bowl, microwave chocolate chips on High in 20-second increments, stirring after each, until just melted, 1 to 2 minutes. Remove from microwave; with wire whisk, whisk in condensed milk. Whisk in 2 egg yolks until blended; refrigerate remaining egg yolk for another use.

3 In another large bowl, with mixer on medium speed, beat egg whites until medium-stiff peaks form (3 to 4 minutes). Add one-third of beaten whites to chocolate mixture, and whisk gently until incorporated. With rubber spatula, gently fold in remaining whites until just incorporated. Divide batter among prepared ramekins. If preparing ahead of time, cover with plastic wrap and refrigerate until ready to bake.

4 Sift confectioners' sugar over tops. Place ramekins in jelly-roll pan for easier handling. Remove plastic wrap and bake 11 to 13 minutes or until tops rise about 1 inch above rim; do not open oven while baking. Serve immediately.

Each serving: About 275 calories, 34g carbohydrate, 8g protein, 15g total fat (8g saturated), 0g fiber, 80mg sodium

Top: Chocolate Soufflé *(above); Bottom:* Panna Cotta with Best Berry Sauce *(opposite).*

Panna Cotta with Best Berry Sauce

Panna cotta, which means "cooked cream" in Italian, is a custard that is served cold with a sauce. Here, we drizzle it with our favorite berry sauce for a festive finish.

Active time: 30 minutes
Total time: 45 minutes plus chilling
Makes: 8 main-dish servings

Panna Cotta

1 envelope unflavored gelatin
1 cup milk
1/2 vanilla bean or 1 1/2 teaspoons vanilla extract
1 3/4 cups heavy or whipping cream
1/4 cup sugar
1 strip (3" by 1") lemon peel
1 cinnamon stick (3 inches)

Best Berry Sauce

3 cups fresh or frozen, thawed berries (raspberries, blueberries, or hulled, sliced strawberries), plus extra for garnish
1/2 to 3/4 cup confectioners' sugar
3 tablespoons water
1 to 2 teaspoons fresh lemon or lime juice

1 Prepare panna cotta: In 2-cup measuring cup, evenly sprinkle gelatin over milk; let stand 2 minutes to soften gelatin slightly. With knife, cut vanilla bean lengthwise in half; scrape out seeds and reserve.

2 In heavy 1-quart saucepan, combine cream, sugar, lemon peel, cinnamon stick, and vanilla bean halves and seeds (do not add vanilla extract yet, if using); heat to boiling over high heat. Reduce heat and simmer, stirring occasionally, 5 minutes. Stir in milk mixture; cook over low heat, stirring frequently, until gelatin has dissolved, 2 to 3 minutes.

3 Discard lemon peel, cinnamon stick, and vanilla bean from cream mixture. (Stir in vanilla extract, if using.) Pour cream mixture into medium bowl set in large bowl of ice water. With rubber spatula, stir mixture until it just begins to set, 10 to 12 minutes. Pour cream mixture into eight 4-ounce ramekins. Place ramekins in jelly-roll pan for easier handling, cover, and refrigerate until well chilled and set, 4 hours or up to overnight.

4 Meanwhile, prepare berry sauce: In nonreactive 2-quart saucepan, combine 3 cups berries, 1/2 cup confectioners' sugar, and water. Cook over medium heat, stirring occasionally, until berries have softened and sauce has thickened slightly, 5 to 8 minutes. Remove saucepan from heat; stir in 1 teaspoon lemon juice. Taste and stir in additional sugar and lemon juice if desired. Serve warm. Makes about 2 cups.

5 To unmold panna cotta, run tip of knife around edges. Tap side of each ramekin sharply to break seal. Invert onto dessert plates. Spoon berry sauce around each panna cotta and sprinkle with fresh berries.

Each serving with 2 tablespoons sauce: About 260 calories, 3g protein, 17g carbohydrate, 20g total fat (13g saturated), 1g fiber, 39mg sodium

HOW WE CELEBRATE CHRISTMAS

"Our typical Christmas celebration is very traditional. Trudie loves all the rituals, so there's a turkey, Christmas pudding. And she insists we all have the presents on Christmas morning, not on Christmas Eve. I am always in favor of the adults doing gifts on Christmas Eve, and the kids in the morning— but I usually lose that argument."

—Sting

CRANBERRY TRIFLE *(opposite)*

Cranberry Trifle

Assembling this trifle is a piece of (pound) cake.

Active time: 30 minutes
Total time: 50 minutes plus chilling
Makes: 12 servings

2 navel oranges

1 bag (12 ounces) cranberries (3 cups)

1¼ cups water

1 cup sugar

2 tablespoons chopped crystallized ginger

¼ teaspoon ground cinnamon

⅛ teaspoon ground allspice

1 cup heavy cream

1 package (3 to 4 ounces) instant vanilla pudding and pie filling

2 cups milk

1 frozen pound cake (16 ounces), cut into ¾-inch cubes

1 From oranges, grate 1 teaspoon peel and place in 4-quart saucepan. With knife, remove all remaining peel and white pith from oranges. Holding each orange over same saucepan to catch juice, cut sections from between membranes and drop into pan; squeeze juice from membranes into pan and discard membranes.

2 Set aside several cranberries for garnish. In same saucepan, stir remaining cranberries with water, sugar, ginger, cinnamon, and allspice. Heat to boiling over high heat, stirring often. Reduce heat to medium and cook 15 to 17 minutes, stirring occasionally, until cranberries pop and sauce thickens slightly. Remove from heat; cool to room temperature.

3 Meanwhile, in bowl, with mixer on medium speed, beat cream until soft peaks form. In large bowl, with whisk, whisk pudding mix and milk until completely combined. Immediately fold whipped cream into pudding until blended.

4 In 3-quart glass trifle bowl or other serving bowl, place one-third of cake. Spoon one-third cranberry mixture (about 1 cup) over cake, spreading evenly to side of bowl. Top with one-third of pudding (about 1¼ cups). Repeat layering twice more. Garnish with reserved cranberries.

5 Cover trifle with plastic wrap and refrigerate at least 4 hours or up to 2 days.

Each serving: About 375 calories, 4g protein, 53g carbohydrate, 17g total fat (10g saturated), 2g fiber, 285mg sodium

TRIFLE: THEME & VARIATIONS

Most trifle recipes have three elements in common: strips or cubes of cake for their base, a rich custard sauce for pouring between layers, and fresh fruit. Whipped cream, nuts, candied fruit, jam, and brandy or fruit-flavored liqueur are all popular add-ins. Try one of these delectable variations.

• **Use plain or chocolate** sponge cake or a fruit-flavored pound cake instead of plain pound cake.

• **Drizzle the cake** with a little brandy or orange-flavored liqueur, and/or brush it with orange, apricot, or strawberry jam.

• **Substitute 3 cups** of whole, sliced, or diced fresh fruit—strawberries, pears, peaches, or bananas—for the cranberries.

• **Prepare a homemade custard** instead of the instant pudding mix: In 4-quart saucepan, heat 2½ cups milk and ¾ cup sugar on medium just to boiling. Remove saucepan from heat. In medium bowl, whisk together ½ cup milk, ⅓ cup cornstarch, and ⅛ teaspoon salt; beat in 2 large egg yolks. Stir small amount of hot milk mixture into egg yolk mixture; gradually stir yolk mixture back into milk mixture in pan. Cook on medium heat, stirring constantly, until mixture thickens and boils. Pour into clean bowl and refrigerate until cold, at least 3 hours.

Citrus Trifle

Store-bought pound cake and vanilla pudding make this impressive dessert a snap to prepare.

Active time: 10 minutes
Total time: 10 minutes plus chilling
Makes: 10 servings

3 (11-ounce) pound cakes, cubed
3 cups vanilla pudding
1 (10-ounce) jar lemon curd
5 medium oranges, sliced into half moons
2 cups whipped cream
Orange peel

1 Layer cubed pound cake in 4-quart trifle bowl with vanilla pudding, lemon curd and orange slices. Cover, refrigerate 4 hours or overnight, then top with whipped cream and orange peel.

Each serving: About 615 calories, 9g protein, 83g carbohydrate, 27g total fat (4g saturated), 3g fiber, 467mg sodium

Top: CITRUS TRIFLE *(above)*;
Bottom: NO-BAKE PUMPKIN CHEESECAKE
MINI TRIFLES *(opposite)*.

No-Bake Pumpkin Cheesecake Mini Trifles

Luscious pumpkin cheesecake gets reimagined as individual trifles for a modern holiday dessert bar.

Active time: 25 minutes
Total time: 40 minutes, plus chilling
Makes: 8 servings

1 (8-ounce) brick cream cheese, softened
1/2 cup packed dark brown sugar
1 (15-ounce) can pure pumpkin
1 1/2 teaspoons vanilla extract
1 teaspoon pumpkin pie spice
2 cups heavy cream, cold
2 tablespoons plus 1/2 cup granulated sugar
2 cups crumbled ginger cookies or graham crackers
1 1/4 cup chopped candied nuts
2 tablespoons water

1 With mixer on medium speed, beat cream cheese until fluffy. Gradually beat in brown sugar until smooth. Add pumpkin, vanilla and pumpkin pie spice. Mix until smooth, scraping side of bowl as needed; set aside. In separate bowl, with mixer on medium-high speed, beat cream until soft peaks form. Gradually beat in 2 tablespoons granulated sugar until stiff peaks form.

2 In medium bowl, combine cookies and 1 cup chopped nuts; divide half among 8 parfait glasses. Divide half of pumpkin mixture among glasses, followed by half of whipped cream. Repeat layering of cookies, pumpkin and whipped cream. Cover and refrigerate at least 3 hours or up to 1 day.

3 Line cookie sheet with foil. Spray foil with nonstick cooking spray. In small saucepan, heat 2 tablespoons water and remaining 1/2 cup granulated sugar to boiling on medium-high; cook until golden. Working quickly, stir in remaining 1/4 cup nuts, then spread mixture onto prepared foil in thin layer. Cool completely. Break into small shards. To serve trifles, garnish with brittle.

Each serving: About 660 calories, 7g protein, 61g carbohydrate, 45g total fat (21g saturated), 4g fiber, 305mg sodium

Red Velvet Holiday Trifle

Start with your favorite red velvet cake mix, then throw together this impressive dessert in three easy steps.

Active time: 25 minutes
Total time: 25 minutes plus standing and cooling
Makes: 20 servings

1 box Red Velvet cake mix

GANACHE
2 cups half-and-half
1 cup heavy cream
20 ounces semisweet chocolate chips

WHIPPED CREAM
6 cups heavy cream
16 ounces mascarpone (at room temperature)
3/4 cup sugar
2 teaspoons vanilla extract
1/4 teaspoon salt

1 Prepare cake mix according to package instructions. Cool and reserve.

2 Prepare the Ganache: In saucepan, bring half-and-half and heavy cream to simmer, stirring often. Add chocolate chips to heatproof bowl and pour cream mixture over. Let stand 5 minutes, then whisk until blended. Let cool completely.

3 Prepare the whipped cream: Using mixer with whisk attachment, beat heavy cream, mascarpone, sugar, vanilla extract, and salt on low until blended. Increase speed to high; beat until stiff peaks form. Refrigerate until assembly.

3 Assemble: Break cake into chunks. Layer in a deep glass trifle bowl, starting with Ganache. Refrigerate until serving. Garnish with cake crumbs.

Each serving: About 760 calories, 8g protein, 49g carbohydrate, 62g total fat (35g saturated), 2g fiber, 235mg sodium

Meyer Lemon Pudding Cakes

Half custard, half cake, these sweet-tart desserts are chiffon light.

Active time: 25 minutes
Total time: 1 hour
Makes: 8 cakes

⅓ cup plus ¼ cup sugar, plus additional for ramekins
¼ cup all-purpose flour
¼ teaspoon salt
2 to 3 Meyer or regular lemons
3 large eggs, separated
2 tablespoons butter or margarine, melted and cooled
1 cup whole milk
1 pint raspberries for garnish
Fresh mint sprigs for garnish

1 Preheat oven to 350°F. Grease eight 4- to 5-ounce ramekins; sprinkle with sugar, shaking out any excess.

2 On sheet of waxed paper, with fork, combine flour, ⅓ cup sugar, and salt. From lemons, grate 1½ tablespoons peel and squeeze ½ cup juice. In large bowl, with wire whisk, beat egg yolks and lemon peel and juice. Whisk in butter and milk. Gradually whisk in flour mixture.

3 In another large bowl, with mixer on medium, beat egg whites until foamy. Gradually beat in remaining ¼ cup sugar until soft peaks form, 2 to 3 minutes.

4 Add one-third beaten whites to yolk mixture and, with rubber spatula, stir gently until incorporated. Gently fold in remaining whites until just incorporated. With ladle, divide batter evenly among prepared ramekins.

5 Arrange ramekins 1 inch apart in large (17" by 13") roasting pan. Fill pan with enough hot water to come halfway up sides of ramekins. Carefully transfer pan to oven and bake 30 to 35 minutes or until cakes are golden brown and tops rise ½ inch above rims.

6 Cool cakes in pan on wire rack 5 minutes. Carefully transfer ramekins to wire rack to cool 15 minutes longer.

7 Run thin knife around edge of one ramekin. Place small serving plate on top of ramekin and invert plate and ramekin together; remove ramekin. Repeat with remaining ramekins. Garnish each cake with a couple of raspberries and a mint sprig; serve warm.

Each cake: About 170 calories, 4g protein, 25g carbohydrate, 6g total fat (3g saturated), 3g fiber, 145mg sodium

Wine-Poached Pears

Dessert doesn't get any simpler or more elegant than this red-wine-drenched stunner.

Active time: 10 minutes
Total time: 50 minutes plus chilling
Makes: 8 servings

1 bottle (750 milliliters) Shiraz or red Zinfandel wine
2 cups water
1 cup sugar
4 star anise
8 medium Bosc pears with stems

1 In 5- to 6-quart Dutch oven, heat wine, water, sugar, and star anise just to boiling on high heat, stirring to dissolve sugar.

2 Meanwhile, peel pears, leaving stems on. With melon baller or small knife, core pears through blossom (bottom) end.

3 Place pears in wine mixture; heat to boiling. Cover and simmer on low 10 to 15 minutes, until pears are tender but still hold their shape, turning occasionally.

4 Transfer pears to platter; discard star anise. Heat wine mixture to boiling on high. Cook 20 minutes, uncovered, to thicken liquid and reduce to 1½ cups.

5 Cover pears and syrup separately; refrigerate 6 hours or up to 3 days. To serve, spoon syrup over pears.

Each serving: About 190 calories, 1g protein, 46g carbohydrate, 1g total fat (0g saturated), 4g fiber, 10mg sodium

Top right: TIRAMISÙ *(opposite)*;
Bottom right: WINE-POACHED PEARS *(above)*.

Tiramisù

In Italian, tiramisù *means "pick me up"—a perfect description of this light-as-a-feather dessert.*

Active time: 20 minutes
Total time: 25 minutes plus chilling
Makes: 9 servings

2/3 cup hot water
2 tablespoons brandy
1 tablespoon instant espresso powder
1/4 cup plus 1 tablespoon sugar
1/4 cup whipping cream
1 box (8 ounces) Neufchâtel cheese, softened
1/4 cup low-fat (1%) milk
1/2 teaspoon vanilla extract
4 ounces sponge-type ladyfingers (30 halves)
1 tablespoon cocoa powder

1 In small bowl, stir together hot water, brandy, espresso powder, and 1 tablespoon sugar until sugar dissolves. In medium bowl, with mixer on medium speed, beat cream until soft peaks form when beaters are lifted.

2 In large bowl, with mixer on medium-high speed, beat cream cheese and remaining 1/4 cup sugar until fluffy, about 4 minutes. Continue beating; add milk and vanilla in a slow, steady stream. Beat until well mixed and fluffy, about 2 minutes. With spatula, gently fold whipped cream into cream cheese mixture.

3 In 9-inch-square baking dish, arrange half of ladyfingers, flat sides up, in single layer. Pour half of brandy mixture evenly over; let stand until absorbed.

4 Spread half of cream cheese mixture evenly over ladyfingers. Top with remaining ladyfingers, flat sides up. Brush remaining brandy mixture over ladyfingers, allowing liquid to be absorbed before each addition. Spread evenly with remaining cream cheese mixture.

5 Sift cocoa powder evenly on top. Cover with plastic wrap and refrigerate at least 4 hours or overnight. Garnish with chocolate curls, if desired.

Each serving: About 175 calories, 4g protein, 18g carbohydrate, 9g total fat (5g saturated), 0g fiber, 180mg sodium

COOKIES, BROWNIES & BARS

Traditional Cutouts

This recipe provides the perfect base for all your Christmas cookies. Keep them simple or make them magnificent by putting your own twist on these butter-based beauties.

Active time: 35 minutes
Total time: 55 minutes
Makes: about 2¹/₂ dozen

2¹/₄ cups all-purpose flour
1 teaspoon baking powder
¹/₂ teaspoon baking soda
³/₄ cup butter
³/₄ cup sugar
¹/₂ teaspoon salt
1 large egg yolk
2 tablespoons light corn syrup
1¹/₂ teaspoon vanilla extract
¹/₂ teaspoon almond extract
Ornamental Frosting (right)

1 Preheat oven to 375°F. In medium bowl, whisk flour, baking powder and baking soda; set aside.

2 With mixer on medium high speed, beat butter, sugar and salt until creamy; beat in egg yolk, corn syrup and extracts. With mixer on medium-low speed, beat in flour mixture until just combined.

3 On large sheet of parchment paper, lightly flour half of dough. Roll to ¹/₄-inch thickness. Using 2-inch cookie cutters, cut shapes into dough; gently remove excess dough from around cutters. Slide parchment with cookies onto cookie sheet; place in freezer. Reroll scraps once on another sheet of parchment, then cut shapes; to same sheet in freezer, add cookies. Freeze until stiff, about 30 minutes. Arrange cookies 2 inches apart on a sheet of parchment; place on cookie sheet.

4 Bake 10 to 12 minutes or until golden around edges. Slide parchment with baked cookies onto wire rack; cool completely. With remaining dough, repeat rolling, baking and cooling.

5 Decorate cooled cookies with Ornamental Frosting, as desired.

Each cookie: About 100 calories, 1g protein, 14g carbohydrate, 5g total fat (3g saturated), 0g fiber, 80mg sodium

Ornamental Frosting

In bowl, with mixer on medium, beat **16 ounces confectioner's sugar, 3 tablespoons meringue powder,** and **¹/₃ cup warm water** until blended and mixture is very stiff, about 5 minutes. Tint frosting with **food coloring** as desired; keep surface covered with plastic wrap. With small spatula or decorating bags with small writing tips, decorate cookies with frosting (add warm water to thin as desired). Makes 3 cups.

Clockwise from top left: DRAWING WITH FROSTING (*page 353*); TRADITIONAL CUTOUTS (*above*); PINWHEELS (*page 322*); MAKE MERRY UNDER THE MISTLETOE (*page 256*).

Cocoa Stars

These sugar cookies are a fun way to add chocolate into your Christmas cookie lineup.

Active time: 35 minutes
Total time: 55 minutes
Makes: about 2 dozen

Follow the steps for Traditional Cutouts (page 307) with these modifications: In Step 1, add **¼ cup unsweetened cocoa** to flour. In Step 2, beat in **2 ounces melted bittersweet chocolate** along with **egg yolk.** In Step 3, use 3-inch star-shaped cookie cutters. In Step 4, dust cooled baked cookies with **2 tablespoons confectioners' sugar.**

Each serving: About 145 calories, 2g protein, 19g carbohydrate, 7g total fat (4g saturated), 0g fiber, 145mg sodium

Chocolate-PB Drops

Cookies are always better with chocolate and peanut butter, so spice up your holiday cookie collection with this dynamic duo.

Active time: 35 minutes
Total time: 55 minutes
Makes: about 3½ dozen

Follow the steps for Traditional Cutouts (page 307) with these modifications: In Step 3, do not roll out on parchment. With small (1-tablespoon) cookie scoop, form dough into balls. Place on large cookie sheet, 1 inch apart. Flatten tops slightly. Do not freeze. In Step 4, bake 15 minutes or until golden. In Step 5, drizzle cookies with **2 ounces melted bittersweet chocolate** and **3 tablespoons peanut butter,** heated in separate bowls in microwave. Chill to set (1½ hours).

Each serving: About 85 calories, 1g protein, 10g carbohydrate, 5g total fat (3g saturated), 0g fiber, 88mg sodium

Top: COCOA STARS *(above);*
Bottom: CHOCOLATE-PB DROPS *(above).*

Jammy Thumbprints

Add a little fruit to your holiday cookie swap with these fun and easy-to-make jam cookies.

Active time: 35 minutes
Total time: 55 minutes
Makes: about 4 dozen

Follow the steps for Traditional Cutouts (page 307) with these modifications: In Step 3, do not roll out onto parchment. Roll dough into ½-inch balls, then roll balls in ³/4 cup very finely chopped walnuts or pecans. Place on large cookie sheet, 2 inches apart. With end of wooden spoon handle, make deep indentation in each ball. After freezing, but before baking, add ½ teaspoon apricot or raspberry jam to indentations. In Step 4, cool on sheets 5 minutes before transferring onto wire rack.

Each serving: About 80 calories, 0g protein, 10g carbohydrate, 4g total fat (2g saturated), 0g fiber, 73mg sodium

Spiced Drops

Sometimes a little spice adds a whole lot of sophistication. These irresistible cookies are a great example.

Active time: 35 minutes
Total time: 55 minutes
Makes: about 3¹/2 dozen

Follow the steps for Traditional Cutouts (page 307) with these modifications: In Step 1, add to flour 1¹/2 teaspoons ground cinnamon, 2 teaspoons ground ginger and ¹/4 teaspoon ground cloves. In Step 3, do not roll out on parchment. With small (1-tablespoon) cookie scoop, form dough into balls and roll in ¹/4 cup coarse sugar. Place on large cookie sheet, 1 inch apart. Do not freeze. In Step 4, bake 15 minutes or until edges are set.

Each serving: About 80 calories, 1g protein, 11g carbohydrate, 3g total fat (2g saturated), 0g fiber, 83mg sodium

Top: JAMMY THUMBPRINTS *(above)*;
Bottom: SPICED DROPS *(above).*

Olive Oil Cutouts

A combination of olive oil and butter gives the classic Christmas cookie an exciting update.

Active time: 20 minutes
Total time: 40 minutes
Makes: about 2 dozen cookies

3 cups all-purpose flour
1/2 teaspoon baking powder
3/4 teaspoon salt
1 cup sugar
4 tablespoons butter (no substitutions)
2 large eggs
1 tablespoon vanilla extract
1 teaspoon grated lemon peel
1/2 cup extra-virgin olive oil

1 Preheat oven to 350°F. In large bowl, whisk flour, baking powder, and salt.

2 With mixer on medium speed, beat sugar, butter, eggs, vanilla, and lemon peel until creamy. Beat in oil. Add flour mixture and mix just until combined. Divide dough into 3 equal-size disks. Wrap each in plastic wrap and refrigerate at least 2 hours or until very firm.

3 On large sheet of parchment paper, with floured rolling pin, roll 1 disk dough to 1/8-inch thickness. Using 3- to 4-inch cutters, cut dough into as many cookies as possible, spacing 1/2 inch apart. Slide parchment onto large cookie sheet. Freeze 15 minutes or until firm.

4 With small knife, lift and remove dough between cookies. Wrap and refrigerate scraps. Bake sheet of cookies 10 to 12 minutes or until edges are crisp and golden. Cool on pan on wire rack 5 minutes. Transfer from pan to wire rack. Cool completely. Repeat with remaining dough and scraps, rerolling only once.

5 When cookies are cool, decorate as desired. Allow to dry completely. Store in airtight container (with waxed paper between layers if decorated) at room temperature up to 1 week or in freezer up to 2 months.

Each cookie: About 155 calories, 2g protein, 21g carbohydrate, 7g total fat (2g saturated), 0g fiber, 105mg sodium

Stained Glass Stars

These delicious cookies will look great when you mix things up and get creative with color and frosting.

Active time: 20 minutes
Total time: 40 minutes
Makes: about 3 dozen cookies

Follow the steps for Olive Oil Cutouts with these modifications: In Step 3, use 3- to 4-inch star cutters and cut out the centers of cookies with smaller star cutters. In Step 4, before baking cookies, pile 1/4 to 1/2 **teaspoon crushed red or green hard candies** in centers of cookies, leaving 1/8-inch border around candies. Proceed as directed in Step 4. Store in airtight container at room temperature up to 5 days.

Each cookie: About 110 calories, 1g protein, 15g carbohydrate, 5g total fat (1g saturated), 0g fiber, 70mg sodium.

White-Chocolate-Dipped Biscotti

Dress up these nutty biscotti with a white chocolate dip for a perfect holiday gift. Nestle cookies in cellophane bags tied with a ribbon. They're just the thing for your work colleagues to enjoy during a coffee break.

Active time: 40 minutes
Total time: 1 hour 30 minutes plus cooling
Makes: about 36 biscotti

2 cups all-purpose flour
1½ teaspoons baking powder
¼ teaspoon salt
½ cup butter (1 stick), softened (do not use margarine)
⅓ cup granulated sugar
⅓ cup packed brown sugar
2 large eggs
1 tablespoon vanilla extract
1 cup walnuts (4 ounces), toasted (page 287) and coarsely chopped
12 ounces white chocolate, melted

1 Preheat oven to 325°F. Line large cookie sheet with parchment paper.

2 On waxed paper, mix together flour, baking powder, and salt.

3 In large bowl, with mixer on medium speed, beat butter and both sugars until creamy. Add eggs, one at a time, beating well after each addition. Beat in vanilla. Reduce speed to low; gradually beat in flour mixture just until blended, occasionally scraping bowl with rubber spatula. Stir in walnuts.

4 On a lightly floured surface, divide dough in half. Form each half into 1½-inch-wide log on prepared sheet, spacing 3 inches apart.

5 Bake 30 minutes or until golden brown. Cool on pan on wire rack 5 minutes.

6 Carefully slide logs onto large cutting board. With serrated knife, cut each log crosswise into ½-inch-thick diagonal slices; place, cut side down, on same sheet. Bake 20 to 25 minutes or until golden brown and crisp. Cool completely on pan on wire rack.

7 If desired, dip half of each cooled cookie into melted white chocolate. Let chocolate harden on cookie sheet lined with waxed paper.

8 Store cookies (with waxed paper between layers if chocolate-dipped) in an airtight container at room temperature up to 1 week or in freezer up to 1 month.

Each biscotto (without chocolate): About 90 calories, 2g protein, 10g carbohydrate, 5g total fat (2g saturated), 0g fiber, 45mg sodium.

Chocolate-Raspberry Thumbprints

Chocolate and raspberry make winning sweet-tart partners in these holiday treats.

Active time: 40 minutes
Total time: 1 hour 10 minutes
Makes: about 84 cookies

2³/4 cups all-purpose flour
1/4 teaspoon baking soda
1/4 teaspoon salt
1 cup butter (2 sticks), softened (no substitutions)
³/4 cup sugar
1 large egg
1 teaspoon vanilla extract
2 squares (2 ounces) unsweetened chocolate, melted
1/4 cup unsweetened cocoa
1¹/4 cups sliced natural almonds, coarsely chopped
1/2 cup seedless red raspberry jam

1 Preheat oven to 350°F. On waxed paper, combine flour, baking soda, and salt.

2 In large bowl, with mixer on medium speed, beat butter and sugar 1 minute or until creamy, occasionally scraping bowl with rubber spatula. Add egg, vanilla, melted chocolate, and cocoa; beat until well mixed. Reduce speed to low; gradually beat in flour mixture just until blended, occasionally scraping bowl.

3 With hands, shape dough into 1-inch balls. Place sliced almonds in pie plate; roll balls in almonds to coat.

4 Place balls, 1½ inches apart, on two ungreased large cookie sheets. With thumb or handle of wooden spoon, make small indentation in center of each ball. Fill each indentation with ¼ teaspoon jam. Bake until jam is bubbly and dough is baked through, 14 to 15 minutes, rotating cookie sheets between upper and lower oven racks halfway through. Transfer cookies to wire rack to cool. Repeat with remaining dough and jam.

5 Store cookies with waxed paper between layers, in an airtight container up to 3 days, or freeze up to 3 months.

Each cookie: About 65 calories, 1g protein, 7g carbohydrate, 4g total fat (2g saturated), 1g fiber, 35mg sodium

Christmas Fruitcake Drops

These colorful drop cookies boast an irresistible combination of coconut, chocolate, prunes, and cherries.

Active time: 30 minutes
Total time: 50 minutes plus cooling and setting
Makes: about 36 cookies

1³/4 cups all-purpose flour
1/2 teaspoon baking soda
1/4 teaspoon salt
1 cup packed light brown sugar
6 tablespoons butter or margarine, softened
2 tablespoons vegetable shortening
1 large egg
1 cup pitted prunes, coarsely chopped
1 cup golden raisins
1/2 cup red and/or green candied cherries, coarsely chopped
1/2 cup flaked sweetened coconut
3 ounces white chocolate, chopped

1 Preheat oven to 375°F. Grease two large cookie sheets. In large bowl, combine flour, baking soda, and salt.

2 In another large bowl, with mixer on low speed, beat sugar, butter, and shortening until blended, occasionally scraping bowl with rubber spatula. Increase speed to high; beat until creamy, about 2 minutes. At low speed, beat in egg until blended. Add flour mixture, prunes, raisins, cherries, and coconut; beat just until blended.

3 Drop dough by rounded tablespoons, about 2 inches apart, onto prepared cookie sheets. Bake until edges are golden, 10 to 12 minutes. Cookies will be soft; with wide metal spatula, carefully transfer to wire rack to cool. Repeat with remaining dough.

4 In heavy small saucepan, melt white chocolate over very low heat, stirring frequently, until smooth. Arrange cookies on waxed paper and drizzle with white chocolate. Allow white chocolate to set, refrigerating if needed.

5 Store cookies in an airtight container up to 5 days, or freeze up to 3 months.

Each cookie: About 130 calories, 1g protein, 22g carbohydrate, 4g total fat (2g saturated), 1g fiber, 70mg sodium

Walnut Cookie Balls

A traditional choice for the holiday cookie tray, we think these delicious mouthfuls ought to be enjoyed all year long. They're also luscious made with pecans or toasted hazelnuts.

Active time: 45 minutes
Total time: 1 hour 11 minutes
Makes: about 78 cookies

1 cup butter (2 sticks), softened (no substitutions)
6 tablespoons granulated sugar
$\frac{1}{2}$ teaspoon vanilla extract
2 cups all-purpose flour
$\frac{1}{8}$ teaspoon salt
2 cups walnuts (8 ounces), chopped
$1\frac{1}{4}$ cups confectioners' sugar

1 Preheat oven to 325°F.

2 In large bowl, with mixer on medium speed, beat butter, granulated sugar, and vanilla until creamy, occasionally scraping bowl with rubber spatula. On low speed, gradually beat in flour and salt just until blended, continuing to scrape bowl occasionally. Stir in walnuts.

3 With hands, shape dough into 1-inch balls. Place balls, 1 inch apart, on two ungreased large cookie sheets. Bake until bottoms are lightly browned, 13 to 15 minutes, rotating cookie sheets between upper and lower oven racks halfway through.

4 Place confectioners' sugar in pie plate. While cookies are hot, with wide metal spatula, transfer 4 or 5 cookies at a time to plate with sugar. Gently turn cookies with fork to generously coat. Transfer to wire rack to cool completely. Repeat with remaining dough and confectioners' sugar.

5 Store cookies, with waxed paper between layers, in an airtight container up to 1 week, or freeze up to 3 months.

Each cookie: About 65 calories, 1g protein, 6g carbohydrate, 4g total fat (2g saturated), 0g fiber, 30mg sodium

Top: WALNUT COOKIE BALLS *(above);*
Bottom: CHRISTMAS FRUITCAKE DROPS *(opposite).*

Spritz Cookies

Making these buttery molded favorites is easy with one of the new cookie presses, which offer cookie patterns for every holiday. You can sprinkle the cookies with coarse sugar before baking, or decorate afterwards.

Active time: 35 minutes
Total time: 55 minutes plus cooling and setting
Makes: about 66 cookies

2¼ cups all-purpose flour
½ teaspoon baking powder
½ teaspoon salt
1 cup butter or margarine (2 sticks), softened
½ cup sugar
1 large egg
1 teaspoon vanilla extract
1 teaspoon almond extract
Candy décors (optional)
Ornamental Frosting (page 307; optional)

1 Preheat oven to 350°F. Place two cookie sheets in freezer.

2 On waxed paper, toss together flour, baking powder, and salt.

3 In large bowl, with mixer on medium speed, beat butter and sugar until pale and creamy. Beat in egg, then beat in both extracts. With mixer on low speed, gradually add flour mixture. Beat just until blended.

4 Spoon one-third of dough into cookie press or large decorating bag fitted with large star tip. Onto chilled cookie sheets, press or pipe dough into desired shapes, spacing 2 inches apart. Sprinkle with candy décors before baking, if using.

5 Bake cookies until lightly browned around edges, 10 to 12 minutes (see Tip), rotating cookie sheets between upper and lower oven racks halfway through. Place cookie sheets on wire rack to cool 2 minutes. Transfer cookies to wire rack to cool completely. Rechill cookie sheets and repeat with remaining dough.

6 Decorate cookies as desired with Ornamental Frosting, if using. Set aside to allow frosting to dry.

7 Store cookies in an airtight container up to 1 week, or freeze up to 1 month.

TIP: If you prefer your spritz cookies much lighter in color, bake them 5 to 7 minutes, until set but not golden.

Each cookie: About 50 calories, 1g protein, 5g carbohydrate, 3g total fat (2g saturated), 0g fiber, 20mg sodium

Coconut Macaroons

These flourless cookies are chewy and delicious (and a welcome treat for people who are allergic to wheat or gluten). Bag them in plastic, tie the packet up with a festive ribbon, and attach a gift card.

Active time: 10 minutes
Total time: 35 minutes
Makes: about 42 cookies

3 cups sweetened flaked coconut
¾ cup sugar
4 large egg whites
¼ teaspoon salt
1 teaspoon vanilla extract
⅛ teaspoon almond extract

1 Preheat oven to 325°F. Line two large cookie sheets with parchment paper or foil.

2 In large bowl, stir coconut, sugar, egg whites, salt, and both extracts until well combined.

3 Drop dough by rounded measuring teaspoons, 1 inch apart, on prepared cookie sheets. Bake until set and lightly golden, 25 minutes, rotating cookie sheets between upper and lower oven racks halfway through. Set cookie sheets on wire racks to cool 1 minute. With wide metal spatula, transfer cookies to racks to cool completely. Store in an airtight container up to 3 days, or freeze up to 1 month.

Each cookie: About 40 calories, 1g protein, 6g carbohydrate, 2g total fat (2g saturated), 0g fiber, 32mg sodium

SPRITZ COOKIES *(opposite)*

Brown Sugar and Pecan Fingers

This shortbread-style dough is rolled directly onto the cookie sheet, then cut into slim bars after baking. Present the cookies in a tall glass jar or metal canister.

Active time: 25 minutes
Total time: 45 minutes
Makes: 24 bars

3/4 cup butter or margarine (1 1/2 sticks), softened
1/3 cup packed dark brown sugar
1/4 cup granulated sugar
1 teaspoon vanilla extract
1/4 teaspoon salt
1 3/4 cups all-purpose flour
1/2 cup pecans (2 ounces), chopped

1 Preheat oven to 350°F. In large bowl, with mixer at medium speed, beat butter, both sugars, vanilla, and salt until creamy, about 2 minutes. At low speed, gradually beat in flour until just evenly moistened. With hand, press dough together to form ball.

2 Divide dough in half. Place 1 piece on one side of ungreased large cookie sheet and cover with waxed paper; roll lengthwise into 12" by 5" rectangle. Repeat with remaining dough on other side of same cookie sheet, leaving 1 1/2 inches between rectangles. With fork, prick dough at 1-inch intervals. Press tines of fork along long sides of rectangles to form decorative edge. Sprinkle pecans evenly over rectangles; press gently to make nuts adhere.

3 Bake until edges are lightly browned, 20 to 25 minutes. While pastry is still warm, cut each rectangle crosswise into 12 thin bars. Transfer to wire rack to cool. Store bars in an airtight container up to 1 week, or freeze up to 3 months.

Each bar: About 120 calories, 1g protein, 12g carbohydrate, 8g total fat (4g saturated), 0g fiber, 90mg sodium

Top: BROWN SUGAR AND PECAN FINGERS *(above)*; *Bottom:* WHITE-CHOCOLATE-DIPPED PEPPERMINT STICKS *(opposite)*.

White-Chocolate-Dipped Peppermint Sticks

These festive Christmas cookies look and taste like their namesakes! If you're a fan of dark chocolate, simply substitute it for the white.

Active time: 1 hour
Total time: 1 hour 22 minutes plus chilling
Makes: about 72 cookies

2¾ cups all-purpose flour
¼ teaspoon baking soda
¼ teaspoon salt
1 cup butter (2 sticks), softened (no substitutions)
¾ cup sugar
1 large egg
1 teaspoon vanilla extract
¼ teaspoon peppermint extract
Green and red paste food coloring
5 ounces white chocolate, melted
6 green or red starlight mints, crushed

1 On waxed paper, combine flour, baking soda, and salt.

2 In large bowl, with mixer on medium speed, beat butter and sugar 1 minute or until creamy, occasionally scraping bowl with rubber spatula. Add egg and vanilla; beat until well mixed. Reduce speed to low; gradually beat in flour mixture just until blended, occasionally scraping bowl.

3 Divide dough in half; set aside 1 half. Place other half in bowl and stir in peppermint extract. Divide peppermint dough in half; transfer half to another bowl. Tint 1 portion peppermint dough green and the other portion red.

4 Preheat oven to 350°F. Line 9-inch square metal baking pan with plastic wrap, extending wrap over two sides of pan. Pat plain dough into pan. Freeze 10 minutes. Pat green dough over half of plain dough; pat red dough over other half of plain dough. Freeze 10 minutes.

5 Lift dough from pan using plastic wrap; place on cutting board. Cut dough into thirds so that one third is all red on top, one-third is all green on top, and middle third is half red and half green. Cut each third crosswise into ⅜-inch strips. Twist strips and place, 1½ inches apart, on two ungreased cookie sheets. Bake until golden brown, 11 to 13 minutes, rotating cookie sheets between upper and lower oven racks halfway through. Transfer cookies to wire rack to cool. Repeat with remaining dough.

6 Dip one end of each cooled cookie into melted chocolate and place on waxed paper. Sprinkle chocolate with crushed mints. Refrigerate 15 minutes to set.

7 Store cookies, with waxed paper between layers, in an airtight container up to 1 week, or freeze up to 3 months.

Each cookie: About 75 calories, 1g protein, 9g carbohydrate, 4g total fat (3g saturated), 0g fiber, 50mg sodium

Best Linzer Cookies

A half pound of pecans goes into these tartlike treats filled with raspberry jam.

Active time: 1 hour
Total time: 2 hours plus chilling
Makes: about 48 cookies

2 cups pecans (8 ounces)
1/2 cup cornstarch
1 1/2 cups butter (3 sticks), softened (no substitutions)
1 1/3 cups confectioners' sugar
2 teaspoons vanilla extract
3/4 teaspoon salt
1 large egg
2 3/4 cups all-purpose flour
3/4 cup seedless red raspberry jam

1 In food processor with knife blade attached, pulse pecans and cornstarch until pecans are finely ground.

2 In large bowl, with mixer on low speed, beat butter and 1 cup confectioners' sugar until mixed. Increase speed to high; beat 2 minutes or until light and fluffy, occasionally scraping bowl with rubber spatula. At medium speed, beat in vanilla, salt, and egg. Reduce speed to low; gradually beat in flour and pecan mixture just until blended, occasionally scraping bowl.

3 Divide dough into 4 equal pieces; flatten each into disk. Wrap each disk in plastic and refrigerate 4 to 5 hours or until dough is firm enough to roll.

4 Preheat oven to 325°F. Remove 1 disk of dough from refrigerator; if necessary, let stand 10 to 15 minutes at room temperature for easier rolling. On lightly floured surface, with floured rolling pin, roll dough 1/8 inch thick. With floured 2 1/4-inch fluted round, plain round, or holiday-shaped cookie cutter, cut dough into as many cookies as possible. Change to floured 1- to 1 1/4-inch fluted round, plain round, or holiday-shaped cookie cutter, and cut out centers from half of cookies. Collect small center pieces along with other dough trimmings to reroll; wrap and return to refrigerator. With lightly floured spatula, carefully place cookies, 1 inch apart, on two ungreased large cookie sheets.

5 Bake cookies until edges are lightly browned, 17 to 20 minutes, rotating cookie sheets between upper and lower oven racks halfway through. Transfer cookies to wire rack to cool completely. Repeat with remaining dough and trimmings.

6 When cookies are cool, sprinkle remaining 1/3 cup confectioners' sugar through sieve over cookies with cut-out centers.

7 In small bowl, stir jam with fork until smooth. Spread scant measuring teaspoon jam on top of whole cookies; place cut-out cookies on top.

8 Store cookies, with waxed paper between layers, in an airtight container up to 3 days, or freeze up to 3 months.

Each cookie: About 115 calories, 16g protein, 11g carbohydrate, 8g total fat (3g saturated), 1g fiber, 80mg sodium

BEST LINZER COOKIES (*opposite*)

Dulce de Leche Sandwiches (*opposite*)

Dulce de Leche Sandwiches

A coffee-shop staple in Argentina, traditional alfajores *are a caramel-filled delight.*

Active time: 40 minutes
Total Time: 1 hour
Makes: 3 dozen cookies

Cookies

1 cup all-purpose flour
1⅔ cup cornstarch
1 teaspoon baking powder
¾ teaspoon ground cinnamon
¼ teaspoon salt
10 tablespoons butter, softened
½ cup sugar
½ teaspoon vanilla extract
4 large egg yolks
1 jar (16 oz.) store-bought dulce de leche or about 1 cup
  Slow-Cooker Dulce de Leche (Step 4)
Hazelnut-cocoa spread (optional)
Sprinkles, flaked coconut, mini chips, or chopped nuts
  (optional)

Slow-Cooker Dulce de Leche

1 (14-ounce) can sweetened milk
⅛ teaspoon salt

1 Preheat oven to 350°F. Into large bowl, sift flour, cornstarch, baking powder, cinnamon and salt. With mixer on medium-high speed, beat butter and sugar until creamy. Beat in vanilla, then egg yolks, 1 at a time. With mixer on low, beat in flour mixture until just combined, stopping and scraping down side of bowl occasionally.

2 On lightly floured surface, with lightly floured rolling pin, roll half of dough to ¼ inch thickness. With 1½-inch round cutter, cut out rounds. With small knife or mini offset spatula, transfer rounds to large parchment-lined cookie sheet, spacing 1 inch apart. Reroll scraps once. Bake 12 to 15 minutes or until golden brown on bottoms.

3 Let cookies cool on cookie sheet 5 minutes. Transfer to wire rack to cool completely. Repeat rolling, cutting and baking with remaining dough.

4 Make the Slow-Cooker Dulce de Leche: Transfer sweetened condensed milk to one 1-pint canning jar or two half-pint jars. Stir in salt and seal tightly with lid; place in slow-cooker bowl (if using large jar, lay down sideways) and cover with water. Replace lid on slow cooker and cook on low 8 hours. Carefully remove jar from water and wipe dry. Let cool 1 hour in refrigerator before opening. Makes about 1 cup.

5 To assemble, place dulce de leche in piping bag fitted with star tip. Pipe onto half of cookies. Top with remaining cookies.

6 Cookie sandwiches can be stored in airtight containers in freezer for up to 1 month.

Variations

Hazelnut-Cocoa: Spread half of cookies with 1 teaspoon each hazelnut-cocoa spread instead of dulce de leche.

Fiesta *Alfajores*: After sandwiching, with small knife, spread dulce de leche all over sides of sandwich cookies. Roll in choice of sprinkles, flaked coconut, mini chips, or chopped nuts.

Each sandwich cookie: About 120 calories, 2g protein, 18g carbohydrate, 5g total fat (2g saturated), 0g fiber, 75mg sodium

Whole-Grain Gingersnaps

Offset holiday indulgence with a dose of whole-wheat.

Active time: 25 minutes
Total time: 45 minutes plus chilling
Makes: about 42 cookies

1 cup all-purpose flour
1 cup whole-wheat flour
1 teaspoon ground ginger
1 teaspoon baking soda
½ teaspoon ground cinnamon
½ teaspoon salt
½ cup sugar
6 tablespoons trans-fat-free vegetable oil spread
    (60% to 70% oil)
1 large egg
½ cup dark molasses
Nonpareils or round white sprinkles (optional)

1 On sheet of waxed paper, combine both flours, ginger, baking soda, cinnamon, and salt.

2 In large bowl, with mixer on low speed, beat sugar and vegetable oil spread until blended. Increase speed to high; beat until light and creamy, occasionally scraping down bowl with rubber spatula. Beat in egg and molasses. Reduce speed to low; beat in flour mixture just until blended. Cover dough in bowl with plastic wrap and refrigerate until easier to handle (dough will still be slightly sticky), about 1 hour.

3 Preheat oven to 350°F. With greased hands, shape dough by rounded measuring teaspoons into 1-inch balls. If desired, dip top of each ball in nonpareils. Place balls, 2½ inches apart, on two ungreased cookie sheets.

4 Bake cookies until tops are slightly cracked, 9 to 11 minutes. (Cookies will be very soft.) Place cookie sheets on wire rack 1 minute to cool. Transfer cookies to rack to cool completely. Repeat with remaining dough.

5 Store cookies in an airtight container up to 3 days, or freeze up to 3 months.

Each cookie: About 55 calories, 1g protein, 9g carbohydrate, 2g total fat (0g saturated), 1g fiber, 75mg sodium

Pinwheels

You'll be surprised at how easy it is to shape these pretty treats. Try using several different kinds of jam for variety.

Active time: 35 minutes
Total time: 54 minutes
Makes: 24 cookies

1⅓ cups all-purpose flour
¼ teaspoon baking powder
⅛ teaspoon salt
6 tablespoons butter or margarine, softened
½ cup sugar
1 large egg
1 teaspoon vanilla extract
¼ cup damson plum, seedless raspberry, or other jam

1 In small bowl, stir together flour, baking powder, and salt.

2 In large bowl, with mixer at medium speed, beat butter and sugar until light and fluffy. Beat in egg and vanilla until combined. Reduce speed to low and beat in flour mixture just until combined. Divide dough in half. Wrap each half in waxed paper and refrigerate until firm enough to roll, at least 1 hour or overnight. (If using margarine, freeze overnight.)

3 Preheat oven to 375°F. Remove 1 dough half from refrigerator. On floured surface, with floured rolling pin, roll dough into 10" by 7½" rectangle. With fluted pastry wheel or sharp knife, cut into twelve 2½-inch squares. Place 1 square at a time, 1 inch apart, on two ungreased cookie sheets. Make 1½-inch cut from each corner toward center. Spoon ½ teaspoon jam in center of each square. Fold every other tip in to center. Repeat with remaining squares.

4 Bake until edges are lightly browned and cookies are set, 9 minutes, rotating sheets between upper and lower racks halfway through. With wide metal spatula, transfer to wire racks to cool completely. Repeat with remaining dough and jam.

5 Store cookies, with waxed paper between layers, in an airtight container up to 3 days, or freeze up to 3 months.

Each cookie: About 80 calories, 1g protein, 12g carbohydrate, 3g total fat (2g saturated), 0g fiber, 50mg sodium

Holiday Oatmeal Cookies

Delight family or friends with a cookie kit gift: Layer the dry ingredients for these chewy oatmeal cookies in a mason jar, cover the lid with gingham fabric, and use raffia to attach a wooden spoon and a copy of the recipe.

Active time: 40 minutes
Total time: 1 hour 10 minutes
Makes: 48 cookies

1½ cups all-purpose flour
1 teaspoon baking soda
½ teaspoon salt
1 cup butter or margarine (2 sticks), softened
¾ cup packed brown sugar
½ cup granulated sugar
1 large egg
1 teaspoon vanilla extract
3 cups old-fashioned oats, uncooked
1 cup raisins or dried tart cherries (4 ounces)
1 cup semisweet chocolate chips (6 ounces)

1 Preheat oven to 350°F. On waxed paper, combine flour, baking soda, and salt.

2 In large bowl, with mixer on medium speed, beat butter and both sugars until creamy, occasionally scraping bowl with rubber spatula. Beat in egg and vanilla. Reduce speed to low; gradually beat in flour mixture just until blended, occasionally scraping bowl. With spoon, stir in oats, raisins, and chocolate chips.

3 Drop dough by heaping measuring tablespoons, 2 inches apart, on ungreased large cookie sheet. Bake cookies 13 to 15 minutes or until tops are golden. Transfer cookies to wire racks to cool. Repeat with remaining dough. Store in an airtight container up to 1 week, or freeze up to 3 months.

Each cookie: About 115 calories, 2g protein, 16g carbohydrate, 6g total fat (3g saturated), 1g fiber, 95mg sodium

Top: Pinwheels *(opposite)*; *Bottom:* Holiday Oatmeal Cookies *(above)*.

Lemon Meringue Drops

These melt-in-your-mouth meringues are both crunchy and cloud-light—and require only five ingredients. If you want to make these treats gluten-free, look for McCormick or Spice Islands brand cream of tartar.

Active time: 45 minutes
Total time: 2 hours 15 minutes plus standing
Makes: about 60 cookies

3 large egg whites
1/4 teaspoon cream of tartar
1/8 teaspoon salt
1/2 cup sugar
2 teaspoons freshly grated lemon peel

1 Preheat oven to 200°F. Line two large cookie sheets with parchment.

2 In medium bowl, with mixer at high speed, beat egg whites, cream of tartar, and salt until soft peaks form. With mixer running, sprinkle in sugar, 2 tablespoons at a time, beating until sugar dissolves and meringue stands in stiff, glossy peaks when beaters are lifted. Gently fold in lemon peel.

3 Spoon meringue into decorating bag fitted with 1/2-inch star tip. Pipe meringue into 1½-inch stars, about 1 inch apart, on prepared cookie sheets.

4 Bake meringues until crisp but not brown, 1 hour 30 minutes, rotating cookie sheets between upper and lower racks halfway through. Turn oven off; leave meringues in oven until dry, 1 hour.

5 Remove meringues from oven and cool completely. Remove from parchment with wide metal spatula.

6 Store meringues in an airtight container up to 1 month, or freeze up to 3 months.

Each meringue: About 5 calories, 0g protein, 2g carbohydrate, 0g total fat (0g saturated), 0g fiber, 10mg sodium

Top: Lemon Meringue Drops *(above)*;
Bottom: Peppermint Meringue Twists *(opposite)*.

Peppermint Meringue Twists

Peppermint extract (and a little food coloring) lends these melt-in-your-mouth puffs a holiday twist. Peppermint oil will quickly deflate meringues. For these cookies, choose imitation peppermint extract instead.

Active time: 1 hour
Total time: 3 hours plus standing
Makes: about 12 cookies

4 large egg whites
¼ teaspoon cream of tartar
1 cup confectioners' sugar
¼ teaspoon imitation peppermint extract
Red and green food coloring

1 Preheat oven to 225°F. Line two large cookie sheets with foil.

2 In small bowl, with mixer at high speed, beat egg whites and cream of tartar until soft peaks form. Gradually sprinkle in sugar, beating until whites stand in stiff, glossy peaks. Beat in peppermint extract.

3 Transfer half of meringue mixture to another bowl. Using food colorings, tint meringue in one bowl pale red and meringue other bowl pale green.

4 Spoon red meringue into large resealable plastic bag and cut ¼-inch opening at corner. Repeat with green meringue and second bag. Fit large decorating bag (we used 14-inch size) with basketweave or large round tip (½- or ¾-inch opening). Place decorating bag in 2-cup glass measuring cup to stabilize, fold top third of bag over top of cup to keep top of bag clean. Simultaneously squeeze meringues from both resealable bags into decorating bag, filling decorating bag no more than two-thirds full.

5 Pipe meringue onto cookie sheets, leaving 1 inch between each meringue. If using basketweave tip, pipe meringue into 3- to 4-inch-long pleated ribbons, if using round tip, pipe 2-inch rounds.

6 Bake meringues 2 hours, carefully rotating cookie sheets between upper and lower oven racks halfway through. Turn oven off. Leave meringues in oven at least 30 minutes or overnight to dry.

7 When dry, remove meringues from foil with wide metal spatula. Store, with waxed paper between layers, in airtight container up to 3 weeks.

Each cookie: About 10 calories, 0g protein, 2g carbohydrate, 0g total fat (0g saturated), 0g fiber, 5mg sodium

BEATING EGG WHITES

The secret to light, heavenly meringues is properly beaten egg whites.

Start with room-temperature egg whites to get the fullest volume. If a recipe says to beat whites until "foamy" or "frothy," beat them until they form a mass of tiny clear bubbles. For "soft peaks," beat until the whites form soft rounded peaks that droop when beaters are lifted. For "stiff glossy peaks," beat the whites until they form peaks that hold their shape when the beaters are lifted but are still moist. Overbeaten whites turn lumpy and watery; there is no way to salvage them. Begin again with new egg whites.

Tutti Fruitti Chewy Meringues

These crisp meringue sandwiches, studded with dried pineapple, cranberries, and apricots, are filled with lemon curd.

Active time: 20 minutes
Total time: 1 hour 25 minutes plus cooling
Makes: 2½ dozen meringues

¾ cup dried pineapple, cut up
⅓ cup dried cranberries
⅓ cup dried apricots, sliced
2 teaspoons cornstarch
3 large egg whites
Pinch salt
¼ teaspoon cream of tartar
½ cup granulated sugar
½ teaspoon vanilla extract
½ cup lemon curd
2 drops green food coloring

1 Arrange oven racks in top and bottom thirds of oven. Preheat oven to 225°F. Line two large cookie sheets with parchment paper.

2 In food processor with knife blade attached, pulse dried pineapple, dried cranberries, dried apricots, and cornstarch until finely chopped.

3 In medium bowl with mixer on medium speed, beat egg whites and salt until foamy. Add cream of tartar; beat on medium-high until soft peaks form when beaters are lifted. Sprinkle in sugar 1 tablespoon at a time, beating until sugar has dissolved. Add vanilla; continue beating until egg whites stand in stiff, glossy peaks when beaters are lifted.

Top: TUTTI FRUTTI CHEWY MERINGUES *(above);*
Bottom: MERRY MERINGUES *(opposite).*

4 With rubber spatula, gently fold dried fruit into meringue. Transfer meringue to large resealable plastic bag with corner snipped off. Pipe into 1-inch rounds onto prepared cookie sheets, spacing 1 inch apart. Bake for 1 hour; remove from oven. Cool completely on cookie sheets on wire racks.

5 To assemble, tint lemon curd with food coloring. Spread half of flat sides of cooled meringues with lemon curd mixture. Top with remaining cookies.

Each cookie: About 90 calories, 1g protein, 18g carbohydrate, 2g total fat (1g saturated), 0g fiber, 20mg sodium

Merry Meringues

Blueberry, lemon, mint, and almond infuse our light and airy egg-white kisses.

Active time: 20 minutes
Total time: 1 hour 25 minutes plus cooling
Makes: 5 dozen meringues

3 large egg whites
Pinch salt
¼ teaspoon cream of tartar
½ cup sugar
½ teaspoon vanilla extract
Assorted food coloring pastes and flavor pairings (below)

For Almond: Add ½ teaspoon almond extract, green food coloring.
For Lemon: Add 2 teaspoons freshly grated lemon zest, yellow food coloring.
For Mint: Add ½ teaspoon mint extract, red food coloring.
For Blueberry: Add ¼ cup freeze-dried blueberries, finely crushed; purple food coloring.

1 Arrange oven racks in top and bottom thirds of oven. Preheat to 225°F. Line two large cookie sheets with parchment paper.

2 In medium bowl, with mixer on medium speed, beat egg whites and salt until foamy. Add cream of tartar; beat on medium-high until soft peaks form. Add sugar 1 tablespoon at a time. Beat until meringue stands in stiff, glossy peaks. Beat in vanilla and a flavor, if using (see flavor and color pairings before Step 1).

3 For each color desired, using small brush, lightly paint 3 to 4 stripes of food coloring inside large piping bag fitted with ½-inch plain tip. Divide meringue among piping bags. Pipe meringue into 1½-inch rounds onto cookie sheets, spacing 1-inch apart. Bake 1 hour.

4 Turn oven off. Leave meringues in oven 1 hour with oven door closed. Remove from oven; cool completely. Cookies can be stored in airtight containers at room temperature for up to 2 weeks.

Each meringue: About 5 calories, 0g protein, 2g carbohydrate, 0g total fat (0g saturated), 0g fiber, 10mg sodium

Mint Brownie Bites

Chocolaty and cakey, these brownies get their cooling kick from icing mixed with mint extract and a sprinkling of peppermint candy chunks.

Active time: 35 minutes
Total time: 42 minutes plus cooling
Makes: about 24 cookies

Brownie Bites

2/3 cup all-purpose flour

1/2 cup unsweetened cocoa

1/2 teaspoon baking powder

Pinch salt

3/4 cup granulated sugar

3 tablespoons butter or margarine, melted and cooled

2 tablespoons honey

1 teaspoon vanilla extract

1 large egg white

Topping

1 cup confectioners' sugar

1 tablespoon milk

1 tablespoon butter or margarine, softened

1/2 teaspoon peppermint extract

2 ounces white chocolate, melted and cooled

2 ounces round hard peppermint candies,
   broken into chunks

1 Prepare brownie bites: Preheat oven to 350°F. Grease two large cookie sheets.

2 In large bowl, combine flour, cocoa, baking powder, and salt. In medium bowl, whisk sugar, butter, honey, vanilla, and egg white until blended. Stir sugar mixture into flour mixture; then, with hand, press dough just until blended.

3 With greased hands, shape dough into 1-inch balls and place on prepared cookie sheets at least 2 inches apart; press to flatten slightly. Bake until brownies have cracked slightly, 7 to 8 minutes, rotating cookie sheets between upper and lower oven racks halfway through. Transfer to wire rack to cool.

4 Prepare topping: In medium bowl, whisk confectioners' sugar and milk until smooth. Whisk in butter and peppermint extract, then whisk in melted white chocolate until smooth. Swirl 1 teaspoon topping on each cookie. Top each frosted cookie with 1 chunk candy. Allow chocolate to set.

5 Store cookies, with waxed paper between layers, in an airtight container up to 3 days, or freeze up to 1 month.

Each cookie: About 105 calories, 1g protein, 20g carbohydrate, 3g total fat (2g saturated), 1g fiber, 40mg sodium

Whole-Wheat Sugar Cookies

To get the health benefits of whole-wheat flour without the hearty taste and grainy heft, we added white whole-wheat flour to these cookies. It's available from Gold Medal and King Arthur Flour, among other brands. To create the linzer cookie variation shown in the photo, we sandwiched two of these sugar cookies with jam then sprinkled with confectioners' sugar.

Active time: 1 hour
Total time: 1 hour 20 minutes plus chilling
Makes: about 72 cookies

1 cup all-purpose flour
1 cup white whole-wheat flour
1/2 teaspoon baking powder
1/4 teaspoon salt
1 cup sugar
1/2 cup trans-fat-free vegetable oil spread (60% to 70% oil)
1 large egg
2 teaspoons vanilla extract

1 On sheet of waxed paper, combine all-purpose and whole-wheat flours, baking powder, and salt.

2 In large bowl, with mixer on low speed, beat sugar and vegetable oil spread until blended. Increase speed to high; beat until light and creamy, about 3 minutes, occasionally scraping down bowl with rubber spatula. Reduce speed to low; beat in egg and vanilla, then beat in flour mixture just until blended.

3 Divide dough in half; flatten each half into a disk. Wrap each disk with plastic wrap and refrigerate until dough is firm enough to roll, about 2 hours.

4 Preheat oven to 375°F.

5 On lightly floured surface, with floured rolling pin, roll one piece of dough 1/8 inch thick. With 2-inch cookie cutters, cut out as many cookies as possible; wrap and refrigerate trimmings. With lightly floured spatula, place cookies, 1 inch apart, on ungreased cookie sheet.

6 Bake cookies until lightly browned, 10 to 12 minutes. With thin metal spatula, transfer cookies to wire rack to cool. Repeat with remaining dough and trimmings.

Each cookie: About 35 calories, 1g protein, 5g carbohydrate, 1g total fat (0g saturated), 0g fiber, 20mg sodium

Berry-Orange Linzer Jewels

Prepare sugar cookies as directed above, but in steps 1 and 2, add **1 teaspoon grated orange peel** with egg and vanilla. Chill, roll, and cut as described in steps 3 to 5, but use a scalloped, 2-inch square or round cookie cutter. Use a small star-shaped or other decorative cutter to cut out centers of half the cookies. Bake and cool as described in step 6. When cookies are cool, if you like, sprinkle **confectioners' sugar** through sieve over cookies with cutout centers. From **1/4 cup seedless red raspberry jam**, spread scant 1/2 teaspoon jam on each whole cookie; top with cookie with cutout center. Makes about 36 sandwich cookies.

GINGERBREAD WANDS (*opposite*)

Gingerbread Wands

The magical things about these batons: They're the crispy, sophisticated version of gingerbread men.

Active time: 30 minutes
Total time: 45 minutes
Makes: 7 dozen wands

¼ cup granulated sugar
½ cup light (mild) molasses
1 tablespoon pumpkin pie spice
¼ teaspoon ground black pepper
2 teaspoons. baking soda
½ cup (1 stick) butter melted
1 large egg
3½ cups all-purpose flour
1 large egg white, beaten
Colored decorating sugar, edible glitter and sprinkles
    for decorating (all available at wilton.com)

1 Preheat oven to 325°F. In 4-quart saucepan, combine granulated sugar, molasses, pumpkin pie spice and black pepper, heat to boiling on medium, stirring occasionally. Remove from heat; stir in baking soda, then butter. With fork, stir in egg, then flour until combined.

2 On floured surface knead dough until smooth; divide in half. Wrap 1 piece dough in plastic and set aside. With lightly floured rolling pin, roll remaining half of dough into 12" by 8" rectangle (should be about scant ¼-inch thick). With pizza cutter, cut dough into ¼-inch-wide, 8-inch-long strips. Transfer to large parchment-lined cookie sheet, spacing about 1 inch apart.

3 Lightly brush strips with egg white. Sprinkle with desired decorations. Bake 12 to 15 minutes or until set. Cool on cookie sheet on wire rack. Meanwhile, repeat rolling, cutting, and decorating with remaining dough. Cookies can be stored in airtight containers at room temperature for up to 2 weeks.

Each cookie: About 45 calories, 1g protein, 8g carbohydrate, 1g total fat (1g saturated), 0g fiber, 40mg sodium

Cinnamon Sticks

These delicate cookies get their crunch from finely chopped pecans.

Active Time: 40 minutes
Total Time: 1 hour 30 minutes plus chilling and cooling
Makes: about 10 dozen cookies

3½ cups all-purpose flour
1 teaspoon baking soda
1 teaspoon ground cinnamon
1 cup (2 sticks) butter or margarine, softened
1 cup granulated sugar
1 cup packed brown sugar
2 large eggs
1 cup pecans, finely chopped

1 Line 9" by 5" metal loaf pan with plastic wrap, letting wrap extend on all sides. In medium bowl with wire whisk, combine flour, baking soda, and cinnamon.

2 In large bowl with mixer on medium speed, beat butter and sugars for 2 minutes or until light and fluffy, occasionally scraping bowl with rubber spatula. Add eggs, one at a time, and beat until blended. Reduce speed to low; gradually beat in flour mixture just until blended, occasionally scraping bowl. Stir in pecans.

3 Evenly pat dough into prepared pan. Cover and refrigerate for at least 4 hours or until dough is firm enough to slice.

4 Preheat oven to 325°F. Line large cookie sheet with parchment paper.

5 Invert dough onto cutting board; discard plastic wrap. Cut dough crosswise into ¼-inch-thick slices. Cut each slice lengthwise into ¼-inch sticks. Place sticks, 1 inch apart, on prepared cookie sheet. Bake for 12 to 13 minutes or until golden. Slide cookies, still on parchment, onto wire rack to cool completely. Repeat with remaining dough and cooled, newly lined cookie sheet.

Each cookie: About 50 calories, 1g protein, 6g carbohydrate, 2g total fat (1g saturated), 0g fiber, 30mg sodium.

Glazed Vanilla-Almond Cutouts

Our deliciously decorated crowd-pleasers will stand out in a flurry of Christmas cookies.

Active time: 25 minutes
Total time: 40 minutes
Makes: 4 dozen cookies

2¼ cups all-purpose flour
1 teaspoon baking powder
½ teaspoon baking soda
¾ cup (1½ sticks) butter, softened
¾ cup sugar
½ teaspoon salt
1 large egg yolk
2 tablespoons honey
1 teaspoon almond extract
1 teaspoon vanilla extract

PUMPKIN-SPICE VARIATION
1 tablespoon pumpkin pie spice

1 In medium bowl, whisk flour, baking powder, and baking soda. With mixer on medium-high speed, beat butter, sugar, and salt until creamy. Beat in yolk, then honey and extracts until smooth, stopping and scraping down side of bowl occasionally. With mixer on low, beat in flour mixture until smooth. Divide dough into two pieces. Wrap each in plastic and refrigerate 15 to 30 minutes or until somewhat soft but no longer sticky.

2 Preheat oven to 375°F. On large sheet of parchment, roll 1 piece dough to scant 1/4-inch thickness. With floured 2-inch cookie cutters, cut shapes, then remove dough around them with small knife or mini offset spatula. Slide parchment onto cookie sheet; freeze 20 to 30 minutes, or until firm. On another sheet of parchment, gather scraps and repeat rolling, cutting and removing of excess dough. Freeze shapes until firm. Carefully peel all shapes off parchment and arrange on 1 cookie sheet, 1 inch apart. Bake 10 minutes or until golden.

3 Let cookies cool on cookie sheet 5 minutes. Transfer cookies to wire rack to cool completely. Meanwhile, repeat rolling, cutting and freezing with second piece of dough. Decorate cookies with Ornamental Frosting (page 307), sugar pearls, and decorating sugar as desired. Cookies can be stored in airtight containers at room temperature (with waxed paper between layers) for up to 1 week.

4 For the Pumpkin-Spice variation: Add pumpkin pie spice along with flour.

Each cookie: About 105 calories, 2g protein, 18g carbohydrate, 3g total fat (2g saturated), 0g fiber, 70mg sodium

Chocolate-Citrus Cran Wheels

Orange you glad we baked up the cookie version of choco-dipped fruit slices?! And they're crazy-easy!

Active time: 40 minutes
Total Time: 1 hour 15 minutes
Makes: 4 dozen cookies

2 cups all-purpose flour
¼ teaspoon. baking soda
¼ teaspoon salt
¾ cup dried cranberries
½ cup confectioners' sugar
½ cup granulated sugar
¾ cup (1½ sticks) butter, softened
1 teaspoon orange zest
1 teaspoon vanilla extract
¼ teaspoon ground cinnamon
12 ounces melted white or dark chocolate, for dipping
Dried orange slices (optional)

1 In medium bowl, whisk flour, baking soda, and salt. In food processor, pulse cranberries, confectioners' sugar, and granulated sugar until cranberries are very finely chopped; transfer to large mixing bowl.

2 With mixer on medium-high speed, beat cranberry mixture and butter until combined. Beat in orange zest, vanilla, and cinnamon. Beat in flour mixture until just combined, stopping and scraping down side of bowl occasionally. Divide dough in half. Roll each half into 2-inch-diameter log; wrap tightly with plastic wrap. Refrigerate overnight or up to 1 week.

3 Preheat oven to 350°F. Working with 1 log at a time, cut into 1/4-inch-thick slices; arrange on large parchment-lined cookie sheet, spacing about 1 inch apart. Bake 15 to 17 minutes or until golden brown around edges. Let cool on cookie sheet 5 minutes. Transfer to wire rack to cool completely. Repeat slicing and baking with remaining log.

4 Dip cooled cookies halfway into melted chocolate; decorate with orange slices if desired. Place on waxed-paper-lined cookie sheet. Refrigerate until set. Cookies can be stored in airtight containers in freezer for up to 2 weeks.

VARIATIONS

Cherry-Almond: Replace cranberries with cherries. Add almond extract along with vanilla.

Lemony Apricot: Replace cranberries with apricots. Use lemon zest instead of orange.

Each cookie: About 100 calories, 1g protein, 14g carbohydrate, 5g total fat (4g saturated), 0g fiber, 50mg sodium

Top: Glazed Vanilla-Almond Cutouts *(opposite);*
Bottom: Chocolate-Citrus Cran Wheels *(opposite).*

Matcha Spritz

Matcha green tea powder is ground from the finest Japanese tea leaves. It can be enjoyed as a beverage or as an ingredient in recipes, like these buttery pressed cookies.

Active time: 15 minutes
Total time: 40 minutes
Makes: 3 dozen cookies

½ cup (1 stick) butter, softened
½ cups sugar
4 ounces cream cheese, softened
¼ teaspoon salt
2 ounces white chocolate, melted
1 large egg
1 teaspoon vanilla extract
1½ cups all-purpose flour
1 tablespoon plus 1 teaspoon matcha green tea powder

1 Preheat oven to 350°F. With mixer on medium speed, beat butter, sugar, cream cheese, and salt until smooth. Beat in white chocolate, egg, and vanilla, stopping and scraping down side of bowl occasionally. With mixer on low, beat in flour and tea until just combined.

2 Transfer dough to large piping bag fitted with star tip. Pipe onto large cookie sheet into 2½-inch-round wreaths, spacing about 2 inches apart. Bake 15 to 18 minutes or until golden around edges. Let cool on cookie sheet 5 minutes. Transfer to wire rack to cool completely. Cookies can be stored in airtight containers at room temperature for up to 1 week.

3 For a Cream Cheese variation: Omit matcha. Dip cooled cookie in melted white chocolate, if desired.

Each Cookie: About 75 calories, 1g protein, 8g carbohydrate, 4g total fat (3g saturated), 0g fiber, 50mg sodium

Top: Matcha Spritz *(above);*
Bottom: Lemony Ricotta Pillows *(opposite).*

Lemony Ricotta Pillows

We drizzled icy blue frosting over the Italian family favorite.
(Tell your kids they're Elsa cookies!)

Active time: 30 minutes
Total time: 1 hour
Makes: 3½ dozen cookies

1 lemon
4 cups all-purpose flour
2 teaspoons baking powder
1 teaspoon salt
1¾ cups granulated sugar
1 cup (2 sticks) butter, softened
1 container (15 ounces) ricotta cheese
2 large eggs
2 teaspoons vanilla extract
1¼ cup confectioners' sugar
½ teaspoon water
Blue food coloring
Edible silver stars (optional)

1 Preheat oven to 350°F. From lemon, grate 1 teaspoon zest and squeeze 3 tablespoons juice. In large bowl, whisk flour, baking powder, and salt. With mixer on medium-high speed, beat granulated sugar, butter and lemon zest until creamy. Add ricotta, eggs, and vanilla, beating until combined, stopping and scraping down side of bowl occasionally. Beat in flour mixture until just smooth.

2 Line large cookie sheet with parchment paper. With small cookie scoop (about 2 teaspoons), scoop dough into balls; place on cookie sheet, spacing 1½ inches apart. With fingers, pat each down into flat disk. Bake 15 to 20 minutes or until bottoms are golden brown. Let cool on cookie sheet 5 minutes. Transfer to wire rack to cool completely.

3 Make glaze: In medium bowl, stir together confectioners' sugar, reserved lemon juice and ½ teaspoon water until smooth. Tint with food coloring to desired shade. Place in small plastic bag with one corner snipped off and drizzle all over cookies. Decorate with edible stars if desired. Let stand until set, about 30 minutes. Cookies can be stored in airtight containers in freezer for up to 1 month.

4 For a Chocolate-Glazed Ricotta variation: Omit lemon in cookies. Instead of confectioners' sugar glaze, drizzle with melted dark chocolate.

Each cookie: About 150 calories, 3g protein, 22g carbohydrate, 6g total fat (4g saturated), 0g fiber, 130mg sodium.

HOLIDAY HOSTING SECRET

"I like to make fortune napkins by tucking small notes into the folds. Try sentiments like 'What a great year in friendship' or 'So happy you're here.'"

—Sunny Anderson

Cranberry–Chocolate Chunk Cookies (*opposite*)

Cranberry-Chocolate Chunk Cookies

The addition of cranberries imbues this chewy, chunky cookie classic with holiday spirit. Anyone would be delighted to receive a cookie jar full!

Active time: 30 minutes

Total time: 52 minutes plus chilling

Makes: about 36 cookies

2¹/2 cups all-purpose flour

1 teaspoon baking soda

¹/2 teaspoon salt

³/4 cup butter or margarine (1¹/2 sticks), softened

³/4 cup packed dark brown sugar

¹/4 cup granulated sugar

3 tablespoons light corn syrup

2 large eggs

2 teaspoons vanilla extract

1¹/2 cups walnuts (6 ounces), toasted (page 287) and chopped

1 cup dried cranberries

4 ounces white chocolate, chopped

4 squares (4 ounces) semisweet chocolate, chopped

1 Arrange two oven racks in upper and lower thirds of oven. Preheat oven to 375°F. Line two cookie sheets with parchment paper.

2 On waxed paper, combine flour, baking soda, and salt; set aside. In large bowl, with mixer on medium speed, beat butter, brown and granulated sugars, and corn syrup until just creamy. Beat in eggs and vanilla until blended. Reduce speed to low. Add half of flour mixture, beat until just blended, and repeat with remaining half of flour mixture. Stir in two-thirds of walnuts, cranberries, and white and semisweet chocolates. Refrigerate dough 15 minutes or up to 1 day.

3 Drop dough by rounded tablespoons, 2 inches apart, on prepared cookie sheets (return remaining dough to refrigerator until ready to make next batch). Bake 5 minutes. Working quickly, press some of remaining walnuts, cranberries, and chocolates into cookies. Rotate cookie sheets between upper and lower racks and continue baking until edges are golden brown, 6 to 8 minutes longer.

4 Transfer cookies to wire rack to cool completely. Repeat with remaining dough.

5 Store cookies in an airtight container up to 1 week, or freeze for up to 1 month.

Each cookie: About 170 calories, 2g protein, 21g carbohydrate, 9g total fat (4g saturated), 1g fiber, 75mg sodium

German Chocolate Brownies

These brownies boast a chocolate base and a coconut-pecan topping. They're sure to delight any fan of their namesake layer cake.

Active time: 25 minutes
Total time: 1 hour 10 minutes
Makes: 36 brownies

Brownie
1/2 cup butter or margarine (1 stick)
2 packages (4 ounces each) sweet baking chocolate
1 cup packed brown sugar
3 large eggs, lightly beaten
1 teaspoon vanilla extract
1 cup all-purpose flour
1/2 teaspoon salt

German Chocolate Topping
3 large egg whites
2 cups sweetened flaked coconut
1 cup pecans, toasted (page 287) and chopped
1/2 cup packed brown sugar
1/4 cup whole milk
1/2 teaspoon vanilla extract
1/8 teaspoon almond extract
1/8 teaspoon salt

1 Preheat oven to 350°F. Line 13" by 9" baking pan with foil (see opposite); grease foil.

2 Prepare brownie: In 3-quart saucepan, heat butter and chocolate over medium-low heat until melted, stirring frequently. Remove saucepan from heat; stir in brown sugar. Add eggs and vanilla; stir until well mixed. Stir in flour and salt just until blended. Spread batter evenly in prepared pan.

3 Prepare topping: In medium bowl, with wire whisk, beat egg whites until foamy. Stir in coconut, pecans, brown sugar, milk, vanilla and almond extracts, and salt until well combined. Spread topping over batter.

4 Bake until toothpick inserted 2 inches from edge comes out almost clean and topping turns golden brown, 45 to 50 minutes. Cool completely in pan on wire rack.

5 When cool, lift foil, with brownie, out of pan; peel foil away from sides. Cut lengthwise into 6 strips, then cut each strip crosswise into 6 pieces. Refrigerate in an airtight container up to 1 week, or freeze up to 3 months.

Each brownie: About 150 calories, 2g protein, 18g carbohydrate, 8g total fat (4g saturated), 2g fiber, 85mg sodium

Butter-Almond Thins

These classic cookies can be made well ahead of the holiday rush. They keep in the freezer for up to one month. The recipe makes a big batch, but we bet by December 26, you'll be left only with crumbs.

Active time: 30 minutes
Total time: 50 minutes
Makes: about 84 cookies

3/4 cup (1½ sticks) butter (no substitutions), softened
⅓ cup granulated sugar
½ teaspoon ground cardamom
¼ teaspoon salt
1 large egg, separated
1 teaspoon almond extract
1 teaspoon vanilla extract
2 cups all-purpose flour
2 cups sliced blanched almonds
4 tablespoons confectioners' sugar

1 Preheat oven to 375°F. Grease 18" by 12" jelly-roll pan, line with foil, and grease foil (see below).

2 In large bowl, with mixer on medium, beat butter, granulated sugar, cardamom, and salt until creamy and smooth. Beat in egg yolk and extracts until well mixed. Add flour and beat on low just until clumps form.

3 Scatter clumps evenly on pan. With palm and fingertips, press dough into thin, even layer without any gaps.

4 In medium bowl, whisk egg white until frothy; fold in almonds and 2 tablespoons confectioners' sugar. Spread in even layer over dough, pressing into dough gently. With pizza wheel or sharp knife, cut dough crosswise into 2-inch strips; cut each one crosswise to form 2-inch squares. Cut squares diagonally into triangles. Dust tops with remaining 2 tablespoons confectioners' sugar.

5 Bake 15 to 18 minutes or until golden brown. Cool completely in pan on wire rack. Carefully break cookies into triangles. Store cookies in an airtight container up to 2 days, or freeze up to 1 month.

Each serving: About 45 calories, 1g protein, 4g carbohydrate, 3g total fat (1g saturated), 0g fiber, 25mg sodium

LINING A PAN WITH FOIL

This trick keeps brownies and bars from sticking to the pan—and makes cleanup quick.

Step 1: Turn the baking pan bottom side up. Cover the pan tightly with foil, shiny side out. Remove the foil cover.

Step 2: Turn the baking pan right side up and carefully lift the molded foil into the pan, smoothing the foil to fit it into the edge.

Angeletti

These luscious glazed cookies hail from Italy—consider using red, green, and white décors in honor of its flag.

Active time: 40 minutes
Total time: 54 minutes plus cooling
Makes: about 60 cookies

1/2 cup butter or margarine (1 stick), melted
3/4 cup granulated sugar
1/4 cup whole milk
1 1/2 teaspoons vanilla extract
3 large eggs
3 cups all-purpose flour
1 tablespoon baking powder
1/4 teaspoon salt
2 cups confectioners' sugar
3 1/2 tablespoons water
1/2 cup multicolor candy décors (optional)

1 Preheat oven to 375°F. Grease two large cookie sheets.

2 In large bowl, whisk butter, granulated sugar, milk, vanilla, and eggs until blended. In medium bowl, mix flour, baking powder, and salt. Stir flour mixture into egg mixture until evenly blended. Cover dough with plastic wrap or waxed paper; let stand 5 minutes.

3 With floured hands, shape dough by level tablespoons into 1-inch balls. Place, 2 inches apart, on prepared cookie sheets. Bake until puffed and light brown on bottoms, 7 to 8 minutes, rotating cookie sheets between upper and lower oven racks halfway through. Transfer cookies to wire rack to cool. Repeat with remaining dough.

4 When cookies are cool, whisk confectioners' sugar and water in small bowl, until blended. Dip top of each cookie into glaze and place on wire rack set over waxed paper to catch any drips. Immediately sprinkle cookies with décors, if using. Allow glaze to set, about 20 minutes.

5 Store cookies, with wax paper between layers, in an airtight container up to 5 days, or freeze up to 3 months.

Each cookie: About 75 calories, 1g protein, 13g carbohydrate, 2g total fat (1g saturated), 0g fiber, 55mg sodium

Tin Roof Puffed Rice Treats

These nostalgic cereal treats celebrate the sweet-salty combination featured in tin roof sundaes, a chocolate sundae topped with salted, red-skinned Spanish peanuts popular in the early twentieth century. These no-bake bars are sure kid-pleasers, so they're a great gift for parents! Present them in a square tin with the recipe attached.

Total time: 20 minutes plus chilling
Makes: 16 bars

1/2 cup creamy peanut butter
24 large marshmallows
4 cups puffed rice cereal
2/3 cup semisweet chocolate chips (4 ounces)
2 tablespoons roasted, salted Spanish peanuts, chopped

1 Line bottom of 8-inch square baking pan with foil; spray with nonstick cooking spray.

2 In microwave-safe 4-quart bowl, combine peanut butter and marshmallows. Cover bowl with vented plastic wrap and cook in microwave on High 1 minute, until melted. With rubber spatula, quickly stir in puffed rice until evenly coated. With hand, evenly pat puffed rice mixture into prepared baking pan.

3 In microwave-safe cup, heat chocolate in microwave on High 35 to 45 seconds, or until soft; stir until smooth. With offset spatula, spread melted chocolate on top of puffed rice mixture. Sprinkle with peanuts; gently press so nuts adhere to chocolate.

4 Refrigerate until chocolate is set, 30 minutes. Lift foil, with pastry, out of pan; peel foil away from sides. Cut lengthwise into 4 strips, then cut each strip crosswise into 4 pieces. With small metal spatula, separate treats. Refrigerate bars in an airtight container up to 1 week.

Each bar: About 135 calories, 3g protein, 18g carbohydrate, 7g total fat (2g saturated), 1g fiber, 51mg sodium

Lime Triangles

You can prepare these tart treats up to a day ahead through step 4, but stop before sprinkling on the confectioners' sugar. Store the pan in the refrigerator until you're ready to serve. Sprinkle with confectioners' sugar, then cut the triangles.

Active time: 25 minutes
Total time: 45 minutes plus cooling
Makes: 48 triangles

3/4 cup butter (1½ sticks), cut up and softened (no substitutions)

2¼ cups all-purpose flour

2/3 cup plus 1 tablespoon confectioners' sugar

5 to 6 large limes

6 large eggs

1¾ cups granulated sugar

1 teaspoon baking powder

3/4 teaspoon salt

1 Preheat oven to 350°F. Grease 13" by 9" metal baking pan. Line pan with foil, extending foil over short ends (see page 339); lightly grease bottom and sides of foil. (If you prefer, line pan with nonstick foil and do not grease.)

2 In food processor with knife blade attached, pulse butter, 2 cups flour, and 2/3 cup confectioners' sugar until mixture is moist but crumbly. Dough should hold together when pressed between two fingers. Transfer mixture to prepared pan; spread evenly. With fingertips, press dough onto bottom of pan. Bake 20 to 25 minutes or until lightly browned.

3 While crust bakes, prepare filling: From limes, grate 1 tablespoon peel and squeeze 2/3 cup juice. In large bowl, with wire whisk, beat eggs. Add lime peel and juice, granulated sugar, baking powder, salt, and remaining
¼ cup flour; whisk until well blended.

4 Whisk filling again and pour onto hot crust. Bake 18 to 22 minutes or until filling is just set and golden (filling will jiggle slightly in center). Transfer pan to wire rack. Sift remaining 1 tablespoon confectioners' sugar over hot filling. Cool completely in pan on wire rack.

5 When cool, lift foil, with bars, out of pan and set on cutting board. Carefully peel foil away from sides. If you like, trim edges. Cut bars lengthwise into 4 strips, then cut each strip crosswise into 6 pieces. Cut each piece diagonally in half to form two triangles. Refrigerate any leftovers.

Each triangle: About 95 calories, 1g protein, 14g carbohydrate, 4g total fat (2g saturated), 0g fiber, 85mg sodium

MY MOST MAGICAL CHRISTMAS

"Nothing will ever beat the Christmases I had as a kid. My mother always made it really festive, even if we didn't have much money—which we didn't!"

—Mariah Carey

Figgy Bars with Hard-Sauce Glaze

If these bars remind you of an English steamed pudding, it's no accident. That's exactly the flavor we had in mind—complete with a hard-sauce glaze. Here we've slashed the calories and fat by using lower-fat vegetable oil spread.

Active time: 25 minutes
Total time: 48 minutes plus cooling
Makes: 96 bars

Figgy Bars

10 ounces dried black Mission figs (scant 2 cups), finely chopped

1 cup water

2 cups quick-cooking oats, uncooked

1½ cups packed brown sugar

⅔ cup dark molasses

6 tablespoons reduced-fat vegetable-oil spread (60% to 70% oil)

2 large eggs

1 cup all-purpose flour

1 cup toasted wheat germ

2 teaspoons pumpkin-pie spice

2 teaspoons freshly grated orange peel

1 teaspoon salt

1 teaspoon baking soda

1 teaspoon baking powder

Hard-Sauce Glaze

2 cups confectioners' sugar

⅓ cup brandy

2 tablespoons warm water

1 Preheat oven to 350°F. Lightly spray two 13" by 9" baking pans with nonstick cooking spray. Line both pans with foil, extending foil 2 inches over short sides of pans (page 339). Spray foil with cooking spray.

2 In 4-quart saucepan, combine figs and water; heat to boiling over high heat. Remove saucepan from heat; stir in oats. Stir sugar, molasses, and vegetable-oil spread into fig mixture until blended. Stir in eggs. Add flour, wheat germ, pumpkin-pie spice, orange peel, salt, baking soda, and baking powder and stir until combined. Divide batter equally between prepared pans; spread evenly.

3 Bake bars until toothpick inserted in center comes out clean, 23 to 26 minutes. Cool in pans on wire racks 10 minutes.

4 Meanwhile, prepare glaze: In small bowl, stir confectioners' sugar, brandy, and water until blended.

5 Remove pastry from pans by lifting edges of foil; transfer with foil to racks. Brush both hot pastries with glaze. Cool completely.

6 When cool, cut each pastry lengthwise into 4 strips, then cut each strip crosswise into 6 rectangles. Cut each rectangle on diagonal into 2 triangles.

7 Store bars in an airtight container, with waxed paper between layers, at room temperature up to 1 week, or in refrigerator up to 1 month.

Each bar: About 60 calories, 1g protein, 12g carbohydrate, 1g total fat (0g saturated), 2g fiber, 50mg sodium

Top right: FIGGY BARS WITH HARD-SAUCE GLAZE *(above);*
Bottom right: CRANBERRY SHORTBREAD *(opposite).*

Cranberry Shortbread

Dried cranberries and chopped pistachios add seasonal flavor and flair to these traditional cookies.

Active time: 35 minutes
Total time: 1 hour 25 minutes plus chilling and cooling
Makes: about 60 cookies

1 lemon
1 cups (2 sticks) butter (no substitutions), softened
1¼ cups confectioners' sugar
⅛ teaspoon salt
1 large egg
2¼ cups all-purpose flour
¾ cup dried cranberries
1 cup pistachios, shelled (½ cup), finely chopped
   (optional)

1 Grate 1 tablespoon lemon peel and squeeze
1 tablespoon juice. In large bowl, with mixer on medium
speed, beat butter, sugar, and salt until smooth and
creamy. With mixer running, beat in egg, then lemon
peel and juice, scraping bowl occasionally.

2 Add flour and beat on low until just incorporated. Stir
in cranberries until evenly distributed. Divide dough
among 3 sheets waxed paper and roll into 1-inch logs.
(If dough is sticky, refrigerate for 30 minutes before
rolling.) Wrap logs in waxed paper and refrigerate
45 minutes or until firm.

3 If using, divide pistachios among logs; press into
dough to evenly coat. Wrap tightly in plastic wrap and
refrigerate at least 1 hour or up to 1 week.

4 Preheat oven to 300°F. Line 2 cookie sheets with
parchment paper. In batches, cut logs into ¼-inch-thick
slices. Arrange slices 2 inches apart on cookie sheets.
Bake 25 to 30 minutes or until golden brown. Refrigerate
remaining dough while cookies bake. Cool baked cookies
on wire racks. Repeat with remaining dough.

5 Store cookies in an airtight container up to 3 days, or
freeze up to 1 month.

Each serving: About 60 calories, 1g protein, 11g carbohydrate,
3g total fat (2g saturated), 0g fiber, 35mg sodium

Brown Sugar–Hazelnut Bars

This speedy recipe is the base for the three that follow!

Active time: 15 minutes
Total time: 45 minutes plus cooling
Makes: About 3 dozen

¾ cup butter
½ cup brown sugar
½ teaspoon salt
1 large egg
1½ teaspoon vanilla extract
2 cups all-purpose flour
½ cup hazelnut chocolate spread
1 cup toasted hazelnuts, peeled and chopped

1 Preheat oven to 375°F. Spray 13" by 9" metal baking pan with nonstick baking spray; line pan with foil, then spray foil.

2 With mixer on medium-high speed, beat butter, brown sugar, and salt until creamy. Beat in egg and vanilla. With mixer on low speed, beat in flour until just combined. Transfer to prepared pan. With lightly floured hands, spread into an even layer.

3 Bake 25 to 30 minutes or until deep golden brown around edges. Cool completely on wire rack.

4 Spread crust with hazelnut chocolate spread. Sprinkle with hazelnuts; press to adhere. Using foil, remove bar from pan. Cut into 1½ -inch squares.

Each bar: About 100 calories, 1g protein, 10g carbohydrate, 6 g total fat (3g saturated), 1g fiber, 30mg sodium

Top, clockwise from top: Brown Sugar–Hazelnut Bars *(above),* Pistachio Thins, Apricot Crumb Bars, PB&J Bars *(opposite); Bottom:* "Candy" Bars *(opposite).*

Apricot Crumb Bars

Brown sugar, cinnamon, and apricot jam. Yum!

Active time: 15 minutes
Total time: 45 minutes plus cooling
Makes: About 2 dozen

Prepare Brown Sugar-Hazelnut Bars as directed, with these modifications: In Step 1, for topping, combine in medium bowl 1/2 cup all-purpose flour, 1/4 cup brown sugar, 3 tablespoons softened butter and 1/4 teaspoon ground cinnamon; pinch with fingers until clumps form. In Step 3, bake only 15 minutes, then spread crust with 1/4 cup apricot jam. Sprinkle with topping. Bake 20 minutes or until top is golden brown. Cool completely on wire rack. In Step 4, cut into 2-inch squares.

Each bar: About 165 calories, 2g protein, 23g carbohydrate, 8g total fat (5g saturated), 0g fiber, 107mg sodium

Pistachio Thins

Perfect for the holidays, these crunchy and tasty pistachio cookies are going to become a new family favorite.

Active time: 15 minutes
Total time: 45 minutes
Makes: About 4 dozen

Prepare Brown Sugar-Hazelnut Bars as directed, with these modifications: In Step 1, use 18" by 12" rimmed baking sheet instead of baking pan. In Step 2, to butter, add 1/2 teaspoon ground cinnamon and 1/4 teaspoon ground nutmeg. Press dough into prepared pan in very thin, even layer. Sprinkle with 1/2 cup pistachios, very finely chopped; press nuts into dough. With pizza cutter or very sharp knife, cut dough lengthwise into 3-inch-wide rectangles, then crosswise to form 3-inch squares. Cut squares diagonally into triangles. In Step 3, baking 15 to 17 minutes or until golden. Cool completely on wire rack. Gently break triangles to separate.

Each bar: About 60 calories, 1g protein, 7g carbohydrate, 4g total fat (2g saturated), 0g fiber, 46mg sodium

PB&J Bars

Take your love of peanut butter and jelly to the next level with these easy and delicious bar cookies.

Active time: 15 minutes
Total time: 45 minutes plus cooling
Makes: About 3 1/2 dozen

Prepare Brown Sugar-Hazelnut Bars as directed, with these modifications: In Step 3, after baking while crust is still warm, spread crust with 3/4 cup strawberry jam. Top with 3/4 cup peanut butter chips. Cool completely on wire rack. In Step 4, cut into 1-inch squares.

Each bar: About 95 calories, 1g protein, 12g carbohydrate, 4g total fat (3g saturated), 0g fiber, 60mg sodium

"Candy" Bars

Toffee bits, pretzels, coconut, and chocolate make these bars as rich and delicious!

Active time: 15 minutes
Total time: 45 minutes plus chilling
Makes: About 2 dozen

Prepare Brown Sugar-Hazelnut Bars as directed, with these modifications: In Step 4, spread crust with 3/4 cup caramel sauce. Top with 1/4 cup toffee bits, 1/4 cup broken pretzels, and 1/2 cup toasted coconut. Drizzle with 4 ounces melted bittersweet chocolate. Chill to set (1 1/2 hours). Cut into 2-inch squares.

Each bar: About 185 calories, 2g protein, 24g carbohydrate, 10g total fat (6g saturated), 1g fiber, 146mg sodium

Salted Toffee Rugelach

Salted toffee is a no-fail favorite, but try adding it to rugelach, a delicious cream cheese-based cookie, for a real holiday winner.

Active time: 30 minutes
Total time: 1 hour 10 minutes plus chilling
Makes: 4 dozen cookies

1 cup butter
8 ounces cream cheese
1 teaspoon vanilla extract
3 tablespoons plus ¼ cup brown sugar
2 cups all-purpose flour
½ teaspoon salt
1 cup toffee bits
¾ cup roasted salted almonds
Confectioners' sugar, for dusting

1 Arrange oven racks in top and bottom thirds of oven. Preheat oven to 350°F. Line 2 large cookie sheets with parchment paper.

2 With mixer on medium speed, beat butter, cream cheese, vanilla, and 3 tablespoons brown sugar until well mixed. Add flour and salt; beat on low speed until just combined. Divide dough into 4 equal-sized disks. Wrap in plastic wrap and refrigerate at least 2 hours or up to 24 hours.

3 Meanwhile, in medium bowl, combine toffee, almonds, and remaining ¼ cup brown sugar.

4 On well-floured, large sheet of parchment paper, with floured rolling pin, roll 1 disk into 9-inch circle. Sprinkle with one-quarter of toffee mixture, leaving ½-inch rim. Gently press filling into dough. With sharp knife or pastry cutter, cut circle into 12 even wedges. Starting at outer edge, roll each wedge into crescent. (If dough becomes too soft or sticky to roll, place parchment with dough on cookie sheet and refrigerate 10 minutes or until firmer but still pliable.) Place, point sides down,

Top: SALTED TOFFEE RUGELACH *(above);*
Bottom: WHITE CHOCOLATE–MACADAMIA BARS
and ORANGE GINGER BARS *(opposite).*

on prepared cookie sheet, spacing 1 inch apart. Bake 20 minutes, or until golden brown, switching racks halfway through.

5 Slide parchment with cookies onto wire rack to cool. Repeat with remaining disks of dough and toffee mixture. When cookies are cool, dust with confectioners' sugar. Store cookies in airtight containers at room temperature up to 1 week or in freezer for up to 1 month,

Each cookie: About 120 calories, 1g protein, 10g carbohydrate, 8g total fat (4g saturated), 0g fiber, 105mg sodium

White Chocolate–Macadamia Bars

An easy way to even out the dough for the crust: Cover surface with a large sheet of parchment and press dough down with another 13" by 9" baking pan.

Active time: 25 minutes
Total time: 55 minutes plus cooling
Makes: 4 dozen bars

CRUST

2¼ cups all-purpose flour

⅓ cup granulated sugar

¾ cup cold butter

FILLING

1½ cups packed dark brown sugar

4 tablespoons butter

3 tablespoons light corn syrup

2 tablespoons water

¼ teaspoon salt

1 can sweetened condensed milk

2 teaspoons vanilla extract

1½ cups chopped salted macadamia nuts

1 cup white chocolate chunks

1 Prepare Crust: Preheat oven to 350°F. Line 13" by 9" baking pan with foil. Spray with nonstick cooking spray.

2 In food processor with knife blade attached, pulse flour and sugar until blended. Add butter and pulse until dough begins to form ball. Press dough into bottom of prepared pan in even layer. Freeze 10 minutes.

3 Bake crust 20 to 25 minutes or until golden brown with darker brown edges. Cool in pan on wire rack.

4 Prepare Filling: In 3-quart saucepan, combine brown sugar, butter, corn syrup, water, and salt. Heat to boiling on medium-high, stirring occasionally with heatproof rubber spatula. Stir in condensed milk; return to boiling. Reduce heat to medium-low to maintain simmer. Simmer 10 minutes or until caramel mixture thickens slightly, stirring frequently (especially around edges of saucepan) to prevent scorching. Remove from heat; stir in vanilla. Pour caramel over cooled crust, spreading evenly.

5 While caramel is hot, sprinkle with nuts and chocolate. With spatula, gently push nuts into caramel. Cool completely on wire rack. Refrigerate 30 minutes before cutting. Remove from pan using foil. Cut lengthwise into 6 strips, then crosswise into 8 pieces. Store bars, tightly wrapped in plastic, in refrigerator up to 1 week or in freezer up to 1 month.

Each bar: About 165 calories, 2g protein, 21g carbohydrate, 9g total fat (4g saturated), 0g fiber, 75mg sodium

Orange Ginger Bars

Spiced and sweet, these bar cookies are ideal for the holidays. The classic flavor combination of orange and chocolate, boosted with a hit of candied ginger, makes these bars downright irresistible.

Active time: 25 minutes
Total time: 55 minutes
Makes: 4 dozen bars

Prepare White Chocolate–Macadamia Bars as directed above with these modifications: In Step 5, substitute ½ cup candied orange peel, chopped, and ½ cup crystallized ginger, chopped, for macadamia nuts. Substitute 1 cup semisweet chocolate chunks for white chocolate chunks.

Each bar: About 155 calories, 2g protein, 25g carbohydrate, 6g total fat (4g saturated), 1g fiber, 65mg sodium

1

Abbie — Linzer cookies
Kate — Nut crescents
Alice — Sugar cookies
Susan — Starlight Meringues
Jenny — Oatmeal cookies

Abbie's
Linzer Cookies

2

Susan's
GingerSnaps

Liz's
Meringues

Alice's
Sugar Cookies

3

4

HOST A COOKIE SWAP

It's the easiest party ever! Ask six to ten guests to bring batches of their favorite cookies, then trade. The payoff: Everyone takes home an array of Christmas cookies for a fraction of the effort. Here how to make it come off without a hitch.

1. Master the List

Give guests lots of pre-fete notice (say, one month) so they can fit the cookie prep into their schedules. Pick a convenient time (Sunday afternoons are great) and specify how many cookies to bring; we suggest that each guest bring a half- or full-dozen cookies for each person attending plus an extra dozen for sampling at the party. Besides RSVP'ing, they'll need to let you know what type of goody they'll bring, to prevent four different batches of gingersnaps from showing up; ask attendees to print copies of their recipes to share as well.

2. Create a Staging Area

Decorate the area where the cookies will be displayed: Cover the dining room table or a large folding table with a pretty holiday cloth. Have extra platters on hand to lay out the cookies. In a pinch, cardboard box bottoms can be covered with foil for attractive display. Note who baked what—and alert people of any allergens, like nuts and dairy—on the cookie name cards.

3. Get Fresh

When you're hosting a swap, attending one, or just baking solo, try these Good Housekeeping Test Kitchen tips: Cool treats completely before packing; store in resealable bags, tins, or plastic containers, separating soft and crisp varieties. Slip an apple wedge in with chewy sweets to boost freshness (replace every other day). Most cookies keep at room temperature for one to two weeks, or frozen for a few months. Space out baking for minimal stress.

If you plan to transfer cookies to new vessels for serving, be creative—a bowl or butter dish works as well as a platter; cupcake liners can group tiny treats. Time to send guests packing? Provide plastic wrap or foil so folks can reuse their own carriers.

4. Share the Joy

Remember those less fortunate during the holidays: Ask each guest bake just one more dozen and create a tray or basket of assorted cookies to deliver to your local homeless shelter, hospital, retirement home, or a family in need.

Keep versus Toss

• **Keep** coffee tins, plastic tubs, small gift boxes, or even potato chip tubes for (re)gifting swapped cookies to lucky pals. To package, wrap cleaned vessels in holiday paper. Bows optional.

• **Toss** unreasonable expectations. The yummiest desserts are often the simplest, so don't hesitate to make Grandma's classic recipe. Also avoid cookies that can't sit out for long periods. If they need to be refrigerated after baking, they're not worth your (or your guests') time.

• **Keep** nonsweet snacks on hand so partygoers don't OD on sugar. Fresh veggies and dip, or crackers and cheese, are perfect antidotes. Make sure to have enough drinks available too: coffee, water, tea, or—for the purists—cold milk. This is a great time to pull out the punch bowl and serve a holiday-themed specialty, with or without alcohol.

STRESS-FREE HOLIDAY BAKING

Making Christmas cookies can become a real project. Try our shortcuts: They'll streamline the process and make it more fun, too.

Set Up an Assembly Line

Use parchment paper to line cookie sheets to save time and energy. Place unbaked cookie dough directly on the parchment paper—it eliminates the need to grease the cookie sheets. While the first batch bakes, cut additional sheets of parchment to fit the cookie sheets and arrange more dough on them. When the first batch is done, slide parchment with baked cookies onto a cooling rack, cool the baking sheet slightly (dough will spread on a hot pan), then slide a sheet of parchment with dough onto the cookie sheet and bake.

Cookie Decorator's Tool Kit

When it's time to decorate your Christmas cookies, have these basics at the ready, and it'll be a cinch to make your reindeer, stars, and snowmen look (almost) too good to eat!

• **Wire racks:** Use as a staging area for cookies while your decoration work is in progress.

• **Disposable decorating bags:** For onetime use only, they make cleanup a breeze!

• **Writing tips:** Use a #2 size for piping outlines, decorative lines, and dots; #1 for finer lines and details.

• **Plastic couplers:** Add these devices to the end of a decorating bag so you can easily and quickly change tips.

• **Artists' paintbrushes (various sizes):** Use to brush on decorative finishes like luster dusts. Larger brushes can speed application of thinned icing for filling in bigger spaces.

Freeze Dough for a Snowy Day

Get most of the work out of the way early: Just wrap the dough in foil and place it in heavy-duty resealable plastic bags; freeze for up to a month. When you're ready to bake, proceed as follows:

• **For drop cookies:** Spoon the dough into a plastic freezer-safe container. Let it thaw in the refrigerator for 1 to 2 days before baking.

• **For rolled cookies:** Shape the dough into one or more 1-inch thick disks. Let it thaw in the refrigerator overnight before rolling it out and cutting the cookies.

- **Paste food coloring:** This concentrated gel coloring produces deeper, richer, hues than liquid food coloring.

- **Wooden skewers:** Drag the tips through two wet icings spread side by side to create a marbled effect.

- **Straight- and bent-tip tweezers:** These are ideal for placing small decorative candies or dragées.

- **Luster dust:** This edible powder is available in a wide variety of glimmering hues (see page 353 for tips).

- **Small metal spatula:** This tool comes in handy for applying and smoothing icing.

- **Small offset spatula with tapered blade:** Helps you access hard-to-reach corners.

- **White and colored fine-grade sugars** (also known as sanding sugar): Sprinkle over wet icing for a sparkly finish.

- **Candies:** Decorating is easy with nonpareils, mini M&M's (great for eyes and noses!), small candy-coated gum pieces, jelly beans, spearmint leaves, fruit leather, and other favorites.

TIP: Purchase these tools and edible add-ons at cake-decorating-supply stores, craft stores, or online.

Bake Ahead and Freeze Your Stash

Cool the cookies completely, then wrap and freeze as described below:

- **For fragile, buttery, or crumbly cookies:** Tuck them between layers of waxed paper in airtight freezer containers.

- **For sturdy cookies (gingerbread, drop cookies, biscotti):** Wrap stacks of four or five in foil or waxed paper, then place them in heavy-duty resealable bags.

- **For decorated cookies:** Freeze in a single layer on a cookie sheet until firm, then pack between layers of waxed paper in airtight containers.

- **For brownies and bar cookies:** Cool them completely in the pan set on a wire rack, then slice into bars. Freeze the bars in the pan until firm, then remove from the pan in one piece and wrap in aluminum foil followed by a resealable plastic bag.

Thaw and Share!

The day before you need the cookies, remove from the freezer and allow them to thaw overnight. Prepare a platter of cookies for your party, or package the cookies or bars in gift bags, tins, or boxes lined with tissue paper. Finish with gift tags (see page 399 for ideas).

Decorating bags

Offset spatulas

Candies

Luster dust and extract

QUICK & EASY COOKIE DECORATING

Like cheerfully wrapped packages, cutout cookies with bright trimmings are an essential component of any Christmas celebration. If you don't have time to pipe or paint intricate designs with frosting, here are some playful, easy techniques. These methods work their magic in minutes and are fun to do with kids.

1. Egg Yolk Washes

Beat 1 large egg yolk with ¼ teaspoon water. Divide beaten egg among small cups and tint each with food coloring.

2. Fast Frosting

Whisk 1½ cups confectioners' sugar with 1 to 2 tablespoons milk until blended; tint the mixture with your food coloring of choice and brush or pipe it on.

3. Luster Dust

Use a small artist's brush to paint the dust on a hardened iced surface. If you want only a pale shimmer, dip the brush in the dry luster dust powder and paint it onto the cookie. When subtle color with a metallic sheen is desired, mix ¼ teaspoon luster dust with ¾ teaspoon clear alcohol-based extract, such as lemon or almond. (Do not use water—the dust will be absorbed into the icing, leaving it sticky.) For more intense color, apply a second coat. Since extract evaporates quickly, work in small batches. (Note: Surfaces painted with luster dust dry in minutes.)

4. Piping Icing

You don't have to be a decorating pro to pipe simple designs on cookies. Thin the frosting with warm water to obtain the desired consistency. Then fill a piping bag or resealable plastic bag halfway with frosting. If you're using a plastic bag, use scissors to cut a ¼-inch opening off one corner of the bag. Squeeze the piping bag or plastic bag to create simple outlines or shapes on cookies.

5. Stenciling

Use a matte knife or single-edged razor blade to cut a small star, heart, or other desired stencil from lightweight cardboard. Place the stencil over a brownie or bar; sift confectioners' sugar, unsweetened cocoa, or cinnamon-sugar over the top. Carefully lift off stencil to reveal the design. Repeat with remaining bars.

6. Drawing with Frosting

Frost your cookies with a solid base layer. While the frosting on the base is still wet, fill a decorator's bag with stiff frosting and pipe concentric circles or parallel lines on the cookies. Then, working quickly, before frosting dries, draw a toothpick or the tip of a knife through the lines to create decorative effects as shown in photo.

7. Candyland

Frost cookies with store-bought frosting, then press on chocolate chips, miniature marshmallows, gumdrops, gummy candy, and other favorite candies to create tempting treats.

ICING SNOW: Frost the roof. Pipe on icicles with a pastry bag.

PRETZEL LOGS: Use a serrated knife to "saw" the rods.

SILVER WALKWAY: Pave a path. Glue dragée candies to cookies with icing.

One Wreath, Three Ways

Use a ring-shaped cutter, then decorate your cookie with candies that small fingers can apply with icing.

GUMDROP SLICES

CHOCOLATE CANDIES

CINNAMON-FLAVORED CANDIES

HOME SWEET HOME

Start with a no-bake kit, then get right to the fun part: decorating your prefab gingerbread house with candies, icing, cookies, and more

Xmas Eave

Mints of all stripes adorn this house *(opposite, bottom right)*, but the standout is shimmery fruit leather, cut with a zigzag edge. Little elves can choose their favorite color—or more than one!

PINKING SHEARS

FRUIT LEATHER

Pointers from the GH Pros

Use a Kit The GH Test Kitchens recommend preassembled and unassembled ones from wilton.com; find similar houses at Walmart and Michaels.

Build Ahead The walls and roof can take hours to set. Preassembly will help appease eager junior decorators.

Make "Mistakes" Encourage kids' creativity. The finished product shouldn't look like the too-perfect picture on the box.

Get Handy Broken or cracked gingerbread happens. Premixed icing, which comes with a piping bag, makes repairs easy.

Top: HOUSE MADE OF PRETZEL RODS, WITH WREATH MADE OF COLORED SPRINKLES; *Bottom left:* GINGERBREAD HOUSE WITH GUMDROP SLICE WREATH; *Bottom right:* EAVES MADE OF FRUIT LEATHER.

Have a very Merry Christmas!

Susan

Have a very Merry Christmas!

Chapter 6

The Holiday Wrap-Up

GOURMET GIFTS FROM THE KITCHEN & INSPIRED GIFT WRAPS

This year, do your Christmas shopping in your own kitchen. Create an assortment of enticing preserves, quick breads, and candies, then follow our tips for wrapping them in style. We guarantee these gourmet gifts will be received with delight!

Food Gifts in Jars

Make a big batch of our Caramelized Onion & Bacon Jam, Fig Chutney, or Arrabiata Sauce and distribute to everyone on your list. Or layer a jar with fixings for Curried Lentil Soup; the recipient will appreciate having this fast-to-fix meal on hand in the pantry.

Quick Breads & Granola

Everyone loves to receive a loaf of fresh-baked bread. Tie a bow around a Cape Cod Cranberry Loaf or fill a jar with Puff Pastry Cheese Straws and give it to your neighbor, your hairdresser, or your child's teacher.

Luscious Candies & Confections

Here we share instructions for candies and other nibbles that are fun to make and a joy to give. From Pistachio and Tart Cherry Chocolate Bark to Rocky Road Fudge, these sweet treats are sure to delight the recipients. Or whip up one of the old-fashioned Christmas candies from our archives—there's a reason pralines and peanut brittle are holiday classics.

Gift-Wrapping Know-How

Whether you're wrapping jars of jam or a sweater, setting up a gift-wrapping station will make the process go smoothly. To ensure that your holiday is a green one, check out our tips on how to reuse wrapping paper, ribbons, and trinkets. We also share stunning gift-wrapping ideas to help you wrap every Christmas present with style.

Clockwise from top left: SHRIMP RILLETTES *(page 367)*; CHOCOLATE-DIPPED PRETZELS *(page 386)*; PLAYING WITH LAYERS *(page 399)*.

Recipes

Crafts

PRESERVES, PICKLES & OTHER GIFTS IN JARS

Caramelized Onion & Bacon Jam

This versatile gift can be spread on baguette slices with goat cheese for hors d'oeuvres, used in a grilled cheese sandwich with apples or on pizza dough instead of tomato sauce, or stirred into baked beans.

Active time: 20 minutes
Total time: 1 hour 50 minutes
Makes: 3 cups

1¹/2 pound bacon, finely chopped
3 large onions, finely chopped
1 medium leek, finely chopped
2 cloves garlic, finely chopped
¹/4 teaspoon salt
¹/2 cup balsamic vinegar
¹/2 cup packed brown sugar
¹/2 teaspoon dried oregano
¹/4 teaspoon ground nutmeg
¹/2 teaspoon coarsely ground black pepper

1 In deep 12-inch skillet, cook bacon on medium 30 minutes or until crisp and fat has rendered, stirring occasionally. With slotted spoon, transfer bacon to paper-towel-lined plate. Remove and discard all but 2 tablespoons bacon fat in skillet.

2 To fat in skillet, add onions, leek, garlic, and salt. Cook on medium 50 minutes or until caramelized and soft, stirring occasionally. Add vinegar, sugar, oregano, nutmeg, bacon, and pepper. Cook 15 minutes or until onions are very soft.

3 Transfer mixture to food processor; pulse until finely chopped. Transfer to 4 small jars; refrigerate until cold. Jam may be refrigerated up to 2 weeks.

Each tablespoon: About 45 calories, 2g protein, 4g carbs, 3g total fat (1g saturated), 0g fiber, 95mg sodium.

Arrabiata Sauce

This piquant sauce is seasoned with crushed red pepper and ample garlic. The generous recipe yields enough for six 16-ounce jars for gifts (with a little left over for you).

Active time: 15 minutes
Total time: 1 hour
Makes: 14 cups

¹/2 cup extra-virgin olive oil
6 garlic cloves, crushed with side of chef's knife
4 cans (35 ounces each) Italian plum tomatoes
1 tablespoon salt
1 to 1¹/2 teaspoons crushed red pepper

1 In 8-quart Dutch oven, heat oil over medium heat until hot but not smoking. Add garlic and cook, stirring, 2 minutes; do not brown. Stir in tomatoes with their juice, salt, and red pepper; heat to boiling over high heat. Reduce heat; simmer, uncovered, 50 minutes, or until sauce thickens slightly, stirring occasionally and crushing tomatoes with side of spoon.

2 For smooth, traditional texture, press tomato mixture through food mill into large bowl. Or leave sauce as is for a hearty, chunky texture. Cool sauce slightly then spoon into jar and refrigerate up to 1 week, or spoon into freezer-proof containers and freeze up to 2 months.

Each ¹/4-cup serving: About 30 calories, 1g protein, 3g carbohydate, 2g total fat (0g saturated), 1g fiber, 230mg sodium

Clockwise from top left: Homespun Holiday Wrapping *(page 399);* Caramelized Onion & Bacon Jam *(above);* Giardiniera *(page 369);* Fennel-Roasted Olives *(page 368).*

Freezer Strawberry Jam

If you're the super-organized type who starts planning Christmas in July, this recipe is for you. Peak-of-the-season farmstead berries make for a freezer jam that's fresh tasting even in December.

Active time: 35 minutes plus standing
Total time: 45 minutes
Makes: five 8-ounce containers

5 half-pint freezer-safe containers with tight-fitting lids
1 quart fully ripe strawberries, hulled
4 cups sugar
2 tablespoons fresh lemon juice
3/4 cup water
1 package (1³/4 ounces) powdered fruit pectin

1 Prepare containers and lids (see Tip).

2 In large bowl, thoroughly crush enough strawberries to equal 2 cups. Stir in sugar and lemon juice until thoroughly mixed; let stand 10 minutes.

3 In 1-quart saucepan, combine water and pectin and heat to boiling over high heat. Boil, stirring constantly, 1 minute. Stir pectin mixture into fruit until sugar has dissolved and mixture is no longer grainy, 3 to 4 minutes. A few sugar crystals will remain.

4 Quickly ladle jam into containers to within ½ inch of tops. Wipe container rims clean; cover with lids.

5 Let stand at room temperature until set, about 24 hours. Refrigerate up to 3 weeks, or freeze up to 1 year. To use, place frozen jam in refrigerator until thawed, about 4 hours.

TIP: To store jam long-term in the pantry, you must sterilize the jars and lids. Wash the jars, lids, and screw bands in hot soapy water; rinse. Then submerge the jars in enough cool water to cover and heat to boiling. Remove the pot from the heat, cover it and let sit in the hot water for at least 10 minutes. Place the bands and lids in water and bring to a simmer (180°F). Remove pan from heat, cover, and keep hot until ready to use.

Each 1-tablespoon serving: About 45 calories, 0g protein, 11g carbohydrate, 0g total fat, 1g fiber, 1mg sodium

Fig Chutney

This chutney can be prepared completely up to a week ahead. In fact, that will allow the flavors to blend even more. Give a jar of it as a gift, along with a Zucchini Cheese Loaf (page 374). Tell the recipient to let the chutney stand about an hour at room temperature before serving—or serve it warm.

Active time: 15 minutes
Total time: 40 minutes
Makes: 4 cups

1 tablespoon olive oil
1 onion, chopped
2 Granny Smith apples, each peeled, cored, and chopped
12 ounces dried Calimyrna figs (2 cups; see Tip), each cut into quarters, stems removed
1 cup water
½ cup dry red wine
½ cup sugar
1 teaspoon grated fresh lemon peel
¼ teaspoon salt

1 In 4-quart saucepan, heat oil over medium until hot. Add chopped onion; cook 10 to 12 minutes or until golden, stirring occasionally.

2 To onion in saucepan, add apples, figs, water, wine, sugar, lemon peel, and salt; bring to boil over high heat, stirring occasionally. Reduce heat to medium; cover and cook 10 minutes. Uncover and cook, stirring frequently to prevent scorching, 10 minutes longer or until figs are tender and mixture thickens. Spoon chutney into jars and refrigerate, tightly covered, up to 3 weeks.

TIP: We call for Calimyrna figs because we like the lighter-colored flesh and skin for this recipe, but if you can't find them, black Mission figs will also make delicious chutney.

Each ¼-cup serving: About 100 calories, 1g protein, 23g carbohydrate, 1g total fat (0g saturated), 3g fiber, 40mg sodium

FREEZER STRAWBERRY JAM *(opposite)*

Pear Marmalade

Here, pears are combined with thinly sliced orange peel, fresh ginger, and a touch of allspice to make an unusually delectable marmalade. Use any variety of pear you like. The recipe yields seven 8-ounce jars: Friends and neighbors will be delighted to receive these preserves.

Active time: 30 minutes
Total time: 1 hour 30 minutes
Makes: 7 cups

3 large oranges
6 pounds pears, peeled, cored, and coarsely chopped (12 cups)
2 tablespoons minced, peeled fresh ginger
4 cups sugar
1/3 cup fresh lemon juice
1/2 teaspoon ground allspice
7 half-pint canning jars and lids

1 From oranges, with vegetable peeler, remove peel along with some white pith. Cut enough peel into 2" by ⅛" strips to equal ¾ cup. Remove and discard seeds from orange flesh and coarsely chop enough to equal 1½ cups.

2 In heavy nonreactive 8-quart saucepot, combine pears, oranges and peel, ginger, sugar, lemon juice, and allspice; heat to boiling over high heat, stirring frequently. Reduce heat to medium-high; cook, stirring frequently, until mixture is very thick, about 45 minutes. With spoon, skim off any foam.

3 Spoon marmalade into jars and refrigerate, tightly covered, up to 3 weeks.

Each 1-tablespoon serving: About 45 calories, 0g protein, 11g carbohydrate, 0g total fat, 1g fiber, 0mg sodium

Top: PEAR MARMALADE *(above); Bottom:* FIG AND WALNUT CHEESE BALL *(opposite).*

Fig and Walnut Cheese Ball

You can make these sweet-and-savory cheese balls up to a week ahead, but if you do, hold off on covering them with nuts—they will become soft and chewy. Instead, wrap the balls in plastic and refrigerate them, then roll them in chopped nuts just before gift giving.

Total time: 20 minutes plus chilling
Makes: 3 cheese balls or 24 servings

2 packages (8 ounces each) Neufchâtel cheese
1 cup dried Calimyrna figs (5 ounces), finely chopped, stems removed
1 cup freshly grated Parmesan cheese
2 tablespoons honey
1/2 teaspoon ground black pepper
1 cup walnuts, toasted (page 287) and finely chopped

1 In medium bowl, with mixer on medium speed, beat Neufchâtel 1 minute or until fluffy. Reduce speed to low; beat in figs, Parmesan, honey, and pepper.

2 Place one-third of cheese mixture on sheet of plastic wrap and shape into ball; fold plastic up to enclose cheese ball. Repeat with remaining cheese mixture, making 3 balls. Refrigerate until chilled and firm, at least 1 hour or overnight. Roll chilled balls in chopped walnuts.

3 To serve, if cheese balls have been refrigerated overnight, let stand 30 minutes at room temperature or until soft enough to spread.

Each 1-ounce serving: About 120 calories, 5g protein, 7g carbohydrate, 9g total fat (4g saturated), 1g fiber, 155mg sodium

Butterscotch Sauce

A jar of this classic ice-cream topper makes a great hostess gift. Arrive at the party with this sauce and a tub of premium-brand ice cream. The recipe yields six half-pint jars.

Active time: 5 minutes
Total time: 15 minutes
Makes: 6 cups

4 cups packed light brown sugar
2 cups heavy cream
1 1/3 cups light corn syrup
1/2 cup butter or margarine (1 stick)
4 teaspoons distilled white vinegar
1/2 teaspoon salt
4 teaspoons vanilla extract

1 In 5-quart Dutch oven (do not use smaller pan because mixture bubbles up during cooking), heat brown sugar, cream, corn syrup, butter, vinegar, and salt to boiling over high heat, stirring occasionally. Reduce heat to low; simmer, uncovered, 5 minutes, stirring frequently. Remove saucepan from heat; stir in vanilla. Sauce will have thin consistency when hot but will thicken when chilled.

2 Cool sauce completely, then pour into half-pint jars. Refrigerate up to 2 weeks. Reheat to serve warm over ice cream.

Each 1-tablesoon serving: About 75 calories, 0g protein, 13g carbohydrate, 3g total fat (1g saturated), 0g fiber, 35mg sodium

CURRIED LENTIL SOUP FIXINGS (*opposite*)

Curried Lentil Soup Fixings

Dried lentils and seasonings are layered into a beribboned mason jar to create this inexpensive, one-of-a-kind holiday gift. Add these cooking directions to each label: Place lentil soup mix in 3-quart saucepan with 7 cups water. Heat to boiling over high. Reduce heat to low; cover and simmer 20 to 30 minutes, stirring occasionally. Makes 8 cups soup.

Total time: 5 minutes
Makes: 2 jars soup mix

2 (1-quart) jars with tight-fitting lids
1 pound red lentils
1½ teaspoons salt
6 tablespoons minced dried onion
2 tablespoons curry powder
1 teaspoon garlic powder
1 pound green lentils
2½ ounces dried apple rings, cut into ½-inch pieces
    (1 cup)
2 tablespoons dried parsley leaves

1 In bottom of each glass jar, layer 8 ounces red lentils; top with salt, 3 tablespoons dried onion, 1 tablespoon curry powder, ½ teaspoon garlic powder, 8 ounces green lentils, ½ cup apple pieces, and 1 tablespoon parsley, in that order. Seal jars and store at room temperature up to 1 month.

2 Prepare labels complete with cooking instructions; attach to jars.

Each cup of prepared soup: About 220 calories, 16g protein, 39g carbohydrate, 1g total fat, 14g fiber, 445mg sodium

Shrimp Rillettes

This rich, pâté-like spread, shown in photo on page 358, is served cold as an appetizer on bread or toast. To make rillettes ahead, freeze the spread in jars or ramekins for up to three weeks before giving. Make sure to place the jars in freezer-weight resealable storage bags or wrap the ramekins well in foil before freezing them. Thaw them in the refrigerator overnight and include a French baguette or assorted crackers with the rillettes for serving.

Total time: 20 minutes plus chilling
Makes: 1¾ cups

6 tablespoons butter (no substitutions), softened
1 pound shelled and deveined shrimp
2 tablespoons brandy or dry sherry
¼ teaspoon cayenne (ground red) pepper
2 tablespoons fresh lemon juice
¼ teaspoon salt

1 In 10-inch skillet, heat 2 tablespoons butter on medium-high until melted. Add shrimp and cook 2 minutes or until opaque throughout, stirring frequently. Add brandy and cook 30 seconds. Transfer shrimp mixture to food processor with knife blade attached; pulse until finely chopped.

2 To shrimp mixture in processor, add cayenne, lemon juice, remaining 4 tablespoons butter, and salt; pulse until evenly blended.

3 Transfer shrimp mixture to small jars or ramekins and cover with plastic wrap, pressing wrap directly onto surface of mixture. Refrigerate at least 8 hours to blend flavors or up to 3 days. Let stand 30 minutes at room temperature before serving.

Each serving: About 75 calories, 6g protein, 0g carbohydrate, 5g total fat (3g saturated), 0g fiber, 125mg sodium

Fennel-Roasted Olives

These olives are zesty, tangy, and make a perfect last-minute edible gift.

Active time: 10 minutes
Total time: 40 minutes
Makes: 5 cups

6 cups assorted brine-cured olives (not pitted)
4 cloves garlic, peeled
4 strips lemon zest, each 3 inches long
4 strips orange zest, each 3-inches long
1/2 cup plus 2 tablespoons extra virgin olive oil
1/2 teaspoon black pepper
1 tablespoon fennel seeds
1/2 cup sherry vinegar

1 Preheat oven to 425°F. On large rimmed baking sheet, toss olives, garlic, lemon zest, orange zest, 2 tablespoons olive oil, and black pepper.

2 Spread in single layer. Roast 30 minutes, shaking pan once. Divide olives, garlic and zest among 4 jars; add fennel seeds to each. Pour sherry and remaining olive oil over olives to cover. Store in refrigerate up to 1 month.

Each 1/4 cup serving: About 135 calories, 0g protein, 3g carbohydrate, 13g total fat (2g saturated), 1g fiber, 694mg sodium

Infused Vodkas

These flavored spirits are the best party favor anyone could ask for.

Active time: 10 minutes
Total time: 1 day
Makes: 1 bottle

CHAI VODKA

1 bottle (750 milliliter) vodka
3 cinnamon sticks
2 tablespoons chopped candied ginger
12 black peppercorns
10 whole cloves
10 cardamom pods, lightly crushed

SPICY CITRUS VODKA

1 bottle (750 milliliter) vodka
5 strips grapefruit zest, each 3 inches long
2 jalapeños, sliced

CUCUMBER TARRAGON VODKA

1 bottle (750 milliliter) vodka
1 medium cucumber, thinly sliced
4 large sprigs fresh tarragon

Chai Vodka: Combine vodka, cinnamon sticks, candied ginger, black peppercorns, whole cloves, and cardamom pods. Cover and let stand at least 1 day or up to 3 days. Strain and pour into bottles. Keeps for up to 2 months.

Spicy Citrus Vodka: Combine vodka with grapefruit zest and jalapeños. Cover and let stand 1 day. Strain and pour into bottles. Keeps for up to 2 months.

Cucumber Tarragon Vodka: Combine vodka, cucumber, and fresh tarragon. Cover and let stand at least 1 day or up to 2 days. Strain and pour into bottles. Keeps for up to 2 months.

Each 1 1/2 ounce serving: About 95 calories, 0g protein, 0g carbohydrate, 0g total fat (0g saturated), 0g fiber, 0mg sodium

Giardiniera

This pickled assortment of vegetables is often served as an Italian antipasto. Deliver a jar as part of an Italian gift basket assortment, along with our Fennel-Roasted Olives (opposite), Arrabiata Sauce (page 361), and some gourmet dried pasta.

Active time: 1 hour
Total time: 1 hour 20 minutes
Makes: 5 cups

½ small head cauliflower, cut into small florets
    (1½ cups)
1 large red pepper, cut into 1-inch pieces
1 cup peeled, thickly sliced carrot
2 large stalks celery, thickly sliced
½ (5-ounce) jar green olives, drained
½ cup sugar
2¼ cups distilled white vinegar
¾ cup water
1 tablespoon kosher salt
¼ teaspoon mustard seeds
⅛ teaspoon crushed red pepper

1 In large bowl, combine cauliflower, red pepper, carrot, celery, and olives. In nonreactive 4-quart saucepan, combine sugar, vinegar, water, and salt; heat to boiling over high heat, stirring occasionally. Reduce heat to low.

2 In container with lid, large enough to hold vegetables, place mustard seeds and crushed red pepper; tightly pack vegetables into container and pour hot syrup over, making sure vegetables are completely covered with syrup.

3 Allow giardiniera to cool, then refrigerate in airtight container up to 1 week.

Each ¼-cup serving: 35 calories, 0g protein, 8g carbohydrate, 0g total fat (0g saturated), 0g fiber, 1g fiber, 443mg sodium

Top: INFUSED VODKAS *(opposite);*
Bottom: GIARDINIERA *(above).*

QUICK BREADS & GRANOLA

Chai Spiced Tea Loaves

You know how great chai spice tastes in your tea mug—now try it in these moist and tender loaf cakes. Bake these do-ahead gifts up to three months ahead, then just cool them, wrap them tightly in foil, and freeze. When you're ready, thaw them at room temperature, unwrapped, and giftwrap as desired. If you don't have mini loaf pans, you can find the disposable aluminum ones in your supermarket.

Active time: 30 minutes
Total time: 1 hour plus cooling
Makes: 6 mini loaves

½ cup plus about 1 tablespoon water

1 tea bag (black tea)

3 cups all-purpose flour

2 teaspoons chai spice blend

1 teaspoon baking powder

½ teaspoon baking soda

½ teaspoon salt

¾ cup vanilla low-fat yogurt

1 cup butter or margarine (2 sticks), softened

1 cup granulated sugar

1 cup packed light brown sugar

5 large eggs

1 cup confectioners' sugar

1 Preheat oven to 350°F. Grease and flour six 5¾" by 3¼" by 2" mini metal loaf pans.

2 Bring ½ cup water to boil. Place tea bag in water; press with spoon to submerge. Set aside to steep and cool while continuing with recipe.

3 Meanwhile, in medium bowl, combine flour, chai spice, baking powder, baking soda, and salt.

4 In small bowl, mix yogurt with ⅓ cup cooled tea; discard any remaining tea.

5 In large bowl, with mixer on medium speed, beat butter until creamy, about 1 minute. Gradually beat in granulated and brown sugars. Beat 2 minutes or until fluffy, occasionally scraping bowl with rubber spatula. Reduce speed to low; beat in eggs, one at a time, until well blended. Beat in flour mixture alternating with yogurt mixture, just until combined. Spoon batter evenly into prepared pans.

6 Bake loaves 30 to 35 minutes or until toothpick inserted in centers comes out clean. Cool in pans on wire racks 15 minutes. Run thin knife around loaves to loosen, remove loaves from pans, and cool completely on wire racks, about 2 hours.

7 When loaves are cool, place waxed paper under wire racks. In small bowl, stir confectioners' sugar and remaining 1 tablespoon water until smooth, adding more water, a few drops at a time, if necessary to make thick glaze. Place glaze in heavyweight resealable plastic bag; snip small opening from corner, and drizzle glaze in zigzag pattern over loaves. Let stand until glaze sets, about 30 minutes.

8 Wrap each loaf in plastic or foil. Store at room temperature up to 3 days. Or place wrapped loaves in self-sealing plastic bags, and freeze up to 3 months.

Each serving (¼ loaf): About 225 calories, 3g protein, 32g carbohydrate, 9g total fat (6g saturated), 0g fiber, 195mg sodium

---

Clockwise from top left: CHAI SPICED TEA LOAVES *(above);* OVERNIGHT STICKY BUNS *(page 373);* PUFF PASTRY CHEESE STRAWS *(page 377);* TIE ONE ON *(page 397);* HAZELNUT-HONEY GRANOLA *(page 376)* .

Holiday Bread

This simple stollen, a quick version of the traditional sweetbread, makes a delightful holiday gift. Or serve it for breakfast on Chirstmas morning.

Active time: 10 minutes
Total time: 1 hour 5 minutes plus cooling
Makes: 1 loaf or 16 servings

2⅓ cups all-purpose flour
½ cup sugar
1½ teaspoons baking powder
¼ teaspoon salt
½ cup cold butter or margarine (1 stick)
1 cup part-skim ricotta cheese
1 cup dried tart cherries or other dried fruit, coarsely chopped
⅓ cup pecans, toasted (page 287) and chopped
1 teaspoon vanilla extract
½ teaspoon freshly grated lemon peel
2 large eggs
Confectioners' sugar (optional)

1 Preheat oven to 325°F. Grease large cookie sheet. In large bowl, stir together flour, sugar, baking powder, and salt. With pastry blender or using two knives scissors-fashion, cut in butter until mixture resembles fine crumbs. Stir in ricotta, dried cherries, pecans, vanilla, lemon peel, and eggs until well combined.

2 Turn dough onto lightly floured surface. With floured hands, gently knead two or three times to blend. With floured rolling pin, roll dough into 10" by 8" oval. Fold oval lengthwise, bringing top half not quite whole way over, so that bottom of dough forms 1-inch ledge.

3 Place stollen on prepared cookie sheet. Bake 55 to 60 minutes or until toothpick inserted in center comes out clean. Transfer to wire rack; cool completely. Sprinkle with confectioners' sugar just before serving if you like.

Each slice: About 205 calories, 5g protein, 27g carbohydrate, 10g total fat (5g saturated), 1g fiber, 165mg sodium

Top: HOLIDAY BREAD *(above)*;
Bottom: OVERNIGHT STICKY BUNS *(opposite)*.

Overnight Sticky Buns

Not just sticky but also spicy, nutty, and downright delectable, these breakfast treats must be started the night before you plan to bake them. To give them as a gift, wrap securely in foil and tie with a bow.

Active time: 1 hour
Total time: 1 hour 30 minutes plus rising and chilling
Makes: 20 buns

Dough

¼ cup warm water (105°F to 115°F)
1 package active dry yeast
1 teaspoon plus ¼ cup granulated sugar
¾ cup milk
4 tablespoons butter or margarine, softened
1 teaspoon salt
3 large egg yolks
4 cups all-purpose flour

Filling

½ cup packed dark brown sugar
¼ cup dried currants
1 tablespoon ground cinnamon
4 tablespoons butter or margarine, melted

Topping

⅔ cup packed dark brown sugar
3 tablespoons butter or margarine
2 tablespoons light corn syrup
2 tablespoons pure honey
1¼ cups pecans, coarsely chopped

1 Prepare dough: In cup, combine warm water, yeast, and 1 teaspoon granulated sugar; stir to dissolve. Let stand 5 minutes or until foamy.

2 In large bowl, with mixer on low speed, blend yeast mixture with milk, butter, salt, egg yolks, 3 cups flour, and remaining ¼ cup granulated sugar until blended. With wooden spoon, stir in ¾ cup flour.

3 Turn dough onto lightly floured surface and knead about 5 minutes, until smooth and elastic, working in about ¼ cup more flour to keep dough from sticking.

4 Shape dough into ball; place in greased large bowl, turning dough over to grease top. Cover bowl and let dough rise in warm place (80°F to 85°F), about 1 hour.

5 Meanwhile, prepare filling: In small bowl, combine brown sugar, currants, and cinnamon. Reserve butter.

6 Prepare topping: In 1-quart saucepan, heat brown sugar, butter, corn syrup, and honey over low heat, stirring occasionally, until butter has melted. Grease 13" by 9" metal baking pan; pour brown-sugar mixture into pan and sprinkle evenly with pecans; set aside.

7 Punch down dough. Turn dough onto lightly floured surface; cover and let rest 15 minutes. On lightly floured surface, with floured rolling pin, roll dough into 18- by 12-inch rectangle. Brush dough with reserved melted butter and sprinkle with currant mixture. Starting at one long side, roll up dough jelly-roll fashion; place, seam side down, on cutting board. Cut dough crosswise into 20 slices.

8 Arrange slices, cut side down, on topping in baking pan in four rows of five slices each. Cover pan and refrigerate at least 12 or up to 20 hours.

9 When ready to bake, preheat oven to 375°F. Bake buns 30 minutes, or until golden. Immediately place serving tray or jelly-roll pan over baking pan and invert; remove baking pan. Let buns cool slightly to serve warm or cool completely and wrap tightly in foil to serve later.

Each bun: 290 calories, 12g protein, 5g carbohydrate, 12g total fat (5g saturated fat), 1g fiber, 195mg sodium

Cinnamon Buns

Prepare dough and shape buns as instructed. Omit topping but bake as directed. Invert buns onto cookie sheet; remove baking pan and invert buns on wire racks. In small bowl, mix **1 cup confectioners' sugar** with **5 teaspoons water** until smooth; drizzle glaze over hot buns.

Each bun: 215 calories, 4g protein, 36g carbohydrate, 6g total fat (3g saturated fat), 1g fiber, 170mg sodium

Zucchini Cheese Loaf

This tender zucchini loaf is flavored with Cheddar and Parmesan. The generous dose of black pepper gives the bread a spicy bite, but you can reduce the amount called for or leave it out, if you prefer. Give a loaf to a friend who prefers savory over sweet.

Active time: 15 minutes
Total time: 1 hour 10 minutes plus cooling
Makes: 1 loaf or 12 servings

2^1/2 cups all-purpose flour
4 teaspoons baking powder
1 tablespoon sugar
1^1/2 teaspoons salt
^{1}/2 teaspoon ground black pepper
4 ounces sharp Cheddar cheese, shredded (1 cup)
^{1}/2 cup freshly grated Parmesan cheese
2 cups coarsely shredded zucchini
3 green onions, finely chopped
2 large eggs
^{3}/4 cup milk
^{1}/3 cup olive oil

1 Preheat oven to 350°F. Grease 9" by 5" metal loaf pan. In large bowl, stir together flour, baking powder, sugar, salt, and pepper.

2 In small bowl, combine ¼ cup Cheddar and 2 tablespoons Parmesan; set aside. Stir remaining ¾ cup Cheddar and 6 tablespoons Parmesan into flour mixture. Add zucchini and green onions. In medium bowl with fork, beat eggs; stir in milk and oil. Add egg mixture to flour mixture, stirring just until dry ingredients are moistened (batter will be very thick).

3 Scrape batter into prepared loaf pan and spread evenly with rubber spatula; sprinkle with reserved cheese mixture. Bake 55 to 60 minutes, until toothpick inserted in center of loaf comes out clean. Cool loaf in pan on wire rack 5 minutes. Remove from pan and cool completely on wire rack.

Each slice: About 240 calories, 9g protein, 23g carbohydrate, 12g total fat (4g saturated), 1g fiber, 610mg sodium

Cape Cod Cranberry Loaf

This classic cranberry bread makes a holiday-perfect gift, wrapped in cellophane and tied with a big bow.

Active time: 20 minutes
Total time: 1 hour 15 minutes plus cooling
Makes: 1 loaf or 12 servings

1 large orange
2^1/2 cups all-purpose flour
1 cup sugar
2 teaspoons baking powder
^{1}/2 teaspoon baking soda
^{1}/2 teaspoon salt
2 large eggs
4 tablespoons butter or margarine, melted
2 cups fresh or frozen cranberries, coarsely chopped
^{3}/4 cup walnuts, chopped (optional)

1 Preheat oven to 375°F. Grease 9" by 5" metal loaf pan. From orange, grate peel and squeeze ½ cup juice.

2 In large bowl, combine flour, sugar, baking powder, baking soda, and salt. In small bowl, with wire whisk or fork, beat eggs, butter, and orange peel and juice. With wooden spoon, stir egg mixture into flour mixture just until blended (batter will be stiff). Fold in cranberries and walnuts, if using.

3 Spoon batter into prepared pan. Bake until toothpick inserted in center comes out clean, 55 to 60 minutes. Cool bread in pan on wire rack 10 minutes; remove from pan and cool completely on wire rack.

Each slice without walnuts: About 223 calories, 4g protein, 40g carbohydrate, 5g total fat (3g saturated), 2g fiber, 281mg sodium

CAPE COD CRANBERRY LOAF *(opposite)*

Traditional Irish Soda Bread

This recipe is not just for St. Patrick's Day. In Ireland, soda bread is enjoyed every day with butter and jam or honey.

Active time: 15 minutes
Total time: 1 hour 15 minutes
Makes: 1 loaf, 12 slices

4 cups all-purpose flour, plus additional for dusting
1/4 cup sugar
1 tablespoon baking powder
1 1/2 teaspoons salt
1 teaspoon baking soda
6 tablespoons butter or margarine, chilled
1 1/2 cups buttermilk

1 Preheat oven to 350°F. Grease large cookie sheet. In large bowl, stir together flour, sugar, baking powder, salt, and baking soda. With pastry blender, or two knives used scissor-fashion, cut in butter until mixture resembles coarse crumbs. Stir in buttermilk just until flour is moistened (dough will be sticky).

2 Turn dough onto well-floured surface. With floured hands, knead eight to ten times until combined. (Do not overmix, or bread will be tough.) Shape into ball; place on prepared cookie sheet.

3 Sprinkle ball lightly with flour. In center, cut 4-inch cross about 1/4 inch deep. Bake 1 hour, or until toothpick inserted in center of loaf comes out clean. Remove loaf from cookie sheet and cool completely on wire rack.

Each slice: About 235 calories, 5g protein, 38g carbohydrate, 7g total fat (4g saturated) 1g fiber, 610mg sodium

Soda Bread with Currants and Caraway Seeds

Prepare dough as instructed in step 1 above, adding **1 1/2 cups dried currants** and **2 teaspoons caraway seeds** to flour-and-butter mixture before stirring in butter-milk. Knead dough and bake.

Each slice: About 300 calories, 6g protein, 52g carbohydrate, 7g total fat (4g saturated), 2g fiber, 610mg sodium

Hazelnut-Honey Granola

Present this yummy granola to friends and family in glass canisters, along with the recipe. They'll think of you the next morning as they dig into a bowlful topped with bananas and yogurt.

Active time: 20 minutes
Total time: 50 minutes
Makes: 9 cups or 9 servings

3 cups old-fashioned oats, uncooked
3/4 cup honey
4 tablespoons butter or margarine, melted
1 1/2 teaspoons vanilla extract
1 cup hazelnuts (filberts), whole natural almonds, or both, coarsely chopped
1/2 cup toasted wheat germ
1/2 cup sesame seeds (see Tip)
1 cup dried tart cherries (4 ounces) or dark seedless raisins
1/2 cup dried apricots, cut into thin strips
1/2 cup golden raisins

1 Preheat oven to 350°F. Place oats in two 15 1/2" by 10 1/2" jelly-roll pans. Bake 15 minutes or until lightly toasted, stirring twice.

2 In large bowl, stir together honey, melted butter, and vanilla. Add toasted oats, nuts, wheat germ, and sesame seeds; stir to coat well.

3 Spread oat mixture evenly in same jelly-roll pans; bake until dark golden brown, 15 to 20 minutes, stirring every 5 minutes. Cool in pans on wire racks. Transfer to large bowl and stir in all dried fruit. Store in an airtight container, at room temperature, up to 1 month.

TIP: Sesame seeds contain a high percentage of fat and can go rancid quickly. To maintain freshness, store them in the refrigerator or freezer until you're ready to make the granola.

Each 1/2-cup serving: About 250 calories, 5g protein, 36g carbohydrate, 10g total fat (2g saturated), 5g fiber, 27mg sodium

Puff Pastry Cheese Straws

Our scrumptious cheese straws may lose their crispness if baked too far in advance. To make sure you don't have to rush through the recipe at the last minute, see our tip on how to freeze the unbaked straws, then bake them fresh just before gift-giving time.

Active time: 30 minutes

Total time: 1 hour 30 minutes

Makes: 48 straws

1 tablespoon paprika

1/2 teaspoon cayenne (ground red) pepper

1/4 teaspoon ground nutmeg

1/4 teaspoon salt

1 package (17 to 18 ounces) frozen puff pastry sheets, thawed as label directs

1 large egg white, lightly beaten

8 ounces aged Gouda or Parmigiano-Reggiano cheese, room temperature, finely shredded (2 cups)

1 Grease two large cookie sheets. In small bowl, combine paprika, cayenne, nutmeg, and salt.

2 Unfold 1 puff pastry sheet. On lightly floured surface, with floured rolling pin, roll pastry into 14-inch square. Lightly brush with some egg white. Sprinkle half of paprika mixture on pastry. Sprinkle half of Gouda over paprika. Fold pastry to cover cheese, forming rectangle. With rolling pin, lightly roll over pastry to seal layers together. With knife, cut pastry crosswise into 1/2-inch-wide strips.

3 Preheat oven to 375°F. Place two-thirds of strips, 1 inch apart, on 1 cookie sheet, twisting each to form spiral and pressing ends against cookie sheet to prevent strips from uncurling. (Do not crowd; strips puff while baking.) Place remaining strips on second cookie sheet; set aside. Bake first sheet of strips 15 to 20 minutes or until golden. With spatula, transfer to rack to cool.

4 Meanwhile, repeat with remaining pastry, egg white, paprika mixture, and Gouda, placing one-third of strips on second cookie sheet; bake as above. When first cookie sheet is cool, wash and grease again; use to bake remaining two-thirds strips. (For even cooking, bake only 1 sheet of strips at a time.) Store in an airtight container up to 3 days.

TIP: To do ahead, prepare the pastry strips as above, but do not bake them. Place the pastry strips on two greased cookie sheets, 1/2 inch apart, and twist each into a spiral. Cover loosely with plastic wrap and freeze until firm, at least 4 hours or overnight. Place the frozen cheese straws in a freezer-weight container or resealable storage bag; return them to the freezer for up to one month. When you're ready, preheat the oven and proceed with the recipe as directed in steps 3 and 4.

Each serving: About 75 calories, 2g protein, 5g carbohydrate, 5g total fat (2g saturated), 0g fiber, 75mg sodium

CANDIES & CONFECTIONS

Chocolate Truffles

These bittersweet confections are easy to make—and a perfect gift for the chocolate obsessed. For extra flavor, you can add 2 tablespoons of liqueur, such as Amaretto, to the chocolate mixture.

Total time: 25 minutes plus chilling
Makes: 32 truffles

8 squares (8 ounces) bittersweet chocolate
1/2 cup heavy cream
2 tablespoons Amaretto or other favorite liqueur (optional)
3 tablespoons unsalted butter (no substitutions),
    softened and cut up
1/3 cup hazelnuts (filberts), toasted (page 287) and
    finely chopped
3 tablespoons unsweetened cocoa

1 In food processor with knife blade attached, blend chocolate until finely ground.

2 In 1-quart saucepan, heat cream over medium-high heat to boiling. Stir in liqueur, if using; add mixture to chocolate in food processor and blend until smooth. Add butter and blend well.

3 Line 9" by 5" metal loaf pan with plastic wrap. Pour chocolate mixture into pan; spread evenly. Refrigerate until cool and firm enough to handle, about 3 hours.

4 Place hazelnuts in one small shallow bowl and cocoa in second shallow bowl. Set bowls near workspace.

5 Remove chocolate mixture from pan by lifting edges of plastic wrap and inverting chocolate block onto cutting board; discard plastic wrap. Using knife dipped in hot water and then wiped dry, cut chocolate mixture into 32 pieces. Quickly roll each piece into a ball. Roll half of balls in hazelnuts and other half in cocoa. Refrigerate truffles in an airtight container up to 1 week, or freeze up to 1 month. Remove from freezer 5 minutes before serving.

Each truffle: About 65 calories, 1g protein, 5g carbohydrate, 6g total fat (3g saturated), 1g fiber, 2mg sodium

Salted Caramel Bark

Sweet, salty, and crunchy, you'll want to make this addictive bark in big batches—it's sure to go quickly!

Active time: 5 minutes
Total time: 20 minutes plus chilling
Makes: 8 servings

3 tablespoons corn syrup
2 tablespoons sugar
1/4 teaspoons salt
2 cups roasted salted peanuts
12 ounces semisweet chocolate, melted

1 Preheat oven to 350°F. In large bowl, combine corn syrup, sugar, and salt. Stir in peanuts to evenly coat. Spread in single layer on parchment-paper-lined jelly-roll pan.

2 Bake 15 minutes or until browned and caramelized. Cool completely.

3 Stir into melted chocolate until well coated. Spread evenly on waxed paper-lined pan. Refrigerate until set.

Each serving: About 495 calories, 12g protein, 40g carbohydrate, 34g total fat (13g saturated), 3g fiber, 80mg sodium

Clockwise from top left: DOUBLE-DIPPED BERRIES *(page 384)*; CHOCOLATE TRUFFLES *(above)*; PEPPERMINT STICKS IN PEWTER CUPS; CARAMEL CRUNCH POPCORN *(page 380).*

Caramel Crunch Popcorn

In pursuit of the perfectly easy holiday gift, we dreamed up this homemade version of the rich caramel-covered popcorn and salted-peanut snack everyone loves.

Active time: 20 minutes
Total time: 1 hour 5 minutes
Makes: 24 cups

20 cups popped popcorn
2¹⁄₂ cups salted dry-roasted peanuts
1 cup butter (2 sticks; no substitutions)
1 cup granulated sugar
1 cup packed light brown sugar
¹⁄₂ cup light corn syrup
¹⁄₂ teaspoon baking soda

1 Preheat oven to 250°F. Lightly grease two 15¹⁄₂" by 10¹⁄₂" jelly-roll pans or spray sheets with nonstick cooking spray. Place popcorn in very large bowl; discard any unpopped kernels. Add peanuts; toss to combine. Set aside.

2 In 3-quart saucepan, heat butter, both sugars, and corn syrup on medium, stirring frequently with metal spoon or heat-safe spatula, until butter melts and sugars dissolve, about 5 minutes. Increase heat to medium-high and heat to boiling, about 3 minutes; boil 3 minutes longer. Remove saucepan from heat; carefully stir in baking soda (mixture will bubble vigorously), and pour over popcorn and peanut mixture in bowl. Stir immediately; continue stirring until evenly coated.

3 Divide popcorn mixture between prepared jelly-roll pans; spread evenly. Bake 45 minutes, stirring occasionally and rotating pans between upper and lower racks halfway through.

4 Set pans on wire racks to cool completely, about 1 hour. Break apart any large clusters; store in airtight containers at room temperature up to 2 weeks.

Each ¹⁄₂-cup serving: About 130 calories, 2g protein, 14g carbohydrate, 8g total fat (3g saturated), 1g fiber, 135mg sodium

Chocolate Almond Clusters

Get a head start on holiday gifts with these delicious homemade candies. Our speedy recipe calls for just two ingredients. Present the candies in a tissue-paper-lined gift box—and your work is done!

Active time: 10 minutes
Total time: 45 minutes
Makes: 48 candies

8 ounces semisweet or bittersweet chocolate, chopped
1¹⁄₂ cups roasted, salted almonds (8¹⁄₄ ounces)

1 On large cookie sheet, arrange 48 paper or foil mini-muffin or candy cups in a single layer. (Or, line large cookie sheet with waxed paper.)

2 In large microwave-safe bowl, microwave half of chocolate on High 20 seconds. Stir and repeat until chocolate just melts, about 1 minute 20 seconds total. Stir in remaining chocolate until melted. Cool 3 minutes for a shiny finish.

3 Stir in almonds until evenly coated. With measuring teaspoon, drop 1 spoonful of mixture into mini-muffin cup or onto waxed paper. Repeat with remaining mixture and cups.

4 Refrigerate at least 20 minutes or until set. Chocolate clusters can be refrigerated in an airtight container up to 1 month.

Each candy: About 55 calories, 1g protein, 4g carbohydrate, 4g total fat (1g saturated), 1g fiber, 15mg sodium

Rocky Road Fudge

Peanut butter and two kinds of chocolate chips—semisweet and butterscotch—form the base of this mini-marshmallow-studded fudge. Deliver it in a box, with waxed paper between layers; note on the gift tag that the fudge should be stored in the fridge and will keep for up to two weeks.

Active time: 7 minutes
Total time: 10 minutes plus chilling
Makes: 36 pieces

1 package (12 ounces) semisweet chocolate chips
1 cup butterscotch chips
1 cup crunchy peanut butter
1 tablespoon butter or margarine
1 package (10½ ounces) miniature marshmallows

1 Grease 8- or 9-inch square metal baking pan; line with plastic wrap. In 4-quart saucepan, combine chocolate chips, butterscotch chips, peanut butter, and butter. Cook over medium heat 2 to 3 minutes or just until ingredients are melted, stirring constantly. Remove from heat.

2 Stir marshmallows into fudge mixture. Pour into lined pan; spread evenly. Cover pan with plastic wrap and refrigerate fudge until firm, at least 3 hours.

3 Invert fudge onto cutting board; remove plastic wrap. Turn fudge top side up. Cut fudge into 36 pieces. Refrigerate in an airtight container up to 2 weeks.

Each piece: About 150 calories, 2g protein, 18g carbohydrate, 8g total fat (4g saturated), 1g fiber, 30mg sodium

Top: CHOCOLATE ALMOND CLUSTERS *(opposite)*;
Bottom: ROCKY ROAD FUDGE *(above)*.

Pistachio and Tart Cherry Chocolate Bark (*opposite*)

Pistachio and Tart Cherry Chocolate Bark

Pack this confection in decorative boxes lined with waxed tissue paper or colored cellophane. Make sure to note on the tag that this tart and nutty chocolate bark should be kept refrigerated until ready to enjoy, preferably no longer than one month for best flavor.

Active time: 20 minutes
Total time: 25 minutes plus chilling
Makes: 2½ pounds

1 pound semisweet chocolate, coarsely chopped
8 ounces white chocolate, coarsely chopped
1½ cups shelled pistachios, toasted (page 287)
8 ounces dried tart cherries (1½ cups)

1 Place semisweet chocolate in microwave-safe 8-cup measuring cup or large bowl. Place white chocolate in microwave-safe 2-cup measuring cup or medium bowl. Heat semisweet chocolate in microwave, covered with waxed paper, on High 2 to 3 minutes or until almost melted, stirring once. Remove from microwave and stir until smooth. Heat white chocolate in microwave, covered with waxed paper, on High 1 to 2 minutes or until almost melted, stirring once. Remove from microwave and stir until smooth.

2 Stir 1 cup pistachios and 1 cup cherries into semisweet chocolate; spread mixture to about ¼-inch thickness on large cookie sheet. Spoon dollops of white chocolate onto semisweet mixture. With tip of knife, swirl chocolates together for marbled look. Sprinkle with remaining pistachios and cherries, and press lightly to make pieces adhere.

3 Refrigerate bark 1 hour or until firm. Break into pieces. Refrigerate in an airtight container up to 1 month.

Each 1-ounce serving: About 125 calories, 2g protein, 15g carbohydrate, 8g total fat (4g saturated), 2g fiber, 5mg sodium

Chocolate-Dipped Dried Fruit

Chocolate and dried fruit have a natural affinity for each other. We used dried apricots, apples, pears, and pineapple, but you can use other fruits, such as peaches and mango. Be sure to let the chocolate dry thoroughly before transferring the fruit to waxed-paper-lined gift boxes or tins.

Active time: 10 minutes
Total time: 15 minutes plus cooling
Makes: 33 pieces dipped fruit

4 squares (4 ounces) semisweet chocolate, chopped
1 teaspoon vegetable shortening
1 pound mixed dried fruit, such as apricots, apples, pears, and pineapple
3 ounces crystallized ginger (optional)

1 Place sheet of waxed paper under large wire rack. In top of double boiler or in small metal bowl set over 2-quart saucepan (double-boiler top or bowl should be 2 inches above water), melt chocolate and shortening, stirring frequently, until smooth.

2 With fingers, dip one piece of fruit at a time halfway into chocolate (see Tip). Shake off excess chocolate or gently scrape fruit across rim of double boiler, being careful not to remove too much chocolate. Place dipped fruit on wire rack; allow chocolate to set, at least 1 hour.

3 Layer fruit between sheets of waxed paper in an airtight container. Store at room temperature up to 1 week.

TIP: It's easiest if the larger pieces of fruit are dipped first. Use the smaller pieces to scrape up the melted chocolate remaining in the pan.

Each serving: About 55 calories, 1g protein, 12g carbohydrate, 1g total fat (1g saturated), 1g fiber, 2mg sodium

Double-Dipped Berries

For a dessert that's as luscious as it is lovely, coat ruby-red strawberries in dark or white chocolate and a mantle of coconut flakes or crushed pistachios or almonds.

Active time: 15 minutes plus chilling
Makes: 20 strawberries

1 pound large strawberries (about 20)
3 ounces semisweet, milk, or white chocolate, melted
Toppings: finely chopped pistachio nuts and/or sliced
    almonds, or sweetened flaked coconut

1 Rinse strawberries with cold running water; do not remove stems and/or leaves. Pat strawberries completely dry with paper towels.

2 With fingers, hold 1 strawberry and dip into melted chocolate, leaving part of strawberry uncovered. Shake off excess chocolate. Then dip chocolate-covered cherry in topping of choice. Place berry on large cookie sheet lined with waxed paper. Repeat with remaining strawberries, chocolate, and toppings.

3 Place chocolate-covered strawberries in refrigerator about 15 minutes or until chocolate is set. Strawberries will keep at room temperature up to 2 hours. If not serving right away, refrigerate strawberries up to 4 hours.

Each dipped berry without topping: About 30 calories, 0g protein, 4g carbohydrate, 1g total fat (1g saturated), 0g fiber, 5mg sodium

Sweet and Sassy Nuts

A perfect nibble to set out for unexpected guests.

Total time: 30 minutes plus cooling
Makes: 8 cups

1 large egg white
1/2 cup sugar
1 teaspoon ground cumin
3/4 teaspoon ground chipotle chile pepper
1/2 teaspoon ground cinnamon
8 cups salted fancy mixed nuts (30 to 35 ounces)

1 Preheat oven to 350°F. Grease two 15½" by 10½" jelly-roll pans with vegetable oil or cooking spray.

2 In large bowl, with wire whisk, beat egg white until foamy. Add sugar, cumin, chipotle pepper, and cinnamon, and beat until well combined. Add nuts to egg-white mixture; with rubber spatula, stir until well coated.

3 Spread nut mixture evenly in prepared jelly-roll pans. Bake 20 to 25 minutes or until coating on nuts is golden brown and dry, stirring once and rotating pans between upper and lower racks halfway through.

4 Set pans on wire racks to cool completely, at least 1 hour. When nuts are cool, use hands to gently break apart any large clusters of nuts. Store in an airtight containers at room temperature up to 2 weeks.

Each 1/4-cup serving: About 185 calories, 6g protein, 8g carbohydrate, 15g total fat (2g saturated), 2g fiber, 105mg sodium

MY MOST MAGICAL CHRISTMAS

"On Christmas Eve, my brother used to let me sleep in his bedroom in the spare bed, and we'd sit up all night talking about what Santa would bring us. My brother kept the dream of Santa alive for me longer than it would have been otherwise."

—Reese Witherspoon

Butternut Toffee Crunch

Delight toffee fans with a box of this buttery candy.

Active time: 15 minutes
Total time: 40 minutes plus cooling
Makes: 1³⁄₄ pounds

1³⁄₄ cups sugar
¹⁄₃ cup light corn syrup
¹⁄₄ cup water
1 cup butter or margarine (2 sticks)
2 cups walnuts (8 ounces),
    lightly toasted (page 287) and finely chopped
2 squares (2 ounces) unsweetened chocolate, chopped
2 squares (2 ounces) semisweet chocolate, chopped
1 teaspoon vegetable shortening

1 Lightly grease 15½" by 10½" jelly-roll pan. In heavy 2-quart saucepan, combine sugar, corn syrup, and water; heat to boiling over medium heat, stirring occasionally. Stir in butter.

2 Set candy thermometer in place and continue cooking, stirring frequently, about 20 minutes or until temperature reaches 300°F (hard-crack stage).

3 Remove saucepan from heat. Reserve ¹⁄₃ cup walnuts; stir remaining walnuts into hot syrup. Immediately pour mixture into prepared jelly-roll pan. Working quickly, spread evenly with a rubber spatula. Cool completely.

4 Prepare chocolate glaze: In small saucepan over low heat, melt chocolates with shortening, stirring until smooth. Remove saucepan from heat; cool slightly.

5 Lift cooled toffee out of pan in one piece and place on cutting board. With metal spatula, spread warm chocolate evenly over toffee; sprinkle with reserved walnuts. Let stand until chocolate sets, about 1 hour.

6 With knife, break toffee crunch into serving-size pieces. Store in an airtight container, with waxed paper between layers, at room temperature up to 2 weeks.

Each 1-ounce serving: About 195 calories, 2g protein, 18g carbohydrate, 14g total fat (6g saturated), 1g fiber, 75mg sodium

Crackly Chocolate Almonds

Toasting almonds accomplishes two things: It crisps them up and brings out their flavor. These double-chocolate-dipped nibbles make a sophisticated gift.

Active time: 1 hour 10 minutes
Total time: 1 hour 25 minutes plus cooling
Makes: 8 cups

4 cups whole blanched almonds (1 pound)
1¼ cups sugar
¼ cup water
1 teaspoon vanilla extract
1 pound bittersweet or semisweet chocolate, chopped
⅓ cup unsweetened cocoa

1 Preheat oven to 350°F. Spread almonds in two jelly-roll pans or on two cookie sheets. Bake, stirring occasionally, until toasted, 15 minutes. Cool.

2 Line same pans with parchment. In heavy 4-quart saucepan, combine almonds, sugar, water, and vanilla. Cook, stirring constantly, over medium-high heat until sugar is thick and cloudy and crystallizes on side of pan and almonds are coated and separate, 5 to 6 minutes. With slotted spoon, transfer almonds to jelly-roll pans, leaving excess sugar in saucepan. Spread almonds out; refrigerate until cold, about 45 minutes.

3 Meanwhile, in large microwave-safe bowl, melt half of chopped chocolate in microwave oven on High for 1½ to 2 minutes; stir until smooth. Cool slightly.

4 With hands, transfer almonds from one pan to chocolate in bowl; wipe off any excess sugar on parchment and return parchment to pan. With wooden spoon, stir almonds until completely coated with chocolate; spoon into pan. With fork, spread out almonds and separate as much as possible. Repeat with remaining chocolate and almonds. Refrigerate until chocolate is set, about 1 hour.

5 Sift cocoa into large bowl. Break almonds apart if necessary. Add almonds, in batches, to cocoa, tossing to coat well. (To create variations in color, toss about three-fourths of the almonds in cocoa and leave remaining nuts uncoated.) Place cocoa-coated almonds in sieve and gently shake to remove excess. Refrigerate almonds in an airtight container up to 1 month.

Each ¼-cup serving: About 175 calories, 4g protein, 16g carbohydrate, 12g total fat (3g saturated), 3g fiber, 2mg sodium

Chocolate-Dipped Pretzels

These pretzels are super easy to whip up to give as a gift. Dip them a day ahead and pack them in a box lined with waxed tissue paper. Don't forget to add a note, or simply remind your friends that pretzels are best eaten within a week—not that they'll be around that long!

Total time: 20 minutes plus chilling
Makes: 27 pretzels

8 ounces milk chocolate, broken into pieces
Flaked coconut for topping
Colored sprinkles for topping
27 (8-inch-long) pretzel rods (10-ounce bag)

1 Place chocolate in microwave-safe measuring cup or mug. Heat, covered with waxed paper, in microwave on High 1 to 2 minutes or until chocolate is almost melted, stirring occasionally until smooth.

2 Meanwhile, place each topping choice on separate sheet of waxed paper or on individual plates.

3 Dip 1 pretzel rod at a time in melted chocolate, tipping cup to cover about half of rod. Allow excess chocolate to drip back into cup. Immediately sprinkle coated pretzel with choice of topping. Carefully place coated pretzel rod in pie plate or shallow bowl, leaning uncoated portion on edge.

4 Repeat with remaining pretzels, placing in pie plate so pretzels do not touch, and refrigerate about 20 minutes to set coating. Store pretzels in an airtight container, with waxed paper between layers, up to 1 week.

Each pretzel: About 135 calories, 3g protein, 18g carbohydrate, 6g total fat (3g saturated), 1g fiber, 165mg sodium

CHOCOLATE-DIPPED PRETZELS *(opposite)*

Good Housekeeping

DECEMBER
1935

25 CENTS

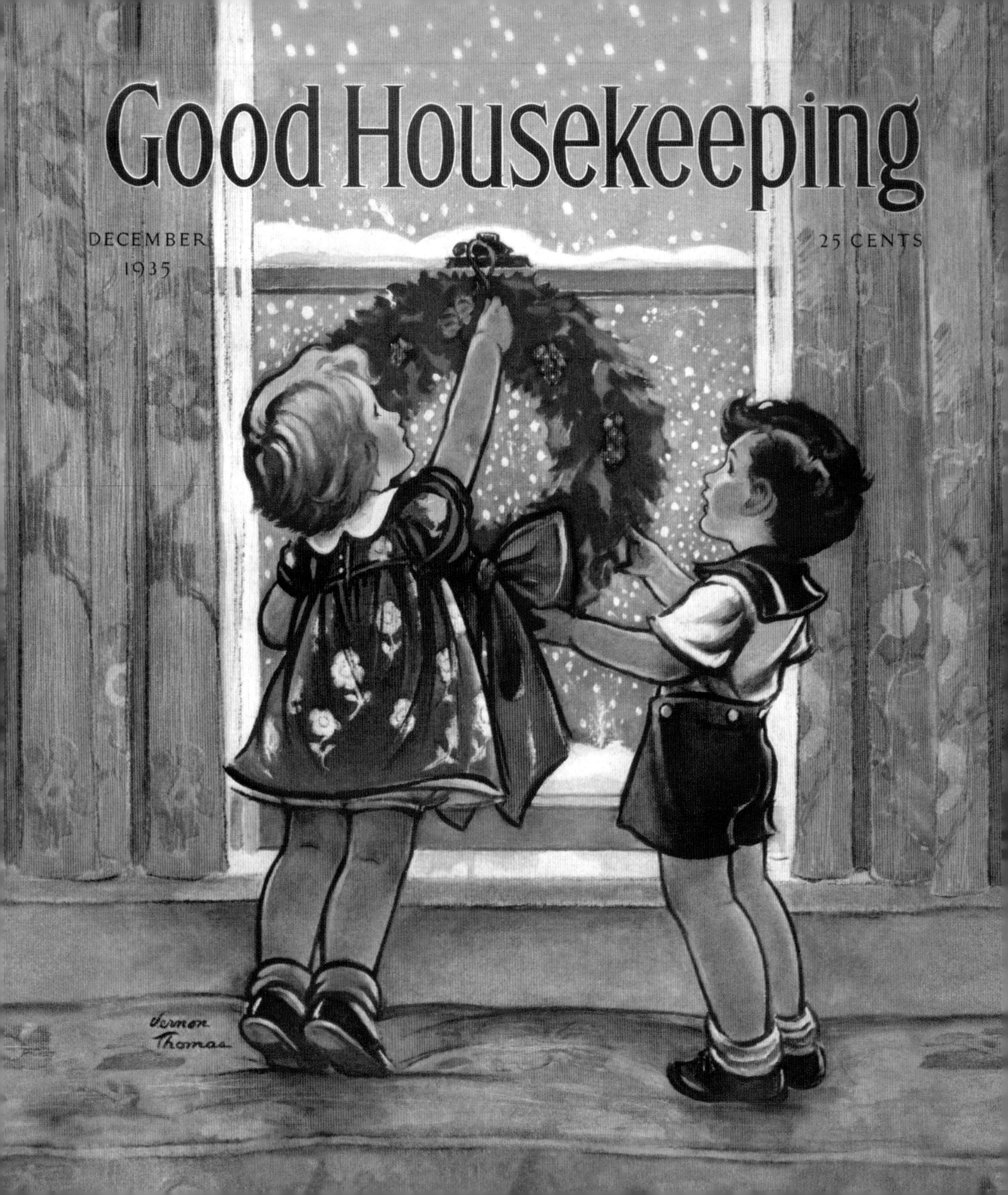

FROM OUR HOLIDAY ARCHIVES:
OLD-FASHIONED CHRISTMAS CANDIES

As the holidays approach, if you have visions of sugarplums dancing in your head, then these festive confections are for you. We've included scrumptious recipes for classics like peanut brittle, fudge, and pralines, as well as Maple Kisses, Sugarplum Puffs, and other creative sweets.

Five-Minute Fudge

1²/₃ cups sugar

2 tablespoons butter or margarine

¹/₂ teaspoon salt

²/₃ cup evaporated milk

1¹/₂ cups semisweet chocolate chips

4 ounces marshmallows, diced

¹/₂ cup chopped walnuts plus additional for sprinkling

1 teaspoon vanilla extract

1 Grease 8-inch-square baking pan.

2 In 2-quart saucepan, combine sugar, butter, salt, and evaporated milk; bring to a boil over medium heat, and boil 5 minutes, stirring constantly.

3 Remove saucepan from heat and add chocolate, marshmallows, chopped walnuts, and vanilla extract. Beat vigorously until marshmallows melt.

4 Pour into prepared pan; sprinkle with additional walnuts. Cool completely. Cut into small squares to serve. Makes 60 candies.

Pralines

3 cups pecan halves

2 cups sugar

1 teaspoon baking soda

1 cup buttermilk

Pinch salt

2 tablespoons butter or margarine

1 Pick through pecan halves and set aside ²/₃ cup perfectly shaped halves for topping. Line a cookie sheet with waxed paper or grease cookie sheet; set aside.

2 In large (8-quart) pot, combine sugar, baking soda, buttermilk, and salt. (If using candy thermometer, set in place.) Cook over high heat, stirring frequently and scraping bottom and crevices of pot, about 5 minutes (candy thermometer should register 210°F). Add butter and 2¹/₃ cups pecan halves. Cook, stirring continuously and scraping bottom and sides of pot, about 5 minutes, until small amount of syrup in mixture added to cold water forms very soft ball (candy thermometer should register 230°F). Remove from heat.

3 Allow mixture to cool for a minute or two. Then, with wooden spoon, beat until thickened and is creamy; immediately drop by tablespoons (or teaspoons for smaller candies) onto prepared cookie sheet. Dot with reserved pecan halves. Makes about 36 pralines.

Peanut Brittle

1½ cups sugar
½ teaspoon cream of tartar
½ cup cold water
1⅔ cups salted peanuts

1 In large saucepan, place sugar, cream of tartar, and water; do not stir. Cook over high heat, shaking pan occasionally, until molasses-colored syrup forms.

2 Quickly stir in peanuts, then pour into well-buttered jelly-roll pan, evenly spreading nut mixture in a single layer. Let cool completely. To serve, break into pieces.

Mixed-Nut Brittle

Combine ⅓ cup each walnut halves, blanched whole almonds, pecan halves, salted peanuts, and hazelnuts. Stir into sugar syrup as described in step 2 and spread, cool, and serve brittle as described.

Chocolate-Peanut Popcorn

2 tablespoons butter or margarine
1 cup semisweet chocolate chips
12 large marshmallows
1 tablespoon water
8 cups popped popcorn
1⅓ cups salted cocktail peanuts

1 In large saucepan over low heat, melt butter. Add chocolate chips, marshmallows, and water, stirring constantly until mixture is melted and smooth.

2 Add popcorn and toss until well coated. Spread out on baking sheet to cool.

3 When cool, toss popcorn with peanuts. Makes about 2 quarts.

Divinity Drops

2⅓ cups sugar
⅔ cup light corn syrup
½ cup water
¼ teaspoon salt
2 egg whites
½ cup chopped Brazil nuts, walnuts, or flaked coconut
½ teaspoon vanilla or almond extract
Chopped nuts, colored sugar, or tinted coconut flakes, for topping (optional)

1 Grease cookie sheet and set aside. In 2-quart saucepan, combine sugar, corn syrup, water, and salt and stir over low heat until sugar is dissolved. Cover pan and bring mixture to boil. Boil 1 minute or until all sugar crystals on sides of pan have melted. Remove cover. (If using candy thermometer, set in place.) Continue gently cooking, without stirring, until small amount of syrup added to cold water forms almost brittle ball (265°F on candy thermometer).

2 Meanwhile, in bowl of standing mixer, beat egg whites until stiff. Slowly pour syrup over egg whites, while beating; continue beating until mixture loses gloss and small amount dropped from spoon holds its shape. With wooden spoon, stir in nuts and vanilla.

3 Drop by teaspoonfuls onto prepared cookie sheet. If desired, sprinkle with nuts, colored sugar, or tinted coconut flakes. Makes about 1½ pounds candy.

TIP: Many candies are made with sugar syrup, and measuring the temperature of the syrup accurately with a candy thermometer ensures the best results. Attach the thermometer to the side of the pan, making sure the tip of the thermometer doesn't touch the bottom of the pan.

To dissolve the sugar crystals that form on the sides of the saucepan, swipe a pastry brush that's been dipped into cold water against the sides of the pan. Otherwise the candy may become grainy.

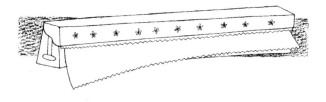

Maple Kisses

1 cup packed light brown sugar
1/2 cup granulated sugar
1/4 cup light corn syrup
1/2 cup evaporated milk
1 tablespoon butter or margarine
1 teaspoon maple extract
1 1/2 cups chopped walnuts

1. Lay sheet of waxed paper on flat work surface. In medium saucepan, combine both sugars, corn syrup, and evaporated milk. Cook over very low heat, stirring constantly, until candy thermometer registers 235°F, or until 1/2 teaspoon sugar syrup dropped in cold water forms a soft ball, about 20 minutes.

2 Remove from heat. With wooden spoon, beat in butter, maple extract, and nuts. Quickly drop mixture, by teaspoonful, onto prepared waxed paper to cool.

3 When set, wrap each kiss in plastic wrap. Store at room temperature, in an airtight container up to 1 week. Makes about 24 candies.

Multicolored Mints

2 1/2 cups sifted confectioners' sugar
7 1/2 teaspoons water
1/4 to 1/2 teaspoon peppermint extract
Red or green food coloring

1 Lay sheet of waxed paper on flat work surface. In top of double boiler, combine sugar, water, desired extract, and a few drops food coloring of choice. Cook over boiling water, stirring constantly, 3 minutes.

2 Remove from boiling water and quickly drop mixture by teaspoonful onto prepared waxed paper. Let stand to cool and harden. With broad spatula, carefully remove from paper. Refrigerate in a loosely covered container up to 1 week. Makes about 20 mints.

Sugarplum Puffs

1 1/2 cups sugar
1/4 teaspoon cream of tartar
6 egg whites
1 1/2 teaspoons vanilla extract
Red and green food coloring
Assorted candies and décors, such as multicolored candy-coated chocolate candies, dragées, snipped gumdrops, red cinnamon drops, colored sprinkles, colored sugar

1 Preheat oven to 200°F.

2 Into small bowl, sift sugar with cream of tartar. In large bowl, with mixer on high speed, beat egg whites until stiff but not dry. Sprinkle in sugar mixture, 1 tablespoon at a time, beating until meringue forms stiff peaks when beaters are raised. Beat in vanilla.

3 Place about one-fourth of meringue in small bowl and gently fold in enough red food coloring to tint meringue bright pink. In second bowl, tint another fourth pale green. Leave remaining meringue white.

4 Cover large cookie sheet with foil. Drop round puffs of tinted and white meringue by quarter-cupfuls, 1 inch apart, on sheet. Decorate puffs with assorted candies and décors.

5 Bake meringues about 2 hours; cool completely on cookie sheet on wire rack. Store in an airtight container, between layers of waxed paper, up to 3 weeks. Makes about 24 candies.

1

2

CREATE A GIFT-WRAPPING STATION

Santa may have a whole workshop—and 364 days to prepare—but you don't. Here's how to handle the holiday present-wrapping rush:

Designate a table, then clear off the surface so you have ample room to spread out and a seat on which to perch. Gather tools that help you work efficiently, like a weighted tape dispenser for grabbing pieces of tape one-handed and sharp scissors (i.e., not the dull kitchen castoffs). Make a list of who's getting what, check it off as you wrap each gift, and finish each present with a well-secured gift tag (so your sister won't end up opening Grandpa's argyle sweater). To make your own easy homemade tags, see "Genius Gift Tags" on page 399. Follow these tips for setting up a station that will make you a gift-wrapping machine.

1. On a Roll

Forget the frustration of tangled ribbon. Stack spools onto a paper-towel holder for easy access, and save leftover pieces of ribbon (that no longer have a spool) on empty paper-towel rolls, using a piece of tape to keep each wrapped tight. Stash the rolls in a handy box, so you know where to find them next year or whenever a wrapping project arises.

ALL WRAPPED UP

Forgo the fruitcake and give the hostess a package of present-wrapping fixings to help ensure that her holidays will be a little less frantic.

It's as easy as lining a decorative box with tissue paper and filling it with a variety of ribbons, gift cards, and tags, glitter, scissors, and snazzy gadgets like a ribbon curler and a pop-up tape dispenser. (You may want to buy a second set of tools to have at the ready in your own gift-wrapping station!)

KEEP VERSUS TOSS

• **Keep** wrapping-paper scraps for year-round use. Small sheets are perfect for creating custom gift tags, scrapbooking, and decoupage. Lay pieces flat (or carefully fold), and store in an expandable accordian folder near the rest of your wrapping supplies.

• **Toss** abused gift wrap (even if it's in a super-cute pattern), battered gift bags, and dog-eared boxes. If the packaging is mangled, it will only distract from your nice gesture. That said, wrinkled fabric ribbon can be saved: Iron it on low heat (you may need a spritz of water) to smooth it out.

• **Keep** unusual papers and trinkets. Recycle magazines and maps to swathe gifts, then salvage ornaments, costume jewelry, and tiny toys to tie on for a personal touch.

2. In the Bag

A hanging toiletry bag makes a perfect trimmings tool kit, since the clear compartments make your equipment accessible, and it can hang out (or get tucked away) when not in use. Arm your arsenal with a hole punch, pen, glue stick, double-sided tape, scissors, gift tags, gift-topping embellishments, and some pretty premade bows.

3. Paper Chase

Corral rolls of wrap in a clean trash bin that you can stow in a closet when not needed. So papers don't unravel and rip, slip thin rubber bands (the thick ones can grab and rumple paper) around the tubes. Also, have some nonseasonal wraps in solid colors or simple patterns to get you through more than one holiday.

THE ULTIMATE GIFT-MAILING GUIDE

Can't visit all your loved ones? Send presents instead—the fastest, cheapest way. Here's how.

Pack Like a Pro

• **Pick the right-size box and don't overstuff;** if you do, the contents are likely to bust out before reaching their destination. Check the bottom flap of the box; it will tell you the maximum weight the container can bear.

• **When you're mailing multiple items, bubble wrap each separately,** then tape them together so they won't clank together during shipping.

• **Before sealing a package, give it a gentle shake.** If you hear anything moving, add padding—newspaper or shredded documents do the trick.

• **To make sure your box is fully reinforced, use the "H" method:** Tape along all the seams—it will look like there's an H on both the top and bottom of your box. And always use real packing tape; the other stuff won't hold up in transit.

Ship Smart

• **Reusing a box?** Strip off old labels, especially the bar codes, so the package doesn't get misrouted by the carrier.

• **Remove batteries** from toys and electronics, if possible. All the jostling can turn them on in transit, and they may burn out before arrival.

• **To make a package waterproof,** line it with a garbage bag.

• **The wrong zip code** can land a package back on your doorstep (weeks later), so check accuracy with the U.S. Postal Service's Zip Code Lookup tool at zip4.usps.com/zip4/welcome.jsp.

Weigh Your Options

• **Click on carrier's sites to schedule pickups.** UPS and FedEx charge for the perk; the U.S. Postal Service doesn't. Pay for postage online and print out shipping labels. To weigh a package at home: Stand on scale with your box, then without, and subtract.

• **Worried about weight?** The U.S. Postal Service has flat-rate boxes that you can fill with your heaviest items, then send to any state—all for one fixed price. (Check rates on shop.usps.com.)

• **Compare postage online** at shippingsidekick.com Enter the weight and destination of your package; the sites will give you rates for all the major carriers, including UPS and FedEx.

Beat Post Office Lines

• **If you decide to mail a gift at the post office,** avoid manic Mondays. (The first day of the week is typically the busiest for shipping).

• **Put minis in the mailbox.** A package weighing less than 13 ounces can be dropped in a mailbox.

Have a very Merry Christmas!

Susan

Have a very Merry Christmas!

To Julie!

GORGEOUS GIFT WRAPS FOR SURE-TO-PLEASE PRESENTS

If you usually just wrap your Christmas presents in red or green paper and call it a day, try these inspired designs, which go way beyond ordinary wrapping paper and ribbon. From rubber stamp monograms and a layered look to seasonal greenery and candy canes, these stunning presentations are (almost) as good as what's inside. And, you can skip the dime-store gift tags: We show how to customize cute tags using basic office and art supplies; turn the page.

1. Candy Cane Christmas

Streamline gift giving by wrapping all your presents in the same pristine white paper, brightened with bold bursts of red and a hint of blue. It's elegant, economical, and easy to customize with tree cuttings, tags, and tempting candies.

2. Can Do

Make a gift card more personal by tailoring the wrap to the item. Here, a home-store certificate nestles in a prettied-up paint can. If you're giving a gift card for a manicure, use a cosmetics bag; for DVDs, try a popcorn box.

3. Tie One On

Dress up a gift with a mini Christmas ornament or jingle bell: The recipient will appreciate the holiday bonus. Select harmonizing hues for the wrapping paper and loop the ornament's hanger through the ribbon before tying a bow.

4. Light Touch

Accent packages with colorful Christmas tree lightbulbs. How to: Hot-glue six bulbs together to form a star shape, then fasten the bauble to a length of ribbon with double-stick tape. Glowing smiles guaranteed.

5. Homespun Holiday Wrapping

With a little imagination, brown parcel paper, some twine, muted ribbon, and nature-made embellishments are all you need to wrap gifts. Here's how: Cover your presents in parcel paper; tie with twine or with ribbon in earthy tones. Then, for a burst of color, use floral wire to attach kumquats, holly sprigs, or other seasonal greenery or fruits to the packages.

6. Play with Layers

Skip holiday-themed gift wrap and go with sweet stripes and cheerful checks. As long as the colors are coordinated, the more patterns you mix, the merrier.

7. Genius Gift Tags

Personalize presents the easy way, using basic office and art supplies. A metal-rimmed tag makes a simple statement. Labeling tags look festive when stamped with holiday motifs or greetings. For a photo card, paste a picture of the gift recipient onto colored paper (especially fun for the wee ones). Reuse old greeting cards by cutting them into simple seasonal shapes like Christmas ornaments, trees, or stars.

To: Sarah
From: Tom

Deck the Halls

Ho! Ho! Ho!

HOLIDAY MENU IDEAS

Looking for meal-planning inspiration?
Choose from these twelve festive menus.

Holiday Open House

Sweet and Sassy Nuts (page 384)

Roasted Red and Green Pepper Quesadillas (page 169)

Pomegranate Margaritas (page 60)

Jicama and Orange Salad (page 87)

Slow-Cooker Chipotle Beef Chili (page 171)

Pimiento Cheese Log (page 47)

Lime Triangles (page 341)

Dark Chocolate–Raspberry Layer Cake (page 267)

See also "Setting Up a Crowd-Pleasing Buffet" (page 164)

Traditional Christmas Dinner

Classic American Relish Tray (page 58)

Roasted-Beet and Pistachio Salad (page 83)

Beef Rib Roast with Creamy Horseradish Sauce and Yorkshire Pudding (page 118)

Braised Wild Mushrooms and Peas (page 214)

Maple-Ginger-Glazed Carrots (page 223)

Dulce de Leche Christmas Wreath (page 272)

Café Brûlot (page 74)

Christmas Brunch Buffet

Christmas Cranberry Juleps (page 60)

Citrus Ambrosia Salad (page 81)

Smoked Salmon Spread and Bagels (page 158)

Bacon French Toast Bake (page 155)

Pineapple-Pom Fruit Melange (page 155)

Cinnamon Crumb Cake (page 275)

Southern Christmas

Blood Orange Mimosas (page 65)

Mustard-Glazed Fresh Ham with Cider Sauce (page 124)

Dill-Pepper Buttermilk Biscuits (page 210)

Sweet Potatoes with Marshmallow Meringue (page 199)

Creamed Spinach (page 222; double the recipe)

Fresh Cranberry-Orange Mold (page 234)

Old-Fashioned Pecan Pie (page 280)

Cranberry Vanilla Cake with Whipped Cream Frosting (page 271)

Turkey with All the Trimmings

Chestnut Parsnip Soup (page 93)

Sage-Orange Turkey with White Wine Gravy (page 138)

Savory Bread Stuffing with Pears (page 206)

Roasted Sweet & Sour Brussels Sprouts (page 219)

Caramelized Onion and Fennel Relish (page 233)

Pumpkin Crème Caramel (page 296)

Cranberry Almond Pie (page 278)

Warm Spiced Cider (page 70)

See also "Our Favorite Sandwich Ideas for Cold Turkey" (page 139)

Southwestern Christmas on the Grill

Spice-Grilled Turkey Breast (page 145)

Accordion Potatoes (page 194)

Kale Salad with Glazed Onions and Cheddar (page 220)

Cranberry-Cornmeal Biscuits (page 210)

Southwestern-Style Cranberry Relish (page 235)

Black-Bottom Chocolate Cream Pie (page 278)

Old-Fashioned Pecan Pie (page 280)

Italian Feast of the Seven Fishes

Ruby Bellinis (page 65)

Salmon Pâté (page 53)

Seafood Salad (page 86; see headnote)

Mussels with Tomato and White Wine Sauce (page 152)

Sole Roll-Ups with Crab Stuffing (page 151)

Italian-Spiced Shrimp Casserole (page 152)

Mixed Winter Greens (page 77)

Sautéed Swiss Chard with Golden Raisins and Capers (page 226)

Lemon-Ricotta Cheesecake (page 266)

Elegant Christmas Celebration for Four

Lacy Parmesan Crisps (page 51)

Champagne Cocktail (page 74)

Mushroom and Wild Rice Soup (page 99)

Roast Duck with Cherry-Port Sauce (page 146)

Tarragon Vegetable Julienne (page 217; halve the recipe)

Fruited Multigrain Pilaf with Almonds (page 201)

Meyer Lemon Pudding Cakes (page 304)

See also "Open Bubbly Like a Pro" (page 62)

Light and Healthy Holiday Dinner

Artichoke and Red Pepper Bruschetta (page 50)

Holiday Spritzers (page 65)

Turkey Breast with Spinach-Herb Stuffing (page 133)

Smashed Potatoes with Yogurt and Chives (page 195)

Tarragon Vegetable Julienne (page 217)

Citrus-Apricot Cranberry Sauce (page 237)

Wine-Poached Pears (page 304)

Lemon Meringue Drops (page 324)

Festive Cocktail Party

Cranberry Mojitos (page 65)

Holiday Champagne Punch (page 67)

Marinated Olives (page 58)

Salmon Pâté (page 53)

Mini Rémoulade Crab Cakes (page 54)

Herbed Gougères (page 51)

Cocktail Meatballs with Creamy Cranberry Sauce (page 37)

Platter of assorted cheeses, bread, and crudité (see "The Perfect Cheese Platter", page 63)

Dessert Buffet

Cranberry Trifle (page 301)

Amaretto Apricot Cake (page 264)

Lemon-Ricotta Cheesecake (page 266)

Cranberry-Almond Pie (page 278)

Chocolate Raspberry Roll (page 263)

White Chocolate–Macadamia Bars (page 347)

Figgy Bars with Hard-Sauce Glaze (page 342)

Mint Brownie Bites (page 328)

New Year's Eve Sit-Down Dinner for Eight

Champagne and Lillet Cocktails (page 62)

Prosciutto-Wrapped Breadsticks (page 40)

Creamy Asparagus Soup (page 96)

Beef Tenderloin with White Wine Sauce (page 113)

Potato Gratin with Gruyère (page 192)

Tarragon Peas with Pearl Onions (page 213)

Ganache Tart with Salted-Almond Crust (page 289)

VOLUME EQUIVALENTS

SMALL VOLUME

Tablespoons	Cups	Fluid Ounces
1 tablespoon = 3 teaspoons		1/2 fluid ounce
2 tablespoons	1/8 cup	1 fluid ounce
4 tablespoons	1/4 cup	2 fluid ounces
5 tablespoons + 1 teaspoon	1/3 cup	2 2/3 fluid ounces
6 tablespoons	3/8 cup	3 fluid ounces
8 tablespoons	1/2 cup	4 fluid ounces
10 tablespoons +2 teaspoons	2/3 cup	5 1/3 fluid ounces
12 tablespoons	3/4 cup	6 fluid ounces
14 tablespoons	7/8 cup	7 fluid ounces
16 tablespoons	1 cup	8 fluid ounces

LARGER VOLUME

Cups	Fluid Ounces	Pints/Quarts/Gallons
1 cup	8 fluid ounces	1/2 pint
2 cups	16 fluid ounces	1 pint
3 cups	24 fluid ounces	1 1/2 pints = 3/4 quart
4 cups	32 fluid ounces	2 pints = 1 quart
6 cups	48 fluid ounces	3 pints = 1 1/2 quarts
8 cups	64 fluid ounces	2 quarts = 1/2 gallon
16 cups	128 fluid ounces	4 quarts = 1 gallon

PAN VOLUMES

Pan Size	Approximate Volume
2 1/2" by 1 1/2" muffin pan cup	1/2 cup
8 1/2" by 4 1/2" by 2 1/2" loaf pan	6 cups
9" by 5" by 3" loaf pan	8 cups
8" by 8" by 1 1/2" baking pan	6 cups
9" by 9" by 1 1/2" baking pan	8 cups
9" by 1" pie plate	4 cups
11" by 7" by 1 1/2" baking pan	8 cups
13" by 9" by 2" baking pan	15 cups
15 1/2" by 10 1/2" by 1" jelly-roll pan	16 cups

EQUIVALENTS FOR DRY INGREDIENTS BY WEIGHT

(To convert ounces to grams, multiply the number of ounces by 30.)

1 oz	=	1/16 lb	=	30 g
4 oz	=	1/4 lb	=	120 g
8 oz	=	1/2 lb	=	240 g
12 oz	=	3/4 lb	=	360 g
16 oz	=	1 lb	=	480 g

METRIC EQUIVALENTS

The recipes in this book use the standard United States method for measuring liquid and dry or solid ingredients (teaspoons, tablespoons, and cups). The information on this chart is provided to help cooks outside the U.S. successfully use these recipes. All equivalents are approximate.

METRIC EQUIVALENTS FOR DIFFERENT TYPES OF INGREDIENTS

A standard cup measure of a dry or solid ingredient will vary in weight depending on the type of ingredient. A standard cup of liquid is the same volume for any type of liquid. Use the following chart when converting standard cup measures to grams (weight) or milliliters (volume).

Standard Cup	Fine Powder (e.g., flour)	Grain (e.g., rice)	Granular (e.g., sugar)	Liquid Solids (e.g., butter)	Liquid (e.g., milk)
1	140 g	150 g	190 g	200 g	240 ml
3/4	105 g	113 g	143 g	150 g	180 ml
2/3	93 g	100 g	125 g	133 g	160 ml
1/2	70 g	75 g	95 g	100 g	120 ml
1/3	47 g	50 g	63 g	67 g	80 ml
1/4	35 g	38 g	48 g	50 g	60 ml
1/8	18 g	19 g	24 g	25 g	30 ml

EQUIVALENTS FOR LIQUID INGREDIENTS BY VOLUME

1/4 tsp		=		=		=	1 ml
1/2 tsp		=		=		=	2 ml
1 tsp	=		=		=		5 ml
3 tsp	=	1 tbsp	=		=	1/2 fl oz	15 ml
		2 tbsp	=	1/8 cup	=	1 fl oz	30 ml
		4 tbsp	=	1/4 cup	=	2 fl oz	60 ml
		5 1/3 tbsp	=	1/3 cup	=	3 fl oz	80 ml
		8 tbsp	=	1/2 cup	=	4 fl oz	120 ml
		10 2/3 tbsp	=	2/3 cup	=	5 fl oz	160 ml
		12 tbsp	=	3/4 cup	=	6 fl oz	180 ml
		16 tbsp	=	1 cup	=	8 fl oz	240 ml
		1 pt	=	2 cups	=	16 fl oz	480 ml
		1 qt	=	4 cups	=	32 fl oz	960 ml
						33 fl oz	= 1000 ml 1 L

EQUIVALENTS FOR DRY INGREDIENTS BY WEIGHT

(To convert ounces to grams, multiply the number of ounces by 30.)

1 oz	=	1/16 lb	=	30 g
4 oz	=	1/4 lb	=	120 g
8 oz	=	1/2 lb	=	240 g
12 oz	=	3/4 lb	=	360 g
16 oz	=	1 lb	=	480 g

EQUIVALENTS FOR COOKING/OVEN TEMPERATURES

	Farenheit	Celsius	Gas Mark
Freeze Water	32°F	0°C	
Room Temperature	68°F	20°C	
Boil Water	212°F	100°C	
Bake	325°F	160°C	3
	350°F	180°C	4
	375°F	190°C	5
	400°F	200°C	6
	425°F	220°C	7
	450°F	230°C	8
Broil			Grill

EQUIVALENTS FOR LENGTH

(To convert inches to centimeters, multiply the number of inches by 2.5.)

1 in	=			=	2.5 cm	
6 in	=	1/2 ft		=	15 cm	
12 in	=	1 ft		=	30 cm	
36 in	=	3 ft	= 1 yd	=	90 cm	
40 in	=			100 cm	=	1 m

REFRIGERATOR AND FREEZER STORAGE GUIDE

Get ready for the holidays: Maximize the longevity of your purchases by freezing them. To avoid freezer burn, leave as little extra air in the storage bag or container as possible. If you take a defrosting shortcut, like zapping edibles in the microwave instead of thawing them in the fridge, fully cook the food before refreezing it.

WHAT TO SAVE	HOW LONG IN FRIDGE (set at or below 40°F)	HOW LONG IN FREEZER (set at or below 0°F)	HOW TO PACKAGE FOR FREEZING
FRUIT			
Juices	Opened, 7 to 10 days Unopened, 3 weeks	8 to 12 months	Pour some off to leave room for expansion; reseal with masking tape; shake after thawing
Bananas, ripe	2 week	8 to 12 months	In peel, in freezer bag (peel may discolor)
Blackberries and raspberries	2 to 3 days	8 to 12 months	Spread on tray and freeze until firm; store in sealed container or freezer bag
Blueberries	10 days	8 to 12 months	In original container, placed in freezer bag
Cranberries	4 weeks	8 to 12 months	In original bag (if unopened) or freezer bag
Grapes	1 to 2 weeks	8 to 12 months	See Blackberries, above (remove stems)
VEGETABLES			
Broccoli and Cauliflower	3 to 5 days	Blanched for 3 minutes, 8 to 12 months*	In freezer bag
Cabbage (shredded or cut into 1½-inch pieces)	1 week	Blanched for 1½ minutes, 8 to 12 months*	In freezer bag
Carrots (cut into ¼-inch cubes)	2 weeks	Blanched for 2 minutes, 8 to 12 months*	In freezer bag
Corn (off the cob)	2 weeks	Blanched for 2 minutes, 8 to 12 months*	In freezer bag
Green beans (trimmed)	1 week	Blanched for 3 minutes, 8 to 12 months*	In freezer bag
Potatoes, small (peeled)	No (they discolor and change flavor)	Blanched for 3 to 5 minutes, 8 to 12 months	In freezer bag

*To blanch vegetables, cook in rapidly boiling water for recommended time. Then cool quickly in ice water bath and drain well. This slows or stops action of enzymes that can cause loss of flavor, color, and texture. Cook frozen vegetables without thawing.

WHAT TO SAVE	HOW LONG IN FRIDGE (set at or below 40°F)	HOW LONG IN FREEZER (set at or below 0°F)	HOW TO PACKAGE FOR FREEZING	
Steaks	3 to 5 days	10 to 12 months	In freezer bag	
Chops	3 to 5 days	4 to 6 months	In freezer bag	
Roasts	3 to 5 days	10 to 12 months	In freezer bag	
Ham, full cooked (whole, half, slices)	Opened, 5 days In vacumn package, 1 month	1 to 2 months	In freezer bag	**MEAT**
Ground	1 to 2 days	3 to 4 months	In freezer bag	
Sausages, raw	1 to 2 days	1 to 2 months	In freezer bag	
Sausages, fully cooked	Opened, 1 week Unopened, 2 weeks	1 to 2 months (opened or unopened)	In original packaging, placed in freezer bag	
Bacon	1 week	1 month (opened or unopened)	In original packaging, placed in freezer bag	
Casseroles, cooked, meat	2 to 3 days	2 to 3 months	In casserole dish, then remove from dish and transfer to freezer bag	
Whole	1 to 2 days	1 year	In freezer bag	
Pieces	1 to 2 days	9 months	In freezer bag	
Ground	1 to 2 days	3 to 4 months	In freezer bag	**POULTRY**
Sausages, raw	1 to 2 days	1 to 2 months	In freezer bag	
Casseroles, cooked, poultry	2 to 3 days	2 to 3 months	In casserole dish, then remove from dish and transfer to freezer bag	
Lean (such as cod, sole, flounder)	1 to 2 days	3 to 6 months	In freezer bag	
Oily (such as salmon)	1 to 2 days	2 to 3 months	In freezer bag	
Smoked (such as salmon in vacuum pack)	Opened, 3 to 5 days Unopened, 1 month	2 months	Place original package in freezer bag	**FISH**
Shellfish (such as shrimp and shucked oysters, scallops, mussels)	1 to 2 days unshucked	3 months shucked	In freezer bag	

WHAT TO SAVE	HOW LONG IN FRIDGE (set at or below 40°F)	HOW LONG IN FREEZER (set at or below 0°F)	HOW TO PACKAGE FOR FREEZING
DAIRY			
Cheese, grated	1 month	3 to 4 months	In freezer bag
Hard cheeses, in blocks (such as Cheddar, Swiss, Parmesan)	Opened, 3 to 4 months Unopened, 6 months	6 months	Cut into smaller portions, wrap each portion in plastic wrap, then place in freezer bag
Soft cheeses (such as Brie, feta, goat)	2 weeks	6 months	See Hard cheeses, in blocks, above
Butter	2 to 3 months	6 to 9 months	For a month or less, in original packaging For longer term, in freezer bag
Egg whites or yolks; beaten eggs	2 to 4 days	6 months	In sealed container closest in volume to amount you're storing; label with number of eggs inside
Milk	1 week	6 months	See Juices, page 380
Cream, heavy cream	Opened, 1 week	6 months (only heavy cream freezes well)	See Juices, page 380
BAKED GOODS			
Breads and rolls, yeast	No (refrigeration makes bread go stale quickly)	3 to 6 months	In original package, then wrapped with foil or plastic wrap, or in freezer bag
Breads, quick (such as zucchini bread, biscuits, or scones)	No (refrigeration makes bread go stale quickly)	3 to 6 months	In freezer bag
Cookies, baked	3 to 5 days (depends on type of cookie)	3 months	In container, separated by layers of waxed paper if frosted or fragile
Cookie dough, raw	1 to 2 days (wrap in plastic)	2 to 3 months	Wrap in plastic wrap, then place in freezer bag
Brownies and bars	2 to 5 days (depends on type of bar)	3 months	Slice bars and place in container, separated by layers of waxed paper
Pies, fruit, unbaked	1 day	2 to 3 months	Wrap pie and pan in plastic, then place in freezer bag
Piecrust, raw	3 to 4 days (rolled in ball and wrapped in plastic)	2 to 3 months	Roll in ball and wrap in plastic, then place in freezer bag

EMERGENCY BAKING SUBSTITUTIONS

Baking powder, 1 teaspoon
Use ½ teaspoon cream of tartar and ¼ teaspoon baking soda (make fresh for each use).

Buttermilk, 1 cup
Place 1 tablespoon vinegar or lemon juice in cup and stir in enough mwilk to equal 1 cup; let stand 5 minutes to thicken. Or use 1 cup plain yogurt or sour cream thinned with ¼ cup milk (there will be some left over).

Cake flour, 1 cup
Place 2 tablespoons cornstarch in cup and add enough all-purpose flour to fill to overflowing; level off top; stir well before using.

Chocolate, semisweet, melted 1 ounce
Use ½ ounce unsweetened chocolate plus 1 tablespoon granulated sugar

Chocolate, unsweetened, melted, 1 ounce
Use 3 tablespoons unsweetened cocoa plus 1 tablespoon vegetable oil, shortening, butter, or margarine.

Cornstarch (for thickening), 1 tablespoon
Use 2 tablespoons all-purpose flour, quick-cooking tapioca, or arrowroot.

Corn syrup, light or dark, 1 cup
1¼ cups granulated or packed brown sugar plus ¼ cup liquid (use whatever liquid the recipe already calls for)

Half-and-Half, 1 cup
Use ⅞ cup whole milk plus 1½ tablespoons butter, or ½ cup light cream plus ½ cup whole milk.

Light brown sugar, 1 cup
Use 1 cup granulated sugar and 1 tablespoon molasses, or use dark brown sugar.

Milk, whole, 1 cup
Use 1 cup nonfat milk plus 2 teaspoons butter or margarine or ½ cup evaporated whole milk plus ½ cup water.

Pine nuts
Use walnuts or almonds.

Sour Cream, 1 cup
Use 1 cup plain yogurt, or ¾ cup sour milk, buttermilk or plain yogurt plus ⅓ cup butter, or 1 tablespoon lemon juice plus evaporated whole milk to equal 1 cup

Yeast, active dry, 1/4-ounce package
Use 0.6-ounce cake, or use one third of 2-ounce cake compressed yeast.

Vanilla extract
Use brandy or an appropriately flavored liqueur.

Whipping Cream (36-40% fat), 1 cup
Use ¾ cup whole milk plus ⅓ cup melted butter. Use this for baking purposes, not for topping.

INDEX

Note: Page numbers in *italics* indicate photographs on pages separate from recipes or crafts.

PHOTOGRAPHY CREDITS

Cover photography: © Stacey Brandford (front); Mike Garten (back)

© Antonis Achilleos: 36 top right, 52 top

age fotostock © Arras K: 95; © Boyny Michael: 378 top right

© Sang An: 313 bottom

© Winnie Au: 160

© Michel Arnaud: 36 center left, 100 bottom & top center, center left & right, top left, 103, 180 left, 244 bottom right, 247, 250, 254 center & center left, 360 top left, 398

© James Baigrie: 19 top, 71, 81 bottom, 112 top, 121 bottom, 132 bottom right, 147, 166, 168, 188 top, 193, 194, 227, 232 center left, 276 center right, 286 top left, 294 top left, 305 bottom, 372 top, 381 bottom

© Monica Buck: 343 top, 348 bottom right

© Justin Coit: 69

© Renee Comet: 98

Corbis © Randy Feris: 32; © LAN: 335; © Splash News: 39 bottom, 80

© Beatriz da Costa: 121 top, 190 bottom left, 221 bottom, 260, 300

© Tara Donne: 94 bottom

Dreamstime © Artzzz: 285; © Elena Elisseeva: 58; © Anne Kitzman: 251 left; © Pablo631: 96; © Danny Smythe: 353; © Sofiaworld: 70; © Ingmar Verveer: 352 bottom center; © Viktarm: 199

© Miki Dusterhof: 246 bottom right, 246 left, 251 right

© Andrew Eccles: 56

FoodPix © Brian Leatar: 144 bottom

Philip Friedman: 18, 84 (boston), 84 (romaine), 200, 280

© Mike Garten: 6, 7 background, 12 top left, 110–111 bottom, 162 163, 218, 238 top, 269 top, 302 bottom, 320, 326 bottom, 327, 330, 333, 334, 360 bottom left & top right, 369 top

© Michele Gastl: 385

Getty Images © Ursula Alter: 243 right; © Brand X Pictures: 31; © Jill Chen: 4 bottom right, 66; © Creative Crops: 397; © Gregg DeGuire: 222; © Foodcollection RF: 15; © Jim Franco: 11 bottom left, 324 top; © Christopher Furlong: 4 bottom left; © Steve Granitz: 153; © Brian Hagiwara: 142; © Sean Justice: 350; © Graeme Montgomery: 30; © Michael Paul: 224; © Siede Preis: 185; © Still Images: 62; © Michael N. Todaro: 119; © Luca Trovato: 91

© Thayer Allyson Gowdy: 352 top left

© Brian Hagiwara: 4 top left, 16, 44 top right, 94 top, 127, 135, 144 top, 148 bottom right, 149, 150 bottom, 202 bottom right

© Lisa Hubbard: 378 top left

iStockphoto © Glenn Barnette: 171; © hanhanpeggy: 84 (frisée); © ivanmateev: 164; © Robert Linton: 139; © Viktor Lugovsky: 84 (arugula); © Okea: 29; © Lisa Thornberg: 399 left; © Camilla Wisbauer: 167

© Frances Janisch: 2, 100 top right, 76 top right, 100 bottom left & right, 100 center, 104,105, 106, 107, 262 bottom right, 266 top, 313 top, 319

© John Kernick: 140, 196 top & bottom, 202 bottom left, 225 bottom, 225 top, 238 bottom, 269 bottom, 282

© Yunhee Kim: 19 bottom, 36 bottom right, 52 bottom, 81 top, 276 top right, 279, 281, 284, 286 bottom, 311, 315, 336, 399 bottom

© Rita Maas: 36 bottom left, 43, 54, 55, 67, 68 bottom left, 93 left & right, 360 bottom right, 363, 364 top, 369 bottom

© Kate Mathis: 4 top right, 10 top, 11 top left, 12 left center, 20, 22, 23, 34 top, 036 top left, 39 top, 41, 35, 40, 42, 47, 59, 64, 76 top left, bottom left & right, 79, 82, 86 bottom, 89, 108, 110 top, 112 bottom left, 114, 122, 125, 132 top, 137, 138, 148 top right, 150 top, 154 bottom left, 159, 170 bottom, 178 bottom center, 184 top left & right, 188–189 bottom, 190 bottom right & left, top left, 204 top, 207, 212 bottom right, left, 215, 216, 232 bottom left, right, 244 top right, 249, 254 center right, 256, 262 left, top & center right, 265, 269, 270, 273, 274, 306 center left, 276 bottom & top right, 294 top right, 298 top, 302 top, 306, 310, 316, 317, 323, 324 bottom, 326 top, 342, 343 bottom, 346 bottom, 346 top, 358 top, 359, 364 bottom, 370 bottom right & top left, 377, 378 bottom left, 387, 382

© Kevin Mazur: 299

© Andrew McCaul: 24, 68 bottom right, 179, 248 right, 348 bottom left & top, 393, 396 right

© Ellie Miller: 352 bottom left

© Laura Moss: 252 left

© Steven Mark Needham: 370 top right, 372 bottom

© Marcus Nilsson: 306 top right, 308, 309, 344, 354, 355

© Helen Norman: 254 bottom left

© Michael Partenio: 4 bottom center, 8, 11 right, 12 right, 27, 34 bottom, 111 top, 112 bottom right, 132 bottom left, 148 bottom left, 154 bottom right & top left, 165, 178 bottom left & top, 180 top & bottom right, 184 bottom left & right, 186, 189 top, 190 top right, 202 top left, 212 center right, 232 top left, 240, 242 bottom, 243 left, 244 top & bottom left, center, 248 left, 253, 254 right, top left, 257, 261 bottom, 294 bottom right, 306 top left, 352 bottom right, 370 bottom center, 396 center right, 378 bottom right, 396 left

© Eric Piasecki: 4 center right, 246 top right, 356, 358 bottom, 399 top right

© Con Poulos: 148 top left, 157, 175, 176 bottom, 242 top, 266 bottom, 289, 294 top right

© David Prince: 44 bottom, 49

Retna Ltd. © Walter McBride: 341

Rex USA © Richard Young: 384

© Sian Richards: 7 inset

© Alan Richardson: 97

Lara Robby: 50, 252 right, 395

© Kate Sears: 12 left bottom, 92, 173, 198, 212 top right, 221 top, 236, 258, 329, 261 top, 297, 305 top, 328, 381 top

Shutterstock © Edith Frincu: 211

© Brian Bowen Smith: 169

StockFood © Callaway Photo: 116; © Mans Jensen; 370 bottom left; © Richard Jung: 338; © Rikki Snyder: 78

© Ann Stratton: 10 bottom, 51, 63, 86 top, 202 top right, 204 bottom, 234, 296, 298 bottom, 351, 352 top right, 375

© Mark Thomas: 44 top left, 117, 154 top right, 176 top, 223, 325, 339, 340

© Wendell T. Webber: 178 bottom right, 183 bottom, 183 top left & right, 254 top center, 276 bottom left, 392 bottom right, 392 left & top right, 394

© Anna Williams: 68 top

The Good Housekeeping Triple-Test Promise

At *Good Housekeeping*, we want to make sure that every recipe we print works in any oven, with any brand of ingredient, no matter what. That's why, in our test kitchens at the **Good Housekeeping Research Institute**, we go all out: We test each recipe at least three times—and, often, several more times after that.

When a recipe is first developed, one member of our team prepares the dish and we judge it on these criteria: It must be **delicious, family-friendly, healthy,** and **easy to make.**

1 The recipe is then tested several more times to fine-tune the flavor and ease of preparation, always by the same team member, using the same equipment.

2 Next, another team member follows the recipe as written, **varying the brands of ingredients** and **kinds of equipment.** Even the types of stoves we use are changed.

3 A third team member repeats the whole process using **yet another set of equipment** and **alternative ingredients.**

By the time the recipes appear on these pages, they are guaranteed to work in any kitchen, including yours. We promise.

HEARSTBOOKS

An Imprint of Sterling Publishing Co., Inc.
1166 Avenue of the Americas
New York, NY 10036

ISBN 978-1-61837-220-8

Distributed in Canada by Sterling Publishing Co., Inc.c/o Canadian Manda Group, 664 Annette Street, Toronto, Ontario, Canada M6S 2C8
Distributed in Australia by NewSouth Books, 45 Beach Street, Coogee, NSW 2034, Australia

For information about custom editions, special sales, and premium and corporate purchases, please contact Sterling Special Sales at 800-805-5489 or specialsales@sterlingpublishing.com.

Manufactured in China

10 9 8 7 6 5 4 3 2 1

www.sterlingpublishing.com